D1247135

Inscribed Landscapes

Inscribed Landscapes

Marking and Making Place

EDITED BY

BRUNO DAVID
MEREDITH WILSON

University of Hawai'i Press
Honolulu

© 2002 University of Hawai'i Press
All rights reserved
Printed in the United States of America
07 06 05 04 03 02   6 5 4 3 2 1

Library of Congress Cataloging-in-Publication Data

Inscribed landscapes : marking and making place / edited by Bruno David and Meredith Wilson.
    p. cm.
  Includes bibliographical references and index.
  ISBN 0-8248-2472-5 (alk. paper)
  1. Human geography.   2. Inscriptions.   3. Monuments.   4. Sacred space.   I. David, Bruno.
  II. Wilson, Meridith.

GF50 .I55 2002
304.2—dc21   2001052824

University of Hawai'i Press books are printed on acid-free paper and meet the guidelines
for permanence and durability of the Council on Library Resources.

Designed by Bookcomp, Inc.

Printed by The Maple-Vail Book Manufacturing Group

CONTENTS

PREFACE

This book is an archaeological and social anthropological exploration of the role of place marking in place making. The approaches taken by the various authors are varied, although all are united in the view that landscapes are not simply "out there," but constructed in social engagement. People physically inscribe spaces, such as in rock-art, monuments, and the like, in the process of *dwelling*. More intimately, people's spatial experiences are inscribed through the senses. Both people and place are codefined in a process of engagement that involves inscription. It is various dimensions of this codefinition that are explored in this book.

The initial seeds for this volume were laid in 1998 when we considered assembling a group of researchers to discuss how the marking of place affects human interaction and perception. At first we were particularly interested in how places marked or decorated with rock-art gained significance as socially marked *territorial* (already-owned) spaces. The psychological and social implications of such a process of place marking are considerable, but have remained largely unexplored by archaeologists.

However, we were not entirely satisfied with the initially bounded archaeological direction for this book. It was clear that it was not *inscriptions* that were at stake, but people's relationships with places in the production of a sense of place and belonging. We thus decided to redirect the book somewhat, to focus less on the fixed landmark and more on the humanization of landscapes, on the process of social and sensual anchorage in place. The book's new direction echoed more closely our intellectual interests and curiosities.

We have followed a number of conventions in the following pages. For one, we write of the nonwritten past as "pre-History" rather than "prehistory." We do this as an attempt to avoid the evolutionary loadedness of the notion of prehistory (while at the same time being well aware of the history of the terms pre-history/prehistory, as influentially used in particular by John Lubbock and Daniel Wilson during the mid- to late nineteenth century).

Following Paul Taçon and Christopher Chippindale's lead (1998, An archaeology of rock-art through informed methods and formal methods, 1–10 in *The Archaeology of Rock-Art*, edited by C. Chippindale and P. S. C. Taçon, Cambridge: Cambridge University Press), we hyphenate "rock-art" to distinguish such practices from the Western artistic program, which is closely tied to a market economy.

We also sometimes refer to radiocarbon dates and sometimes to calibrated ages. Wherever radiocarbon dates are presented, they are listed as "years B.P."; calibrated ages are presented as "years ago." We use the convention C.E. (Common Era = A.D.) and B.C.E. (Before the Common Era = B.C.), in acknowledgment of the widespread use of the Western calendar by people of all faiths.

There are many people who made this book possible. First and foremost we thank the authors themselves for producing what we think is a wonderful set of stimulating essays. Thanks also to the University of Hawai'i Press, and in particular our editor, Pamela Kelley, and copyeditor, Eileen D'Araujo, for their patience and assistance in seeing this book through. Nick Dolby, Colin Hope, Marcia Langton, Ian McNiven, David Mercer, Mariastella Pulvirenti, Lynette Russell, and Sallie Yea read and commented on drafts of various chapters, and two anonymous referees read the entire manuscript—a big thank you to all. Many thanks also to Gary Swinton for drafting most of the figures; Colin Hope for technical advice; the Department of Geography and Environmental Science at Monash University, under whose auspices the volume was edited; Monash University for a Logan Fellowship to B.D.; and Bill Harney and The Wardaman Aboriginal Corporation for permission to reproduce the cover photograph.

ONE

Introduction

Meredith Wilson and Bruno David

*Each way of conceptualising artefacts will tend to bring with it
a particular understanding of society.*
Julian Thomas, *Time, Culture, and Identity*

This book explores various dimensions of inscription as place marking from an archaeological/anthropological perspective. Our focus is the making of place through its physical and metaphysical marking: what Bradley (1997) aptly termed "signing the land." Rock-art, monuments, and other social and personal expressions of place marking signal a cultural presence and give the land social significance. At the same time, it is in the social construction of a sense of place that people's identities unfold.

A book that focuses on place marking in the construction of past and present social landscapes requires a consideration not just of monuments fixed in the landscape, but of their social and, where possible, ontological contexts. We have drawn on two major conceptual themes in this volume in an attempt to explore such contexts: participation and resistance. We explore these themes in this introductory chapter.

Because most of the chapters in this book focus on rock-art as a way of marking place, much emphasis is placed on "art" (Part 1). But the issues we address apply equally to "monuments" (Part 2) and to other forms of inscription, physical and metaphysical (Part 3).

MEANING AND ONTOLOGY

One of the first questions usually asked of an inscription is "what does it mean?" This is a useful place to begin, because "meaning" is a multiladened term and thus a source of much confusion (especially in rock-art research). Most commonly it is taken to refer to a particular individual's or cultural group's understanding of an inscription. In this sense, meaning is about emic understanding, or accessing someone else's experience of the world.

To understand inscriptions such as rock-art, three questions must be asked:

1. What does a picture represent (e.g., a picture of a pig)? Gell (1998:25) described representation

as "the most complicated philosophical and conceptual problem stemming from the production and circulation of works of art." Understanding what a picture represents requires recognizing its visual cues (some pictures are highly schematized versions of their subject). The more informed the "receiver" of an image within the sociocultural milieu in which a picture is found, the more likely the image will trigger recognition. However, there may be more than one "correct" reading of a given picture. Although interpretation may be culturally constrained, representation ceaselessly comes informed by personal experience (history) and context of reading. Because human experience is ongoing, interpretation is in a constant state of flux.

2. What is the sociocultural signification of "pigness"? Knowing that something is a depiction of a pig does not make its cultural meaning transparent. For instance, in many highland New Guinea societies pigs are symbols of wealth, power, and prestige; pig feasts signify a people's ability to muster alliances and elicit the support of ancestors (cf. Rappaport 1968). Marvin Harris (1975) termed this attitude toward pig as "pig loving." But in Jewish and Islamic thought, pigs are imbued with an almost opposite, polluting signification (cf. Douglas 1966), to the extent that their participation in everyday life is encoded and highly restricted. Marvin Harris (1975) termed this attitude toward pigs as "pig hating."

3. What is the place of inscription in the cultural system in question? We may understand the place of pigs in a given social and cultural system, but what of depiction itself? For instance, within modern Western society, a (framed) painting of a pig may be used to decorate an urban home, reminding the dweller of the rural Other. However, within a slaughterhouse it may be used as an advertising tool, to sell pork as a source of food. Depictions need to be considered within their socioaesthetic, display, and communicative contexts.

Thus, in investigating place marking the authors of the chapters in this book do not try to *retrieve* meaning, for meaning varies according to worldview and social (interpretative) context. Rather, through formal or informed methods (Chippindale and Taçon 1998), they seek to identify social codes and hegemonic practices that have resulted in the production of particular senses of place.

Images reflect the inner workings or processes of what Munn (1986:6) called "meaningful order." Such inner workings are not only of "mind," but of bodily engagement in place, perhaps best captured by Heidegger's (1962) word phrase, Being-in-the-world. Meaning and the worldviews from which it derives are historically positioned, situated in time and place.

Some of these ideas are taken up by Georgia Lee in her presentation of petroglyphs on the island of Hawai'i (chapter 6). Petroglyphs are not located everywhere or anywhere, but purposefully positioned in the landscape. They are found in great numbers at some sites, but nearby acres of smooth lava lack any trace of activity. As Lee emphasizes, this pattern suggests that the ancient Hawaiians were culturally selecting places significant to them. The locations of sites were selected because of their special attributes, as informed by worldviews. So-called "power" locations existed. Petroglyphs were juxtaposed to openings in the lava (e.g., collapsed lava tubes) and may have served as a connection to the underworld and the spirits who reside therein. They relate to the idea of *pō*, the underworld (land of spirits), and to its opposite, *ao*, light. In their allusion to Mother Earth and Father Sky, they relate to key elements in Polynesian religious beliefs.

TIME AND PLACE

Time and place locate human action. They operate through *engagement*, not as analytical time slices but as culturally ordered experiences. Marcia Langton (chapter 18) presents an apt analogy demonstrating how time and place are inscribed in the senses through culturally meaningful engagement. In Aboriginal Australia, the identity of the Elders is at one with their ancestral spirits and their clan lands. This construction of identity involves temporal as well as spatial recognition. Langton invites us to understand such constructions by considering the night sky. We in the Western world perceive the stars as located many millions of light years away. What we see is the light of balls of fire emanating across the sky through time. Similarly, for Aboriginal people the land's identity emanates from the ancestral Story (Dreaming) Beings who give it shape and meaning. At the same time, the living Aboriginal person gains her or his inalienable (Dreaming) identity from the ancestors, creating a temporal continuity with originating and yet atemporal Dreaming Beings. Time and space are thus constructed in worldly experience.

STYLE

Sets of social conventions encoded in inscriptions can be termed artistic "traditions." These refer to the way inscriptions are constructed and interpreted, including the employment of perspective, the way images are associated in meaningful sets, and their referential load. The concept of a "tradition" is a useful one, because it refers to a more or less repeated set of cultural expressions. It also implies a meaningful cultural practice in which participants are seen as informed social beings, united by their engagement in a common symbolic system.

In chapter 5, Andrée Rosenfeld considers a long-problematic aspect of the Australian archaeological record in this way. Since the inception of rock-art research in Australia, investigators have considered the rock-art of the arid zone as divisible into two sets: an early engraving tradition, characterized mainly by "simple," nonfigurative geometric and linear motifs; and a later, painted tradition of simple figurative motifs. From her own surveys of both painted and engraved sites in central Australia, Rosenfeld shows that a high level of consistency in the basic motif range of both techniques is apparent. At a broad level, this suggests a strong temporal continuity in the essential features of central Australian rock-art. However, at a finer scale, specific aspects of the art also indicate variation through time and across space. Particular changes in the spatial patterning of certain rock-art features suggest a fundamental alteration of Indigenous geographies through time. Although the distribution of some aspects of the rock-art has remained stable, their meanings and roles in social and cultural life may not have.

In a similar vein, Simon Stoddart (chapter 12) considers long-term change in social geographies via changes in architectural traditions. In pre-Historic Malta, monumental designs changed dramatically over the course of the late Holocene, implying alterations to ritual practices and social circumstances. Implicated in the transformations of architectural traditions are changes in the engagement of people with place.

However, it is generally through the study of *style*, rather than artistic tradition, that the archaeological study of inscriptions has tended to focus. Most studies of style assume that the material world encodes or carries social information. One of the aims of many stylistic analyses has been to figure out how social information is encoded in the material; to understand which variables carry social information and under what circumstances or within which contexts social messaging through objects takes place. Martin Wobst's (1977) theory of "information exchange" is perhaps the most influential study of style. His model emphasized the role of formal variability in information exchange: the greater the stylistic similarities between geographical regions or through time, the greater the communicability via material symbolism (usually taken to mean the more interaction there is likely to be). Similarities are taken to index social proximities and relative degrees of social connectedness.

One of the benefits of models of style that specify its communicative role is that style is seen as active in social process. In this sense style is power: it has the ability to guide behavior, as well as to evoke responses and change. However, interpretations of style based on "information exchange" are usually couched as systemic adaptations. For instance, Wobst argued that the greater the "visibility" of an artifact the better its ability to emit messages. Yet visibility is not so easily measured. To assess the visibility of something requires an understanding of what is seen and not seen by the society in question, rather than a measurement of what the analyst perceives as visible or not. It also reduces the product to its visual qualities when some material items may be remembered or communicated through other means, such as their sound qualities (e.g., musical instruments). Why should visibility be *the* determining factor of messaging ability? Without access to the conditions under which social knowledge is revealed, it is almost impossible to determine whether a space, or an artifact, is itself hidden, deliberately or otherwise. There is a danger of circularity in so-called adaptive interpretations.

Paul Rainbird explores some of these issues in chapter 7. He notes that rock-art researchers have almost always explored style and meaning through visual representation and proposes that an adequate understanding of rock-art may need to go beyond the visual product—the motifs themselves—to consider hitherto largely ignored aspects of meaning. He addresses this issue by reference to the sound of petroglyph production on the island of Pohnpei, in the Federated States of Micronesia, and to a pre-Historic petroglyph site in England.

Style, the Material World, and Agency

Robin Boast (1997) provided a provocative challenge to the concept of style, suggesting it to be a contemporary way of speaking about the world that is based on Cartesian dualism. He argued that style is generally defined in a way that distinguishes "social actors" from the "material world" such that stylized objects are generally conceived of as "out there." In contrast, Boast (1997:188) argued that once made, "the object becomes an actor in its own right, being delegated identities, roles and social status dependent on its constitution within the heterogeneous network." In this way, the object becomes both a *subject* and a form of power.

A similar position on the relationship between people and their physical world is espoused by David and Wilson (1999), who argued that people and things must be considered in relation to each other. It is via such relations, themselves constantly in a state of becoming, that identities are formed and continuously (re)negotiated. In this sense, subjects (i.e., people) are de-centered while retaining their agency, and objects—including rock-art—contribute to the construction of social identity through the process of engagement. The process is dialectic: the material world gaining meaning through participation in the social, and the social world being guided by a historically overdetermined material world.

In chapter 14, Michael Adler conceives of the ancient pueblo landscape of the American Southwest in this light. He suggests that the emergence of centralized pueblo villages represents more than a shift in settlement patterns, but a transformation in organizational principles that operate at different scales of human interaction. Pueblos are seen as central to the formation of identity in this part of the world. They are not just a backdrop for action, but an active location in which social life is engaged. The changing nature of engagement between people, and between people and place through inscriptive behavior, forms a central concern of this book.

Style as Normative Behavior, Style as Power

Because material items affect thought and behavior, they can usefully be thought of as power: a chair not only *represents* sitting, but directs and structures our thinking and bodily postures. An inscription that has existed in the landscape for some time feeds into human experience and impacts on it. It could thus be said that inscriptions are inherently hegemonic.

In chapter 2, Chris Ballard explores how an inscription's message and social context has been used as a source of political power. He documents how places were recently inscribed by the military in West Papua to impose a reign of terror on the local indigenous population. Inscriptions were explicitly used by the institutional elite to remind the passerby of existing power relations and political regimes. Such inscriptions played an active role in controlling people and place.

A further three chapters explore the hegemonic nature of place marking. Sallie Yea (chapter 17) discusses the Sarawak Cultural Village as a political means of appropriating cultural identity for the construction of state identity. Emily Umberger (chapter 13) explores the hegemonic nature of place markings in ancient Mexico, and John Darnell explores the hegemonic role of ancient roads in Egypt's Western Desert (chapter 8).

LANDSCAPES

Paul Taçon explores "landscape" as an archaeological concept in chapter 9, noting that both landscape approaches and the systematic study of rock-art are relatively new to archaeology in many parts of the world.

In recent literature (e.g., Bender 1993; Layton and Ucko 1999) three major formulations of landscape have appeared:

1. Landscape as "out there," a measurable, physical world independent of human signification. Such a conception is abundant in much positivist literature.
2. Landscape as *representation* of the world (as in "landscape paintings"), much the domain of art historians (e.g., Cosgrove and Daniels 1988).
3. Landscape as the engagement of people in

place, as experience of the world (e.g., Rodman 1992; Thomas 1993b). In this sense, landscapes are meaningful, socially constructed places involving bodily and cognitive experience.

In this book we are primarily concerned with the third definition. Landscapes exist in relation to the human actors who engage with them and imbue them with meaning. Bender (1993:2) noted that sometimes "the engagement will be very conscious—a way of laying claims, of justifying and legitimating a particular place in the world—sometimes almost unconscious—part of the routine of everyday experience."

All landscapes embody memories, and through mnemonics the past is continuously drawn into the present as identities are crafted. Because inscriptions are often permanent or long-lasting marks in the landscape, they engage the viewer as a memory trigger. Even after the "original" meaning(s) of an inscription is forgotten, the mark—"fixed" in the landscape—participates in peoples' constructions of their worlds.

This theme is taken up by Michael Allen and Julie Gardiner in their discussion of the British Mesolithic (chapter 10), and by Chris Scarre (chapter 11) for the Neolithic of central Brittany. Allen and Gardiner examine recent evidence for several large postholes that are found close to Stonehenge and other special ritual places. These postholes are interpreted as remnants of pine posts, erected during the eighth–seventh millennia B.C.E. The implication is that the locations of megalithic sites were already places of social importance long before the erection of the megaliths.

Scarre's chapter describes one of the largest complexes of Neolithic monuments in the area of Saint-Just, central Brittany, which spans a period of over two millennia (ca. 4500–2000 B.C.E.). The monuments include standing stones, stone rows, and a series of chambered tombs—many showing successive stages of remodeling and reuse. These constructions were the work of small-scale societies, perhaps partially nomadic in character. Scarre suggests that the way in which the Saint-Just landscape was marked over time implies that it was a place of special attention for these communities.

Landscapes are thus inscribed not just through physical marks such as monuments or rock-art, but through a social engagement that serves to anchor people in place. In chapter 15, Mariastella Pulvirenti explores how Italian migrants in Australia anchor themselves in their new country through home ownership. Her chapter is specifically concerned with how the security of home *ownership* is experienced as a sense of emplacement—it is through territoriality, not just use, that anchorage is achieved. Pulvirenti notes that relationships with place emerge through social participation, and that the social creation of place and belonging are integral to the negotiation of identity, including gendered, ethnic identities. As a monument in the landscape, the home can be seen, in the words of Paul Carter (chapter 16; personal communication), as a "fantasy of *writing* a new country."

Landscape and Resistance

Julian Thomas (1993a) and Barbara Bender (1999) recently discussed a component of landscapes that has remained undertheorized in archaeological discourse. This is the concept of *resistance*, as formulated by Foucault (1990, 1997a:166–173, 1997b:282–300). Resistance is present wherever there is power (Foucault 1990:95). Power, wrote Foucault

(1997a:169), "is a strategic relation which has been stabilised through institutions." Without resistance, "there would be no power relations. Because it would simply be a matter of obedience. You have to use power relations to refer to the situation where you're not doing what you want. So resistance comes first, and resistance remains superior to the forces of the process; power relations are obliged to change with the resistance. So I think that *resistance* is the main word, *the key word*, in this dynamic" (Foucault 1997a:167). In this sense, a person or thing (e.g., rock-art) is not constituted *by*, but *in* relations of power and resistance (Foucault 1997b:290).

Ian McNiven and Lynette Russell (chapter 3) discuss Australian Aboriginal resistance to invasion not as something that takes place outside established cultural practices, but through them. They argue that Australian Aboriginal responses to European invasion tend to be discussed in the literature in terms of social and material innovations. Social practice on the "other side" of the colonial frontier is rarely considered in discussions of resistance.

Bruno David and Meredith Wilson (chapter 4) note that landscapes of northern Australia have long been informed by the Dreaming. During the 1870s, however, Westerners began invading Indigenous lands, bringing guns, cattle, exclusionary practices (e.g., fencing, an aggressive policing of the land), and an attitude of ownership insensitive to the land's Indigenous spiritual (Dreaming) existence. These changes involved an abrupt appropriation of country and flagrant dismissal of Indigenous law. The organizational system that linked individuals, groups, homelands, and the ancestral order was upturned. Suddenly and with no explanation, access to sacred places was denied and rituals could often not be performed in their appropriate places.

It therefore comes as no surprise to find that during this time of upheavel, a culture of resistance emerged in northern Australia that involved the marking of place. In Wardaman country, rock outcrops began to be decorated with large, domineering paintings signifying the presence of the spirits that gave the land its identity. These were not representations, but the spirit Beings themselves "sitting" in place. We suggest that the emergence of these new art conventions was a direct response to an unprecedented experience of social turmoil.

CONCLUSION

Accepting that structure (as order) is integral to communication, we treat inscriptions as patterned symbolic expressions that facilitate the transmission of ideas. Place markings are not found randomly across the landscape, but rather are an ordered component of socially constructed space. If inscriptions can be seen in their symbolic and hegemonic capacity, they become a conduit for understanding social experience and social action. A social analysis of inscriptions requires:

1. Understanding the rules or conventions of composition; and
2. Determining which parts of the social landscape these rules/conventions extend into (see also Bradley 1997).

We thus conceive of place markings not simply as *signs* loaded with conscious, intended messages, but rather as the result of relations between people, places, and things that have emerged from historical circumstances (however perceived). The aim of analysis is not to recover what marks "meant" to the artists or users, but the underlying graphic structures and how they are engaged in everyday society, from participation to resistance. Ultimately, we are not aiming to address *intention* (as cognitive, hegemonic awareness), but rather the social conditions (as hegemonic forces) that shaped and constrained intention.

With these points in mind it is not difficult to see how the notion of style can be put to use in regional studies of place marking and place making. Style is not something that is "out there," but rather a structured system of coherence produced via ongoing relations between people and place.

In this book we focus on place and place marking, and in the process gain an understanding of the different ways people have constructed their lived environments, past and present. It can never be known whether the control of space conceived by the analyst matches the perception of the people in the past who used it, but as Thomas (1993b:93) stated, people were obviously influenced by the space they occupied and used; space, "not the subject, was what was being controlled."

Each chapter in this book in one way or another does away with the dichotomy between mind and the material world, favoring an approach that sees the object as "integral to social process" (Thomas 1996b:10). People, places, and things are constantly engaged in a process of inscribing place. Through this process identities unfold in a continual process of (re)negotiation.

The chapters in this book are divided into three sections. Part 1 focuses on rock-art, Part 2 focuses on monuments, and Part 3 describes how the physical and metaphysical articulate to inscribe places with meaning. In the final chapter of the book (chapter 19), Jimmy Weiner invites us to accept that "the traces of people's actions left on the earth and in the environment generally also leave traces in people's consciousness." Such traces include physical marks such as monuments or rock-art, but also include various forms of "imaginal markings," such as the song-poetry, or *sorohabora*, of the Foi of Papua New Guinea. Through recitation of the *sorohabora*, deceased relatives are remembered. Because these poems are rich in spatial references, place is memorialized in social consciousness. Weiner's chapter serves as an apt reminder that inscription is not just about physical marking, but concerns the social creation, communication, and experience of place.

REFERENCES

Bender, B. 1993. Introduction: Landscape—Meaning and Action. In *Landscape: Politics and Perspectives*, edited by B. Bender, 1–17. Oxford: Berg.

———. 1999. Subverting the Western Gaze: Mapping Alternative Worlds. In *The Archaeology and Anthropology of Landscape: Shaping your Landscape*, edited by P. J. Ucko and R. Layton, 31–45. One World Archaeology 30. London: Routledge.

Boast, R. 1997. A Small Company of Actors: A Critique of Style. *Journal of Material Culture* 2 (2): 173–198.

Bradley, R. 1997. *Rock Art and the Prehistory of Atlantic Europe: Signing the Land*. London: Routledge.

Chippindale, C., and P. Taçon. 1998. *The Archaeology of Rock-Art*. Cambridge: Cambridge University Press.

Cosgrove, D., and S. Daniels (editors). 1988. *The Iconography of Landscape*. Cambridge: Cambridge University Press.

David, B., and M. Wilson. 1999. Re-Reading the Landscape: Place and Identity in Northeastern Australia during the Late Holocene. *Cambridge Archaeological Journal* 9:163–188.

Douglas, M. 1966. *Purity and Danger*. London: Routledge and Kegan Paul.

Foucault, M. 1990. *The History of Sexuality: An Introduction*. Vol. 1. New York: Vintage Books.

———. 1997a. Sex, Power, and the Politics of Identity.

In *Michel Foucault: Ethics—Subjectivity and Truth*, edited by P. Rabinow, 163–173. New York: The New Press.

———. 1997b. The Ethics of the Concern for Self as a Practice of Freedom. In *Michel Foucault: Ethics—Subjectivity and Truth*, edited by P. Rabinow, 281–301. New York: The New Press.

Gell, A. 1998. *Art and Agency: An Anthropological Theory*. Oxford: Oxford University Press.

Harris, M. 1975. *Cows, Pigs, Wars, and Witches: The Riddles of Culture*. New York: Vintage Books.

Heidegger, M. 1962. *Being and Time*. Oxford: Blackwell.

Layton, R., and P. J. Ucko. 1999. Introduction: Gazing the Landscape and Encountering the Environment. In *The Archaeology and Anthropology of Landscape: Shaping your Landscape*, edited by P. J. Ucko and R. Layton, 1–20. One World Archaeology 30. London: Routledge.

Munn, N. 1986. *The Fame of Gawa: A Symbolic Study of Value Transformation in a Massim (PNG) Society*. Cambridge: Cambridge University Press.

Rappaport, R. A. 1968. *Pigs for the Ancestors: Ritual in the Ecology of a New Guinea People*. New Haven: Yale University Press.

Rodman, M. C. 1992. Empowering Place: Multilocality and Multivocality. *American Anthropologist* 94: 640–656.

Thomas, J. 1993a. The Politics of Vision and the Archaeologies of Landscape. In *Landscape: Politics and Perspectives*, edited by B. Bender, 19–48. Oxford: Berg.

———. 1993b. The Hermeneutics of Megalithic Space. In *Interpretative Archaeology*, edited by C. Tilley, 73–97. Oxford: Berg.

———. 1996a. *Time, Culture, and Identity: An Interpretive Archaeology*. London: Routledge.

———. 1996b. A Precis of Time, Culture, and Identity. *Archaeological Dialogues* 3 (1): 6–46.

Wobst, M. 1977. Stylistic Behaviour and Information Exchange. In *For the Director: Research Essays in Honour of James B. Griffin*, edited by C. E. Cleland, 317–342. Museum of Anthropology Anthropological Papers 61. Ann Arbor: University of Michigan.

PART I
ROCK-ART

TWO

The Signature of Terror

Violence, Memory, and Landscape at Freeport

CHRIS BALLARD

The notion of a "culture of terror," developed by ethnographers of Latin America and given wider currency through the writing of Michael Taussig, resonates powerfully with conditions around the world's richest mining operation, Freeport's Grasberg mine in the Indonesian province of Papua or Irian Jaya.[1] Taussig (1987) described how a climate or culture of terror, the perpetual imminence of the threat of death, can create a "space of death," an imaginary zone in which fear blocks the senses as violence and representations of violence achieve a near-perfect circle of mirrors reflecting terror back upon both perpetrators and victims. Neither cultures of terror nor spaces of death, however, have been explored in any depth in terms of their topographic arrangement, the nature of their inscription in a specific landscape. How does death—or, more accurately, the terror of an unfamiliar, unexpected, or violent death—come to inhabit a landscape? How is the land itself marked, manipulated, and deployed in the orchestration of terror? And if landscapes, by definition, invoke perspective and the scope for different readings, how are these markings received by different audiences?

I address these questions by considering the history of violence around the Freeport mine, in an attempt to understand the operation of a technology of terror through the deployment of a particular iconography. The manipulation of a layered series of images and other prompts for the memory allows the very meaning of the landscape for a community, and thus the literal base of its identity, to be reconfigured. These images both record and recall violent events, conferring upon those who have the power to inscribe the landscape in this way a degree of control over the summoning of memories of the past and the heightening of terror and uncertainty about the future. In a companion paper (Ballard 2000), I considered the performative aspects of violence at Freeport and elaborated upon the relationship between violence and terror. Here I focus on the manner in which death and the terror of dying are implanted in the landscape and rendered perpetually present for its inhabitants, as an echo of violence that persists through the intervals between episodes of murder, torture, and disappearance. The manner in which bodies become absent and are then re-presented is mediated by an iconography of violence, which introduces signs that stand for these absences (Graziano 1992:73).

Recent studies of political iconography in violent contexts have tended to focus on the symbolism of community resistance and sectarian distinction. The graphic and political sophistication apparent in the graffiti and murals of Northern Ireland and Palestine has required that close attention be paid to the identity of the intended audiences for these images and slogans. Although Catholic murals in Belfast, often restricted to clearly defined working-class neighborhoods, are at one level emblems of resistance to Protestant domination and British rule (Sluka 1992), they are also, and perhaps just as powerfully, a means of policing community will, "part of an inwardly focused propaganda which largely ignores debate" (Jarman 1993:118). Murals have multiple audiences, but consideration of their location, their content, and their immediate historical context yields a much richer sense of their reception and their efficacy as interventions in relations of power, both between and within communities.

Of particular relevance to the Freeport case is Peteet's (1996:140) observation that an analysis of the way in which graffiti are read forces enquiry to extend beyond the simple binary of domination and resistance. Palestinian graffiti have provided the community with a voice, a means of access to communal memory, and a public affirmation of allegiance to different Palestinian factions; but the fact that most graffiti are rendered in Arabic means that Israeli soldiers, although keenly aware of the role of graffiti as a challenge to authority, remain largely ignorant of their content (Peteet 1996:150). Local historical context, relations of power, and the positions of image makers and image readers are thus vital to an adequate analysis of what, following Poole (1997), we might think of as a "visual economy" of political violence. The notion of visual economy introduces the sense of a systematic production, exchange, and reproduction of images and interpretations in whose organization the relations of power feature prominently.

Around the Freeport mine, the more obvious iconography of murals and graffiti has been overwhelmingly that of the state and its armed forces, and the multiple interpretations of these images and the intentions of their makers demand attention. An analysis of the patterned appearance of the state's images is potentially revealing of the structured nature of its attempts to dominate the community and thus capable of identifying the means of subverting their intended effects. Yet this is not to portray the communities of the mine area as passive consumers of some discourse of the dominant. Much as armed forces and communities alike participate in novel "vocabularies of terror" (Suárez-Oroco 1992:235) to manage and communicate conditions of radical violence, an iconography of terror requires the participation of both the army, as producers of the images, and the community, as active readers and interpreters. The capacity and the will to read and interpret, however the message might be transformed in the act of communication, necessarily implicate the audience as culturally fluent agents, fully capable of response. At Freeport, where the community's response has not thus far taken the more obvious forms of murals or graffiti, other, more subtle means of resisting the intended import of these images and insisting on the integrity of the community can be identified.

CONTEXTS FOR VIOLENCE AT FREEPORT

Irian Jaya has had a deeply troubled history of incorporation within the Republic of Indonesia since the colonial territory of Dutch New Guinea was transferred to Indonesia via the interim authority of the

United Nations in 1962 (Budiardjo and Liong 1988; Défert 1996; Osborne 1985; Saltford 2000). The Indonesian military campaign to seize the western half of the island of New Guinea from the Dutch played a role in creating the international pressure that led to the transfer, and the army thereafter displayed a tendency to regard the possession of Irian Jaya and its resources as a right of conquest. Popular uprisings during the 1960s were brutally suppressed. After the crushing in 1977 of a provincewide insurrection led by the poorly equipped Free Papua Movement (Organisasi Papua Merdeka, or OPM), Irian Jaya became one of three provinces, along with East Timor and Aceh, in which the military exercised almost complete control (Aditjondro 1994; Robinson 1998).

The Freeport mine played an important role in the history of Irian Jaya under Suharto's New Order regime. The 1936 discovery of a substantial copper deposit at the Ertsberg ("Ore Mountain") in the Central Highlands of Dutch New Guinea had led to further exploration in 1960 by an American mining company, Freeport Sulphur (Wilson 1981). When Suharto came to power in 1965, Freeport was the first foreign company to sign a major investment contract with Indonesia, forming a local subsidiary, P.T. Freeport Indonesia. Initially a medium-sized copper and gold venture centered on the Ertsberg, the Freeport mining complex rose dramatically to global prominence after the 1988 discovery of the Grasberg, the world's richest copper-gold deposit, with an estimated reserve value in 1998 of US$54 billion. The newfound strategic significance of the mine for Indonesia resulted in a substantial increase in troop numbers around the mine and the local townships of Timika and Tembagapura, exacerbating existing tensions between the army, the mining company, and the Indigenous communities of the

wider region. In the absence of an effective, functioning local civilian administration, the security forces, including both army and police units, are in many respects the representatives of the state, and their actions are commonly viewed locally as reflections of the will of a distant and fundamentally malign state.

The traditional landowners of the highland mining area, the mining township of Tembagapura and its surrounds, are the Amungme, a language community of about 8,000 people, divided between urban residents of the lowland towns of Timika and Akimuga, and the inhabitants of rural hamlets scattered across a dozen narrow highland valleys cut into the southern slopes of the Central Range.[2] Although both the 1936 and 1960 reconnaissance expeditions were peacefully received, the Amungme reacted almost immediately to the start of mine construction in 1967 with a strong show of protest. They had been neither consulted about plans for the mine nor compensated for the loss of land, productive trees, or gardens.

Much as the miners themselves were in awe of the technical demands and the scale of construction at the Ertsberg (see Wilson 1981), so too the Amungme were initially overwhelmed by the accompanying environmental destruction of the headwater areas where the mine is located. As the presence of the mine failed to translate into shared benefits or wealth for the community, Amungme protests grew more forceful, culminating in the closure of exploration camps, which were marked off with cross-shaped *em jinkong* sticks forbidding further trespass. A 1974 agreement between the company and the community, mediated by the government and the army, was widely considered by the Amungme to have been forced upon them. When a small group of OPM fighters with Amungme leaders walked from neighboring Papua

New Guinea to Akimuga in 1977, many Amungme, including those few with jobs at Freeport, joined with them in an attack upon the mine. The army's response was devastating, putting almost the entire community into flight, with many families spending a year or more hiding in the forest. The 1977 uprising introduced a new era in relations between the community on one hand and the mine and the military on the other, characterized by a profound mutual enmity and distrust.

Although there had been a permanent police presence at the mine since the initial construction phase, the army appears not to have been involved at this early stage in direct conflict with the Amungme community, restricting its activities largely to the suppression of separatist sentiments among better-educated mine workers from other parts of the province and occasional intervention in interclan feuding. After the 1977 uprising, army units stationed around the mine began increasingly to focus their attention upon the community, and numerous Amungme were killed or assaulted in individual incidents during the 1980s. In the aftermath of the discovery of the Grasberg ore body in 1988, army interest in the new economic opportunities on offer in the Freeport area intensified, and a more coordinated campaign of arrest, torture, and disappearance appears to have begun in 1991–1992. In response to a new program of mining exploration across the Central Highlands, riding on the success of Freeport's Grasberg discovery, the OPM launched a series of acts of open defiance during 1994, raising the independence movement's banned "Morning Star" flag in several Amungme settlements. This renewed OPM activity then provoked or legitimated an intensification of the army's terror campaign, and relatives of known OPM members were abducted and executed during the latter half of 1994.

At dawn on the morning of Christmas Day, December 1994, a large crowd of Amungme and other highlanders raised the Morning Star flag on a small hill in the Wa Valley, overlooking the mining town of Tembagapura, a peaceful but astonishing act of defiance. The first troops to approach the gathering opened fire, wounding two men, one of whom, Naranebelan Anggaibak, was then captured. Reports from Amungme eyewitnesses detailed how Naranebelan was dragged behind a car by a noose around his neck to the army checkpoint near the Amungme settlement of Banti, a short distance from Tembagapura. By the time he was delivered to the Banti checkpoint, he was dead, and his body was then suspended by the ankles from a post opposite the checkpoint. Banti villagers, forced to file past the corpse on their way to church services that morning, were taunted by the surrounding soldiers asking whose pig, whose dog, this was. Naranebelan's relatives were refused permission to take the corpse for burial, and it was removed and probably thrown by the army into a steep ravine along the road between Tembagapura and Timika, where other bodies have been disposed of in a similar manner. That day, and for the next few weeks, terrible violence was unleashed on the community, as individuals were killed in public, others disappeared, and leading men and women in the Amungme community were arrested, held in shipping containers, and tortured.[3] As the army rushed in reinforcements, it also expanded its area of operations to the more distant Amungme settlements, establishing garrisons in each of the valleys. A pattern developed of intermittent outbreaks of violence coupled with periods of uneasy calm, which continued for more than three years until 1998.[4]

A number of questions hang over some of the incidents that were used to justify the increase in military numbers around Freeport, from a unit of less than 100 troops before 1977 to at least 1,850 soldiers by 1996. Shootings of Freeport workers along the road between Tembagapura and Timika in late 1994, attributed to the OPM, were almost certainly the work of army units on "black operations," designed to create a climate of fear and place pressure on the mining company to fund the presence of more troops. Likewise, a series of riots in Tembagapura and Timika over three days in March 1996, reported around the world and widely attributed at the time to Amungme dissatisfaction with the company, appears to have been instigated and directed by troops in civilian clothing carrying walkie-talkies.[5] Again, the company's response was to welcome further reinforcements and submit to the financial costs involved.

After 1996, each of the military's different services insisted on being represented in the Timika area, and police, army, navy, air force, and even armored car units have been stationed there, largely at Freeport expense. The key units, in terms of confrontation with the Amungme community, are the red-bereted elite troops of the Special Forces Command (Kopassus); a unit of the army's Strategic Reserve (Kostrad) tasked specifically with the defense of the mine as a designated National Asset; the poorly trained Territorial troops (Korem) of the regional Trikora Military Command; and the elite paramilitary Police Mobile Brigade (Brimob). Competing business interests, legal and illegal, operated by each of these different units, have led to frequent clashes among them, often resulting in firefights and the loss of life.[6] This summary history of violence at Freeport establishes the range of actors in the area and supplies a context within which the place of violence in the landscape and its iconographic representation can be addressed.

THE CORPSE AS SIGN, AND THE SIGN OF THE CORPSE

Violence, a seemingly infinite category of activity and effect, assumes a more focused role in the context of a culture of terror. Elsewhere I advance the argument that violence and terror are mutually supportive, with violence at its most effective when enacted in a climate of terror, and terror continues and extends the work of violence (Ballard 2000). Though Taussig (1987:51f) alerted us to the dangers of seeking to distinguish the rational from the irrational in accounting for terror, the maintenance of a culture of terror involves a degree of conscious coordination and planning—a structured *mise-en-scène*, or material organization of the act of representation. There is no requirement that the actual agents of terror be capable of articulating this structure to fulfill their role; military hierarchies of command are designed precisely to distance the infliction of pain from its conception. But the patterned form of military or paramilitary campaigns of terror, and the parallel reproduction of highly elaborate and specialized forms of torture imply a network for the communication of techniques and technologies of terror that matches the traffic in more conventional forms of military knowledge and hardware (Nordstrom 1995).

Drawing on Elaine Scarry's *The Body in Pain* (1985), I propose that the deliberate enactment of terror upon a community follows closely her distinction of the three central features of the torture of individuals: the infliction of pain "in ever-intensifying ways"; the objectification of pain, in which the effects of pain are rendered visible for other observers; and the denial of the objectified pain, an act that is itself construed as evidence of the power of the torturer. In much the same way, communities that become the target of campaigns of terror are subjected to a series of increasingly graphic forms of violence, in which the effects of violence are objectified and displayed before the community. The power of the state is then doubly confirmed by its capacity to deny the violence and to call into question the very absence of the disappeared.

James Siegel (1998) argued convincingly that Suharto's New Order regime employed violence along precisely these lines during a campaign to eliminate urban gangs in the capital of Jakarta during the 1980s. Beyond the immediate objective of creating the appearance of order for an international audience, Suharto sought to communicate to his political rivals and to the nation at large the extent of his control, both of events and of their meaning. The corpses of young men, bearing the tattoos associated with gang membership, assumed the function of signs, "left in the streets [to] keep the moment of disappearance from life vivid, retaining that moment in the present" (Siegel 1998:111). At Freeport, the steady increase in the frequency of violence during the early 1990s was matched by the development of an increasing sophistication in the manner in which bodies, parts of bodies, and the signs of bodies were deployed to amplify the effects of violence and thus to brand the brief eruptions of violence upon the communal memory. If, as in Jakarta, these corpses have functioned as signs of death for the Amungme community, the Amungme landscape has also been seeded with signs that themselves recall the corpses.

In common with most rural Melanesian communities (Ballard 1997), Amungme ground their identity upon the familiar features of the surrounding landscape, endowing it with a cosmography in which the land and the people account for one another's presence. Amungme land and Amungme people were allocated to each other in the foundational epoch recounted in myths. Mountains assume a particular cosmological significance as the final residences of the spirits of patrilineal ancestors, and each peak is thus associated with a specific patriclan.[7] In addition to this "mountain orientation" (Ellenberger 1996:146) mediated by ancestral spirits, Amungme cosmography conceives of a landscape possessed and inhabited by female earth spirits. The most significant of these female spirits, Tu Ni Me Ni, represents the ultimate locus of fertility in the Amungme cosmos, the source both of nourishment and of retribution, propitiated during periods of stress through a network of sites such as pools and pandanus groves. She is often described as embodying the landscape, with her head in the mountains, her breasts and womb in the valleys, and her legs stretched out toward the distant coast (see, for example, Beanal 1997).

Mining in the Amungme landscape has thus been quite literally an assault upon the body of Amungme belief and the foundations of Amungme identity. Individual peaks, such as the Grasberg and Ertsberg, have been leveled or reduced to deep pits, lakes associated with earth spirits filled in with mine waste, and sacred sites in the valleys destroyed in the construction of the mine's infrastructure. Because the Amungme clearly link the activities of the mining company and the presence of the army, referring to the latter as "Freeport's savage dogs" (*anjing galak dari Freeport*), the company's assault on the landscape is perceived as another facet of the army's assault upon the community. Freeport's ebullient chief executive officer, Jim-Bob Moffett, has done little to counter this perception in describing the Grasberg ore body in corporeal terms, as "a volcano that's been decapitated by nature, [where] we're mining the esophagus, if you will" (Project Underground 1998:14).

The Amungme landscape operates as a sign in and of itself, inconceivable without the knowledge and presence of the Amungme community. Memory supplies the necessary markers of identity and ownership, in associating particular locations with former settlement or garden sites and with all of the remembered incidents of a community's history. The crossed *em jinkong* sticks placed around the mine by Amungme during construction are of a universal form, indistinguishable one from another, indicating the displeasure of the owner at finding evidence of trespass in a garden or along a path.[8] Within small-scale communities such as the Amungme hamlets of the highlands, the ownership of a specified area of land, although not immune from dispute, requires no physical signs that proclaim an individual's identity; the presence of trees and gardens identifiable as the produce of the owners or their kin, or the capacity to correctly identify and name the features of the landscape, are sufficient in themselves.

The land acquires significance through a dense microhistory of these acts of naming, acts that include the use of a location for activities such as gardening, hunting, settlement, or ritual performance. Violence and death are already present in this named landscape, emplotted in the form of burial sites or the locations of deaths during interclan wars. But these are deaths that have been rendered meaningful for Amungme through a range of conventional practices, including mortuary payments and war compensation, and the proper interment of bodies. In contrast, uncompensated or unreciprocated deaths at the hands of the military, particularly where the bodies have not been made available, have produced a disordered landscape of "corpses out of place" (Warren 1993:31).

In the absence of corpses, which Amungme relatives are often refused permission to bury (as in the

case of Naranebelan's body), the sites of murder or of the initial display of the body assume a particular threat of their own. If the "sight of torture is itself a torture," as Fabri (1995:150) observed of the creation of violence as a spectacle in Guatemala, it is equally the case that the *site* of torture or other violence can be refashioned as an instrument of terror. The passage of Naranebelan's body, from the hillside where he was captured, via the road along which he was dragged, to the post (which still stands), and thence to the ravine where he is presumed to lie, has endowed these locations with an unprecedented and terrifying significance for the Amungme of the Wa Valley. The growing number of these sites of murder, of torture, of arrest, and of the disposal of bodies is sufficient to form a topographic grid or layer composed of the memories of these events of unaccountable violence. Amungme people traversing the landscape by foot or in vehicles point out these locations, recounting and reliving the events.

An additional and corresponding layer of significance has recently been draped over the landscape, this time in the form of a series of graphic images engraved and painted by the security forces. During the most recent phase of violence, in the 1990s, these images first appeared around the vicinity of the army and police posts, initially in the form of the insignia of units stationed there, as bored soldiers and police passed their time reproducing their divisional emblems on walls or on prominent boulders, an activity common enough to military units everywhere. In late 1996, the elite Kopassus unit stationed at Tsinga village carefully engraved and painted a large rock in front of their mess with a skull bearing their distinctive red beret (Figure 2.1). A similar image of a skull, this time weeping blood from the cracks around the face—like a corpse trapped in an eternal torture, portending perhaps the capacity of

FIGURE 2.1. Kopassus (Special Forces) insignia engraved and painted onto a boulder at Tsinga village (photo taken in 1997). The acronym RPKAD beneath the skull stands for "Regimen Para Komando Angkatan Dara," the precursor to Kopassus during the period 1955–1971, famous for its role in the invasion of Dutch New Guinea; the wings and anchor indicate the airborne and naval capabilities of this elite unit.

the state to pursue people beyond death—appeared later in front of the army post at Banti. For the illiterate majority of the Amungme population, for whom the unit names and insignia are not always intelligible, the meaning of the skulls is an unmistakable warning of the fate of those who resist the army.

To mark the Indonesian Independence Day celebrations in August 1997, the road from Tembagapura town down to the Amungme village of Banti was adorned with a pair of columns, forming a cer-

emonial gateway to the village. On three of the four faces of either column an anonymous artist had produced the requisite multicolored images of the military heirs of the Indonesian revolution, dropping by parachute into a hell of explosions, piloting fighter jets diving with guns blazing, or driving a tank across a battlefield (Figure 2.2). The mine's tramway was depicted, as were several curious images, including a soldier wearing a badge with the acronym AEA used by Freeport's medical services contractors (who ran a clinic in the village of Banti), and a jar enigmatically marked "Ovaltine." Above the tank rose the figure of a bare-chested Amungme warrior, patriotically sporting a red-and-white headband and raising a clenched fist, with an Indonesian red-and-white (merah putih) flag in the other hand (Figure 2.3).

FIGURE 2.2. Indonesian Independence Day gateway erected on the road to Banti village, 1997.

FIGURE 2.3. Indonesian Independence Day gateway erected on the road to Banti village, 1997.

These are images with complex genealogies and an equally intricate communicative intent. As statements of the permanent presence and eternal vigilance of the military, they signal the army's goal of pervading all aspects of Amungme life, much as it monitors the movements of each individual through the issue of passes for travel between valleys and enters the classroom through the ubiquitous presence of mock rifles carved from wood with which pupils conduct their compulsory marching exercises. Scarry (1985:52) identified torture's goal of fashioning a "totality of pain" for the victim, and the intention for terror is perhaps a similar aspiration to a totality of representation, in which all aspects of a community's life come to reflect the will of the state.

For Amungme, the images are doubly potent through their capacity to summon up the memory of violent events and thus the enduring threat of further violence. The images themselves are almost invariably violent, as illustrated by the use of skulls and the themes of the panels of the Independence Day gateway. However, the particular significance of army unit designations and the ideological import of Independence Day celebrations and their symbolism more generally are not clearly recognized by many Amungme. Instead, the violence that is summoned up for Amungme through these images is the specific violence of the past enacted upon kin and neighbors, and of the perpetual threat of its resurgence. Where the bodies of the murdered, the tortured, and the disappeared are not made available for mourning and for appropriate reception in the Amungme landscape and memory, the army's graffiti come to stand instead for the absent corpses: as signs of corpses that are themselves signs of the power of the state.

If these images are evidently directed in part toward the Amungme, they also serve to speak to other audiences in quite different ways. During 1998, a further addition to this landscape of novel images was a rash of graffiti painted by the elite Police Mobile Brigade (Brimob). In large, white lettering, the acronym BRIMOB appeared on cliff faces and boulders along the length of the road between Tembagapura and the Amungme settlement of Banti (Figure 2.4). Because much of the previous unit-specific imagery had been confined to the immediate vicinity of army and police posts, this was something of a departure in its attempt to mark out a new territory for inscription; the sole Brimob post in the valley was one positioned above the gate at the bottom end of Tembagapura, controlling access from the Banti road. Unadorned by any attempt at

FIGURE 2.4. Brimob (Police Mobile Brigade) graffiti on the Tembagapura-Banti road, 1998.

representation beyond the simple reproduction of the acronym, the Brimob graffiti assumed a literate audience. However, literate Amungme read this graffiti not as a warning to them, but as an unmistakable sign of interunit rivalry: a territorial challenge by the elite police to the Kostrad army units, much envied for their access as Freeport's official guards to seemingly unlimited company largesse and expanded opportunities for graft and theft from the mine and the company's townships.

One of the enduring features of the long history of violence at Freeport has been the question mark about the company's complicity in the army's atrocities, an accusation leveled at Freeport by both the Amungme community and international observers, but denied by the company. Although this is not the place to offer definitive pronouncements on such a complex topic, it is valid to seek to understand the role of Freeport staff as another potential audience for the army's graffiti. Here, perhaps, the issue of

complicity between image and audience is brought most powerfully into focus, because staff whom I questioned about the emergence of the army and police insignia appeared genuinely ignorant of their presence. The army and police pose no threat to their existence, and Freeport staff have rarely been the targets of violence. Only a small proportion of the staff ventures down to Banti, or to remote villages such as Tsinga, and thus have the opportunity of encountering these images, suggesting that the army has observed fairly carefully the principle of "line of sight." But those Freeport staff who are exposed to the graffiti are also largely unaffected by them, viewing them as an integral part of the social landscape. Though these graffiti function as land mines for the memories of passing Amungme, Freeport staff can apparently move freely among them without triggering their charges. However, surrounded as they are by a community subjected to more than two decades of state violence, the ability of Freeport staff to remain oblivious to the potential significance of army graffiti is itself a form of knowledge, a will to ignorance.[9]

RESISTANCE (*AVANT LA LETTRE*)

What Taussig referred to as "the problem of writing effectively against terror" (1987:3) is the risk we run of representing terror as a rational economy of behavior, and thus of extending its reach. This is to contribute, in effect, to the torturer's goal of creating a totality of representation, in which the efficacy of torture or terror is made evident through the fashioning of the victim (or the writer) as another mouth for the truths of the state. A common response to this problem has been to perceive, in even the most mundane actions, the seeds of a coherent project of resistance (Ortner 1995). Inspired by a commendable wish to portray communities as agents in their own right and not simply as passive consumers of the truths of others, studies of resistance tend to focus on conscious and unambiguous acts of reaction to domination (see also McNiven and Russell, this volume).

Without diminishing the scale or dismissing the impact of the army's onslaught on the community and the mine's assault on the land, it must also be observed that the Amungme have succumbed neither to the violence nor to the terror. As a community, Amungme have continued to escape the circle of mirrors, the totality of representation that I identify as the goal of the state operating through its security forces, and their success in this evasion can perhaps be characterized as a form of resistance. But to describe the various ways in which this is effected as a single, coherent strategy of resistance is to obscure several complex operations of power and to conflate conscious and unconscious acts and their intended and unintended consequences. At one level there appears to be a curious silence on the part of the Amungme in response to the iconography of terror described here. Thus far there has been no countericonography—no Amungme graffiti and very little graphic art—to challenge the images deployed around the Freeport mine by the security forces. The one exception to this observation is the raising of the Morning Star flag, a singular act of defiance that has historically provoked violent repression from the army and police. But Amungme have conventionally disputed identity and land through a politics of residence and of naming, rather than through an iconography of graphic symbols denoting status. Amungme resistance might be said to revolve around an insistence on the primordial link between Amungme and their landscape, and a confidence that Amungme people have a privileged access to the meaning of the land and the knowledge of its names. In linking the violence of the security forces to the presence of the mine, Amungme accord a central role in their analysis of terror to the mine's assault on their land. It is no accident, in this light, that one of the principal demands of Amungme leaders during recent negotiations with Freeport has been the restoration of Amungme names to those elements of the landscape whose significance has been obscured by Indonesian or American terms.

Amungme resistance has also drawn strength from the failure of the state to incorporate the community successfully in a symbolic relationship characterized by domination through the imposition of a common graphic vocabulary or visual economy. The symbols and imagery of the state, which are deployed to such effect elsewhere in Indonesia (Siegel 1998), are often imperfectly recognized and received by Amungme and thus limited in their effect. Bourdieu (2000:175) observed that the efficacy of symbolic domination rests upon the capacity of the state, through lengthy processes of inculcation and incorporation, to naturalize "common symbolic forms of thought, social frames of perception, understanding or memory."[10] Where these familiarizing conditions are not met—where the symbolism of national Independence Day is poorly understood, for example—the "submission" of the dominated cannot be secured. The state's frustration at the incomplete incorporation of the Amungme—their failure to recognize and correctly interpret their symbolic relationship—sets the stage for recourse to physical violence, which has the effect of still further alienating the Amungme. If the Indonesian state's strategic marginalization of communities such as the Amungme is a theater of statehood directed principally toward the cosmopolitan centers of Java (Tsing 1993), it is a strategy that also serves to undermine the efficacy of the state's symbolic dominance, through its failure to inculcate the logic and the grammar of domination among these marginalized communities.

NOTES

This chapter was prepared with the kind permission of the Traditional Amungme Council/Lembaga Musyawarah Adat Suku Amungme (LEMASA). Access to the Freeport area was made possible through the work of the UNCEN-ANU Baseline Studies (UABS) Project between 1996 and 1998, which was funded and supported by the Universitas Cenderawasih, The Australian National University, and P.T. Freeport Indonesia. A very large number of people, many of whom cannot be identified for various reasons, have contributed materials and ideas that inform this paper, but I am responsible for the argument put forward here and any factual inaccuracies. I especially thank Yunus Omabak and the Amungme communities of the Wa, Tsinga, and Aroa Valleys, and my colleagues in the UABS Project. The chapter was prepared during periods spent as a visitor at the Amsterdam branch of the International Institute of Asian Studies and at the Centre de Recherche et de Documentation sur l'Océanie of the Centre National de la Recherche Scientifique at Marseille.

1. Formerly known as Irian Jaya, a name widely associated with the New Order regime of former President Suharto, Indonesia's easternmost province was renamed "Papua" in January 2000 by the newly elected president, Abdurrahman Wahid (however, Indonesia's Parliament had not yet ratified this change by January 2001). Though Papuans now refer to their territory as West Papua, Irian Jaya is used in this chapter to retain the historical flavor of the New Order regime under which these events took place.

2. The lowland portion of the Freeport mining lease is owned largely by Kamoro-speaking communities (though this ownership is not recognized by the state) (Widjojo 1997). The apparent absence of overt conflict between Kamoro people and the army poses intriguing questions, which space does not permit me to explore here, about the nature of resistance under different historical and cultural conditions.

3. A preliminary but incomplete account of these events is given in a report published by the Australian Council for Overseas Aid (ACFOA 1995).

4. Details of the long list of massacres and other abuses of basic human rights during 1994–1998 are beyond the scope of this chapter, but have been described in a series of reports by church groups and other nongovernment organizations (see ACFOA 1995; Catholic Church of Jayapura 1995; ELSHAM 1997, 1999; Robert F. Kennedy Memorial Center for Human Rights and the Institute for Human Rights Studies and Advocacy. 1999).

5. In fact, Amungme appear to have been only marginally involved in these riots, which largely involved migrants from other parts of Irian Jaya.

6. See Robinson (1998) and Kammen (1999) for further discussions of the role of business interests in similar conflicts within the security forces in Aceh and East Timor.

7. Ellenberger's (1996:144f) detailed account of the role of mountains in the beliefs of northern Amungme, or Damal, accords closely with my own more limited enquiries among Amungme.

8. The Amungme assumption of the transparency of the message of the *em jinkong* sticks placed around the mine during the construction phase, as claims by landowners prohibiting further trespass, was sorely misplaced. Freeport workers read the sticks instead as "hex sticks" (see, for example, Wilson 1981:168), designed to bring misfortune down upon the mine—evidence, for the miners, both of the "primitive" mentality of the Amungme and of their fundamental opposition to the entire mining project.

9. Elsewhere (Ballard 2000) I address in more detail the question of Freeport's apparent "will to ignorance" and also describe how the army has sought to attract Freeport's attention more directly and to inculcate a sense of terror in the company.

10. "Symbolic violence is the coercion which is set up only through the consent that the dominated cannot fail to give to the dominator (and therefore the domination) when their understanding of the situation and relation can only use instruments of knowledge that they have in common with the dominator, which, being merely the incorporated form of the structure of the relation of domination, make this relation appear as natural" (Bourdieu 2000:170).

REFERENCES CITED

ACFOA. 1995. *Trouble at Freeport: Eyewitness Accounts of West Papuan Resistance to the Freeport-McMoRan Mine in Irian Jaya, Indonesia and Indonesian Military Repression, June 1994–February 1995.* Melbourne: Australian Council for Overseas Aid.

Aditjondro, G. J. 1994. *In the Shadow of Mount Ramelau:* *The Impact of the Occupation of East Timor.* Leiden: Indonesisch Documentatie- en Informatiecentrum.

Ballard, C. 1997. It's the Land Stupid! The Moral Economy of Resource Ownership in Papua New Guinea. In *The Governance of Common Property in the Pacific Region*, edited by P. Larmour, 47–65. Canberra: National Centre for Development Studies and Resource Management in Asia-Pacific Project.

———. 2000. Performing Violence: An Anatomy of Terror at Freeport. Paper presented at the Séminaire sur la Violence Coloniale, SHADYC-CNRS, La Vieille Charité, Marseille, France.

Beanal, T. 1997. *Amungme: Magaboarat Negel Jombei-Peibei.* Jakarta: WALHI.

Bourdieu, P. 2000. *Pascalian Meditations.* Cambridge: Polity Press.

Budiardjo, C., and L. S. Liong. 1988. *West Papua: The Obliteration of a People.* Surrey: Thornton Heath.

Catholic Church of Jayapura. 1995. *Violations of Human Rights in the Timika Area of Irian Jaya, Indonesia.* Melbourne: Australian Council for Overseas Aid.

Défert, G. 1996. *L'Indonésie et la Nouvelle-Guinée-Occidentale. Maintien des Frontières Coloniales ou Respect des Identités Communautaires.* Paris: L'Harmattan.

Ellenberger, J. D. 1996. The Impact of Damal World View on the Formation of a Local Theology in Irian Jaya. Ph.D. thesis, Fuller Theological Seminary, Pasadena, California.

ELSHAM. 1997. *Bella dan Alama Berdarah.* Jayapura: Lembaga Studi dan Advokasi Hak Asasi Manusia, December.

———. 1999. *Operasi Militer Pembebasan Sandera dan Pelanggaran Hak Asasi Manusia di Pegunungan Tengah Irian Jaya: Menyingkap Misteri Misi Berdarah ICRC, Keterlibatan Tentara Asing dan Tentara Nasional Indonesia.* Jayapura: Lembaga Studi dan Advokasi Hak Asasi Manusia, August.

Fabri, A. 1995. Memories of Violence, Monuments of History. In *The Labyrinth of Memory: Ethnographic Journeys*, edited by M. C. Teski and J. J. Climo, 141–158. Westport: Bergin and Garvey.

Graziano, F. 1992. *Divine Violence: Spectacle, Psychosexuality, and Radical Christianity in the Argentine "Dirty War."* Boulder: Westview Press.

Jarman, N. 1993. Intersecting Belfast. In *Landscape: Politics and Perspectives*, edited by B. Bender, 107–138. Oxford: Berg.

Kammen, D. 1999. Notes on the Transformation of the East Timor Military Command and Its Implications for Indonesia. *Indonesia* 67:61–76.

Nordstrom, C. 1995. Contested Identities/Essentially Contested Powers. In *Conflict Transformation*, edited by K. Rupesinghe, 93–115. London: St. Martin's Press.

Ortner, S. 1995. Resistance and the Problem of Ethnographic Refusal. *Comparative Studies in Society and History* 37 (1): 173–193.

Osborne, R. 1985. *Indonesia's Secret War: The Guerilla Struggle in Irian Jaya.* Sydney: Allen and Unwin.

Peteet, J. 1996. The Writing on the Walls: The Graffiti of the Intifada. *Cultural Anthropology* 11 (2): 139–159.

Poole, D. 1997. *Vision, Race, and Modernity: A Visual Economy of the Andean Image World.* Princeton: Princeton University Press.

Project Underground. 1998. *Risky Business: The Grasberg Gold Mine. An Independent Annual Report on P.T. Freeport Indonesia, 1998.* Berkeley, Calif.: Project Underground.

Robert F. Kennedy Memorial Center for Human Rights and the Institute for Human Rights Studies and Advocacy. 1999. *Incidents of Military Violence against Indigenous Women in Irian Jaya (West Papua), Indonesia.* Washington: Robert F. Kennedy Memorial Center for Human Rights and the Institute for Human Rights Studies and Advocacy.

Robinson, G. 1998. *Rawan* is as *Rawan* Does: The Origins of Disorder in New Order Aceh. *Indonesia* 66:127–156.

Saltford, J. 2000. United Nations Involvement with the Act of Self-Determination in West Irian (Indonesian West New Guinea) 1968 to 1969. *Indonesia* 69:71–92.

Scarry, E. 1985. *The Body in Pain: The Making and Unmaking of the World.* Oxford: Oxford University Press.

Siegel, J. T. 1998. *A New Criminal Type in Jakarta: Counter-Revolution Today.* Durham: Duke University Press.

Sluka, J. A. 1992. The Politics of Painting: Political Murals in Northern Ireland. In *The Paths to Domination, Resistance, and Terror*, edited by C. Nordstrom and J. Martin, 190–216. Berkeley: University of California Press.

Suárez-Oroco, M. 1992. A Grammar of Terror: Psychocultural Responses to State Terrorism in Dirty War and Post-Dirty War Argentina. In *The Paths to Domination, Resistance, and Terror*, edited by C. Nordstrom and J. Martin, 219–259. Berkeley: University of California Press.

Taussig, M. 1987. *Shamanism, Colonialism, and the Wild Man: A Study in Terror and Healing.* Chicago: University of Chicago Press.

Tsing, A. L. 1993. *In the Realm of the Diamond Queen: Marginality in an Out-of-the-way Place.* Princeton: Princeton University Press.

Warren, K. B. 1993. Interpreting *La Violencia* in Guatemala: Shapes of Mayan Silence and Resistance. In *The Violence Within: Cultural and Political Opposition in Divided Nations*, edited by K. B. Warren, 25–56. Boulder: Westview Press.

Widjojo, M. S. 1997. *Orang Kamoro dan Perubahan. Lingkungan Sosial Budaya di Timika, Irian Jaya.* Jakarta: LIPI.

Wilson, F. K. 1981. *The Conquest of Copper Mountain.* New York: Atheneum.

THREE

Ritual Response

Place Marking and the Colonial Frontier in Australia

Ian J. McNiven and Lynette Russell

It is time that Australian historians sought to understand the Aboriginal
response to conquest and dispossession. To do so it is necessary to seriously
explore *the farside of the frontier* and the underside of the caste barrier.
Henry Reynolds, *Aboriginal-European Contact History* (emphasis added)

Historical scholarship over the past two
decades has seen a growing awareness of
colonial processes and in particular the
dramatic and often violent events of the colonial
frontier. For Indigenous people, depopulation and
dispossession are all-too-familiar themes of colonialism. In Australia, rewriting these violent themes
into colonial history has undermined European narratives of colonialism by introducing Indigenous
stories of agency, resistance, and survival from the
frontier. Historical sources alone are, however, inad-
equate for the task of exploring activities on the far
side of the frontier, because without Indigenous
voices the process of rewriting will continue to be a
colonial enterprise, appropriating, suffocating,
ignoring, or otherwise marginalizing non-European
views and experiences of the past.

Australian archaeologists have begun to make
contributions to writing so-called "alternative" contact histories. In this connection, Birmingham
(1992:178) identified two key questions that guide
research on Australian contact sites: "First, how is
the documentary record confirmed, complemented
or challenged by the archaeological evidence? Second, what further questions arise from queries or
gaps in the documentary record for which the
archaeologist is likely to find answers?"

In her own study, Birmingham (1992) found
that Aboriginal Tasmanians at Wybalenna reserve
resisted colonial domination by strategically resisting different aspects of European culture. Related
studies have also investigated accommodation and
resistance at other early-European frontier sites such
as homesteads (Murray 1993) and shepherd's huts
(Wolski 2000). On a narrower scale, investigations
have shown the social, economic, and perhaps even
ceremonial circumstances in which Aboriginal people appropriated, enculturated, and used items of

"European" material culture such as bottle glass (Wolski and Loy 1999) and clay tobacco pipes (Courtney and McNiven 1998).

Accommodation and resistance are models of frontier dynamics that have become central in Australian contact historiography. In most cases, historical research has focused on the frontier as the point of Aboriginal-European interaction and dispossession. In this sense, Australian contact archaeology has followed suit. This research focus privileges both physical encounters and secular activities as frontier dynamics. In this chapter, we concur with recent developments in Australian contact historiography that a broadened perspective on frontier dynamics is required that includes activities that took place on the "farside" of the frontier. The issue we explore is Aboriginal ceremonies and rituals, especially those associated with the marking of place such as with rock-art, which aimed to affect the nature of frontier encounters and control of lands. Research in this area is well established in North America (e.g., Drooker 1996; Klassen 1999; Miller and Hamell 1986; Stoffle et al. 2000) and Africa (e.g., Jolly 1996, 1999), but few Australian researchers apart from historian Henry Reynolds (1981) have appreciated the potential significance of these nonsecular responses as a frontier dynamic.

Following Reynolds, we believe that an essential feature of most frontier encounters is resistance and the control of resources and land. For European historians, frontiers have tended to be represented as geographical phenomena that divided landscapes into civilized and uncivilized realms. Although it is beyond the scope of this chapter to critique the concept of frontiers in Australian contact historiography, we do note that the idea of a frontier as somehow marking a line of European conquest was a colonial illusion (see Russell 2001a). In reality, frontier encounters were extremely complex affairs that could be violent or peaceful at different times and at different places. Furthermore, European colonizers may have partitioned the landscape into conquered and unconquered spaces, but Aboriginal people neither acknowledged conquest nor ceded sovereignty to the colonizers. Thus, frontier dynamics are not only about encounters between people, but clashes over the power to control lands. So how have Australian contact historians approached this dynamic and what historical evidence exists to lay the foundations for archaeological explorations of ritual responses by Aboriginal people to invasion?

FRONTIER DYNAMICS AND RITUAL RESPONSE

Beginning with the foundational work of Rowley (1972) and later Reynolds (1978, 1981), historical research in Australia shifted focus from memorializing European explorers to an exposition of the "hidden" and often violent dimensions of Australia's nineteenth-century colonial frontier (Broome 1982; Critchett 1990; Elder 1988; Evans et al. 1975; Loos 1982; Reynolds 1981; Rowley 1972). Other researchers have been concerned with histories considerably after first contact and explored accommodation, cultural survival, and negotiations between Europeans and indigenes (Attwood 1989; Beckett 1987; Fels 1988; McGrath 1987). Out of these various contact histories a nuanced and complex picture of resistance and survival has developed.

Henry Reynolds has taken an explicitly political position dedicated to shedding light on the concealed dimensions of frontier violence and exposing the equally hidden "farside" or "other side" of the frontier. However, in reality the use of European archival records in this endeavor often perpetuates a European perspective, because the vantage point remains from the European "side" of the frontier. For the historian confined to the use of early European documents, the other side of the frontier can only ever be gazed at from a distance. This issue is most relevant regarding early European recordings of their frontier clashes with Aboriginal people. Reynolds, aware of this problem, saw the need for documentation of Aboriginal oral testimonies to provide an inverted and more balanced perspective on frontier dynamics. Although oral testimony has been argued by some to overemphasize Aboriginal agency and control, its use has, nonetheless, proliferated. Beginning in the late 1980s numerous books appeared documenting the "hidden histories" of Aboriginal Australians as told by themselves. These histories reveal that the violence of the nineteenth century pastoral frontier continued well into the twentieth century (e.g., Huggins and Huggins 1994; Rose 1991; Rosser 1987; Trigger 1991). Although the passage of time has greatly lessened our ability to retrieve Aboriginal perspectives on specific frontier clashes before the mid-nineteenth century, it is equally clear that many stories from that era have been passed down to the present day (e.g., Baker 1999; Henderson 1999; McKellar 1984; Poignant 1996; Simon 1987). The contact history of Aboriginal people and Europeans concerns not only violent contacts but also negotiated encounters. As Reynolds (1978:52) noted, "Resistance has been a constant motif of black history; but it has never been the only one." Aboriginal and Torres Strait Island people entered into negotiations with Europeans to precipitate trade (e.g., McBryde 1989; McNiven 2001), peace (e.g., Reynolds 1978), and work arrangements (e.g., Anderson 1983; McGrath 1987). Similar negotiated trade agreements took place historically between Aboriginal peoples of northern Australia and visiting Macassan bêche-de-mer fishermen from Indonesia (MacKnight 1976). Aboriginal people also acted as guides for European explorers, showing "safe" pathways through an Aboriginal sociopolitical landscape, pointing out water holes, and even supplying food (Reynolds 1990a, 1990b; Ryan 1996).

It is something of an irony that Australian frontier historiography has, by focusing on encounters between Europeans and Aboriginal people, actually directed intellectual attention away from Aboriginal activities taking place on the "farside" of the frontier. This in effect perpetuates the colonial silencing of Aboriginal history. From a European historian's perspective, Thorpe (1996:40, Thorpe's emphasis) noted that when the *encounters themselves* are the "major focus" of research, "other, arguably more significant, features of such relations recede from view." In a similar fashion, we contend that what Aboriginal people were doing out of the sight of the Europeans was instrumental in directing the nature of frontier encounters. This raises the important question of how it is possible to understand frontier dynamics when direct intercultural encounters tended to be sporadic and the "farside" of the frontier was for the most part what took place *beyond the gaze* of Europeans. This observation applies equally to Aboriginal people removed to government reserves. Indeed, life on some of the expansive reserves became a microcosm of wider frontier dynamics as Aboriginal people continued both subsistence and ceremonial activities without the knowledge of Europeans (e.g., Birmingham 1992; L'Oste-Brown et al. 1995; Trigger 1991). "First contact" situations with European survey expeditions, shipwrecked sailors, and others can also yield insights into Aboriginal activities well beyond European settlement boundaries. In many instances, detailed written or oral knowledge on these activities has not survived, and it is in this capacity that contact archaeology has a key role to play.

In Australia perhaps the least known of all activities to occur on the "farside" of the frontier are ceremonies and rituals, many of which involved place marking. Indeed, as Langton (this volume) has noted, ceremonies and rituals were crucial to the process of constructing place. That Aboriginal people often interpreted the presence of Europeans within the spiritual realm is indicated by numerous first-contact narratives documenting Aboriginal people identifying Europeans as ghosts or the returned dead (often specific relatives) (e.g., Barrett 1948; Howitt 1904:442–446; Schaffer 1995). Equally significant is the fact that some early contact narratives hint that Aboriginal people were undertaking ceremonial and ritual activities aimed at affecting the nature of Aboriginal-European encounters. Aboriginal Australians carried out a wide range of ceremonies involving the sorcerous activities of "clever-men" who aimed to rid their lands of Europeans and exact revenge for wrongdoings. The most famous of these anti-European ceremonies were those associated with the Mulunga "cult" that originated in northwestern Queensland and spread across much of the continent during the late nineteenth and early twentieth centuries (Hercus 1980; Mulvaney 1976:90–92; Swain 1993: 224–233). Missionary Otto Siebert observed that the ceremony involved Aboriginal people dressed up as Europeans carrying sticks representing rifles. The rite climaxed with a spirit figure using her magic to destroy the "European" dancers and "whites and all that belonged to them." This was intended as "an act of revenge carried out on all whites" for the murder of a "number of natives" (Siebert 1910 cited in Swain 1993:227), possibly

the Kalkadoon people massacred at Battle Mountain in 1884 (Swain 1993:230).

In another example, a ceremony was observed in northern Queensland in 1874 whereby Aboriginal people made two effigies of Europeans and after "war songs and dances, attacked the effigies with their tomahawks and cut them to pieces" (Reynolds 1981:74). For southeastern Cape York, Trezise (1969:110) speculated that the ritual "cannibalism" of Europeans and Chinese practiced by Aboriginal people during the nineteenth century may have been performed in the "hope of absorbing their 'cleverness,' thus helping to defeat them in the relentless warfare raging at the time."

The cessation of so-called "increase" ceremonies with the onset of European incursions was an alternative strategy used to facilitate the removal of Europeans. Newland (1926) observed that in the late nineteenth century, certain Aboriginal people of western New South Wales put a halt to rain increase ceremonies during the drought season to ruin cattle and sheep stations and drive out Europeans. Among the Kamilaroi of north-central New South Wales, Parker (1905:48–49) recorded that a "clever-man" placed his "rain-stone" into a fire to bring a drought, believing that "if all the sheep died the white fellows would go away again, and then, as long ago, the black fellows' country would have plenty of emu and kangaroo." Recently, Bruno David (personal communication, 1999) documented how in 1992 an elder of the Yir-Yiront people of northern Queensland, while performing a fish increase ceremony, excluded sending fish to a particular water hole known to be favored by European fisherpersons. The purpose of this exclusion was twofold: first, not to waste sending fish to a place where they would be fished and eaten, often in large numbers, by Europeans; and second, to make that part of the river a less attractive camping place to Europeans and deter the non-Indigenous exploitation of Yir-Yiront lands and resources. In this sense, there was a change in place marking through a change in ceremonial activity aimed at altering the land's fecundity, in resistance to European incursions.

European-introduced diseases could also be controlled by ceremonies. The squatter E. M. Curr (1887a:681) described a large mounded sculpture of a snake "about 100 feet or yards long" located "close to the Murray River" in southeastern Australia that was used to "charm away the small-pox." In the Port Phillip Bay region of Victoria, Aboriginal people believed that smallpox was the product of Mindi, a malevolent spirit, and in 1840 performed a ceremony to "send this plague forth" to destroy Europeans as revenge for the "incarceration of some hundreds of their number by the military and police authorities" (Parker cited in Smyth 1878, 1:446).

Not all ceremonies were aimed at removing or harming Europeans. Rituals were also performed to increase contact with Europeans and facilitate access to European goods. In the 1840s, castaway Barbara Thompson recorded how the Naghi Islanders of Torres Strait (northeastern Queensland) developed an increase ceremony to encourage European sailing ships to stop off at their shores to trade goods. The ceremony included a dance performed by two Islanders acting as Europeans, legs painted white and wearing European shirts and special masks adorned with red ochre and fragments of silk handkerchief (McNiven 2001; Moore 1979:199). A similar observation was made during the 1870s on Fraser Island off the central Queensland coast, where Aboriginal people performed a simple ritual to acquire European items: "If a schooner is passing the Mission about sunset, the natives will sometimes throw sand up into the air, and blow with their mouths towards the sun, in order to make the sun go under quickly, and thus compel the schooner to come to an anchor for the night in the channel, near the Mission, and enable them to get on board [for] tobacco, biscuits, &c., which the captains generally supply them with" (Fuller 1872 cited in Curr 1887b:145; see also Courtney and McNiven 1998).

Are these historical snippets of ritual activities mere glimpses of an otherwise invisible domain of Aboriginal responses to European invasion? If so, it is here that archaeology has the potential to make important contributions to contact history and frontier historiography. However, can these ritual activities be recovered archaeologically? We argue that in many respects they can and that rock-art has a central place in this endeavor.

CONTACT ROCK-ART AND RITUAL RESPONSE

If rock-art is a form of place marking, then we could expect to find traces of Indigenous responses to European incursions in the archaeology of rock-art. However, such research has rarely been carried out in Australia. Archaeologists for the most part identify rock-art from the period after European contact using Aboriginal informants (e.g., Hascovec and Sullivan 1989) or archaeologically by depictions of "European" motifs such as guns and in rare instances by the use of "European" pigments (e.g., Mulvaney 1989). As Frederick (1999) noted, the archaeological identification of rock-art is problematic because it inadvertently *defines* contact rock-art as rock-art with "European" motifs. Consequently, many Indigenous responses will remain hidden unless they are expressed by new and recognizable motif *forms* of purportedly non-Indigenous material objects, rather than by reference to artistic practices that can be shown to relate people to the land and to address aspects of social relations. It is for this reason that Frederick (1999:134) offered the following definition of contact rock-art that we use in this paper: "Contact rock-art . . . refers to rock-art/markings produced within a context of cross-cultural exchange. In general terms this exchange, whether it be a fleeting encounter or a sustained relationship, does not and will not always relate to a specific event or date but marks the beginning of a process of awareness of or interaction with another cultural group. In this way, contact rock-art may have been made during and/or after interaction (direct or indirect) between cultural groups."

It is important to remember that images of contact themes are not the only rock-art produced after European contact. There have been several anthropological studies that have documented twentieth-century Aboriginal rock-art painters working in a traditional manner with no reference to European people or objects (e.g., Hascovec and Sullivan 1989; Layton 1992).

The issue of the "visibility" of contact sites is not unique to rock-art. Wolski (2000) noted that similar problems confront the identification of Aboriginal contact camp sites. Sites with flaked bottle glass and/or other items of European origin are defined as contact sites; sites without such items (e.g., stone artifact scatters) are defined as precontact sites. Numerous anthropologists have recorded the production and use of stone tools in contemporary Aboriginal communities, which clearly is at odds with definitions of pre- and postcontact site types based on the absence and presence of European materials (Gould et al. 1971; Hayden 1981; Horne and Aiston 1924; Jones and White 1988; Thomson 1964; Tindale 1965; see also Head and Fullagar 1997:422–423). The circularity of defining contact

rock-art simply by the presence of "European" images privileges acculturation as a major frontier dynamic. As Frederick (1999:133) noted: "An over emphasis on motifs or materials that appear to be introduced can imply that subjugation of Indigenous graphic systems, design vocabularies and the social institutions governing the graphic system is an inevitable outcome of contact."

Further problems arise when rock-art investigations overuse secular interpretative frameworks. Although there exists a number of important exceptions to this view (see later in this section), in a general sense it is true that "European" images tend to be interpreted as secular illustrations of cross-cultural encounters; images of guns are representations of frontier violence; depictions of horses and sheep are representations of strange new animals, and images of people with hats are representations of Europeans (Chaloupka 1979; Layton 1992:76–77; Mulvaney 1989). Frederick (1999:133–134) questioned why such simple, secular interpretations of the art are put forward when the wealth of ethnographic information reveals the mythological significance and complex iconography of Aboriginal rock-art (see also Layton 1992). Images that are perceived as secular to a European audience are not necessarily seen as secular by the artists. Again, to quote Frederick (1999:134): "Contact rock-art is not merely a passive reflection of the changing times, it also demonstrates the measures Indigenous Australians took towards securing their own social, economic and cultural survival in a transforming world."

A secularist interpretation of contact rock-art also plays into the hands of the popular truism that postcontact or modern expressions of Aboriginality are inauthentic (Russell 2001b; Wolfe 1999). By assuming that, after the impact of Europeans, rock-art becomes a simple recording system ties into questions of authenticity and hybridity. In this scheme only that which was in place before colonization can be described as "traditional." Rock-art made from non-Indigenous materials and/or including non-Indigenous motifs is somehow considered less authentic; they have been transformed and are now "postcontact," hybrid, or appropriated. Many researchers hold such views almost inadvertently, yet this nonetheless aids the disempowerment of Aboriginal agency and control.

A focus on secular interpretations of contact rock-art also has parallels with interpretations of contact material culture. Recent historical and archaeological research in North America indicates that beyond the realm of direct encounter, "European" items imported via Indigenous trade networks mostly impacted the nonsecular domains of Native American life. Miller and Hamell (1986: 316) observed that the bulk of European items located in archaeological sites dating to the early contact era are found "directly alongside spiritually charged native items in ceremonial contexts" (see also Brown 1979:154; Drooker 1996:172). For instance, it is believed that bottle glass was "incorporated into the native thought-world as a replacement for traditional divining implements" such as crystal quartz (Miller and Hamell 1986:316).

Despite the American experience, "European" items found in Australian Aboriginal contact sites (excluding burials) continue to be interpreted within a secularistic paradigm. The problematic nature of this approach is best exemplified by fragments of bottle glass. These items are invariably seen as resulting from nonreligious technology—the production of cutting and scraping tools (e.g., Cooper and Bowdler 1998; Thorpe 1924). Recent use-wear and residue studies reveal the validity of this assumption in certain contexts (Wolski and Loy 1999). However, we note with

some interest that among nineteenth-century ethnologists, the most commonly documented function of bottle glass fragments is as sorcery objects used by "medicine men" (e.g., Chief Commissioner of Police 1887:147; Howitt 1904:358, 408; Muirhead 1887: 29; Smyth 1878, 1:474). Cursory examination of museum collections reveals that fragments of glass were also incorporated into ceremonial regalia (e.g., Leipzig Museum, I.J.M., personal observation, 1994). Ironically, the best-documented example of Aboriginal bottle glass flaking is Kimberley "spearheads," many of which were used as ceremonial trade items (e.g., Akerman 1979). More extreme is Thomson's (1949: plate 5) recording of a glass bottle that had been "elevated to the level of a ceremonial totem of the Mildjingi clan" in Arnhem Land. All these examples reinforce McBryde's (1989:181) comment that we know very little about what happened to European items once they passed into Aboriginal hands. What is certain is that European items became imbued with Aboriginal values once they entered the Aboriginal world. The same can be said of the place of rock marking and how it was used during the period of response to the early and later European encounter.

Frederick's (1999) perceptive insights into the nature of contact rock-art set the scene for invigorated investigations of the place of rock-art in cross-cultural encounters. In terms of this study, the pathway we follow takes us over to the "farside" of the colonial frontier. We are concerned with two major issues: first, the ceremonial and ritualistic function of contact rock-art, and second, how the production of this art might relate to controlling European activities and affecting (as opposed to illustrating) intercultural encounters.

Unfortunately there is only meager evidence for rock-art aimed at exacting and maintaining positive relations with Europeans. Furthermore, such evidence is often vague and open to speculation. Could it be that iconic representations of "European" material culture were associated with ceremonies aimed to acquire these items? This potential connection between rock-art and increase ceremonies was revealed by Rose (1942:175), who recorded that an Aboriginal man on Groote Eylandt (Northern Territory) had repainted the edge of a steel ax image "in order to make his own axe sharp." In a similar fashion, it is possible that some paintings of guns were related to rain increase ceremonies. Meston (1896 cited in Layton 1992:104) recorded that certain Aboriginal people in northern Queensland "thought guns were the source of thunder and lightning."

As expected, most available information on the ritual role of Aboriginal contact rock-art indicates that it was associated with controlling dispossession of Aboriginal lands by European invaders. Here we identify two major forms of this art—*sorcery rock-art* aimed at controlling the killing of Aboriginal people either by murder or from introduced diseases, and *territorial rock-art*, which aimed to reaffirm Aboriginal ownership and control of their lands.

Sorcery Rock-Art

Percy Trezise was one of the first Europeans to document Aboriginal sorcery rock-art (see also Mulvaney 1992). At Crocodile Gallery 1 in southern Cape York Peninsula, northern Queensland, Trezise recorded four large anthropomorphs oriented horizontally that show no obvious associations with Europeans (Trezise 1971:19). Aboriginal informants Caesar LeChu and Willy Long identified two of the anthropomorphs as Europeans and two as "native policemen." The Native Police was a government instrument made up of Aboriginal men. The two painted native policemen wear the "peaked cap of the early police uniform" and the "upper chest and arms have been over-painted with what appears to be a charcoal-clay mixture, to represent shirts" (Trezise 1971:19). These images were associated with sorcery aimed at killing the Native Police, who were considered to be traitors. A large, 5-m-long snake is seen injecting poison into the foot of one of the figures. According to Caesar LeChu, the "seven white hand stencils along the snake" represent the "signatures of the small guerilla band harrying the Black Police" (Trezise 1993:51). Nearby at Pig Gallery are further sorcery paintings of Europeans that "have been repainted or touched up, and additions made, probably during a repeat performance of a sorcery ceremony" (Trezise 1971:30). As with the other sorcery figures, the Pig Gallery figures have linear motifs at their sides that are thought to be rifles. Another sorcery figure at LeChu Site has one of these linear motifs at its side in addition to a stone ax painted over the head (Cole 1992:168, 1995:65). At Emu Gallery, Trezise (1971:25) documented other horizontally oriented anthropomorphs identified as "sorcery-motivated paintings of white men" by his informants. Trezise (1993:52) reflected on the broader significance of this site: "We camped under bloodwoods outside the Emu Gallery. It was a sad haunted place for each of us. We felt the presence of those desperate people who had fled here to their stronghold to employ bitter sorcery against the invaders, after they had found their spears useless against Snider rifles. The silence of the bush around the long-abandoned sites was mute evidence that sorcery had failed."

Farther to the west, Chaloupka (1993:207) suggested that certain parts of Arnhem Land saw a "dramatic" increase in postcontact sorcery rock-art that he associates with controlling the impact of European-introduced diseases (cf. Kimber 1988). However, in something of a twist, many Aboriginal people attributed these diseases not to the newcomers but to Indigenous sorcery activities. The increased occurrence of sorcery paintings was the result of attempts to punish Aboriginal people thought responsible for causing these afflictions. This situation has parallels with ceremonies in southeastern Australia during the nineteenth century that were aimed at curbing the impact of smallpox and the malevolent spirit that caused it (see earlier in this chapter).

Territorial Rock-Art

Queensland's Central Highlands reveals the largest stencil rock-art tradition in the world, with thousands of sites containing stencils ranging from full human bodies to hafted stone axes and various other items of material culture (Morwood 1984; Quinnell 1976; Walsh 1979, 1984, 1988). The region is also known for its complex and elaborate Aboriginal mortuary ceremonies which are manifested archaeologically by bark "cylinder" coffins (often decorated) placed inside naturally weathered recesses within sandstone cliff faces (McNiven 1996; Robins and Walsh 1979; Walsh 1987). Although none of the burials has been radiometrically dated, many of the bark coffins exhibit steel ax cut marks indicating a postcontact (post-1840) date. From a detailed investigation of crypts in the Chesterton Range, Walsh (1987:117) found that most burials were located on prominent outcrops, with no sites "recorded in settings which could be termed 'concealed' or without any view" (Walsh 1987:117).

The obtrusiveness of burials was enhanced greatly by rock paintings around the entrances to crypts. Significantly, Walsh (1987:133) noted that this "burial art" dates mostly to the last few hundred years. Furthermore, he noted that the Chesterton Range area exhibits the "most highly developed" and highest concentration of burial art (Walsh 1988: 128) *and* the highest concentration of postcontact burials within the region (Walsh 1987:120). As such, he believed that the elaboration of burial crypts may have been a postcontact "innovation" (Walsh 1987:120). Following on from these observations, McNiven (1996) hypothesized that this "innovation" may have been a response to the extremely violent colonial frontier of the Central Highlands region. That is, Aboriginal people of the Central Highlands elaborated their burial crypts to create highly visual, spiritually charged markers on the landscape to reinforce their control of the land in the eyes of European invaders. Although it is acknowledged that the burials-as-resistance hypothesis is tentative, it is consistent with observations from other parts of Australia where burials (particularly obtrusive burial forms such as rock outcrop crypts and mounded burial grounds) could be used by Aboriginal people as general signifiers of land ownership/tenure (e.g., Pardoe 1988; see also Ingold 1986: chap. 6; Pearson 1999:135) and more specifically as social boundary markers identifying different territorial domains (e.g., Tindale 1974:66). In the Central Highlands, the broad distribution of burials suggests that they functioned as general markers of land tenure. A concentration of postcontact burials in the Chesterton Range—the "tribal" boundary between the Pitjara and Nguri peoples (Tindale 1974:183–184)—supports arguments for increased expressions of territoriality, as highly visible and elaborate burial art became an important response to European invasion.

Rock-art of the Wardaman people of the Northern Territory provides an opportunity for a more ethnographically informed examination of the associations between rock-art, land ownership/control, and responses to European invasion (David et al. 1990, 1994; Merlan 1989). Recent ethnographic research with the Wardaman has revealed that their "country" is divided into different estates that have both general and specific cosmological ("Dreaming") associations. Land ownership for clans is legitimated by associations with specific Dreaming identities that express themselves visually as rock paintings across the landscape. These visual expressions link specific places with specific clans and underwrite the local land tenure system. It is this linking of places with specific groups that led David et al. (1994:249) to conclude that Wardaman rock-art is also "closely linked with territorial concerns."

Excavations across Wardaman country indicate that the visual expression of Dreaming entities was elaborated in the period after European contact in the mid-nineteenth century. In particular, paintings of large paired anthropomorphs, of which the Lightning Brothers are the most famous, seem to date mostly to the period after European contact. David et al. (1990:82) suggested that because these figures are "expressions of the identity of the Dreaming Beings which are associated with the land on which the paintings occur, it is possible that a post-contact origin to such paintings signals the emergence of a very specific form of territorial marker." Furthermore, "The establishment of such territorial markers throughout Wardaman country re-enforced established land divisions, and this may or may not have been linked to the perceived threats resulting from European invasion of Wardaman country" (David et al. 1990:83).

A strategic part of the visual reaffirmation of Wardaman land ownership and control appears to have been an increase in the size of paintings expressing Dreaming entities. For example, the largest paintings in Wardaman country are the paired anthropomorphs that are up to 4.5 m tall in the case of the Lightning Brothers at Yiwarlarlay (David et al. 1991:373). Thus, elaboration of an existing rock-art tradition, both in terms of the scale and extent of paintings, was a feature associated with Aboriginal responses to European colonial invasion in the Central Highlands and in Wardaman country (see David and Wilson, this volume, for a detailed discussion of the Wardaman example).

CONCLUSIONS

Australian contact history after the 1970s, and subsequently contact archaeology, has been defined to a large extent by the heuristic model of a frontier. As we have observed, this model was an important step in disentangling previous histories that neglected or skimmed over dispossession and depopulation. However, the frontier model is now seen to have severe limitations because Aboriginal actions are interpreted in terms of reactions to a frontier with an illusory geographical specificity. Archaeologists, too, have on occasion been led by the idea that the land at contact could be divided into colonized and uncolonized categories. These arbitrary units, divided as they are by an imaginary line, should not be allowed to limit our understandings of the contact period. Aboriginal people saw all of their territory, both that occupied by invaders and that which was not, as their own. In this sense, the European construction of a geographical frontier reveals its illusory status (see Wolski 2001). Actions aimed at removing Europeans or controlling their actions need to be viewed with an appreciation that Indigenous perceptions of "place" were dramatically different from that of the Europeans. Postcontact rock-art and the appropriation of new materials and objects should not be seen as necessarily secular activities related to acculturation but as possible attempts to regain control over land and resources. We argue that it is only when frontiers are conceptualized as multivalent categories that it will be possible to develop a much more subtle sense of the early contact period.

Across their lands Aboriginal responses to European invasion were physical and spiritual, many and varied. To the European observers overt actions such as skirmishes and battles were juxtaposed by the covert actions of theft and the slaughter of grazing animals. What was not observed and for the most part remains poorly understood were those interactions that took place within the realm of the spirit world and Indigenous knowledge and experience of place and existence itself. By extending a counter-reading of sketchy historical sources to include archaeological evidence such as contact rock-art, we have revealed the existence of a postcontact Indigenous landscape that was regulated by ceremonial strategies and systems of place marking designed to combat European colonialism. This was a landscape that may very well have appeared to the invaders as obtainable, its inhabitants passive and acquiescent. Far from merely fleshing out historical narratives of contact life, this chapter has highlighted archaeology's unique position to identify otherwise invisible domains of postcontact activity.

Material culture frequently manifests elements of what Nicholas Thomas (1991) called entanglement. Entangled objects need to be understood in terms of the relationships out of which they have developed. Postcontact rock-art can provide a unique understanding of the complicated relationships between colonizer and colonized. It is up to the contact archaeologist to determine whether or not he or she can contribute to this understanding and deliver

new insights into the dynamics of intercultural encounters. However, it is not simply a case of contact historians continuing to expose "hidden history" (both oral and documentary) and contact archaeologists uncovering "missing history" whose shadow forms the archaeological record. Each discipline can act as a counterpoint to the other to create a new epistemological arena that exposes the past and its unfamiliarity.

NOTE

Thanks to Nathan Wolski and Bain Attwood for numerous stimulating discussions on contact archaeology and frontier historiography.

REFERENCES CITED

Akerman, K. 1979. Trade and Material Culture in the Kimberley Region. In *Aborigines of the West*, edited by R. M. Berndt and C. H. Berndt, 243–257. Perth: University of Western Australia Press.

Anderson, C. 1983. Aborigines and Tin Mining in North Queensland: A Case Study in the Anthropology of Contact History. *Mankind* 13 (6): 473–497.

Attwood, B. 1989. *The Making of the Aborigines*. Sydney: Allen and Unwin.

Baker, R. 1999. *Land is Life: From Bush to Town: The Story of the Yanyuwa People*. Sydney: Allen and Unwin.

Barrett, C. 1948. *White Blackfellows: The Strange Adventures of Europeans Who Lived among Savages*. Melbourne: Hallcraft.

Beckett, J. 1987. *Torres Strait Islanders: Custom and Colonialism*. Cambridge: Cambridge University Press.

Birmingham, J. 1992. *Wybalenna: The Archaeology of Cultural Accommodation in Nineteenth Century Tasmania*. Sydney: The Australian Society for Historical Archaeology Incorporated.

Broome, R. 1982. *Aboriginal Australians*. Sydney: George Allen and Unwin.

Brown, I. W. 1979. Functional Group Changes and Acculturation: A Case Study of the French and the Indian in the Lower Mississippi Valley. *Midcontinental Journal of Archaeology* 4 (2): 147–165.

Chaloupka, G. 1979. Pack-Bells on the Rock Face: Aboriginal Paintings of European Contact in Northwestern Arnhem Land. *Aboriginal History* 3 (2): 92–95.

———. 1993. *Journey in Time*. Sydney: Reed.

Chief Commissioner of Police. 1887. Great Sandy or Fraser's Island. In *The Australian Race*, edited by E. M. Curr, 144–147. Vol. 3. Melbourne: John Ferres.

Cole, N. 1992. "Human" Motifs in the Rock Paintings of Jowalbinna, Laura. In *State of the Art: Regional Rock Art Studies in Australia and Melanesia*, edited by J. McDonald and I. P. Hascovec, 164–173. Occasional AURA Publication No. 6. Melbourne: Australian Rock Art Research Association.

———. 1995. Rock Art in the Laura-Cooktown Region, S.E. Cape York Peninsula. In *Quinkan Prehistory: The Archaeology of Aboriginal Art in S.E. Cape York Peninsula, Australia*, edited by M. J. Morwood and D. R. Hobbs, 51–70. Tempus 3. St. Lucia: Anthropology Museum, University of Queensland.

Cooper, Z., and S. Bowdler. 1998. Flaked Glass Tools from the Andaman Islands and Australia. *Asian Perspectives* 37 (1):74–83.

Courtney, K., and I. J. McNiven. 1998. Clay Tobacco Pipes from Aboriginal Middens on Fraser Island, Queensland. *Australian Archaeology* 47:44–53.

Critchett, J. 1990. *A Distant Field of Murder: Western District Frontiers 1834–1848*. Melbourne: Melbourne University Press.

Curr, E. M. 1887a. The Ovens, Caves, Paintings, and Sculptures of Our Blacks, and Also the Question of Whether the Present Race Were the First Inhabitants of Australia. In *The Australian Race*, edited by E. M. Curr, Vol. 3, 675–681. Melbourne: John Ferres, Government Printer.

———. 1887b. Great Sandy or Fraser Island. In *The Australian Race*, edited by E. M. Curr, Vol. 3, 144–149. Melbourne: John Ferres, Government Printer.

David, B., I. McNiven, J. Flood, and R. Frost. 1990. Yiwarlarlay 1: Archaeological Excavations at the Lightning Brothers Site, Delamere Station, Northern Territory. *Archaeology in Oceania* 25: 79–84.

David, B., I. McNiven, and J. Flood. 1991. Archaeological Excavations at Yiwarlarlay 1: Site Report. *Memoirs of the Queensland Museum* 30 (3): 373–380.

David, B., I. McNiven, V. Attenbrow, J. Flood, and J. Collins. 1994. Of Lightning Brothers and White Cockatoos: Dating the Antiquity of Signifying Systems in the Northern Territory, Australia. *Antiquity* 68:241–251.

Drooker, P. B. 1996. Madisonville Metal and Glass Artifacts: Implications for Western Fort Ancient Chronology and Interaction Patterns. *Midcontinental Journal of Archaeology* 21 (2): 145–190.

Elder, B. 1988. *Blood on the Wattle: Massacres and Maltreatment of Australian Aborigines since 1788*. French's Forest: Child and Associates.

Evans, R., K. Saunders, and K. Cronin. 1975. *Exclusion, Exploitation and Extermination: Race Relations in Colonial Queensland*. Sydney: Australian and New Zealand Book Company.

Fels, M. 1988. *Good Men and True: The Aboriginal Police of the Port Phillip District 1837–1853*. Melbourne: Melbourne University Press.

Frederick, U. K. 1999. At the Centre of It All: Constructing Contact through the Rock Art of Watarrka National Park, Central Australia. *Archaeology in Oceania* 34:132–144.

Gould, R. A., D. A. Koster, and A. H. L. Sontz. 1971. The Lithic Assemblage of the Western Desert Aborigines of Australia. *American Antiquity* 36 (2): 149–169.

Hascovec, I., and H. Sullivan. 1989. Reflections of an Aboriginal Artist. In *Animals into Art*, edited by H. Morphy, 57–74. London: Unwin.

Hayden, B. 1981. *Palaeolithic Reflections: Lithic Technology and Ethnographic Excavations among Australian Aborigines. Canberra: Australian Institute of Aboriginal Studies.

Head, L., and R. Fullagar. 1997. Hunter-Gatherer Archaeology and Pastoral Contact: Perspectives from the Northwest Northern Territory, Australia. World Archaeology 28:418–428.

Henderson, J. 1999. Sent Forth a Dove: Discovery of the Duyfken. Nedlands: University of Western Australia Press.

Hercus, L. A. 1980. "How We Danced the Mudlungga": Memories of 1901 and 1902. Aboriginal History 4 (1): 4–47.

Horne, G., and G. Aiston. 1924. Savage Life in Central Australia. London: Macmillan and Co.

Howitt, A. W. 1904. The Native Tribes of South-east Australia. London: Macmillan and Co.

Huggins, R., and J. Huggins. 1994. Auntie Rita. Canberra: Aboriginal Studies Press.

Ingold, T. 1986. The Appropriation of Nature: Essays on Human Ecology and Social Relations. Manchester: Manchester University Press.

Jolly, P. A. 1996. Symbiotic Interaction between Black Farming Communities and the South-eastern San: Some Implications for Southern African Rock Art Studies, the Use of Ethnographic Analogy, and the Cultural Identity of Hunter-Gatherers. Current Anthropology 37:277–305.

———. 1999. Modelling Change in the Contact Art of the South-eastern San, Southern Africa. In The Archaeology of Rock-Art, edited by C. Chippindale and P. S. C. Taçon, 247–267. Cambridge: Cambridge University Press.

Jones, R., and N. White. 1988. Point Blank: Stone Tool Manufacture at the Ngilipitji Quarry, Arnhem Land 1981. In Archaeology with Ethnography: An Australian Perspective, edited by B. Meehan and R. Jones, 51–87. Canberra: Department of Prehistory, Research School of Pacific Studies, Australian National University.

Kimber, R. G. 1988. Smallpox in Central Australia: Evidence for Epidemics and Postulations about the Impact. Australian Archaeology 27:63–68.

Klassen, M. A. 1999. Icon and Narrative in Transition: Contact-Period Rock-Art at Writing-On-Stone, Southern Alberta, Canada. In The Archaeology of Rock-Art, edited by C. Chippindale and P. S. C. Taçon, 42–72. Cambridge: Cambridge University Press.

Layton, R. 1992. Australian Rock Art: A New Synthesis. Cambridge: Cambridge University Press.

Loos, N. 1982. Invasion and Resistance: Aboriginal-European Relations on the North Queensland Frontier 1861–1897. Canberra: Australian National University Press.

L'Oste-Brown, S., L. Godwin, G. Henry, T. Mitchell, and V. Tyson. 1995. "Living under the Act": Taroom Aboriginal Reserve 1911–1927. Cultural Heritage Monograph Series, Vol. 1. Brisbane: Queensland Department of Environment and Heritage.

MacKnight, C. C. 1976. The Voyage to Marege': Macassan Trepangers in Northern Australia. Melbourne: Melbourne University Press.

McBryde, I. 1989. " . . . To Establish a Commerce of This Sort"—Cross-Cultural Exchange at the Port Jackson Settlement. In Studies from Terra Australis to Australia, edited by J. Hardy and A. Frost, 169–182. Occasional Paper No. 6. Canberra: Australian Academy of the Humanities.

McGrath, A. 1987. Born in the Cattle. Sydney: Allen and Unwin.

———. 1995. A National Story. In Contested Ground: Australian Aborigines under the British Crown, edited by A. McGrath, 1–54. Sydney: Allen and Unwin.

McKellar, H. 1984. Matya-Mundu: A History of the Aboriginal People of South West Queensland. Cunnamulla: Cunnamulla Australian Native Welfare Association.

McNiven, I. J. 1996. Ethnological Specimens or Aboriginal Graves? Managing Aboriginal Burial Crypts of the Central Queensland Highlands (Stage 1)— Preliminary Assessment and Recommendations. Report to Queensland Department of Environment and Heritage, Central Coast Region, Rockhampton.

———. 2001. Torres Strait Islanders and the Maritime Frontier in Early Colonial Australia. In *Colonial Frontiers: Indigenous-European Encounters in Settler Societies*, edited by L. Russell, 175–197. Studies in Imperialism Series. Manchester: Manchester University Press.

Merlan, F. 1989. The Interpretive Framework of Wardaman Rock Art: A Preliminary Report. *Australian Aboriginal Studies* 2:14–24.

Miller, C. L., and G. R. Hamell. 1986. A New Perspective on Indian-White Contact: Cultural Symbols and Colonial Trade. *The Journal of American History* 73 (1): 311–328.

Moore, D. R. 1979. *Islanders and Aborigines at Cape York*. Canberra: Australian Institute of Aboriginal Studies.

Morwood, M. J. 1984. The Prehistory of the Central Queensland Highlands. *Advances in World Archaeology* 3:325–380.

Muirhead, J. 1887. Belyando River. In *The Australian Race*, edited by E. M. Curr, Vol. 3., 26–31. Melbourne: John Ferres, Government Printer.

Mulvaney, D. J. 1976. "The Chain of Connection": The Material Evidence. In *Tribes and Boundaries in Australia*, edited by N. Peterson, 72–94. Canberra: Australian Institute of Aboriginal Studies.

———. 1989. *Encounters in Place: Outsiders and Aboriginal Australians 1606–1985*. St. Lucia: University of Queensland Press.

Mulvaney, K. 1992. Who Paints for a Killing: Gurindji Sorcery Painting of Palngarrawuny. In *State of the Art: Regional Rock Art Studies in Australia and Melanesia*, edited by J. McDonald and I. P. Hascovec, 216–225. Occasional AURA Publication No. 6. Melbourne: Australian Rock Art Research Association.

Murray, T. 1993. The Childhood of William Lanne: Contact Archaeology and Aboriginality in Tasmania. *Antiquity* 67:504–519.

Newland, S. 1926. *Memoirs of Simpson Newland*. Adelaide: F. W. Preece and Sons.

Pardoe, C. 1988. The Cemetery as Symbol: The Distribution of Prehistoric Aboriginal Burial Grounds in Southeastern Australia. *Archaeology in Oceania* 23:1–16.

Parker, L. K. 1905. *The Euahlayi Tribe: A Study of Aboriginal Life in Australia*. London: Archibald Constable.

Pearson, M. P. 1999. *The Archaeology of Death and Burial*. Phoenix Mill: Sutton.

Poignant, R. 1996. Ryko's Photographs of the "Fort Dundas Riot": The Story So Far. *Australian Aboriginal Studies* 2:24–41.

Quinnell, M. C. 1976. Aboriginal Rock Art in Carnarvon Gorge, South Central Queensland. Master's thesis, University of New England, Armidale.

Reynolds, H. 1978. Aboriginal-European Contact History. *Journal of Australian Studies* 3:52–64.

———. 1981. *The Other Side of the Frontier: An Interpretation of the Aboriginal Response to the Invasion and Settlement of Australia*. Townsville: History Department, James Cook University.

———. 1990a. The Land, the Explorers and the Aborigines. In *Through White Eyes*, edited by S. Janson and S. Macintyre, 120–131. Sydney: Allen and Unwin.

———. 1990b. *With the White People: The Crucial Role of Aborigines in the Exploration and Development of Australia*. Ringwood: Penguin.

Robins, R. P., and G. L. Walsh. 1979. Burial Cylinders: The Essence of a Dilemma in Public Archaeology. *Australian Archaeology* 9:62–76.

Rose, D. B. 1991. *Hidden Histories: Black Stories from Victoria River Downs, Humbert River and Wave Hill Stations*. Canberra: Aboriginal Studies Press.

Rose, F. 1942. Paintings of the Groote Eylandt Aborigines. *Oceania* 13:170–176.

Rosser, B. 1987. *Dreamtime Nightmares*. Ringwood: Penguin.

Rowley, C. D. 1972. *The Destruction of Aboriginal Society*. Ringwood: Penguin.

Russell, L. 2001a. Introduction. In *Colonial Frontiers: Indigenous-European Encounters in Settler Societies*, edited by L. Russell, 1–20. Studies in Imperialism Series. Manchester: Manchester University Press.

———. 2001b. *Savage Imaginings: Historical and Contem-*

porary Constructions of Australian Aboriginalities. Melbourne: Australian Scholarly Publications/Arcadia.

Ryan, S. 1996. *The Cartographic Eye: How Explorers Saw Australia*. Cambridge: Cambridge University Press.

Schaffer, K. 1995. *In the Wake of First Contact: The Eliza Fraser Stories*. Cambridge: Cambridge University Press.

Simon, E. 1987. *Through My Eyes*. Blackburn: Collins Dove.

Smyth, R. B. 1878. *The Aborigines of Victoria: With Notes Relating to the Habits of the Natives of Other Parts of Australia and Tasmania*. 2 vols. Melbourne: John Ferres, Government Printer.

Stoffle, R. W., L. Loendorf, D. E. Austin, D. B. Halmo, and A. Bulletts. 2000. Ghost Dancing the Grand Canyon: Southern Paiute Rock Art, Ceremony, and Cultural Landscapes. *Current Anthropology* 41: 11–38.

Swain, T. 1993. *A Place for Strangers: Towards a History of Australian Aboriginal Being*. Cambridge: Cambridge University Press.

Thomas, N. 1991. *Entangled Objects: Exchange, Material Culture and Colonialism in the Pacific*. Cambridge, Massachusetts: Harvard University Press.

Thomson, D. F. 1949. *Economic Structure and the Ceremonial Exchange Cycle in Arnhem Land*. Melbourne: Macmillan and Co.

———. 1964. Some Wood and Stone Implements of the Bindibu Tribe of Central Western Australia. *Proceedings of the Prehistoric Society* 30:400–422.

Thorpe, B. 1996. *Colonial Queensland: Perspectives on a Frontier Society*. St. Lucia: University of Queensland Press.

Thorpe, W. W. 1924. Aboriginal Adaptability. *The Australian Museum Magazine* 3 (10): 337–339.

Tindale, N. B. 1965. Stone Implement Making among the Nakako, Ngadadjara and Pitjandjara of the Great Western Desert. *Records of the South Australian Museum* 15 (1): 131–164.

———. 1974. *Aboriginal Tribes of Australia*. Berkeley: University of California Press.

Trezise, P. J. 1969. *Quinkan Country: Adventures in Search of Aboriginal Cave Paintings in Cape York*. Sydney: A. H. and A. W. Reed.

———. 1971. *Rock Art of South-east Cape York*. Australian Aboriginal Studies No. 24. Prehistory and Material Culture Series No. 4. Canberra: Australian Institute of Aboriginal Studies.

———. 1993. *Dream Road: A Journey of Discovery*. Sydney: Allen and Unwin.

Trigger, D. 1991. *White Fella Comin'*. Melbourne: Cambridge University Press.

Walsh, G. L. 1979. Mutilated Hands or Signal Stencils? A Consideration of Irregular Hand Stencils from Central Queensland. *Australian Archaeology* 9:33–41.

———. 1984. Managing the Archaeological Sites of the Sandstone Belt. Report, Queensland National Parks and Wildlife Service, Brisbane.

———. 1987. The Chesterton Range: Its Sites and Management. Report (Draft). Queensland National Parks and Wildlife Service, Brisbane.

———. 1988. *Australia's Greatest Rock Art*. Bathurst: Brill–Robert Brown Associates.

Wolfe, P. 1999. *Settler Colonialism and the Transformation of Anthropology*. London: Cassells.

Wolski, N. 2000. Brushing against the Grain: Excavating for Aboriginal-European Interaction on the Colonial Frontier in Western Victoria, Australia. Ph.D. thesis, University of Melbourne, Melbourne.

———. 2001. All Is Not Quiet on the Western Front: Rethinking Resistance and Frontiers in Aboriginal Historiography. In *Colonial Frontiers: Indigenous-European Encounters in Settler Societies*, edited by L. Russell, 216–235. Studies in Imperialism Series. Manchester: Manchester University Press.

Wolski, N., and T. H. Loy. 1999. On the Invisibility of Contact: Residue Analysis of Aboriginal Glass Artefacts from Western Victoria. *The Artefact* 22:65–73.

FOUR

Spaces of Resistance

Graffiti and Indigenous Place Markings in the Early European Contact Period of Northern Australia

BRUNO DAVID AND MEREDITH WILSON

The words *graffito* and *graffiti* originate from the Italian *"graffiare"* (to scribble), "graffito" and *"graffio"* (a scratch), and ultimately from the Greek *"gráphein"* (mark, draw, or write). "Graffiti" was first used in the English language in 1851, when Daniel Wilson[1] discussed the Scandinavian runes in the Neolithic chambered tomb of Maeshouse (Maeshowe) in Orkney, Scotland. This 4,700-year-old tomb had been entered by Vikings during the Norse settlement of Orkney in the mid-twelfth century C.E. The Vikings had marked the rocks with twenty-four runic inscriptions—the largest set of runic inscriptions in the world—and some drawings (Oram 1997:214–215). The inscriptions echo strangely the familiar writings of modern graffiti: "Haermund Hardaxe carved these runes," "these runes were carved by the man most skilled in runes in the Western Ocean," "Benedikt made this cross," and "Ingigerth is the most beautiful of women" (Mackenzie-Winters 2000; see Barnes 1995 for full texts and discussion of interpretations).

It was not until 1877, however, when Amelia Edwards (1877:653) published a description of her adventures up the Nile River, that the word *graffiti* was first used in the English language to describe recently made inscriptions. Edwards noted that the ancient Egyptian tombs at Bab-el-Molûk, Thebes, were "visited by crowds of early travellers, who have as usual left their neatly-scribbled graffiti on the walls." The tombs' defacement with modern (and older) writings was lamented by Edwards as a violation of the sanctity of the long-dead kings of the Great Valley. In truth, however, the writings on the walls were as much a violation of Amelia Edwards' own nostalgic imaginings of a past long gone.

Amelia Edwards' reactions to the graffiti at Thebes aptly address the main ideas explored in this chapter. Inscriptions are not simply writings in place, but the actions of people who write themselves into the landscape and in the process encroach on the sanctuary of other personal spaces. But we suggest that inscriptions are also more than this. In that they are an assertion of a right to be-in-place, inscriptions represent a resistance to sociogeographical exclusion. Such acts of resistance vary according to the social circumstances underpinning them.

The first part of this chapter considers modern-day graffiti as the product of an inherently territorial and resistive act. An example of rock-art is then discussed in view of graffiti-associated behavior. This example is presented in an attempt to theorize various bodies of rock-art in a new way—as a mobilization of the right to be-in-place in a context of resistance.

GRAFFITI

The Oxford English Dictionary defines graffiti as "a drawing or writing scratched on a wall or other surface." In common parlance, however, graffiti[2] has a more pointed definition, referring to unsolicited inscriptions in public spaces. As a form of inscription usually practiced *outside* the censoring arm of the power elite, graffiti confronts and contradicts the ordered and ordering space of institutionalized life.[3] Thus by definition, graffiti is imbued with a polluting and vandalistic quality irrespective of its decorative potential. It threatens the status quo not just because of the words or images written, but by the fact that its execution in public spaces lies outside the control of existing social forces.

Graffiti is thus a particular kind of inscription in public space—the written voice of people actually or potentially subordinated by public sentiment and expectation. Such voices *include* the subordinative propaganda of those in a position of power who express resistance to other social forces (see Ballard, this volume, for examples). When inscriptions cease to be seen as polluting (in the sense of Mary Douglas [e.g., 1966]), they cease to be graffiti, instead becoming public art or street decoration in the eyes of the controlling institutions.

One of the differences between graffiti performed as propaganda by the power elite (e.g., politicians seeking votes) and that undertaken in resistance to those elites concerns a balance of powers. A common thread is that in both cases the writing inscribes the protagonist onto the land *as a right of place* and self-determination. Because graffiti is in the public eye, the behavioral censorship of what Stenson (1997:528) called the "moral entrepreneurs—urban managers, politicians, police and commercial interests" is questioned and resisted. In Stenson's (1997:528) words, "graffiti as a crime of style offers active, playful anarchistic resistance. . . . This is seen as part of a wider battle to reclaim control over the streets and other so-called public spaces, seen as increasingly under the control of government and corporate authorities" (see also Ferrell 1996). In marking place, *ownership* is claimed over space and over the *right* to place. Graffiti, like all place marking, is a territorial concern.

Graffiti is also often said to represent the anonymous voice, because the act of inscription is usually undertaken beyond the gaze of censoring authorities (e.g., Blake 1981; Ferrell 1995; Gonos et al. 1976). Nonetheless, graffiti in its final form offers insight into the relationships between inscriber, inscription, and societal power relations. As we hope to demonstrate in this chapter, it is these relationships that offer lessons about inscriptive behavior more generally.

The usefulness of graffiti for the study of rock-art thus emerges from a basic characteristic: graffiti represents an inscription of the self in various kinds of social spaces and has the ability to mobilize sentiment. Rock-art is rarely seen in this light, as actively engaged and engaging, being more commonly treated as stylistic silence. What parallels are there between the practice of graffiti and the practice of rock-art; between the sociopolitical contexts in which both are practiced, the physical space in which they are rendered, and the relations between inscriber, inscription, and recipient? First let us consider some of the ways individual and social voices can be heard through the medium of graffiti. This discussion will in turn provide a contemporary springboard for examining more ancient forms of speaking through images. We are not looking to extrapolate contemporary explanations into the past, but rather to examine more generally social mechanisms of inscription and their territorial implications. The key point is that *all* inscription is about the politics of turf; inscriptions colonize space.

GRAFFITI AS NORM AND RESISTANCE

Stocker et al. (1972) argued that graffiti is an indicator of social values. Although their work focused in particular on the sexual dimensions of Western graffiti, their conclusions have much broader implications:

1. "Graffiti are an accurate indicator of the social attitudes of a community and their thematic content will discriminate similar communities with different socio-political ideation";
2. Most so-called "deviant" graffiti are a result of societal denunciation of particular practices or ways of being. With changing values normalizing or accepting past deviance, the incidence of such graffiti will decrease;
3. "The difference between men's and women's graffiti is due to childhood socialisation; and, if there is a change in amount and kind of women's

and men's graffiti, then there has been a change in some aspect of women's [and presumably men's] socialisation" (Stocker et al. 1972:358). The implication is that graffiti is socially produced and sensitive to societal change.

In making these conclusions Stocker et al. were concentrating on the written messages rather than on the act of marking place. They suggested that these messages could be read more or less directly, as an echo or track of the social use of space and societal norms. These views have subsequently been questioned, an alternative position being that "as we look at culture through the window afforded us by any expressive outlet, what we see has been modified by the peculiar nature of the medium" (Gonos et al. 1976:40). Instead of graffiti mirroring cultural norms and power relations, the "anonymity" that defines its production allows the graffitist "opportunities to use language, and present beliefs and sentiments, which are not acceptable in ordinary social life" (Gonos et al. 1976:42). Gonos et al. (1976) proposed that the need to write particular graffiti is continually changing. The pressure or compulsion to write certain types of graffiti is strongest when a value has a "life" outside of the established value system that has been institutionalized in community norms or enforced by the power elite.

Liminality

The studies of Stocker et al. and Gonos et al. articulate opposing positions and interpretations of graffiti. In some ways, Blake (1981:99) unified aspects of the two approaches by describing graffiti as "behavioural residues." Following Victor Turner (e.g., 1987), Blake used the concept of *liminality* to address human behavior in space: "liminal spaces are transitional areas where social boundaries are blurred and normal rules of conduct and role expectations are held in abeyance or even in opposition" (Blake 1981:95). Blake found that graffiti occurs in many places with high degrees of liminality (e.g., bus back seats, elevators), with the toilet usually being treated as the most liminal space of all (Blake 1981:96). Because graffitists can transcend social boundaries in liminal spaces, they can express themselves and inscribe those spaces in ways that also transcend established norms. The effect is to question such norms and to resist the possibility of exclusion in the process.

RESISTANCE AND POWER

Place marking is not just an assertion of power, but an expression of resistance. Foucault (e.g., 1990) has repeatedly stated that resistance is present wherever there is social power. He noted that

> resistance is never in a position of exteriority in relation to power. . . . there is a plurality of resistances, each of them a special case: resistances that are possible, necessary, improbable; others that are spontaneous, savage, solitary, concerted, rampant, or violent; still others that are quick to compromise, interested, or sacrificial; by definition, they can only exist in the strategic field of power relations. But this does not mean that they are only a reaction or rebound, forming with respect to the basic domination an underside that is in the end always passive, doomed to perpetual defeat. Resistances do not derive from a few heterogeneous principles; but neither are they a lure or a promise that is of necessity betrayed. They are the odd term in relations of power; they are inscribed in the latter as an irreducible opposite. Hence they too are distributed in irregular fashion: the points, knots, or focuses of resistance are spread over time and space at varying

densities, at times mobilizing groups or individuals in a definitive way, inflaming certain points of the body, certain moments in life, certain types of behaviour. . . . Just as the network of power relations ends by forming a dense web that passes through apparatuses and institutions, without being exactly localised in them, so too the swarm of points of resistance traverses social stratifications and individual unities. (Foucault 1997:169)

Emplaced Resistance

By virtue of the fact that *individuals* are emplaced in a *social* world, places are institutionalized in relations of interpersonal power. A consideration of graffiti brings out the political nature of all inscriptions, that place marking is about writing the self onto the land. Place markings of all forms, not just graffiti, are territorial endeavors, inscribing the land with an identity that identifies the marker with the place *irrespective of the written message*. The process of place marking *takes place* in the need for a social recognition in opposition to or anticipation of the possibility of exclusion. It is the possibility of exclusion, real or imagined, actual or potential, that is resisted in place marking, that signals the territorial imperative.

If this is so, then changes in patterns of place marking in the archaeological record imply changes in social circumstances and patterns of resistance. These insights show promise for a new understanding of preexisting marks in place, such as rock-art. We explore this with respect to rock-art in Wardaman Aboriginal country, Australia. Discussion focuses on the nature of inscriptive behavior during the early European contact period, when the exclusion or threat of exclusion of Indigenous peoples from their traditional lands were at their most extreme.

THE ROCK-ART OF WARDAMAN COUNTRY, AUSTRALIA

First some background on Wardaman country and Wardaman relations with the land to set the scene. The Wardaman are an Aboriginal language group of the Victoria River district, in Australia's Northern Territory (Figure 4.1). Wardaman country is located some 70 km southwest of the modern town of Katherine. Covering a vast expanse of land (ca. 200 by 150 km in area) roughly quadrilateral in shape, it is delimited to the north by Scott Creek, Romula Knob in the southeast, and the Victoria River crossing in the southwest. Wardaman country is surrounded by distinctive but related Aboriginal language groups and territories: Jaminjung to the west, Dagoman to the north, Yangman to the east, Mudburra to the south, Ngarinyman and Ngaliwurru to the southwest (Merlan 1994, 1998). Kin, exchange, and other cultural relations are close between mem-

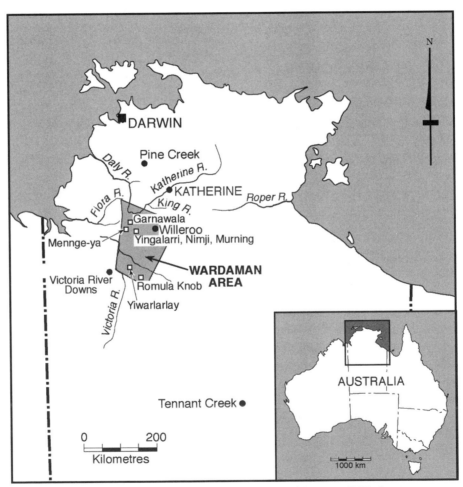

FIGURE 4.1. Map of north-central Australia showing location of Wardaman country and key sites.

bers of the various language groups, especially to the west and south where a number of common cultural practices are observed (e.g., the eight-class kinship system, and various initiation practices such as subincision). All of these cultural practices are immersed in the Dreaming—they are explained by, emerge from, and structured through the Dreaming (see Langton, this volume, for a discussion of Aboriginal relations with the land in another part of Australia).

Language, Territory, and the Dreaming

When Europeans first arrived in Australia, some 250 Aboriginal languages were spoken across the continent; Wardaman was one of these. Sutton (1991:50) noted that what Aboriginal languages mark "are the lands whose owners under Aboriginal customary law were given particular languages during the mythic foundation of the world, the Dreaming, and it plots those land/language associations. It is a general rule in Aboriginal Australia that languages are held to have originated when Dreamings (Ancestral Beings, totemic heroes) invested the land with meaning and with human beings." In other words, Wardaman country represents the lands whose owners under customary law were given the Wardaman language during the creative acts of the Dreaming. The people who trace their ancestry as Wardaman hold exclusive primary Indigenous associations with both the land and the language. As Kearney (1988:7–9) wrote, "[t]he land, conceived in religious terms, is considered as having a cultural identity which it projects onto those people who are affiliated to its sites. It also projects that identity on to the . . . language which is considered to be the property of the people affiliated to that land. . . . The group as so conceived is said to be 'local' in the sense that it is territorially-based in [that] territory."

Among the Wardaman today and during the early European contact period there are various ways in which people are linked with the land. Wardaman people generally recognize nonlocalized matri-totems (the *ngurlu*); assign subsection partly, though not exclusively, through the mother; and practice a matrifocal system of parent-child relationship. There exists a matrifiliative complementary relationship to land, with patrifiliation being primary (F. Merlan, personal communication, 1993). Wardaman people, wrote Merlan (1994:6),

speak of different territorial sub-groupings, to which recruitment is normatively in the male line, as having different *madin* "languages," or "words." Each such identifiable grouping is said to have minimally one, sometimes more, special words that are "their" language. Typically, these are said to be either the sound made by, or the language spoken by, principal mythological figures saliently associated with given Wardaman sub-territories. For example, an important mythological association with the sub-country just west of Willeroo Station homestead running westerly to Garnawala (Mount Hogarth) is *gulirrida* "peewees," which are abundantly represented in some of the spectacular rock paintings in this area. The "language" or "word" of the peewees, and therefore of the grouping of people patrifiliated to this area, is said to be *mamunda-jgani*, a form for which no etymology can be given. A few of the "words" for particular sub-groupings may have etymologies in other languages of the Victoria River area. At least one is clearly onomatopoetic (e.g., standardization of a bird cry).

During the recent past, Wardaman country was divided into eleven totemically based territorial estates, each of which recognized a cosmological identity with specific Dreaming Beings, such as *gulirrida* (peewees) in the just-mentioned example

(Merlan 1989, 1994). In addition to the localized Dreamings of the various estates there were also traveling Beings who cut across patri-estates, such as Gorondolni, the Rainbow Serpent. Other Dreamings were restricted to individual locations only, such as *gandawag*, the Moon at Jalijbang. While the entire landscape thereby gained its identity and was made discontinuous by its affiliations with disparate localized and landed Dreaming Beings and events, some of which identified patri-estates and others that were located on the land but did not signify patri-estates, the entire landscape was united into a cosmological whole by its common participation in a unified system of beliefs informed by the Dreaming. In this sense, the way in which the various estates were divided and interlinked at various levels reflects the pattern of Wardaman land tenure, land use, identity, and cosmology. The land was inscribed with meaning, and all things present were sensual proof of the truth of those meanings.

The Dreaming and Wardaman Rock-Art

Thus it is in the Dreaming that Wardaman ontology is centered. Dreaming realities are expressed everywhere—in the mountains, rivers, trees, and rock outcrops. The landscape consists of a complex patchwork of Dreamings crisscrossed by nonlocal, traveling ones, both of which give identity to the land and link Wardaman country with neighboring lands. Individual places identified as of specific significance to Wardaman people take many forms, from features such as water holes or hills to smaller objects such as rocks or prominent trees, including individual or complexes of rock shelters. Thus although anthropogenic inscriptions in the form of rock-art tend to be found in the Victoria River district wherever there are rock outcrops and rock shel-

ters, it is the entire landscape that was created by the Dreaming Beings and that affirms and reaffirms the reality that is the Dreaming, including the "art" that strikingly and visually dominates many of the rock outcrops (David et al. 1994).

Paintings and engravings in Wardaman country portray specific historical events and/or designate the identity of the local Dreaming spirits who give identity to places (e.g., David et al. 1994; Merlan 1989). Because people's own identities are defined by their Dreaming, rock-art represents an assertion of the self in place—part of the general process of inscription already noted in relation to graffiti.

Two types of rock-art are identified today by Wardaman elders: "art" that is a visual manifestation of the Dreaming Beings themselves (*buwarraja*) and art created by people (*bulawula*). *Bulawula* rock-art concerns art that was undertaken during very recent times, usually by known individuals. Typically it portrays historical events (e.g., droving scenes) or historical characters, such as individual station managers. Much *bulawula* art consists of European objects such as guns and pipes, but this is not always the case. The historical status of *bulawula* art is not well understood, however. It is uncertain, for instance, whether or not such art emerged only with the advent of Europeans during the 1880s. Nevertheless, it always appears to be of recent character (i.e., *bulawula* art tends to have a fresh appearance, and in oral tradition it relates to the period of European contact or to rock pictures that traditional owners have no knowledge of and cannot easily position within their own Dreaming understanding). *Bulawula* art is uncommon compared with the abundant *buwarraja* rock-art of Wardaman country[4] (David et al. 1990; Flood 1997; Flood and David 1994; Flood et al. 1992). However, even though *bulawula* art is a mode of inscribing the self onto the land, for the purpose of this chapter we are more interested in the art recognized as *buwarraja* by Wardaman Elders.

Buwarraja rock-art consists predominantly of figurative paintings, abstract abrasions, and abstract and animal track peckings. The abrasions and the peckings tend to be small in size, usually less than 30 cm in maximum length. Their antiquity is poorly understood, but the oldest known examples are at least 5,000 years B.P., as evident by the presence of engravings on an exfoliated slab excavated by John Mulvaney (1975) in stratigraphic contexts at the Ingaladdi (Yingalarri 1) site. Similar peckings have recently been dated by Watchman et al. (2000), who, using accelerator mass spectrometry (AMS), have radiocarbon dated carbon-bearing laminae accumulated above an engraving at the site of Yiwarlarlay. The results show that a macropod track was engraved shortly before ca. 3,000 years B.P. Abraded grooves, however, are also known to have continued to be made into ethnographic times, into the late twentieth century C.E. The creation of abrasions thus has an antiquity spanning from at least 5,000 years B.P. to the twentieth century C.E., whereas peckings date at least to the mid- to late Holocene and likely also to the early Holocene/late Pleistocene because they are often heavily patinated.

Buwarraja rock paintings include all the large images; the highly decorated figures of animal and human shape. They also include many abstract figures. The age of these paintings is not easily determined, but painting activity is known to have continued into ethnographic times because of the presence of European items in the art and the testimonies of Wardaman Elders. The total absence of extinct animals such as thylacines (Tasmanian tigers) implies that painting activity was unlikely to have been intensive before ca. 3,500 years B.P. Watchman et al. (2000) reported clear traces of earth pigments trapped as laminae in rock surface crusts at Yiwarlarlay, AMS dated to less than ca. 3,000 years B.P. Most telling, the archaeological excavation of seven rock shelters within Wardaman country has revealed in each major increases in deposition rates of stratified fragments of ochre during the late Holocene, particularly during the last millennium. This is despite the excavation of a number of late Pleistocene and early Holocene sequences. The implication is a major increase in the incidence of painting activity during the late Holocene, coincident in time with major increases in intensities of site and regional land use. This implies that place marking in Wardaman country, as a means of inscribing the self onto the land, intensified with increasing social interaction (and likely also absolute populations).

Of particular interest to this chapter are the changes that take place in the rock-art with the advent of European invaders late in the nineteenth century C.E. The advent of Europeans does not just signal the beginnings of new, European-based motif forms (many, but not all, of which are *bulawula*) (such as guns and cattle-droving scenes; e.g., Figure 4.2), but also a restructuring of existing artistic conventions associated with *buwarraja* rock-art. Throughout the Victoria River district, preexisting conventions of polychrome painting, striping, anthropomorphism, and juxtapositioning of specific motifs were combined to produce complex images of gigantic proportions, all of which have a very recent appearance. Such paintings are not particularly common, only ever occurring singularly in any given rock outcrop or patri-estate. But when they do occur, they visually dominate the landscape in a way that the earlier art does not. In all cases, these paintings have a Dreaming significance that links the art to the place's Dreaming status and to the individuals of the appropriate Dreaming affiliation.

FIGURE 4.2. Depictions of European contact scenes, Yiwarlarlay.

There are five documented examples of such rock-art in Wardaman country. The best known of these sites is the Lightning Brothers of Yiwarlarlay (Delamere Station). David et al. (1990) reported on the Lightning Brothers story, as it was told by the senior Wardaman custodian of the site and other Wardaman elders in 1989. The story goes: Yagjagbula and Jabirringi are brothers. Yagjagbula is the younger. He is tall and handsome, but Jabirringi is short and not so attractive. Both brothers are of the Jabijin subsection. Yagjagbula has a wife, Gulliridan, and Jabirringi is married to Ganayanda (some people say that Jabirringi was promised to Ganayanda, but that both brothers could potentially have married her because of their shared subsection affiliation). Each day one of the brothers goes hunting for food, bringing the day's catch back to camp where it is shared by all. One day it is Yagjagbula who hunts; the next it is Jabirringi.

One day Jabirringi returns from the hunt to hear Ganayanda whispering with Yagjagbula in a secluded break in the rock. Suspicious, he investigates and finds them copulating. Jabirringi throws a spear at Yagjagbula, who evades it. A fight breaks out, with each brother taking his position on the plains at Yiwarlarlay. Spears and boomerangs are thrown, producing the lightning and thunder. The lightning strikes the sandstone outcrop at Yiwarlarlay and splits the rock in two. The frogs come up from the south to watch the fight, clapping their thighs rhythmically. Wiyan, the rain, was heading north to the Yingalarri water hole, but gets distracted as it passes near Yiwarlarlay (at the same time, the Rainbow Serpent, Gorondolni, flashes at the rain to warn it not to advance to Yingalarri). It metamorphoses into the rain rock Ngalanjarri nearby (Figure 4.3) (Flood and David 1994). Eventually Yagjagbula hits Jabirringi across the forehead with his boomerang. Some say that Jabirringi's headdress is

FIGURE 4.3. The rain, metamorphosed into rain rock Ngalanjarri in the Dreaming.

knocked off; others say that Jabirringi is decapitated. In either case, Yagjagbula wins the fight[5] (David et al. 1990).

The Lightning Brothers are impressive, polychrome anthropomorphs (Figure 4.4); Ganayanda is a small depiction at the side of Yagjagbula. At more than 4 m in height, Yagjagbula is one of the largest known anthropomorphs in the world; Jabirringi is only slightly smaller. Together, these three paintings cover a significant portion of the rock wall surface in the main shelter at Yiwarlarlay. At least some parts of the two large anthropomorphs identified by Wardaman elders as the Lightning Brothers at Yiwarlar-

lay date to the end of the nineteenth–early parts of the twentieth centuries C.E. When the Lightning Brothers were first reported by D. S. Davidson in 1936, only the upper portions of the two anthropomorphs (Yagjagbula and Jabirringi) were striped; the bottom half was only outlined. A few years later, Barrett and Croll (1943) published their own account of the site. Comparing their photograph of the site with Davidson's, Arndt (1962:165) concluded that paint had been added to the main figures since Davidson's visit. Arndt (1962:165) further noted Harney's (1943) comment that he witnessed the paintings being retouched during the mid-twentieth

FIGURE 4.4. Yagjagbula (*left*) and Jabirringi (*right*), the Lightning Brothers at Yiwarlarlay.

century C.E. By 1956, when Arndt visited the site, the paintings were said to be complete. Arndt's interviews with Wardaman elders revealed certain details of major interest for this chapter. He noted:

> [Kulumput claimed that] the Lightning Brothers originally "camped" on the Victoria River, where several neighbouring tribes were free to visit them. When the country and the people were divided between rival pastoral interests it was no longer practical for the Wardaman people to visit the Lightning Place. The Wardaman elders at Delamere Station decided that the Lightning Brothers could "camp" at the Rain Place near the homestead, so that they could be seen by the rising generation. A contemporary of Kulumput, Emu Jack, "dreamed" (visualised) the design and did the

painting. The task was delayed by station and tribal duties and was not finished until he was in bush-retirement prior to his death "near the end of the Japanese war [World War II, 1939–1945]." (Arndt 1962:169)

Archaeological excavations undertaken at Yiwarlarlay in 1989 confirmed the post-European age of all known painting activities at this site.

Lightning Brothers paintings at Yiwarlarlay are the most researched case we have of large, paired, striped polychrome anthropomorphs in the Victoria River district, but there are other examples. At Garnawala (Figure 4.1) the large, paired, striped anthropomorphs are *djangural*, Dreaming Beings who look over the young *yirmi nyonong* Dreaming Beings nearby. David et al. (1994:247) reported on the Dreaming story associated with these pictures, as recorded from Wardaman elders Elsie Raymond and Tarpot Ngamunagami between 1988 and 1991. The story tells of two sisters who are chased from Port Keats by Gorondolni, the Rainbow Serpent. They in turn are chased by a diver duck and a flying fox, who are in turn followed by numerous animals—kangaroos, emus, peewees, dingoes, and others. The Dreaming Beings pass through Garnawala on their way southeast. The Rainbow Serpent arrives at a place near the Yingalarri water hole, where he plays his didgeridoo. The diver duck approaches the Rainbow Serpent, who is not paying close attention to what is happening around him. The diver duck drags a spear along the ground between his toes. Undetected by the Rainbow Serpent, he manages to get close and spears him.

At Mennge-ya (Figure 4.1), the large, paired, striped figures are *menngen*, White Cockatoo Dreamings (Figure 4.5). In the rock shelter two large polychrome anthropomorphs dominate the walls. They are female White Cockatoos, and the wives of old man White Cockatoo who resides at Winybarr a few kilometers away. Elsie Raymond, a Wardaman Elder, recounted the White Cockatoo story in June 1989 (Merlan 1994:509–510):

old man white cockatoo was there for them at Winybarr
they went walkabout from there to Geberrung and what's it?
Old Willeroo
they pulled up kapok
and in the afternoon the two went home to Winybarr, they gave him food
they went back to white cockatoo place
they slept
early they went from there
they went in the morning
they went to Old Willeroo
they got kapok
food
they dug and in the afternoon went home
all the time like that
they went back to Winybarr and gave it to the old man
food
they went from him to the white cockatoo place
to go in/under as dreaming
they went in as dreaming.

The White Cockatoos of Mennge-ya gather the native cotton (kapok) to feed their husband, old man White Cockatoo, at Winybarr. They then return to Mennge-ya, the White Cockatoo place, where they sit in the rock as the Dreaming.

Mennge-ya was excavated in 1989 by Val Attenbrow (Attenbrow et al. 1995). David et al. (1994) argued that the paintings of the White Cockatoos have been repainted many times since their initial creation. Their first painting corresponds to a period of increase in ochre deposition rates, shortly after an uncalibrated radiocarbon determination of

FIGURE 4.5. The White Cockatoos, *menngen*, at Mennge-ya.

380 ± 60 years B.P. (Wk 1822). This means that the first archaeological signs of the White Cockatoo paintings appear very late in the second millennium C.E., consistent with the European contact period.

There are also similar paired, striped polychrome anthropomorphs at Nimji, where they are *gulirrida*, peewees (magpie lark). At Murning nearby, similar paintings are *gornbu*, hawk Dreaming Beings. In each case the paintings visually and spatially dominate the rock panels. In each case also they appear to have been originally freshly painted or can be shown for taphonomic reasons to have a limited antiquity (see Frost et al. 1992 for further details). The paintings are always identified by Wardaman

Elders as being of the identity of the land on which they are found.

What is of interest to us here is that the large, domineering paintings appear to have emerged only during the early European contact period. In this capacity they map not just the land, but a frontier situation of invasion and threats to land tenure. Let us examine in some detail the nature of this frontier situation to better understand the place of such rock-art in the Wardaman landscape.

Contact History: Land, Cattle and the Frontier Violence

European incursions into the Victoria River district began in 1839 when Stokes briefly explored the lower reaches of the Victoria River, followed by Gregory who traversed the length of the river in 1855–1856. Although these explorations were fleeting, they revealed the region's grazing potential to the broader Australian community.

Sections of the Victoria River district proper began to be permanently stocked with cattle in 1883, when Wave Hill and Victoria River Downs (VRD) Stations began in earnest (see Riddet 1990 for early European impressions of the Victoria River district's fine pastures). Auvergne, Newry, Leguna, and Kilfoyle Stations were taken up soon after, and Inverway and Bradshaw Stations in the 1890s (Ogden 1989; Riddet 1990). The stations were large, each measuring in the thousands of square kilometers and carrying thousands of head of cattle (e.g., Auvergne carried a stock of 7,000 cattle in 1886 when it was established). European traffic in the Victoria River district was fast gaining momentum, with access to the land being of primary importance. As Berndt and Berndt (1987: 6) noted, "stocking the land for pastoral purposes disturbed Aboriginal waterholes and drove away wild game. This led at times to expressions of open hostility, including cattle-spearing. Pastoralists clamoured for retaliation, asking for police protection and threatening (sometimes putting these threats into effect) to 'take the law into their own hands.'" In 1887, the Government Resident wrote of the "usual course of procedure" in the cattle stations (cited in Berndt and Berndt 1987:6):

A capitalist or syndicate applies for or buys at auction the leases for a certain number of hundreds or thousands of square miles of country, carefully following the permanent watercourses, and including the permanent lagoons and waterholes. The aborigines who have the vested rights of hoary antiquity are only considered by the State to the extent of the above-recited clause in the pastoral lease. Afterwards the squatter or his manager comes on to the country with his overland herds, and usually tries to cultivate friendly relations with the natives. How often these kindly-meant attempts are frustrated is only known by those who have attempted them. In nearly all cases the early results of the white man's intrusion is a permanent feud between the blacks and whites. The blacks frighten and spear the cattle and hold themselves in readiness to attack boundary rider and stockman, or to make a raid upon outstations or the storeroom. The whites look well to their Winchesters and revolvers, and usually proceed on the principle of being on the safe side. It is an affectation of ignorance to pretend not to know that this is the condition of things throughout the back blocks of the new country of Australia.

In 1889 (cited in Berndt and Berndt 1987:6), he further wrote that "The primary fact which philanthropists must accept is that the aborigines regard the land as theirs, and that the intrusion of the white man is a declaration of war, and the result is simply 'the survival of the fittest.' . . . I am well aware that there are many odious things done by whites, but I believe I express the opinion of nine-tenths of those who have taken their lives in their hands and gone into the back blocks when I say that occupation of the country for pastoral purposes and peaceable relations with the native tribes are hopelessly irreconcilable."

A major issue during this early contact period was land. The incoming Europeans had their sights on rich grazing and, to a lesser extent, mining opportunities, but the land was already occupied by people perceived as threatening savages. Not to be outdone, a more efficient warring technology coupled with a preconception that the land was "empty" (*terra nullius*) led to land acquisitions legitimated under the form of pastoral leases, authorized by the Colonial Secretary. The results were devastating for the local Aboriginal people, whose lives, spirituality, and identities were firmly grounded in their homelands. Rose (1992:14) noted that "while Townsend was manager of VRD (1904–1919), a large group of Ngarinman and Ngaliwurru people (language groups neighbouring the Wardaman) had congregated in a valley near the VRD homestead in order to perform ceremonies. They were attacked before dawn, and most or all of them were killed." She (Rose 1992) listed numerous eyewitness accounts of similar events from both Aboriginal and European people, a few of which we cite here:[6]

> Native life was held cheap, and a freemasonry of silence among the white men, including often the bush police, helped keep it that way. In far-off Perth, clerics and various "protection" societies tried to get at the truth of stories of native killings . . . but up in the north men kept their mouths shut. The basic philosophy . . . was that the cattlemen had battled their way into this empty land

> with great hardship and high cost in lives and money; that they were there to stay, and if the wild blacks got in the way, or in other words speared men and killed and harassed cattle, they would be relentlessly shot down. It was as simple and as brutal as that. (Broughton 1965:53, writing of his experiences in 1908, cited by Rose 1992:9)

> The business of establishing a cattle empire depended upon killing. To the new station you brought working blacks from some far country— no conspiracies, they were terrified of the "bush niggers." . . . There was "quiet nigger" country and "bad nigger" country, but on most of the far out stations cattle-killers were a grievous trouble for thirty or forty years. (Hill 1970:175, cited by Rose 1992:10)

Rose (1992:12) noted that what Europeans "call 'bad nigger' country was country in which Aboriginal people were able to resist invasion." Francesca Merlan (1994:558–562) reported from elders oral stories of murder in Wardaman country. The following is by Claude Manbulloo as recorded in June 1989 and tells of Europeans shooting her father's father on Delamere Station:

> my
> old
> my father's father
> whites
> shot him
> at Delamere
> where the windlass is, they used to get water, the
> old women
> my old father's father
> went for water
> he was perishing for water
> he went
> to the well
> white people saw him

and they shot him
with a rifle
and they called him "Back George" for good and
all [from where he was wounded]
where he might have been getting water
I've seen that well too
when I was little

This initial period of European contact was what Daly Pulkara, a Ngarinman man, has called "banging, banging time," in reference to the sound of gunshots (Read and Read 1991:7). The "frontier" conflicts led to an increasing difficulty of access to some traditional lands by local Aboriginal groups. In some cases, this was due to the presence of pastoral homesteads or pastoral camps. In other cases, it was due to the European appropriation of watering places or other focal points for pastoral activity. The following account is by the first manager of VRD Station: "During the last ten years, in fact since the first white man settled here, we have held no communication with the natives at all, except with the rifle. They have never been allowed near this station or the outstations, being too treacherous and warlike" (Crawford 1895:180, cited by Rose 1992:13).

The most notorious killer of the early contact years was the only policeman in the entire region, Constable W. H. Willshire. In January 1892, the owners of VRD Station requested from the government a Native Police post in the region to curb Aboriginal resistance. In May 1894, the government acquiesced, posting Constable Willshire to Gordon Creek, between VRD, Willeroo, and Auvergne Stations (Reid 1990). Willshire reported one account of events as he surprised a group of Aboriginal people in a gorge near the Wickham River in August 1894 (cited by Reid 1990:125): "The war cry sounded through the tribe, and they picked up their spears and commenced climbing the precipitous sides. As there was no getting away the females and children crawled into rocky embrasures, and there they remained. When we had finished with the male portion we brought the black gins and their offspring out from their rocky alcoves. . . . There were some nice-looking boys and girls among them. One girl had a face and figure worthy of Aphrodite. . . ." Rose (1992:12) cited another account dated to June of that same year: "Next morning we went on, picked up another set of tracks on Black Gin Creek, followed them up, and at 3 p.m. came upon a large mob of natives camped amongst rocks of enormous magnitude and long dry grass, growing like a thick crop of wheat on the side of a mountain. They scattered in all directions, setting fire to the grass on each side of us, throwing occasional spears, and yelling at us. It's no use mincing matters—the Martini-Henry carbines at this critical moment were talking English in the silent majesty of those great eternal rocks" (Willshire 1896:40–41, cited by Rose 1992:12).

The memory of such events were passed down in Aboriginal lore. Riley Young Winpilin, an Aboriginal man from the Victoria River district, recalls being cautioned about openly resisting the Europeans by community Elders:

Old people reckon: "Ah! You'll get shot! Don't worry about it, if he wants to fight you. Just give it away. Don't fight him. Old men got flogged. Old women got bashed. He can bust your eye. He can bust your nose. Don't worry about that. Don't worry about him. If [he wants to] fight, give it away. Because olden times, you know, you can get shot like a dog. They shoot you like a dog and just let you burn on the fire." (Rose 1991:xix)

We couldn't, we didn't have any help behind [no one to back us up]. You know, we tried, but sort of frightened for—Aboriginal people [were] too frightened he might get shot. Like all my grandfa got shot before. That kind of law; they were frightened. . . . [They thought]: "Long as you can look after the land. Keep the place, right thing. . . . We might do something more sometime. We might turn the law someday. Any year's time." (Rose 1991:xxi)

By the 1930s, within the first 50 years of European intrusion, many Victoria River district groups were almost entirely exterminated, including the Karangpurru who had numbered more than 500 in 1880, the Bilinara, the Dagoman, and at least one portion of Ngarinman. Rose (1992:7) estimated that "Over the years, somewhere between 86.5 per cent and 95.6 per cent of the Aboriginal population of the VRD area was lost." Although other (related) factors such as disease were also involved, to a very significant degree the losses can be directly attributed to the shooting of Aboriginal people.

It is within this early European contact situation that the large, paired, striped figures of the Victoria River district were painted. We suggest that the timing of their production was not coincidental, indicating instead an act of territorial resistance and the mobilization of solidarity. In the next section we explore the major links between these inscriptions, land, and resistance, as previously brought out in our consideration of graffiti.

DISCUSSION

Let us revisit the key points made about place markings in the first part of this chapter so as to highlight their relevance to the Wardaman case study.

1. Place is socially constructed.
2. A person is continuously (re)defined through

her or his emplacement (e.g., the coidentification of people and place through one's Dreaming ancestry in Wardaman country). Because place is *socially* produced, people ceaselessly define themselves and their emplacement in relation to others.

3. Because inscriptions in places are undertaken by people affected by social circumstances, inscribed places are sites of institutionalization.

4. Place marking is about the occupation of space as one's own. It represents resistance to (the possibility of) exclusion and the affirmation of emplacement within an institutionalized landscape. Such institutionalization (or social normalization) of life creates the existence of an (excluded) Other. Inscribed places are thus sites of resistance against marginalization as the excluded Other.

5. Although place marking as a process is an act of resistance, individuals and groups inscribe their landscapes in different ways and in various degrees, depending on the particular nature of perceived or operating social relations of power, of domination and subordination.

Even if the content (the message) of Wardaman paintings does not spell out "resistance," the act of inscribing them does. Such inscriptions are exemplars of how rock-art serves as a means of affirming the truth of one's inalienable links with place while simultaneously indicative of operating social forces, social tensions, and social resistances. In this chapter we have explored with Wardaman rock-art of the early European contact period how marks in place can inform the archaeologist on social dynamics and resistances over both the long and short terms. Understanding the resistive nature of place markings generally promises to shed new light on the archae-ological past and to enable a reconceptualization of regional social dynamics (including the pre-Euro-pean contact period) through time.

The Wardaman example can be compared with other contemporary examples of place marking per-formed under duress, as is common in much graf-fiti. Such examples need not focus on the messages of the markings per se, but on the social contexts in which they were produced. During ethnographic times, rock-art in Wardaman country was inti-mately linked with place, the Dreaming Beings that gave the land its identity, and the people who were affiliated with the land. *Buwarraja* rock-art was visual proof of the Dreaming itself. The Dreamings map(ped) the land and people's relationships with the land, as did the art. In marking the Dreaming, rock-art was thus a signpost to the identity and his-tory of people and place.

The advent of Europeans at the end of the nine-teenth century C.E. brought new pressures and threats. In particular, access to land became increas-ingly denied through military-style enforcement. Such exclusions amounted to no less than the denial of emplaced identities. In traditional law, War-daman individuals possessed specific rights of access and responsibilities to their own lands, but not to the lands of others. Unlike the modern traveler, the Wardaman could not just move on to new places. Individual identities were molded with the Dream-ings who resided in place via ancestral connections (see also Langton, this volume). The incursion of Europeans thus led to the development of geo-graphical enclaves of resistance (among other forms of resistance). In such places, the land was marked with new symbols of its Dreaming identity. The Wardaman paintings inscribed in place strategies of resistance, mapping the Indigenous self onto the land and affirming established territorial rights in the process. The new rock-art asserted existing sys-tems of land ownership and social affiliations, and acted to muster solidarity in resistance to European visions of territory. At the turn of the nineteenth century when European-Wardaman relations were at their most violent and when Indigenous lands were most threatened by the arrival of the European invaders, resistance by the Wardaman was in part operationalized by modifying existing inscriptive practices to fit the new social circumstances of exclusion. The newly inscribed sites became *spaces of resistance.*

NOTES

1. It is interesting that this publication also saw the first use of the word "prehistoric" in the English language (Bogucki 1999; Chippindale 1988).

2. We use the word *graffiti* here both as the plural of *graffito* and in its singular form as the entire body of unso-licited inscriptions in fixed places.

3. So-called "graffiti" walls allocated for public writ-ings by city councils or other controlling powers are attempts at appropriating place by those institutions and to appropriate also the right of the public voice. Because the writings on allocated "graffiti" walls concern solicited inscriptions in public spaces, they do not fall under the definition of "graffiti" considered here.

4. It is interesting that it appears that the motifs found in *bulawula* rock-art, and their degree of compositional complexity, can fairly easily be differentiated from *buwarraja* art. The former tends to be monochrome and relatively small; the latter is often polychrome and can be large. As already noted, contact subjects are often depicted in *bulawula* art, but almost never in *buwarraja* art. A detailed exploration of these themes is warranted, but has not yet been attempted.

5. Wardaman Elders recount how Jabirringi's head-dress/head could be seen as a relatively small but conspicuous rock at Yiwarlarlay until recent times, when it was stolen by people of European descent.

6. See Read and Read (1991) for numerous examples of Indigenous narratives from the Victoria River district.

REFERENCES CITED

Arndt, W. 1962. The Interpretation of the Delamere Lightning Painting and Rock Engravings. *Oceania* 32:163–177.

Attenbrow, V., B. David, and J. Flood. 1995. Mennge-ya 1 and the Origins of Points: New Insights into the Appearance of Points in the Semi-arid Zone of the Northern Territory. *Archaeology in Oceania* 30: 105–120.

Barnes, M. P. 1995. The Interpretation of the Runic Inscriptions of Maeshowe. In *The Viking Age in Caithness, Orkney and the North Atlantic*, edited by C. E. Batey, J. Jesch, and C. D. Morris, 349–369. Edinburgh: Edinburgh University Press.

Barrett, C., and R. H. Croll. 1943. *The Art of the Australian Aboriginal*. Melbourne: The Bread and Cheese Club.

Berndt, R. M., and C. H. Berndt. 1987. *End of an Era: Aboriginal Labour in the Northern Territory*. Canberra: Australian Institute of Aboriginal Studies.

Blake, C. F. 1981. Graffiti and Racial Insults: The Archaeology of Ethnic Relations in Hawaii. In *Modern Material Culture: The Archaeology of Us*, edited by R. A. Gould and M. B. Schiffer, 87–99. New York: Academic Press.

Bogucki, P. 1999. *The Origins of Human Society*. Oxford: Blackwell Publishers.

Chippindale, C. 1988. Invention of Words for the Idea of "Prehistory." *Proceedings of the Prehistoric Society* 54:303–314.

David, B., I. McNiven, J. Flood, and R. Frost. 1990. Yiwarlarlay 1: Archaeological Excavations at the Lightning Brothers Site, Delamere Station, Northern Territory. *Archaeology in Oceania* 25:79–84.

David, B., I. McNiven, V. Attenbrow, J. Flood, and J. Collins. 1994. Of Lightning Brothers and White Cockatoos: Dating the Antiquity of Signifying Systems in the Northern Territory, Australia. *Antiquity* 68:241–251.

Davidson, D. S. 1936. *Aboriginal Australian and Tasmanian Rock Carvings and Paintings*. Memoirs of the American Philosophical Society 5.

Douglas, M. 1966. *Purity and Danger*. London: Routledge and Kegan Paul.

Edwards, A. B. 1877. *A Thousand Miles up the Nile*. London: Routledge.

Ferrell, J. 1995. Urban Graffiti: Crime, Control, and Resistance. *Youth and Society* 27 (1): 73–92.

———. 1996. *Crimes of Style: Urban Graffiti and the Politics of Criminality*. Boston: Northeastern University Press.

Flood, J. 1997. *Rock Art of the Dreamtime: Images of Ancient Australia*. Sydney: Angus and Robertson.

Flood, J., and B. David. 1994. Traditional Systems of Encoding Meaning in Wardaman Rock Art, Northern Territory, Australia. *The Artefact* 17:6–22.

Flood, J., B. David, and R. Frost. 1992. Dreaming into Art: Aboriginal Interpretations of Rock Engravings—Yingalarri, Northern Territory, Australia. In *Rock Art and Ethnography in Australia*, edited by M. Morwood and D. R. Hobbs, 33–38. Occasional AURA Publication 5. Melbourne: Australian Rock Art Research Association.

Foucault, M. 1990. *The History of Sexuality: An Introduction*. Vol. 1. New York: Vintage Books.

———. 1997. Sex, Power, and the Politics of Identity. In *Michel Foucault: Ethics—Subjectivity and Truth*, edited by P. Rabinow, 163–173. New York: The New Press.

Frost, R., B. David, and J. Flood. 1992. Pictures in Transition: Discussing the Interaction of Visual Forms and Symbolic Contents in Wardaman Rock Pictures. In *Rock Art and Ethnography in Australia*, edited by M. Morwood and D. R. Hobbs, 27–32. Occasional AURA Publication No. 5. Melbourne: Australian Rock Art Research Association.

Gonos, G., V. Mulkern, and N. Poushinsky. 1976.

Anonymous Expression: A Structural View of Graffiti. *Journal of American Folklore* 89:40–48.

Harney, W. E. 1943. *Taboo.* Sydney: Australasian Publishing Company.

Kearney, W. J. 1988. *Jawoyn (Katherine Area) Land Claim. Report 27.* Canberra: Australian Government Publishing Service.

Mackenzie-Winters, J. 2000. *Orkney Archaeological Sites.* http://www.scotland-inverness.co.uk/ork-arch.htm.

Merlan, F. 1989a. The Interpretive Framework of Wardaman Rock Art: A Preliminary Report. *Australian Aboriginal Studies* 2:14–24.

———. 1989b. Survey of Aboriginal Sites in the Northwest of the Northern Territory. Report to the Australian Heritage Commission, Canberra.

———. 1994. *A Grammar of Wardaman: A Language of the Northern Territory of Australia.* Berlin: Mouton de Gruyter.

———. 1998. *Caging the Rainbow: Places, Politics, and Aborigines in a North Australian Town.* Honolulu: University of Hawai'i Press.

Mulvaney, D. J. 1975. *The Prehistory of Australia.* Harmondsworth: Pelican.

Ogden, P. 1989. *Bradshaw via Coolibah: The History of Bradshaw's Run and Coolibah Station.* Darwin: Historical Society of the Northern Territory.

Oram, R. D. 1997. *Scottish Prehistory.* Edinburgh: Birlinn.

Read, P., and J. Read. 1991. *Long Time, Olden Time: Aboriginal Accounts of Northern Territory History.* Alice Springs: Institute for Aboriginal Development Publications.

Reid, G. 1990. *A Picnic with the Natives: Aboriginal-European Relations in the Northern Territory to 1910.* Carlton: Melbourne University Press.

Riddet, L. A. 1990. *Kine, Kin and Country: The Victoria River District of the Northern Territory 1911–1966.* Darwin: Australian National University North Australia Research Unit.

Rose, D. B. 1991. *Hidden Histories: Black Stories from Victoria River Downs, Humbert River and Wave Hill Stations.* Canberra: Aboriginal Studies Press.

———. 1992. *Dingo Makes Us Human: Life and Death in an Australian Aboriginal Culture.* Cambridge: Cambridge University Press.

Stenson, K. 1997. Review of "Crimes of Style: Urban Graffiti and the Politics of Criminality." *Sociological Review* 45 (3): 527–529.

Stocker, T. L., L. W. Dutcher, S. M. Hargrove, and E. A. Cook. 1972. Social Analysis of Graffiti. *Journal of American Folklore* 85:344–366.

Sutton, P. 1991. Language in Aboriginal Australia: Social Dialects in a Geographic Idiom. In *Language in Australia*, edited by S. Romaine, 49–66. Cambridge: Cambridge University Press.

Turner, V. 1987. *The Anthropology of Performance.* New York: PAJ Publications.

Watchman, A., B. David, I. J. McNiven, and J. Flood. 2000. Micro-Archaeology of Cortex from Engraved and Painted Rock Surfaces at Yiwarlarlay, Northern Territory, Australia. *Journal of Archaeological Science* 27:315–325.

Wilson, D. 1851. *The Archaeology and Prehistoric Annals of Scotland.* Edinburgh: Shetland and Knox.

FIVE

Rock-Art as an Indicator of Changing Social Geographies in Central Australia

ANDRÉE ROSENFELD

The rock-art of central Australia is characterized by a long-standing graphic tradition based on relatively simple forms of circles, arcs, lines, and track motifs. Over time there are some changes in the expression and in the combinations of these graphic forms, and new forms, including rare figurative motifs, appear in the very recent art, but there are no identifiable stylistic breaks. Sites identified as "early" on archaeological criteria are integral to current mythological meanings encoded in the land, and the motifs are for the most part easily interpreted by custodians in terms of these current meanings.

The archaeology of central Australia, however, indicates significant cultural change in this region during the Holocene and especially during the last millennium. Smith and Thorley have both argued for fundamental changes in the social dynamics of Aboriginal culture. Smith took a broad regional view and argued for fundamental changes in population densities, mobility patterns, and alliances, in part as a result of the introduction of new extractive technologies in the late Holocene (Smith 1996); Thorley (1998a,b) in focusing more narrowly on the Palmer River catchment questioned the impor-

tance of demographic increase and emphasized changes in land use and territoriality during the recent Holocene. Kimber (1996) reconstructed an admittedly speculative history for the century or so preceding white colonization of the Center, focusing particularly on the impact on demography of diseases introduced by coastal contact with Macassans to the north and Europeans in the south and east, and he argued (inter alia) for an intensification of ritual. All three agree that Aboriginal culture has undergone significant transformations in the recent past in the areas of technology, subsistence strategies, and the demographics of mobility and territoriality. It is improbable that such transformations did not also require reformulations of the legitimating ideologies that underly social praxis.

The impact of this dynamic history on rock-art is, of course, not explicit in its current exegesis, because Aboriginal metaphysics is underscored by a precept of unchangeability of the created world, but it raises questions on the extent to which changes in sociopolitical structures in central Australia may be further illuminated by the rock-art.

The near-permanent nature of rock-art means that much of it will outlive the period and cultural context of its production, leaving marked places in the land that pertain to an earlier social geography. If we take the essence of a geography to be the enculturation of natural space, its primary mechanism involves the identification and naming of nodes in a spatial continuum (i.e., places whose significance derives from assigned cultural meanings). Most geographies comprise generic named entities (rivers, mountains, woodland, etc.), but it is the identified and named individual features and "places" that structure a sociopolitical framework of space (i.e., "country") and in this way serve to define and to articulate a shared identity by its legitimate users. A cohesive ontology of country requires an explanatory framework, generally with both spatial and temporal referents and frequently legitimated by a supernatural, creative, or a heroic ancestry. The legitimacy of ownership can be expressed in a variety of ways, including associated knowledge or, more visibly, by permanent marking, which includes rock-art.

In Australian Aboriginal geographies of country such explanatory frameworks are encoded in the mythology of the creative actions of supernatural beings whose activities took place in a remote and timeless past, often glossed as "the Dreamtime." It is often the combined activities of a number of creative beings within a definable area that serve to define "country." These creative beings are also ancestral to the human communities whose "country" they define, and as such their interactions as embodied in "country" also define the relational framework for human groups. Thus, throughout the continent, the manifestations of ancestral beings in the land and the social identities of its custodians are inextricably linked. The web of meanings that link places into a geography of country also serves to define the social identities of persons and to articulate their place in society.

Some of the ancestral beings traveled widely, each creating its own features in the land that it traversed. In this way, shared identities emerged between segments of territorial groups that crosscut territorially defined identities. The degree to which the mythologies of different parts of the continent comprise localized or wide-ranging ancestral beings varies. This results in communities who place differing emphasis either on regionally fairly closed networks of social interaction or alternatively on articulating networks that extend the social relations of locally defined identity well beyond the bounds of "country."

The way rock-art is located within the cultural praxis of such metaphysics is of interest to archaeology, because it is one of its more enduring expressions.

ROCK-ART IN THE CENTRAL RANGES

With its long graphic continuity the rock-art of central Australia, where a dynamic Aboriginal culture is firmly rooted in past traditions, offers the potential to explore this issue.

The rock-art of this region has not been widely published, though some very weathered and ancient looking petroglyph sites of the region were key sites in Edwards' (1971) identification of a "Track and Circle" tradition, later redefined as the Panaramitee tradition by Maynard (1979). Edwards' publications make passing mention of more recent pigment art, but these were not pertinent to his interests at the time. Pigment art sites are briefly reported from the earliest literature for this region, in the records of the Horn Expedition (Stirling 1896) and by Spencer and Gillen (1994:614 ff.), but have attracted little subsequent interest. Strehlow (1964) noted that for ceremonial purposes rock-art was subsidiary in importance to sand painting and body decoration, and his treatment of it was therefore brief. More recently, the requirements of land claim and of site protection legislation have resulted in a number of reports that include rock-art recordings and that are archived in the several heritage management and other agencies. Access to information in these documents, however, depends on the nature of the contemporary significance of the sites.

Gunn (1995, 2000) examined the general characteristics of rock-art through central Australia. In taking a very broad view of this region he demonstrated that there is greater regional diversity than has generally been considered. In this chapter, a narrower regional focus is taken, concentrating on rock-art sites in the western Central Ranges, an area west and southwest of Alice Springs that more or less corresponds to the region of the Western Arrernte and their immediate neighbors. It comprises rock-art sites in the West McDonnell Range and farther south in the George Gill Range where West Arrernte traditions link up with territory of Matutjara speakers (often loosely referred to as Luritja). Some other localities are included—notably the early petroglyph site of Ewaninga, 35 km south of Alice Springs, and the very large rock shelter of Puritjarra in the Cleland Hills, which lies in very different sand plain and dune country, some 350 km west of Alice Springs.

The data for this chapter were obtained from available published and archival material and from additional field surveys. This additional material was recorded in part for management purposes, and the detail with which sites were investigated is therefore quite variable. At Puritjarra the recording was undertaken during a two-week field project in conjunction with Mike Smith's archaeological investi-gation at the site (Smith 1989; the Puritjarra Excavation Report is in preparation).

CHRONOLOGY OF CENTRAL AUSTRALIAN ROCK-ART

Chronology must clearly be a central consideration in any study of the dynamics of land marking. The chronology of rock-art in central Australia is difficult to define, but temporal trends can be established. Figurative charcoal drawings of people in clothing and of horses establish its continuity into the period after European colonization in the late nineteenth century. This almost certainly applies to the total assemblage of charcoal drawings that always overlie paintings in situations of superpositioning (Frederick 1997, 1999). Weathering conditions and patina can suggest a general indication of age (e.g., "ancient" for deeply patinated and fractured petroglyphs and "recent" for pigment art on shelter walls in the very friable Merinee sandstone of the George Gill Range). At some sites an internal sequence can be established for the rock-art, and at Puritjarra some temporal indicators are available from the excavation.

It has generally been considered that the petroglyphs are ancient and date back at least to the late Pleistocene. Edwards argued for an early date on the grounds of their patina and the absence of dingo tracks, and Maynard, who included the Tasmanian petroglyphs in the Panaramitee, argued for a date before the separation of Tasmania from the mainland. A reevaluation of the Tasmanian rock-art has caused its similarity to that of the mainland sites to be questioned (Rosenfeld 1991a:137) and shown their age to be mid–late Holocene (Brown 1991). However, the very deep patina, rock fractures across motifs, and slippage at several central Australian petroglyph sites, notably at Ewaninga, do indicate a considerable time span for the accumulation of this assemblage.

At Puritjarra the petroglyphs, consisting almost entirely of single circular motifs, are executed on boulders that have fallen from the shelter roof. They show a twofold patina sequence of a glossy red (?silica) skin that is now partly exfoliating, but in the protected hollows of the petroglyphs is covered with a pale buff cemented dust. This patina sequence has been observed on petroglyphs at several other rock shelters, notably the Wanga East shelter in the George Gill Range. It demonstrates changing conditions of patination within the shelters, and that the petroglyphs were executed when microclimatic conditions differed from current ones and were more humid. More-humid conditions obtained in the region during the earlier part of the Holocene. Furthermore, at Puritjarra Smith (1996:67) obtained charcoal from a level immediately below one of the fallen blocks with petroglyphs that yielded a date of 13,570 ± 100 years B.P. (ANU 7469), thus providing an age *post quem* for the petroglyphs.

On the evidence from Puritjarra, it may be suggested that petroglyphs with similar patina conditions found in several of the rock shelters in the George Gill Range probably date to the same general period, and in view of its overall condition a similar antiquity may well apply to the "classic Panaramitee" site of Ewaninga. However at other localities the situation is less clear. Already in 1983 Forbes had found from her analysis of trends in motif types and patina at N'Dahla Gorge that neither the motif definition nor the chronology of the "Panaramitee" tradition are as clear-cut as had been postulated. At the Roma Gorge sites (west of Glen Helen), petroglyphs show a great diversity of patina as well as a diversity of motif types, indicating that the practice of rock engraving was long-lived and subject to innovation.

At Wallace Rock Hole the morphology and erosional sequence of the rock shelter yielded an opportunity to analyze the sequential development of a petroglyph site with changing trends in motif preference and the introduction of new motifs (Rosenfeld 1996). Absolute ages could not be established in this exposed shelter, but the patina conditions of the petroglyphs range from a glossy skin to no visible patina. Furthermore, at a nearby locality in the Wallace Rock Hole gorge, an engraved track motif is superimposed on an elongated wet-milling groove, a grain preparation technology that dates back no farther than 3,000 years B.P., only becoming prevalent in the last 800–1,000 years (Smith 1986, 1996). This demonstrates the continuity of technique and of some motifs into the late Holocene (Rosenfeld 1996:254).

For reasons of preservation much pigment art of central Australia cannot be "ancient," because many shelter walls are visibly unstable, showing extensive areas of spalling and weathering, in some cases with patches of freshly fallen sand grains on the shelter floor. This is particularly severe in several sites within the Watarrka National Park. Moreover, some pigment art retains a streakiness and a grading of paint thickness on the wall that attests to its execution as finger paintings and also to its relatively recent origin.

The rock surface at Puritjarra is considerably more stable. This shelter contains a complex sequence of painted panels with some superimposition (see Rosenfeld and Smith's rock-art report, in press, for a full discussion of the rock-art at this site); it also possesses a group of faded motifs so close to the current floor level that their assignment to a period of lower ground level is highly probable. Excavations reveal human occupation and the use of ochre dating back at least 32,000 years (Smith 1989, 1996). In the Pleistocene levels, ochre fragments occur in central areas of the shelter, whereas in levels above ca. 13,000 years B.P. ochres are found in close proximity to the shelter wall and comprise a variety of pigments, including some yellow and white (Smith et al. 1998: Table 1 [279]). Because of this spatial patterning within the site, Smith suggested that ochre in the earlier levels may have been used mainly for body painting, and that painting on the rock wall postdates the 13,000-year period (Smith et al. 1998:280). This does not, of course, date any surviving paintings.

This brief discussion of chronology indicates that both petroglyphs and pigment art have been practiced in the region throughout the Holocene and probably from the very late Pleistocene. Although many patinated petroglyphs are likely to date to an early phase of this era, petroglyphs as a whole span most, if not all, of this period up to the recent past. Surviving pigment art is for the most part restricted to the late Holocene, though at Puritjarra some could be somewhat earlier.

THE ROCK-ART SITES

The majority of art sites are rock shelters, but petroglyphs also occur on exposed rock surfaces in gorges, creek beds, or near other sources of water.

This survey of rock-art sites is necessarily skewed toward localities that are not subject to culturally restricted access. It includes sites of known sacred significance that may be visited, although in such cases only general information on their totemic affiliation is freely available. It is clear from the literature that a number of restricted access sites do contain rock paintings, and their generalized characteristics can be taken into consideration. Petroglyphs, however, are not described in the available sources for restricted access localities in the area under consideration.

Pigment art is found almost exclusively in shelters or on protected cliff surfaces, but one instance of very faint traces of a pigment design of joined circles was identified on a boulder in the Kings Canyon creek bed. This was located close to a water hole, the rock borders of which contain engraved motifs of circles that lie below water level after periods of good rain. Clearly, the pigment motif on the boulder must have been fairly recent, but the weathered petroglyphs, even if periodically submerged, have some antiquity.

Paintings at Restricted Sites

Paintings at restricted, or formerly restricted, localities consist largely of formally structured designs. Emily Gap (Walsh 1988: pl. 58) and Jesse Gap both contain large striped designs of alternate red and white stripes. Similarly structured paintings are described for Antiara (Undiara) (Stirling 1896:67, pl. 1bis). Striped designs are also recorded for the restricted men's locality at Lilla, in red and yellow, and from at least two other localities in the Waterhouse Range and in the vicinity of Tyler Pass in the West McDonnell Range (none of which I could view). It seems that these striped designs mark localities of very powerful mythological significance. Access to Emily and Jesse Gaps (and Heavytree Gap) was formerly restricted to initiated males (Spencer and Gillen 1968: 424ff., Willshire 1888:4), and Stirling commented on the great reluctance of his informants at Undiara. Panels of circle and arc forms characterize restricted localities in the Rodinga

Range (Walsh 1988: pl. 53) and in the George Gill Range (Hamilton and Vachon 1985).

The Lilla Rock Shelters

At Lilla, on the southern margin of the George Gill Range, Aboriginal custodians have approved guided tourist access to two shelters that were said to have formerly been restricted sites (U. K. Frederick, personal communication). One is a former women's birthing site with only circular and arc-based motifs; on a cliff nearby is a small, striped motif. The other is the larger shelter at Lilla, which local guides indicate was at one time a boys' initiation site. It contains a lower panel with formal circular motifs and an anthropomorphic design (Figure 5.1). This latter shelter, which has a surface scatter of artifacts and grindstones, also contains more recent paintings on a

higher panel of the wall that consist of track alignments and hand stencils (Rosenfeld 1991b). Nearby, a currently restricted men's site is said to have formal motifs, including a large, striped design, and another restricted site is above the water hole.

The artesian water hole of Lilla, on Reedy Creek, is located on the southern edge of the George Gill Range. These form the northern boundary for the Matutjara whose territory comprises the sand hill country and Lake Amadeus basin to the south. Lilla is currently an important mythological place where the possum totem leaves his beloved Matatjura sand hill country to travel into the range of the Western Arrernte. The locality (within the Lilla assemblage) denoting this link between Matatjura and Western Arrernte is the restricted-access shelter above the water hole, which contains a formal arrangement of circle and arc designs (Hamilton and Vachon

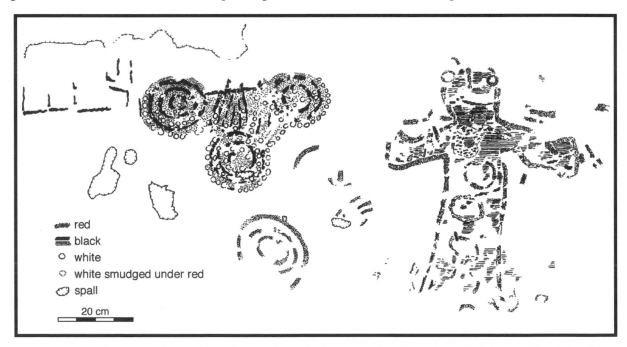

FIGURE 5.1. Anthropomorphic and circular motifs on the lower panel at the main rock shelter of Lilla, Watarrka National Park.

1985:38). These appear fresh (illustrated in Walsh 1988: pl. 55) and more recent than the fading anthropomorphic and associated motifs at the lower, larger shelter.[1] The mythological stories recounted by the guides for the anthropomorphic and associated figures at the former boys' initiation site deal with less far-traveled totems.

The artesian water hole at Lilla provides reliable water even in severe droughts; the place must have been important throughout human occupation of the region. The absence of any identified ancient rock-art among the Lilla shelters highlights the partial nature of rock-art (archaeological evidence) in marking important localities. In view of the friable nature of the rock surfaces the totality of the Lilla rock-art assemblage can reliably be assumed to belong to the late Holocene. The seeming freshness of the motifs at the restricted site and the introduction of new imagery appropriate to mark the current culturally structured meaning of the place suggest that the significance of Lilla as "place in country" has undergone some changes even during the late Holocene period. Furthermore, it is evident that particular shelters within the Lilla complex have undergone changes in function and in accessibility, and that this process is still ongoing today. There have been innovations in the graphic structures of formal designs and in their precise location within the place. This should caution against the extrapolation into the deeper past of the current significance of the place as a boundary and link between the sand hill country to its south and the Central Ranges to the north.

Puritjarra

Puritjarra is a very large rock shelter in the Cleland Hills in sand dune country some 350 km west of Alice Springs. Pigment art covers almost the entire length of the shelter wall, some 40 m long, comprising numerous hand and other stencils, some handprints and alignments of macropod tracks, of bird tracks, and other track motifs.[2] The macropod track alignments tend to meander along the rock wall, sometimes for several meters; the bird track alignments are much shorter and tend to move vertically up the wall. The direction of movement can be discerned even for single-line macropod track designs from the unevenness of the pigment that reflects the pressure of the finger stroke used to depict them.

Prominent among the more recent paintings at the site are two panels of white paintings with formal motifs that display single bird track (emu) motifs, not visually rendering movement of the bird. The associated formal motifs comprise mainly circles in the earlier panel and an elongate form with lateral projections in the more recent panel (Figures 5.2 and 5.3).

At the base of the shelter wall, near ground level, are four faint motifs in black and red pigment, clearly more ancient than the white panels and of quite different form. They are variants of a motif structured on a line with sets of arcs on either side (Figure 5.4). It is evident that the formal visual symbols appropriate to expressing the site's significance have changed over time.

These earlier motifs at Puritjarra have analogues in very recent paintings in a formal shelter in the northern sector of the George Gill Range (Figure 5.5), suggesting that earlier linkages of Puritjarra, as expressed visually in surviving paintings, lay in the direction of the George Gill Range to the southeast. The formal use of the emu track motif that characterizes the recent panels at Puritjarra has not been identified in any locality in the area of the George

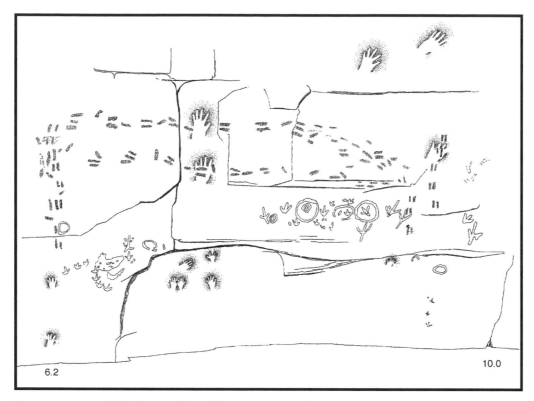

FIGURE 5.2. Panel of white circles and iconic emu tracks over red paintings of meandering alignments of macropod tracks and hand stencils. Puritjarra rock shelter, Cleland Hills.

FIGURE 5.3. Panel of white motifs of iconic bird tracks and elongate forms with lateral projections over older red and black paintings. Puritjarra rock shelter, Cleland Hills.

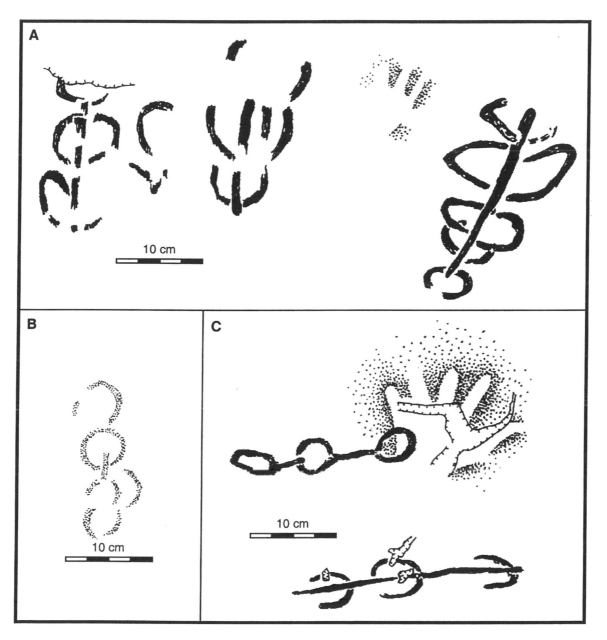

FIGURE 5.4. Line and arc-based motifs in red and black pigment, all occurring low on the shelter wall, Puritjarra rock shelter, Cleland Hills.

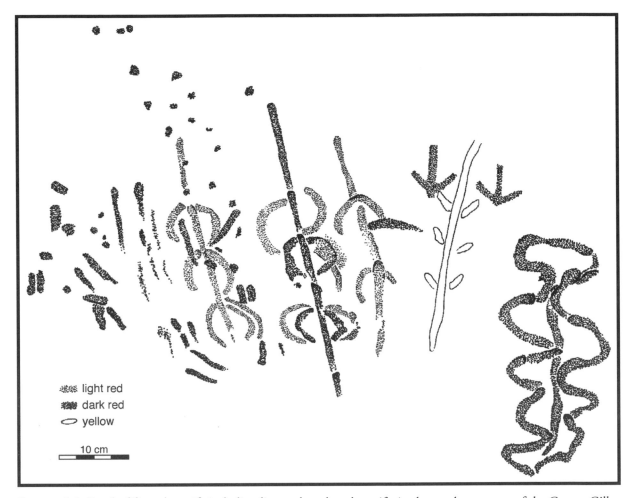

FIGURE 5.5. Panel of formal motifs including line and arc-based motifs, in the northern sector of the George Gill Range, Watarrka National Park.

Gill Range, but it is the principal formal design at Ruguri, a powerful emu Dreaming site in Warlpiri country to the north of Puritjarra.

Smith et al. (1998) documented analogous changes in the sources of ochres at Puritjarra. Ochres from the Karrku mine in Warlpiri country are virtually the only red ochres in the uppermost levels of the last 700 years or so and occur also throughout the Pleistocene–early Holocene levels. During the intervening early-mid Holocene period

Karrku ochres decrease in importance and virtually drop out in the mid Holocene levels when they are replaced by a variety of local pigments and red ochre from Ulpunyali near the George Gill Range (Smith et al. 1998:279–80).

It can be suggested, therefore, that the earlier line and arc motifs of Puritjarra denote its significance in the geographic linkages of this site to the southeast during the mid-late Holocene period, but that with the abandonment of this southeastern link during the last millennium new and different symbols became appropriate to express the site's place in its geographic web of connections to the north.

Smith et al. (1998:286–288) provided a comprehensive discussion of the implications of the changes in the derivation of ochres in the context of other archaeological and linguistic evidence. The evidence from the rock-art, of changes in its iconography, and of the distribution of related motifs in other regions is fully compatible with their argument and serves to suggest approximate ages for the paintings.

The presence at Puritjarra of formal panels as well as stencils (including many children's stencils) and track meanders also suggests that the social contexts of discrete painting episodes at the site have varied and have alternated.

Ewaninga

The Ewaninga petroglyphs are located on a small group of rock outcrops near an ephemeral clay pan, concentrating on a large, steep rock surface that faces the clay pan (Brown 1993). They are patinated with a glossy skin and in some instances truncated by rock fractures. Motifs consist of single and rare double concentric circles, few spirals, arcs, meandering lines, pits, and small bird tracks and emu tracks, the latter in a short alignment on one boulder. The petroglyphs are essentially linear in design and fairly deeply pecked. A few are shallower, with some motifs created by pecked-out areas (intaglio). These include the same motif range, but with the addition of macropod tracks, one disk, and one concentric circle of four circles. Although these are also patinated, there is one clear instance of superpositioning of this technique over deeper linear engraving. This is on a boulder below the main surface but partly obliterated by later rock slippage.

A small group of quite different motifs, fresh looking, very lightly pecked, and partly abraded, is located in a hidden niche formed by the fracture and slippage of boulders under the main surface. These motifs consist of variations on an oval form topped by a plumelike design. Their patina and location clearly indicate a much more recent addition to the site that postdates the fracture and slippage of blocks into their current configuration.

The Ewaninga outcrop, with its clay pan and small lunette, forms a striking landmark in sand plain country. At least two instances for some change in the execution of petroglyphs can be identified on grounds of technique and patina. In the earlier instance essentially the same motifs were repeated but supplemented by macropod tracks, suggesting that a slight modification to the assemblage was required to encode its cultural meanings at that period. In the recent past, only quite novel motifs were executed, suggesting a more fundamental reformulation of the site's meaning(s).[3] The site is now a significant location on a rain Dreaming track from Koperilya Springs near Hermannsberg in West Arrernte country that then traveled east and north through Alyawara country and into northwestern Queensland (Conservation Commission of the Northern Territory information panels 1995). The antiquity of most of the petroglyphs and evidence for ongoing engraving indicate that the site has remained a meaningful place in Indigenous geographies of the region over a considerable period of time; however its significance in articulating with other localities appears to have been subject to change.

Wallace Rock Hole

A more specific instance of changes in a site's linkage can be documented at Wallace Rock Hole in the

James Range. Here the petroglyphs are located through much of the gorge, concentrating near the water hole and above this on the floor of a wide and open rock shelter. An analysis of the site and interpretation of its internal chronology are discussed elsewhere (Rosenfeld 1996). Some trends in motif preferences over time can be discerned, notably in the development of concentric circles from few to numerous, and in the addition of a greater diversity of track shapes, including the addition of macropod tracks. Among the more recent, less-patinated petroglyphs are motifs of long bands of curvilinear meandering lines identified by Glenys Porter, one of the senior female custodians for the site, as witchety grub Dreaming tracks. Finally, on an isolated boulder near the mouth of the gorge is an unpatinated pecked and abraded motif. This consists of an elongated form with small lateral projections near its top and a three-pronged base, and next to it a single pair of macropod tracks. This motif differs from other petroglyphs at the site in every respect of form, technique, location, and patina.

The Aboriginal community of Wallace Rock Hole is promoting visits to the site as part of its tourism venture, and it was in the process of erecting a chain barrier and clearing the shelter of fallen rocks that further engravings, mainly of circles, were uncovered on the shelter floor. The senior custodian at the time identified these as denoting one of the principal totemic figures of the locality, not identified among any of the previously visible petroglyphs. This totem links Wallace Rock Hole with Imanda on the Hugh River (see later in this section) and with the Serpentine Gorge, for which he was also a senior custodian. Circles at the site are variously identified, but to an outsider there are no systematic visible clues that differentiate them.

Concentric circles were pointed out as impor-

tant, referring to "law." Because it was inappropriate to give me more specific exegesis, one of the senior custodians, Peter Bulla, explained the significance of the several enclosed circles as denoting the "coming together" of many people, animals, plants, food—"everything held together." The space outside the circles represented the exclusion of others. The concentric circle motif is thus perceived (by him) as a powerful symbol of inclusion-exclusion and thus implicitly of the mythologically structured links between people and between people and (the resources of) their country. It is tempting to suggest that the trend toward increasing the number of circles among the more recent petroglyphs of this configuration is a reflection of the increased complexity of the web of social links that resulted from higher population densities during the late Holocene, as evidenced from the archaeological record (Smith 1996). However, this possible interpretation should be considered with caution, because it assumes continuity of the narrative tradition and associated meanings. At other rock shelter petroglyph sites of the region considered "early" on grounds of patina, circles are nearly all single and only rarely display concentric circles of more than two circles.

Aboriginal custodians identify many of the track motifs quite specifically, including those of the extinct "mala" (hare wallaby). Many of the bird tracks on exposures within the gorge, where they are subject to periodic flooding and thus unlikely to have survived from the earliest periods of the site's engraving, are of waterbirds, especially duck and pelican. These birds feature in the site's current mythological links with Imanda (near Bad Crossing) on the Hugh River and Irbmankara (Running Waters), a reliable water hole on the Finke River. These aspects of the site's significance are freely spoken of, but were not pointed out among the highly patinated petroglyphs.

The most powerful totemic link of the site, however, concerns a dangerous totem, the bat, whose raids were repelled at Wallace Rock Hole by the principal totem, newly identified among the recently uncovered petroglyphs in the rock shelter. This myth also links Wallace Rock Hole with Imanda (and other localities) but cannot be recounted freely, as was the link expressed by the waterbirds. Imanda is the *pmara kutata*[4] for the bat totem (Strehlow 1947:74) and hence a particularly powerful and restricted locality. The only petroglyph that denotes the bat at Wallace Rock Hole is the fresh-looking pecked and abraded motif on the isolated boulder near the mouth of the gorge. It is a motif from the more recent design vocabulary of the region, and its addition unambiguously expresses what has become the most powerful totemic link of the site.

It appears, therefore, that the principal current mythological linkage of the site is relatively recent, although the site's location as intermediate between Imanda and Irbmankara may predate this, as evidenced by the tracks of waterbirds among petroglyphs of probably intermediate age. The long continuity of graphic form as evidenced among the majority of petroglyphs cannot be interpreted as evidence of a continuation of meanings, nor of the site's role within the same political or social geography, despite the fact that some (not all) ancient track motifs and circles can be read in terms of current meanings.

Other Petroglyph Sites

There are several further petroglyph localities within the region that appear to have been used over a protracted period and which show a diversity of motifs. At Rainbow Valley, Kimber (1991) distinguished between older and more recent petroglyphs on grounds of patina and some superpositioning.

Although the overall range of motifs is the same, mainly tracks and simple circle motifs, he stated that the older petroglyphs tend to be executed with greater precision of form. For the pigment art in the shelters of Rainbow Valley he suggested a four-stage sequence, but that they are all relatively "recent." These paintings include circles and tracks, but also hand stencils and a range of new motifs. In one of the shelters these comprise a formal arrangement of an oval with plumelike top, bracketed between sets of parallel arcs, again suggesting a reformulation of the meanings encoded at this locality. The site is currently associated with a grass seed totem and bears witness to the practice of rubbing patches of rock in ritual, partly abrading some earlier petroglyphs.

At the main site of Roma Gorge petroglyphs include both patinated, mainly circular forms and a number of diverse forms with various degrees of wear and patina (Taçon 1992). Because of periodic vigorous flow during flooding in the gorge, a relative chronology based on wear and patina is difficult to establish. Clearly, both Rainbow Valley and Roma Gorge have been significant geographic markers over a long period of time and both are significant in current mythology and territorial affiliation.

Some ancient petroglyph sites, however, appear no longer to play any meaningful role in concepts of "country." Smaller assemblages of ancient-looking petroglyphs occur on a creek bed and in at least two rock shelters in the George Gill Range: the Wanga East shelter on the southern slopes (Rosenfeld 1991b:9–11) and Site 5 in the Upper Reedy Creek catchment (Smith and Rosenfeld 1992:25–30). Neither of these rock shelters is closely associated with reliable water, though they are within easy walking of ephemeral sources. At both rock shelters an age of terminal Pleistocene–early Holocene is posited on the basis of the two-stage patina sequence discussed earlier for the Puritjarra petroglyphs. The motif range is very limited, consisting almost exclusively of simple circles and bird tracks, with pits, arcs, and one spiral at Wanga East. The Upper Reedy Creek Site 5 shelter has large numbers of incised grooves mainly on the shelter wall, but also cutting across some petroglyphs, and at the Wanga East shelter, also, incised grooves postdate the petroglyphs, and there is some casual pigment art in the form of hand stencils. Both shelters have a surface scatter of recent artifacts.

These shelters show evidence of use during the recent Holocene and are located in country for which the custodians today identify significant sites, yet the petroglyph shelters appear to be either unknown or not considered of specific significance.[5] The role of these localities in marking country has been replaced by other features (some of which are rock-art sites) in the contemporary mythology and geography for the same landscape.

Paintings in Camping Sites

The majority of known pigment art sites are camping sites with artifact scatters, grinding stones, charcoal, and sometimes cut wood, attesting to the recent use of some of these places (Smith and Rosenfeld 1992). At these localities the dominant motifs are hand and other stencils and a range of track motifs and alignments. It has been conventional to consider tracks in broad categories of bird, macropod, and other animal tracks. The form and configurations of tracks within these categories also differ, and Aboriginal informants often distinguish different species within these categories. However, because there can be formal variation within a single track alignment, caution is indicated in extrapolating such identifications to strictly archaeological contexts.

Alignments of tracks are common in occupation sites, but appear to be few or absent at the restricted sites or on panels with predominantly formal motifs (see earlier in this chapter). In the secular context of habitation sites macropod tracks are frequently shown wandering extensively across a rock surface, sometimes rising out of, or disappearing into, natural fissures or hollows. They are mostly lines of short, parallel strokes rarely showing the lateral toe, and they may be elaborated with tail or tail and front paw marks. Bird track alignments are characteristically much shorter than macropod track lines, or alternatively bird tracks are shown as a cluster of small track motifs.

The distinction between configurations of track alignments and (most instances of) single track designs appears to be significant. Single track motifs, which may be a repeated motif within a panel but not arranged so as to denote movement, are generally shown with more formal detail of lateral toe and sometimes heel for macropods, and as toes and heel configurations for birds, almost certainly denoting emu. As shown earlier for Puritjarra, the single "emu" track motifs are components of assemblages of formal motifs in two of the more recent panels of that site. At the petroglyph site of Wallace Rock Hole a single pair of macropod tracks on the formal "bat" panel and an isolated pair of recent macropod tracks on the main shelter floor are both more figurative than the linear forms usually used in macropod track alignment designs.

It seems that as a general trend the distinction between these track configurations has implications for the contextual significance of the art. Track alignments denoting the movement of the creature recall the sand markings sometimes made to punctuate a narrative and may be considered illustrative designs. An isolated track appears as "iconic," focusing on the symbolic values encoded in the concept of the creature.[6] This could explain the dominance of iconic uses of track motifs in sites or panels with formal designs that relate explicitly to mythological values. Although the illustrative alignments of tracks may also evoke these values, their narrative could also have been understood at less esoteric levels and hence be the more appropriate visual form in secular contexts of painting.

I have argued elsewhere (Rosenfeld 1993, 1999) that stencils are qualitatively different from graphically structured images and operate as personal markers. They are particularly abundant at camping sites in the George Gill Range and in small shelters nearby, and not uncommonly include children's stencils.

Other marks that I argued evoke individual presence rather than mythologically structured identity are the incised grooves that are found in many petroglyph sites and also in sites where they are the sole evidence of former human activity. At Wallace Rock Hole, such grooves were pointed out on one occasion as the spear-sharpening marks of men preparing for war, and on another occasion as marks made by men coming together to "make peace" after a fight. Although these explanations may seem contradictory, they do emphasize their significance as individual participatory marks, rather than as referents to mythological meanings.

These grooves are short incisions into the rock that may form extensive clusters or alignments along natural projections or edges of rocks. They do not form patterned configurations. At Puritjarra and at the two petroglyph rock shelter sites in the George Gill Range, incised grooves postdate the petroglyphs. At Wallace Rock Hole incised grooves cut into older petroglyphs and are absent from the more recently exposed petroglyph surfaces. On this evidence it appears that incised grooves are essentially Holocene and were in vogue during a restricted period within that time. The distribution of localities with incised grooves within the Upper Reedy Creek catchment reveals a quite different marking of country than do the recent archaeology and pigment art of that area (Smith and Rosenfeld 1992:21).

The technique of incision, however, is also found in some of the more recent pigment art sites in the George Gill Range, where a superpositioning of incised groove over pigment attests to the use of this technique during the very recent past. In these instances, however, the technique of incision has frequently been utilized to form three-pronged motifs resembling a bird track and other simple linear designs. It is not clear how incised groove designs relate to the unpatterned use of this technique.

DISCUSSION

Gunn (1995) argued for marked regional variation of rock-art through the arid zones of central Australia, and this survey serves to confirm his views and to add further detail to his argument.

In addition to regional variation as emphasized by Gunn, within-region variation of rock-art relating to the significance of the site can be documented, at least for the late Holocene period in the western Central Ranges. As foreshadowed by Spencer and Gillen (1968:614), two broad categories of rock-art may be identified. On the one hand is a body of informal "story line" art with statements of individual presence, which is widespread and generally associated with habitation debris. The other is a body of formal motifs generally of greater graphic complexity, which is the dominant (or only) art at a site. Several categories of formal designs can be recognized that are probably more locally restricted than the informal body of motifs:

- striped motifs, seemingly appropriate for men's restricted localities,
- circle and arc-based motifs in both men's and women's restricted sites, but also in sites not, or no longer, restricted,
- the "line and arcs" motif formerly at Puritjarra, and recently in northern Watarrka,
- iconic emu track in pigment art at Puritjarra, but probably only as ancient petroglyphs in the western Central Ranges,
- rare figurative motifs including anthropomorphic forms.

Localities marked with rock-art therefore can fulfill a variety of functions in central Australia. They may be mythologically powerful places that articulate the conceptual geography as well as the political geography, and these tend to have formally controlled designs. Places marked with rock-art are also camping or casual shelters. These articulate the daily economic and social geographies of groups, which may transcend formal political boundaries, and they tend to contain informal designs of track lines, hand stencils, prints, and object stencils. Finally, localities that contain both may have oscillated over time in the degree of access and/or restriction placed on them, or in the social context of successive rock-art making episodes.

Underlying this regional and functional variability of the rock-art is a continuity of essential motif vocabulary that testifies to an enduring graphic tradition. Some localities, furthermore, display evidence of repeated episodes of marking, attesting to the enduring nature of their role in the sociopolitical geographies of the region. In all these instances, however, additions to the motif assemblages comprised a very small number of new or different motifs that indicate modifications to the integration of these sites and their prior rock-art within the dynamics of social and territorial relations. As discussed elsewhere, the very nature of the graphic tradition of central Australia lends itself to the dynamics of cultural praxis without necessarily requiring significant recasting of form (Rosenfeld 1991a:141–142). However, as shown by petroglyphs at Ewaninga and Wallace Rock Hole, and some of the pigment art at Rainbow Valley, the addition of new motifs appears to be pertinent to the recasting of the meanings understood in the older marks.

Furthermore, where this could be identified, earlier (?mid-Holocene) additions tended to embody relatively minor variations of form, but it is only among very recent-looking petroglyphs and pigment art that fundamentally new and different graphic structures arise, adding further evidence to the rapidly changing nature of Aboriginal society in this region during the late Holocene.

NOTES

I want to thank the many people who facilitated my fieldwork in the Center, particularly Dick Kimber and Mike Smith and the rangers at Watarrka National Park. Andrew Bridges of the Conservation Commission of the Northern Territory (now the PWCNT) negotiated permission from Aboriginal custodians to record in Watarrka National Park and provided logistical assistance. I am indebted to the Wallace Rock Hole community and especially Ken and Glenys Porter, who enabled me to record and study the petroglyphs there. I particularly want to thank Winifred Mumford for valuable assistance in the field and for her outstanding draftswomanship in preparing the drawings of rock-art. The research was funded by grants from the Australian Institute of Aboriginal and Torres Strait Islander Studies and the Australian Research Council small grants fund.

1. The Lilla water hole has been used as a cattle watering place, and this has undoubtedly contributed to the

worn appearance of paintings on the lower panel. However, the contrast in the state of preservation between lower and upper panels is marked and, together with some repainting of the circular motif on the lower panel, seems to confirm a chronological sequence at the site.

2. A full description and recording of the rock-art at Puritjarra is given in a forthcoming paper (A. Rosenfeld and M. A. Smith, in press), Puritjarra Excavation Report, in preparation).

3. Instances of the addition of novel motifs to early petroglyph sites have been noted elsewhere in Australia, notably in at least two early petroglyph sites in Cape York Peninsula, where the addition of one pair of macropod tracks appears to have brought early assemblages into the ambit of the recent visual language of the region in which macropod images and tracks feature prominently (Rosenfeld 1981:86).

4. *Pmara kutata* is "the 'everlasting home' where the most honoured totemic ancestors . . . lived from the beginning, and where they went for their final sleep . . ." (Strehlow 1947:112).

5. The Upper Reedy Creek area had not been visited for a very long period of time; some of the custodians knew it only from oral tradition, and one remembered camping there as a young child. The Wanga East site, on the other hand, is within the vicinity of land that is frequented fairly regularly by its custodians.

6. See also Strehlow (1964, especially pp. 46–47), who described the use of sand paintings to enliven narrative, whereas more formal treatment of the same motif structures is used in sacred designs.

REFERENCES CITED

Brown, R. 1993. Ewaninga Rock Carvings Conservation Reserve: Site Recording and Condition Assessment. Report to the Conservation Commission of the Northern Territory, Alice Springs.

Brown, S. 1991. Art and Tasmanian Prehistory: Evidence for Changing Cultural Traditions in a Changing Environment. In *Rock Art and Prehistory: Papers Presented to Symposium G of the AURA Congress, Darwin, 1988*, edited by P. Bahn and A. Rosenfeld, 96–108. Oxford: Oxbow Monograph 10.

Edwards, R. 1971. Art and Aboriginal Prehistory. In *Aboriginal Man and Environment in Australia*, edited by D. J. Mulvaney and J. Golson, 356–367. Canberra: Australian National University Press.

Forbes, S. 1983. Aboriginal Rock Engravings at N'Dahla Gorge. In *Archaeology at ANZAAS 1983*, edited by M. Smith, 199–213. Perth: West Australian Museum.

Frederick, U. K. 1997. Drawing in Differences: Changing Social Contexts of Rock Art Production in Watarrka (Kings Canyon) National Park, Central Australia. Master's thesis, Australian National University, Canberra.

———. 1999. At the Centre of It All: Constructing Contact through the Rock Art of Watarrka National Park, Central Australia. *Archaeology in Oceania* 34:132–144.

Gunn, R. 1995. Regional Patterning in the Aboriginal Rock Art of Central Australia: A Preliminary Report. *Rock Art Research* 12 (2): 117–127.

———. 2000. Central Australian Rock Art: A Second Report. *Rock Art Research* 17 (2): 111–126.

Hamilton, A., and D. Vachon. 1985. Lake Amadeus–Luritja Claim Book. Alice Springs: Central Land Council.

Kimber, R. G. 1991. Rainbow Valley: Aboriginal Rock Art Survey. Report to the Conservation Commission of the Northern Territory, Alice Springs.

———. 1996. The Dynamic Century before the Horn Expedition: A Speculative History. In *Exploring Central Australia, Society, the Environment and the 1894 Horn Expedition*, edited by S. R. Morton and D. J. Mulvaney, 91–102. Chipping Norton: Surrey Beatty and Sons.

Maynard, L. 1979. The Archaeology of Australian Aboriginal Art. In *Exploring the Visual Art of Oceania*, edited by S. M. Mead, 83–110. Honolulu: University Press of Hawai'i.

Rosenfeld, A. 1981. *Early Man in North Queensland: Art*

and Archaeology in the Laura Area. Terra Australis 6. Canberra: Australian National University Press.

———. 1991a. Panaramitee: Dead or Alive? In *Rock Art and Prehistory: Papers Presented to Symposium G of the AURA Congress, Darwin, 1988*, edited by P. Bahn and A. Rosenfeld, 136–147. Oxbow Monograph 10. Oxford.

———. 1991b. Rock Art in Watarrka National Park. Report to the Conservation Commission of the Northern Territory on Fieldwork in 1990.

———. 1993. A Review of the Evidence for the Emergence of Rock Art in Australia. In *Sahul in Review: Pleistocene Archaeology in Australia, New Guinea and Island Melanesia*, edited by M. A. Smith, M. Spriggs, and B. Fankhauser, 71–80. Canberra: Research School of Pacific Studies, Australian National University.

———. 1996. The Thuiparta rock engravings at Erowalle, Wallace Rock Hole, James Range, NT. *Tempus* 6:247–255.

———. 1999. Rock Art and Rock Markings. *Australian Archaeology* 49:28–33.

Rosenfeld, A. and M. A. Smith. In press. Rock-art and the History of Puritjarra Rock Shelter, Cleland Hills, Central Australia. *Proceedings of the Prehistoric Society.*

Smith, M. A. 1986. The Antiquity of Seedgrinding in Arid Australia. *Archaeology in Oceania* 21:29–39.

———. 1989. The Case for a Resident Human Population in the Central Australian Ranges during Full Glacial Aridity. *Archaeology in Oceania* 24:93–105.

———. 1996. Prehistory and Human Ecology in Central Australia: An Archaeological Perspective. In *Exploring Central Australia: Society, the Environment and the 1894 Horn Expedition*, edited by S. R. Morton and D. J. Mulvaney, 61–73. Chipping Norton: Surrey Beatty and Sons.

Smith, M. A., and A. Rosenfeld. 1992. Archaeological Sites in Watarrka National Park: The Northern Sector of the Plateau. Report to the Conservation Commission of the Northern Territory on Fieldwork in 1991.

Smith, M. A., B. Fankhauser, and M. Jercher. 1998. The Changing Provenance of Red Ochre at Puritjarra Rock Shelter, Central Australia: Late Pleistocene to Present. *Proceedings of the Prehistoric Society* 64:275–292.

Spencer, B., and F. J. Gillen. 1968. *The Native Tribes of Central Australia.* New York: Dover Publications. Original publication 1899, London: Macmillan and Co.

Stirling, E. C. 1896. Anthropology. In *Report on the Work of the Horn Scientific Expedition to Central Australia: Part IV, Anthropology*, edited by B. Spencer, 1–157. Melbourne: Melville, Mullen and Slade.

Strehlow, T. G. H. 1947. *Aranda Traditions.* Melbourne: Melbourne University Press.

———. 1964. The Art of Circle Line and Square. In *Australian Aboriginal Art*, edited by R. Berndt, 44–59. Sydney: Ure Smith.

Taçon, P. S. 1992. The Roma Gorge Rock Art Complex: An Assessment and Description. Report to the Conservation Commission of the Northern Territory, Alice Springs.

Thorley, P. B. 1998a. Shifting Location, Shifting Scale: A Regional Landscape Approach to the Prehistoric Archaeology of the Palmer River Catchment, Central Australia. Ph.D. thesis, Northern Territory University, Darwin.

———. 1998b. Pleistocene Settlement in the Australian Arid Zone: Occupation of an Inland Riverine Landscape in the Central Australian Ranges. *Antiquity* 72:34–45.

Walsh, G. L. 1988. *Australia's Greatest Rock Art.* Bathurst: Brill–Robert Brown Associates.

Willshire, W. H. 1888. *The Aborigines of Central Australia with a Vocabulary of the Dialect of the Alice Springs Natives.* Adelaide: Bristow, Government Printer.

SIX

Wahi Pana

Legendary Places on Hawai'i Island

GEORGIA LEE

The island of Hawai'i has been the subject of much archaeological attention, particularly since the 1950s. One dominant theme has been changing relations between people and between people and place through the course of (pre)history, perhaps best examplified by Kirch's evolutionary approach to the emergence of Hawaiian kingdoms (e.g., Kirch 1997). Yet until recently one aspect of the archaeological record has been largely ignored by professional researchers: rock-art. This is perhaps surprising, because the island of Hawai'i is rich in petroglyph sites. It is even more surprising when it is realized that ethnographic details relating to rock-art can be shown to shed some light (albeit limited) on people's relations to place. The art not only reflected people's cultural practices, but contributed to their social (re)production.

The Hawaiian example is useful because petroglyphs can be shown to have been purposefully ordered in the landscape: the ancient Hawaiians were *selecting* places that were significant to them. As Wilson and David note in chapter 1, this enables us not to *retrieve* meaning, but *"to identify social codes . . . that have resulted in the production of particular senses of place."* It is by understanding place

marking, including rock-art, as ordered by world-views that people's relations with place can be approached. In this way, this chapter treats the Hawaiian cultural landscape as meaningfully constituted; by considering the ethnographic record, place markings are shown to be intimately linked to worldviews.

HAWAI'I: BACKGROUND

In early surveys and studies, the petroglyphs of Hawai'i received sporadic attention, and few sites were scientifically investigated. The first publication to bring petroglyphs to the general audience was *Hawaiian Petroglyphs*, by J. Halley Cox and Edward Stasack (1970). At that time, many key persons in Hawaiian studies believed that the petroglyphs were idle activities, lacking religious overtones. In several publications following *Hawaiian Petroglyphs*, rock carvings were described as discrete objects and were rarely studied in their physical and archaeological contexts.

The studies upon which this chapter is based are unusual in Pacific rock-art research, because complete inventories were recorded for the sites documented (cf. Lee and Stasack 1999). All the petroglyphs in the study were recorded in their associated surroundings and contexts, and placed into a computerized database that ultimately totaled more than 32,000 petroglyphs. The database enabled us to determine that motif variation was related to site type. Although this was intuitively felt, the absolute numbers provided verification and illuminated site usage.

Petroglyphs are not randomly distributed in the Hawaiian Islands. They are concentrated at certain sites on Hawai'i Island (the Big Island), leaving adjacent acres of smooth lava without any trace of activity. Of the many caves on the Big Island, only a few contain panels of petroglyphs on their cave walls. This distribution of rock-art sites in the landscape, coupled with ethnographic details (see later in this chapter), indicates that certain sites had spiritual associations and that the ancient Hawaiians were selecting places in their environment for activities that involved the making of petroglyphs.

Throughout Polynesia certain locales were considered sacred. These might be mountains, caves, or oddly shaped rock formations. It is not surprising, therefore, that Hawai'i's petroglyphs are not randomly distributed across the landscape; they were created in relation to cultural beliefs and practices, sometimes involving rituals or offerings. Some sites have attributes such as openings in the earth (e.g., caves, fissures); other sites are along ancient trails, and some are clearly related to current or recent religious sites (*heiau*). A few distinctive sites are connected to status locales, where chiefs resided. At these diverse sites, the motifs vary according to both function and to the spatial structure of sociocultural organization: sites that emphasize anthropomorphic petroglyphs generally are placed where some ritual activity was determined and, in at least one instance, the petroglyphs mark a boundary between two districts. Trail sites feature geometric designs. The famous *pu'u* (hill) at Pu'uloa stands apart for its relationship to the *piko* ceremony (see details later in this chapter).

In addition to site variation, petroglyph motifs depicting anthropomorphs evolved over time, from stick figures to triangle torso figures and then to more elaborate muscled anthropomorphs. A time frame for such developments has been determined by archaeological excavations (Cleghorn 1980; Hammatt and Folk 1980). Thus, for Hawaiian petroglyphs, we are dealing with spatial, temporal, sociostructural, and functional relationships.

Little detailed ethnographic material exists about the petroglyphs of the Hawaiian Islands. The most often quoted is Ellis (1979:203), who made a trip around the Big Island in 1823 and noted some petroglyph sites. Although his explanations are based upon comments by one informant and appear superficial, they have been cited often, and many later writers have suggested that the petroglyphs were of little importance due to some of Ellis' remarks (Lee and Stasack 1999:86).

In contrast, in 1914 Beckwith (n.d.) recorded the custom of placing the umbilical stump (*piko*) of a newborn into a "*piko* hole"; her field notes have proved to be of great value for understanding the ceremonial use of petroglyphs at some sites. The practice of making a cupule (a small, worked depression) as part of the *piko* ceremony (to ensure long life for a newborn) must have been a significant one judging from the thousands of cupules at some sites. The *piko* custom, alive when Captain Cook "discovered" the Hawaiian Islands in 1778, mystified Dr. Samwell who was on Cook's ship. He wrote in amazement about the scramble to place babies' *piko* into various crevices and cracks on ships. As Captain Cook was believed to be the god Lono, what better place to deposit a *piko*! The practice of making a *piko* (cupule) for the newborn has been revived in recent years in an effort to rejuvenate ancient ways.

RELIGIOUS MANIFESTATIONS

So-called "power" locations were those where the carving of a petroglyph appears to have been a means of gaining *mana* (spiritual power) or conferring a blessing. Usually associated with openings in the earth (caves, cracks, or collapsed lava tubes), these locales may be considered as a connection to the underworld and its residing spirits. Relating to the idea of *pō*, the underworld (land of spirits), and its opposite *ao*, light, these concepts allude to Mother Earth (*Papa*) and Father Sky (*Wākea*) and arc key elements in understanding religious beliefs in Polynesia. Lava arises from the depths and becomes land. Natural openings in the earth's crust relate to entrances or access to the underworld and the powers therein. The idea of the birth of prehuman forms in the nether regions of *pō*, then moving up to the coming of people, and the image that ushers in the world of humans (*ao*), corresponds to the genealogical history of Hawai'i's line of chiefs, with the center of the earth being the *piko* or navel (Beckwith 1970:312–313). It is clear that special places in the landscape not only reflected, but actively reinforced legends in a concrete way, enabling power to be extracted from them by the creation of petroglyphs. Rock-art, as place marking, thus played a crucial role in the *construction* of the experienced world and social identity.

As examples of sites that connect to the underworld, I turn to a cave on the west coast of the Big Island and a cave in the Ka'ū Desert, Hawai'i Volcanoes National Park. I also consider the island's major site, Pu'uloa, also in Hawai'i Volcanoes National Park (Figure 6.1).

Kalaoa 'O'oma

Kalaoa 'O'oma consists of three major lava tubes that radiate from a collapsed sink. The caves were used over a considerable time span for occupation, refuge, and burial. The north tube contains 12 m of petroglyphs. It was here that Hammatt and Folk (1980) excavated a platform against the petroglyph wall, uncovering more pictures in the process. The site was dated to around 1700 C.E.

The motifs on the panel include images of human figures, many with canoe paddles or other

FIGURE 6.1. Map of Hawai'i Island showing locations of sites discussed in this chapter.

like objects raised overhead (Figure 6.2). Paddles had enormous significance throughout Polynesia. They could relate to status, or to founding ancestors; a paddle became an extension of the person using it. Steering paddles were given names, and even the mythical canoes of the gods had their steering paddles named. Paddles were weapons for fighting canoes, and, at times, ceremonial paddles were used in religious dancing. The petroglyph panel may have commemorated a ritual, a status burial, or venerated a famous canoe paddler or warrior. Its location in the darkened recesses of the cave suggests that it somehow related to nonpublic space.

Hilina Pali

There are 17 m of petroglyphs inside the Hilina Pali cave, in the Ka'ū Desert. Archaeological excavations inside the cave date the occupation to 1540–1720 C.E. (Cleghorn 1980:20). The partly buried lower levels contain stick figures, and the upper levels have triangle-torsoed figures, providing a clue to the development of anthropomorphs in Hawaiian rock-art. Based upon his archaeological findings, Cleghorn (1980:30) estimated that the form of the human figures changed around 1600 C.E.

Hilina Pali's petroglyphs also include bird-headed figures, turtles, roosters, dogs, fishhooks, and human feet (or footprints). Again, geometric motifs are absent. This pattern is consistent throughout other caves in the Ka'ū District.

The caves/lava tubes of the district were considered as special places in the landscape and appear to be correlated with the underworld, as documented ethnographically. Burials and offerings are often associated, found deep within the cave recesses.

Pu'uloa

Located on the bleak, windswept slopes of Kīlauea Volcano, the great site at Pu'uloa (hill of long life) is on the inland fork of an old Hawaiian trail that runs across the north part of a pressure dome (*pu'u*) and continues beyond. Pu'uloa lacks an accessible lava tube but does have a small cave shelter on the east side. The main focus of the site is the large pressure dome that rises above the adjacent fields of *pāhoehoe* (smooth lava). Deep fissures run across the dome and

FIGURE 6.2. The panel inside the cave at Kalaoa, with figures holding paddles aloft.

these appear to have been the central point for much of the petroglyph making on the *pu'u* (Figure 6.3). Petroglyphs are on the mound and extend both west and north, continuing along the trail to the northeast for 500 m. There is no nearby occupation site.

Pu'uloa contains at least 24,000 petroglyphs (84% are cupules), far exceeding the number of cupules at other sites on the island and giving us ample evidence of the importance of the place in the lives of early Hawaiians. That *piko* (cupule) making and use was still going on in the late 1800s is evident from the work of anthropologist Martha Beckwith, giving us a specific function for at least some of the thousands of cupules

at the site (Figure 6.4). *Piko* were placed wherever the family thought they would do the most good for the child and the child's family. In that sense, *piko* places were associated with life powers; engagement with such places, through place marking, activated such powers. At Pu'uloa, what was sought after was long life.

Aside from making a small depression in the lava to contain the umbilical stump, it is also likely that *piko* were placed inside the large cracks that run through the mound at Pu'uloa, and a cupule was then made to record or to symbolize that event: cupules placed on vertical surfaces in the narrow crevices at Pu'uloa indicate that these, at least, were

FIGURE 6.3. Fissures running through the *pu'u* at Pu'uloa.

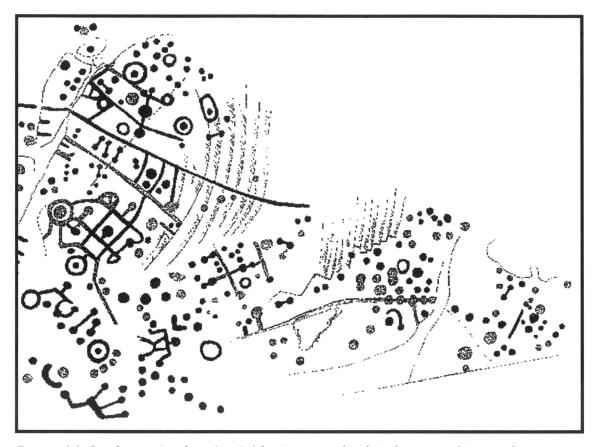

FIGURE 6.4. Cupules covering the *pu'u* at Pu'uloa, interspersed with circles, cups and rings, or lines connecting the cupules. Most cupules are small (4–5 cm diameter).

symbolic (Figure 6.5). The interpretation of cupules as repositories or symbols for the placement of an infant's umbilical stump is consistent with Polynesian tradition and has also been recorded for Easter Island, suggesting a common heritage and the existence of *piko* symbolism during ancestral times (dating back at least to a time when ancestral Hawaiians and Easter Islanders were in contact; this implies an ancestral central Polynesian origin around the mid to late first millennium C.E.) (Lee and Stasack 1999:88).

The *pu'u* was the focus for the *piko* ceremony, but Pu'uloa is much more than cupules. Petroglyphs cluster along the trail that runs through the site (Fig-

ure 6.6), and most of these are geometric designs, including circles, cups and rings, lines, plus some anthropomorphs. Also recorded were historic ships and copperplate lettering, further evidence that the site was used into historic times.

The trail that passed through the site may have served as a connection between villages or as part of the annual *makahiki* celebration, as indicated by the presence of a motif that bears close resemblance to the banner held aloft during the circumnavigation of the island by those participating in the festival (Figure 6.7). If this interpretation is correct, it appears that several ritual events were happening at this site: the *piko* ceremony, symbols made along the trail by those

FIGURE 6.5. Cupules carved on vertical surfaces in the cracks, Puʻuloa.

FIGURE 6.6. The trail at Puʻuloa, associated with circular motifs. Foot traffic through the years has obliterated many petroglyphs.

passing through, and a few pictures that seem to suggest the *makahiki*.

SITES THAT FOCUS ON RITUAL ACTIVITY

Kaeo 1

Kaeo 1, the center of the extensive site at Puakō in southern Kohala, is a site that appears to have been a focus for specific ritual activity, at least during the recent past. What comes across most forcefully at Kaeo is the density of carving and superimposition of images, particularly at one end of the site where a natural rise in the lava forms a slight dome. This is the central point of the site, with designs carved and recarved, one over another, suggesting that the location of the site was an important factor.

There is a high incidence of female images with prominent vulvae as well as pairs of baby-sized foot-

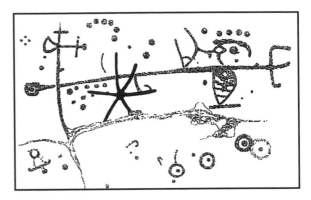

FIGURE 6.7. A figure at Puʻuloa that may be a Lono image, related to the *makahiki* festival.

prints (*wāwae*). The tiny footprints are often associated with adult-sized footprints. Human images branch off from central figures, and tiny figures occur beneath the shoulders of larger anthropomorphs (Figure 6.8). It may be that Kaeo was a place where the transformation of an individual was made to the status of family *ʻaumakua* (guardian spirit) (Barrow

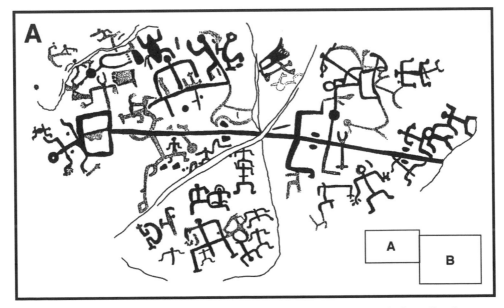

FIGURE 6.8. Kaeo 1 petroglyphs are densely carved and have suggestions of *ʻohana* (family, group, kin group, related), with connecting figures, small feet, and a huge "*moʻo*" (lizard or reptile) that spans the central portion of the site. *Moʻo* can be translated as "backbone," as in family genealogy.

1999). The site of Kaeo 1 has a preponderance of "stick" figures, the earliest form of anthropomorph in Hawaiian rock-art. Although we lack absolute dates, we therefore assume that this is an early site.

As my recording team was documenting the petroglyphs in 1997, a young Hawaiian family came to the site, bringing a *pū'olo* (offering bundle). They walked around the site for some time, apparently considering various options, and then put the bundle at the center of the slight mound where the carvings are most dense: the site, with its carvings, continues to hold special significance to local people to this day.

Status Concerns

Two sites contain motifs replete with status concerns, providing evidence of chiefly ritual activity. These motifs are very different from those found in caves, but they are also found in the great site at Pu'uloa and at Kaeo 1 at Puakō.

Ka'ūpūlehu

Ka'ūpūlehu, on the Kona coast, was a ritual status center and was a known residence of a great chief of the area. The site is remarkable for its delightful lagoon, fine beach, and, according to legend, a spring of fresh

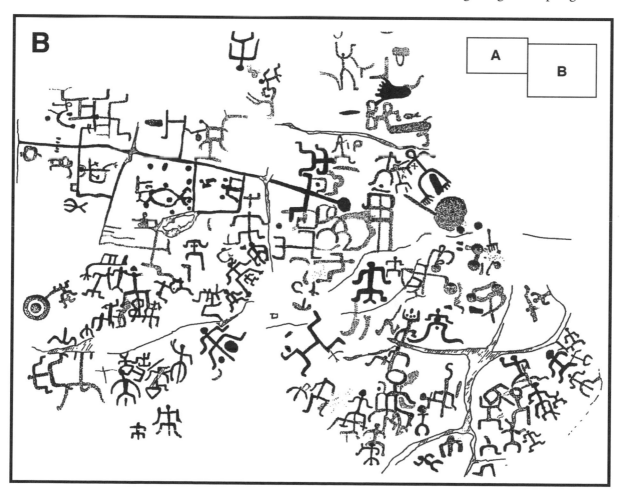

water. Divine intervention by the god Kāne is said to have provided the name for the site.

Ka'ūpūlehu's petroglyphs represent the finest images in Hawaiian rock-art; and some of the motifs are unique in the Islands. Artistry, in most instances, is outstanding, in the sense that the carvings exhibit special technical skill (Figure 6.9). The images differ enough from those at other locales in Hawai'i to suggest that the site related to distinctive activities or contexts, probably dealing with status, ritual, and sailing canoes. Canoes were renowned status markers and belonged to chiefs. Some motifs suggest a cult relating to the demigod Māui.

Today no *heiau* is visible, but an immense lava flow overtook a part of the site in 1800–1801 C.E., covering an area just north of the petroglyph site.

We do not know what it may have inundated. Part of the petroglyph field was covered also; petroglyphs disappear beneath the wall of lava toward the northern end of the site.

Ka'ūpūlehu has anthropomorphs and sets of pictures with chiefly attributes that display such status items as *kāhili* and feathered headdresses. *Kāhili* were ceremonial objects carried by honored retainers and used like fly whisks (Rose et al. 1993). The handles of some were made of human leg bones. Elaborate headdresses are shown on many of the anthropomorphs, and several of these have fishing lines in hand, with a hook and fish on the end. These are reminiscent of the myths of Māui who "fished up the Islands" (Figure 6.10).

Petroglyphs of huge crab-claw sails are the outstanding motif here, composing 25% of the pictures. Because only sails are indicated, it appears that "sail" metonymically implied "canoe." These are beautifully designed, large and elegant with sweeping curves. Some are associated with small anthropomorphs, and a few have pennants flying from the top or display ribbing. A panel of seven large and

FIGURE 6.9. Ka'ūpūlehu's is notable for its finely made petroglyphs. This chiefly figure sports an elaborate feathered headdress.

FIGURE 6.10. *Kāhili* (fly whisks) were status emblems. This chiefly figure at Ka'ūpūlehu wears a headdress and is flanked by *kāhili*. The figure holds a long fishing line with a hook and fish.

elegant sails in a row is without parallel in the Islands (Figure 6.11). Crab-claw sails went out of fashion by 1800, two decades after contact with the West.

The site also has two large kite designs, a rarity in Hawaiian rock-art (Figure 6.12). It may be that these refer to the demigod Māui, because Hawaiian legend describes his activities with a kite, such as controlling the wind or snaring the souls of those who have done evil (Beckwith 1970:109).

The "sacrifice scene" is unique in Hawaiian rock-art. Although it may represent a funeral or a sacrifice, the image is of two anthropomorphs carrying a body slung beneath a long pole (Figure 6.13). This motif may have been made to commemorate the killing of the captain of an American ship by the resident chief, Kame'eiamoku, in the nineteenth century (Kuykendall 1938:24).

Papamū are game boards pecked into the lava for playing a checkerlike game called *kōnane*, a kingly pursuit. Eighteen are found at Ka'ūpūlehu,

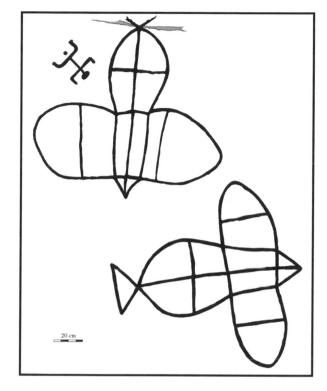

FIGURE 6.12. Kites in Polynesia were used in divination and figure prominently in some legends of the demigod Māui. Ka'ūpūlehu.

FIGURE 6.11. Crab-claw sails are a prominent motif at Ka'ūpūlehu. Made of elegant curves, some have pennants flying or ribbing. Note small human figures associated with the sails. On the left are a paddle and trident.

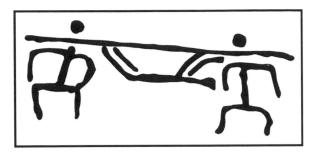

FIGURE 6.13. This appears to be a sacrifice scene, Kaʻūpūlehu.

evidence for high-ranking activities at the site (in contrast, there are none at Puʻuloa). The majority of the anthropomorphs at Kaʻūpūlehu have triangular torsos, and many are also muscled. These forms are later in time than the stick figure type, leading to the supposition that this site dates from a somewhat later time period than Kaeo 1 at Puakō.

Kahaluʻu, Kona

Kahaluʻu's petroglyph site is located next to Keʻekū *heiau* on the ocean's edge at Kailua-Kona. The site is under water at high tide. This area was once home to the kings of leeward Hawaiʻi, and in this area can be found at least ten major *heiau*, plus shrines, small temples, and a royal residential complex. It has long been recognized as a major center of power (Tuggle and Tomonari-Tuggle 1999:3, 11).

The petroglyphs were first recorded in 1906 by Stokes (1910:45), who had been told that one figure represented the slain Māui king Kamalalawalu, whose "body was brought to Kahaluʻu, a picture of it made on the rock, and his body sacrificed in the nearby heiau of Keʻeku." Other motifs here include images that include birth (and reproduction/potency), ceremony, death, and the relationship to the adjacent *heiau* (Tuggle and Tomonari-Tuggle 1999:10).

This site fits well with the type of status place we see at Kaʻūpūlehu, one that is associated with power, chiefdom, legend, and sacrifice.

BOUNDARIES

Boundaries were of great importance in ancient Hawaiʻi. They were *kapu* (sacred, forbidden), and travel across them was forbidden except during the *makahiki*. A line of individual petroglyph sites stretches out from Kaeo 1 at Puakō for a distance of 1.7 km. It has been suggested (Bishop Museum Department of Anthropology report, 1964) that the motifs may have bordered a trail. However, Lee and Stasack (1999) failed to find any trace of such a trail. Rather, the petroglyphs were placed along an ancient boundary separating the *ahupuaʻa* (land division) of Lālāmilo from that of Waikoloa. Petroglyphs are absent for tens of meters on either side of this decorated line. The motifs are different from those found at recognized trail sites, such as ʻAnaehoʻomalu and Puʻuloa.

TRAILS

ʻAnaehoʻomalu

We have already noted the trail at Puʻuloa, with its focus on geometric motifs. ʻAnaehoʻomalu, on the Kona coast, is a similar site. A trail runs through ʻAnaehoʻomalu, and foot traffic through the centuries has obliterated some of the petroglyphs (Figure 6.14). The site formerly was in a desolate sea of *pāhoehoe* that stretched for miles, but today its nucleus is all that is left, surrounded by a lush golf course, a fake lake, and a resort.

FIGURE 6.14. Trail through 'Anaeho'omalu.

Aside from a sprinkling of anthropomorphs and a few other motifs such as feet, fishhooks, and a cape, the site features elaborate circular motifs with interior designs, enclosures (lines pecked around a picture, perhaps to give the image added significance), cup and ring designs, and cupules. In discussing circular things, Valeri (1985:89) stated that in Hawai'i there was "meaning in abstract theory rather than mundane . . . circular things and things capable of circular movement considered divine— sun, moon, . . . circles are complete and self-sufficient." In this context, the predominance of circles at 'Anaeho'omalu implies a preoccupation with abstraction. The geographical focus of the site is a collapsed lava tube, located at a slight rise in the landscape. Surrounding this opening in the earth are cupules, cup and ring designs, circles, and other geometric forms. The significance of the high density of petroglyphs near this opening in the earth, on a raised section of the landscape, may have had as much to do with the land's morphology—ladened with socially constructed meaning—as with the petroglyphs themselves.

DISCUSSION

It is not possible to enter the minds of those ancient Hawaiians who made the petroglyphs. But by considering Hawaiian worldviews, as recorded by early explorers and anthropologists, it becomes possible to identify what the rock-art meant to its creators and users, at least in the recent past. And as hinted by the occurrence of the *piko* ceremony in different parts of Polynesia, such beliefs may have some antiquity, dating back at least to the end of the first millennium C.E. Many petroglyphs contained hidden and multiple, secret meanings (*kaona*), and such information was restricted to a select group. Motifs related to belief, power, prayer, offering, and magic.

Hawaiian petroglyphs are intimately related to their geographical settings. They should not be considered as isolated artistic products, but as markings *in* and *of* place. We thus find petroglyphs on or near unusual rock formations, shrines, lava tubes, cracks in the earth, or at the point of a sweeping vista. Mythical and legendary places in the landscape— those places given special meaning by their association with essential life forces or with the deeds of founding ancestors—were attractive to petroglyph makers. It comes as no surprise to note, therefore, that petroglyphs are often located in places where the rock surface does not appear to be well suited to marking (because of its mechanical properties), implying that it is place and place marking, more so than the petroglyphs themselves, that are of significance. Thus the petroglyphs gained significance in their *association* with place; and in the process of being marked, the significance of the places themselves was heightened, inscribed with the powers that made them special in the first place. There is a dialectic here, a re-enforcing rhythm that enabled place to speak through symbol and symbol to speak through place. Valeri (1985:101) noted that *mana* may come from the gods, but potent speech and correct ritual actions were required for its successful transfer to people. We could say this in different terms: rock-art expressed a world order, and that order came into being by a perpetuation of certain forms of inscription (including rock-art).

REFERENCES CITED

Barrow, L. 1999. *ʻAumakua* (Guardian Ancestors) in the Context of Current Hawaiian Religious Beliefs. *Rapa Nui Journal* 13 (2): 49–56.

Beckwith, Martha. n.d. Unpublished Field Notes. Department of Anthropology, Hawaiian Sources Collection, Bernice P. Bishop Museum, Honolulu.

———. 1970. *Hawaiian Mythology*. Honolulu: University of Hawaiʻi Press.

Cleghorn, P. L. 1980. The Hilina Pali Petroglyph Cave, Hawaii Island. Report, B. P. Bishop Museum, Honolulu.

Cox, J. H., and E. Stasack. 1970. *Hawaiian Petroglyphs*. Honolulu: Bishop Museum Press.

Ellis, W. 1979. *Journal of William Ellis*. Rutland, Vermont: Charles E. Tuttle Co.

Hammatt, H. H., and W. H. Folk. 1980. Archaeological Excavations within the Proposed Keahole Agricultural Park: Kalaoa-Oʻoma, Kona, Hawaii Island. Report, State of Hawaiʻi, Department of Agriculture.

Kirch, P. 1997. *Feathered Gods and Fishhooks*. Honolulu: University of Hawaiʻi Press.

Kuykendall, R. S. 1938. *The Hawaiian Kingdom*. Vol. 1. 1778–1854. Honolulu: University of Hawaiʻi Press.

Lee, G., and E. Stasack. 1999. *Spirit of Place: Petroglyphs of Hawaiʻi*. Los Osos: Easter Island Foundation.

Rose, R., S. Conant, and E. P. Kjellgren. 1993. Hawaiian Standing Kahili in the Bishop Museum: An Ethnological and Biological Analysis. *Journal of the Polynesian Society* 102:243–304.

Stokes, J. F. G. 1910. Notes on Hawaiian Petroglyphs. *Occasional Papers of the Bernice Pauahi Bishop Museum* 4 (4): 33–71.

Tuggle, D., and M. Tomonari-Tuggle. 1999. The Petroglyphs of Kahuluʻu, Kona, Hawaiʻi. *Rapa Nui Journal* 13 (1): 3–13.

Valeri, V. 1985. *Kingship and Sacrifice: Ritual and Society in Ancient Hawaii*. Chicago: University of Chicago Press.

SEVEN

Making Sense of Petroglyphs

The Sound of Rock-Art

Paul Rainbird

The standard interpretative strategy in rock-art studies is one that privileges the visual propensities over other forms of meaning production. In this chapter I examine how the production of petroglyphs impacts on another of the human senses, that of hearing. I propose that in certain contexts the meaning of petroglyphs may not be solely, or most importantly, in the motifs themselves, but also in the noise of their manufacture. We tend to view rock-art only as the end product of a process of social engagement. I argue instead that its social significance may lie in its production. In this sense, rock-art can be considered as a by-product of meaningful social action. I explore this idea through specific case studies derived from fieldwork on the island of Pohnpei in the Federated States of Micronesia and on Ilkley Moor in West Yorkshire, United Kingdom.

THE SOCIALITY OF SOUND

Each of the senses—vision, touch, smell, taste, and hearing—is activated as one experiences being in the world. However, the five senses identified in Western conceptions are not universally recognized as discrete sensual categories; perceptions are culturally specific (e.g., Classen et al. 1994; Finney 1995; MacGregor 1999:263–264). Nevertheless, it may be assumed that hearing, although in Western society not considered the most acute of the human senses, is something generally shared by our species. In archaeology and rock-art studies we obviously privilege the visual aspects because, although perspective may change, the material can be *seen*; that is, it can be viewed and appreciated as a direct manifestation of the past. The other senses are usually regarded as ephemeral and difficult to capture in the present. However, a more fully interpretative archaeology requires us to attempt to consider other sensual experiences to provide the broader experiential context for social action. In relation to the current interest in the phenomenology of landscapes, Tilley (1999:180) pointed out that "[w]hen we consider landscape we are almost always thinking about it primarily in terms of a visual construct. . . . Landscapes are not just visionscapes but also soundscapes, touchscapes, smellscapes. . . ."

Here I am concerned with soundscapes. I suggest

that in marking place, social action is not restricted to just visual phenomena. For example, Ingham et al. (1999) researched the social geographies of warehouse parties in the city of Blackburn, England. The warehouse party was a phenomenon of the late 1980s where the music of choice was "house" style, often associated with the drug Ecstasy, and where empty spaces such as warehouses were used to hold large dance parties, usually lasting for one night only. The nonregulated organization of these events soon led to legislation restricting their occurrence, and they were, for the most part, stamped out in urban environments by the passing of the draconian Criminal Justice and Public Order Act of 1994. Ingham et al. (1999) set out to establish how the short-lived phenomenon of warehouse parties created new soundscapes for derelict industrial buildings. They found that the "academic challenge [is] to overcome the neglect of ephemeral spaces and the ways in which the dynamic of sound interacts with the dynamic of space; and therefore to encounter and examine the critical difference between the mental construction of a sonorous world on the basis of essentially static soundmarks, as against dynamic, impermanent, fuzzily bounded soundspaces" (Ingham et al. 1999:300). Soundmarks are supposed to be analogous to landmarks and be unique to particular places or communities (Schafer 1976, 1977; Westerkemp 1994 cited in Ingham et al. 1999:286).

In general, the soundscapes conceived of in social geography have been dominated by music (e.g., Smith 1997; see also the review of "acoustic ecology" by Waterman 2000), to the detriment of the development of a more fully contextualized understanding that may include the more mundane facets, including human utterances, that have an equal role in establishing the social understanding of place. In anthropology Gell has gone some way to adding this

extra, required dimension. Ethnographic experience among the Umeda of northwestern Papua New Guinea highlighted for Gell (1995) that he was a "pronouncedly visual thinker." His desire to get above the forest and thus through vision to place himself spatially in the landscape was frustrated by the thick forest and lack of a vantage point. He found that the visual world in which he had been socially inculcated was there, in the forest, of very close range and inhibiting in establishing the parameters of the world beyond the intimate. He realized that the world of the Umeda went far beyond the visual. The villagers created much of their world through sound; "one can hear bush activities in progress; chopping, pounding sago, and the standard location-giving 'whoops' uttered by parties of Umeda on the move" (Gell 1995:239–240). Gell's experiences remind us that the world is not simply that of a visual landscape, but also one of soundscape and soundmark in everyday practice.

Elsewhere in the tropical Pacific material items have been linked to sound production. In Vanuatu, Clausen (1960, quoted in Tilley 1999:128) found that hardwood slit drums connected people "with the otherwise unknown world of the ancestral ghosts whose voices they represent and who live on—literally feed on—the psychic essence of the boars that are sacrificed to them. Slit-drums thus constitute a psychic medium of communication with the spirit world. . . ."

In the Caroline Islands much is made in archaeological reports and ethnographic texts of shell jewelry found in excavations and recorded as traditionally worn by both men and women. Discussion of such items of bodily ornamentation has usually focused on the aesthetics of the visual impact, but Steager (1979), writing of the people of Puluwat Atoll, found that the sensual focus of the local people may have been rather different. Thus Steager

(1979:351) wrote that "[o]ne elderly woman provided me with a clue as to the rationale behind these ornaments. She described to me her childhood memories of the lovely sound these ornaments made as people awakened and moved about in the dark predawn hours. She also described the sound they made during dances, especially men's dances, which included a great deal of vigorous jumping and stamping."

These examples illustrate that although sound events are ephemeral, they participate in a sense of being and may even leave material residue. Attempts to consider senses beyond the visual in the past can only be a benefit to a closer understanding of the different social worlds that existed.

SENSUAL ARCHAEOLOGIES

Archaeological interpretation has slowly been going beyond the visual to incorporate the other senses to more broadly contextualize human experience in the past. A number of these sensual approaches in archaeology have been conducted in relation to megalithic architecture. Lynch investigated the role of acoustics in passage-grave type tombs (1973) and choices of color in their construction (1998). Devereux and Jahn (1996) explored acoustical resonance in a variety of enclosed pre-Historic sites, and Watson and Keating (1999) also tested the effects of sound within megalithic tombs and compared this with how sound is altered within comparatively open stone circle settings. Much of this sound research in archaeology has been reviewed by Lawson et al. (1998) and complements phenomenological studies of aspects of megalithic architecture (e.g., Richards 1993; Thomas 1993), and others have explored sensual biographies for various items of material culture. For instance, MacGregor (1999)

considered the touch sensitivity of ancient carved stone balls from Scotland, and Edmonds (1999) commented on the pain and sound of flint knapping. Hamilakis (1998) pursued interests in the sensual aspects of food and drink consumption.

Rock-art studies have also gone beyond the traditional visual interpretations of images with a certain amount of consideration having been given to other sensual aspects of locational choice. Scarre (1989) reported on work that has identified "points of resonance" that appear to be associated with images in French Palaeolithic cave sites, and Dayton (1992) reported on similar work by Steven Waller in which he concluded that "the best way to appreciate the sophisticated art of our ancestors is to make noise." For Waller this was a universal feature because all rock-art sites he had tested in Europe, North America, and Australia revealed unusual acoustic propensities. Other painted caves in Europe have also had aspects of their sensual sound importance identified through the discovery of "lithophones" (Charatan 1998; Dams 1984). Lithophones are natural formations in caves that when hit with stone or wood, rather like a xylophone, will produce a constant variety of notes that can be used to construct music. Bone flutes contemporary with the art at these sites are also known, and it has been proposed that rites, replete with musical accompaniment, may once have been associated with the paintings.

I now turn to my two case studies, starting with the petroglyphs from Pohnpei Island in the tropical Northwest Pacific.

POHNPAID, POHNPEI

The Pohnpaid petroglyph site is located in the southeast of the island of Pohnpei, in the eastern Caroline Islands of Micronesia. Pohnpei is a mountainous island, volcanic in origin, and covered in the lush vegetation typical of its tropical Pacific location. The region of Micronesia is not well known for its rock-art (Rainbird 1994), but the Pohnpaid site stands out as being special in having over 750 individual petroglyphs. The motifs include forms identified as footprints, handprints and fish, as well as repeated forms that cannot be identified as a specific material item (geometric and more abstract compilations). I do not provide further details here because these and other features of the site have been presented elsewhere (Rainbird 1998, in press; Rainbird and Wilson 1999).

This chapter derives from an experience similar to that described for Gell above, because it was not planned during the initial stages of my research at Pohnpaid. While I was in the process of making a standard record of the petroglyphs at Pohnpaid, a few local children visited the site and began to beat sticks against the rock. These children are aware, as their ancestors must have been, that different parts of the exfoliating volcanically derived outcrop produce different sounds. The sounds produced when the rock is beaten with a stick are of high resonance, and experiments using stone—not directly on the decorated rock surfaces—indicate that loud and resonating sounds may be heard far beyond the boundaries of the Pohnpaid site itself.

The location of the outcrop on which the petroglyphs occur allows for broad views across and into the valley below (Figure 7.1). The valley is the area of human habitation, but the forest allows no direct views of human activity apart from the smoke rising from stone ovens and fires. The forest is "agroforest," consisting almost exclusively of trees of subsistence importance. Studies from the neighboring island of Kosrae suggest that such forests were actively promoted from the time people first settled the island (Athens et al. 1996; Rainbird 1995).

With no direct visual associations across the neighboring valley, could it be that the petroglyphs of Pohnpei have made their mark by ordering an earlier soundscape? The petroglyphs are not made today and have not been in living memory. Some of the motifs appear to be unique, but others have correlations that indicate that they may have been made around 2,000 years ago.

Soundscape in this forest environment has been important in the recorded past and continues to be important in the present day. Apart from the crescent-shaped basalt slabs that emanated a bell-like tone that was reported by Christian (1899:92), the traditional preparation of *sakau*—more commonly known elsewhere in the Pacific as *kava* (Lebot et al. 1992)—leads to much noisemaking. *Sakau* preparation requires crushing the roots of the *Piper*

FIGURE 7.1. View from Pohnpaid.

methysticum plant by hammer stone on a basalt pounding stone. Each community has developed its own rhythms as groups of men perform this solemn task (Riesenberg 1968). The noise of the pounding resonates through the forest, indicating to all that preparations for specific communal, but restricted, ritual events have begun.

Petersen (1995) noted the essential importance of *sakau* in Pohnpeian society. He found that it is valued above any other element of the social order, and, although some other texts dispute this, unlike many other *kava*-using societies was and is available to all members of society through a relaxed but ritualized process. Males are usually responsible for the preparation of the drink, but in all sections of the island one of the first four coconut cupfuls is designated for a woman (usually the wife of the highest-ranking male). The complex social ranking that is almost bound to exist at any gathering involving *sakau*, because of the complex and wide-ranging dual titular system of each of the five sections of the island, is observed but unspoken. O'Connell (1972:141) in his early nineteenth-century sojourn noted how the tempo of the pounding rhythm changed to correspond to the composition of the gathering: "If a head chief be present the blows are given thus, in perfect time: one, two, three—then a pause,—one,—another pause,—one, two, three. If a petty chief is the highest in rank present, the blows are one, two,—a pause,—one,—another pause,—one, two."

Accentuating the aural senses, the sound of *sakau*, with its complex associated meanings of power, hierarchy, community, and history, pervades and creates the soundscape (Rainbird 1998). Ignoring the bell-like tones emanating from the center of production is extremely difficult because the sound passes easily across boundaries that inhibit the visual: notions of inclusion or exclusion are accentuated. I imagine a similar scenario during the production of the petroglyphs; the sound of rock hammering against rock would have emanated beyond the boundaries of the visual. The community in earshot would have understood the sound and its associated meanings. Sound (rather than the petroglyphs themselves) may have been the one sensual experience shared by all during the process of image production, creating a sense of place in an aural world.

ILKLEY MOOR, ENGLAND

On the other side of the world from Pohnpei, and beginning perhaps 2,000 years earlier (Neolithic or Early Bronze Age [Beckensall 1999:1; Keighley 1981]), the petroglyphs on Rombalds Moor, of which Ilkley Moor is a part, were being hammered out of the rock. Situated on the east Pennine edge of West Yorkshire, this area boasts the highest concentration of petroglyphs in the British Isles, with some 297 engraved rocks recorded (Ilkley Archaeology Group [I.A.G.] 1986:7).

The engravings are, for the most part, limited to a small range of motif types consisting of cupules (cup marks), cup marks enclosed by a ring or rings (cup and ring marks), and on occasion lines joining these other motifs (grooves). More complex motifs have been recorded, but are rare. The distribution of carved stones is one that appears to favor the moorland edge either set back a few meters or on the point where the land falls steeply into the valley of the River Wharfe. However, this is a modern phenomenon, because a great deal of quarrying has taken place (Beckensall 1999:71; I.A.G. 1986:12) and has eaten at the moorland edge, providing a false impression of the past spatial distribution of the petroglyphs. A number of carved rocks are also positioned on the lower valley slopes.

Bradley (1997) considered this group of petroglyphs in his broader examination of the Atlantic tradition of rock carving that is found along the western Atlantic seaboard from Spain to Scotland. For Bradley (1997:4) it was a visit to Ilkley Moor that sparked his interest in rock-art studies, and he found that considering the petroglyphs within a landscape archaeology approach allowed for the possibility of new interpretations as to their role in pre-Historic society. Previous work had proposed that these carvings may have served as markers on long-distance trade routes or that they were distributed in relation to Bronze Age farming areas (see Bintliff 1988). However, Bradley (1997:4) found that some of the most elaborately engraved rocks were located in places that "commanded extensive views over the lower ground." He interpreted the engravings as located on the edge of contemporary settlement rather than within the farming areas. This view finds support in recent studies that found that although many flint artifacts show that the area was used from the Mesolithic onward, "the absence of settlement sites suggests that the area was used for pastoral and hunting activities" (Beckensall 1999:73). Bradley (1997) proposed that in this Atlantic tradition the engraved stones may mark places of movement and be indicators of territory in those Late Neolithic and Early Bronze Age societies which were not as sedentary and agriculturally based as had previously been supposed. In doing this, Bradley highlighted the visual aspects of these inscribed landscapes: at Ilkley Moor, the carvings themselves are read as visual text ("Signing the Land" is the subtitle of his book) and the intervisibility of lowland or other carved rocks is taken to indicate the broader spatial referents of these marks.

With these issues in mind Kate Howell and I visited the carved rocks of Ilkley Moor and found a different picture emerging. We found that although some of the most elaborately carved rocks did have extensive views, these views were distant ones and did not provide visual links with the lowland area directly below the moor. Here I provide two examples:

The "Badger Stone" (No. 88, I.A.G. 1986) is one of the most commonly photographed of the local group, with deeply incised cup marks, rings, and linking grooves on its southwestern face. Facing the inscribed panel of the Badger Stone the vista that attracts the eye is to the northwest, where Wharfedale is cut deeply into the Pennine chain of hills (Figure 7.2). This direction provides the only view, at some considerable distance, of the lowland bottoms.

The "Haystack" or "Cottage" Rock (No. 141, I.A.G. 1986) is so named due to its large size and roof-shaped profile. Cup marks, rings, and grooves are spread spectacularly across the whole of the "roof." Once again the vista here is not the local valley bottom that is obscured by the moor edge, but the valley of the River Wharfe as it spreads out east into the lowlands of West Yorkshire and the Vale of York. As with the Badger Stone, it appears that if a visual reference is being made it is to more distant rather than to local lowland settlement areas.

Two problems then arise from a vision-dominant sensual understanding of the Ilkley Moor rock carvings. The first is that much of the apparent moor edge distribution is an artifact of postmedieval quarrying that has altered the potential vistas from some sites. Second, any visual reference was apparently not being made in relation to the local communities in the immediate lowland area. A further problem with an ocular-centric interpretation arises when a fuller consideration of the carved rocks at Ilkley is

FIGURE 7.2. View from the Badger Stone, Ilkley Moor (photo courtesy of Jennie Hawes and Andrew Parker).

attempted taking account of those located on the lower valley sides and the paleoenvironmental context of those on the moor top.

Carved rocks at Ilkley are not restricted to the moor top, but are also found on earthfast boulders in the rough, rock-strewn slope leading to the valley bottom. These petroglyphs, although not necessarily the most elaborate, appear never to have had the potential for the broad vistas exhibited by many of their counterparts on the moor top. How then can these be fitted within an interpretation that favors intervisibility? But it may be premature to interpret

these as different. The paleoenvironmental research of Bannister (1985) concluded that major woodland clearing did not occur on the moor top until the Middle or Late Bronze Age, after the supposed inscribing of the majority of the stones. Indeed she stated that, "[t]he wide distribution of cup-and-ring rocks, and in particular their abundance on the apparently uninhabited western side of the moor, suggests that these rocks are not associated with agriculture or settlement, and may instead be the work of early Bronze Age hunters" (Bannister 1985:167).

For the petroglyphs of Ilkley Moor it may be

inappropriate to favor the visual aspects over the aural. If we consider the aural propensities, then we find that gritstone geology does not resonate with the bell-like tones of the rock from Pohnpei, but the dull thud of stone against stone does carry. We should also not necessarily imagine a person hammering alone; communal rhythmic hammering will raise the level of the noise created. Such a communal performance, like dancing or *sakau* preparation, acts socially as a recursive phenomenon that reinstitutes and may even remake community ties. The secondary production of petroglyphs may act as mnemonic soundmarks for periodic events at these locales.

Locating specific noise in Pohnpei, where the modern trappings of motor vehicles, aircraft, televisions, and radios are still few and far between, is far easier than on Ilkley Moor, where there is the constant rumble of traffic from below and from above the regular drone of planes climbing from Leeds/Bradford Airport. But we know that this was not always the case, and Sherratt (1991) reminded us of the dramatic impact the first church bells must have had as they resonated across the medieval landscape. The noise caused by making the petroglyphs at Ilkley would transcend the boundaries of the visual.

DISCUSSION

Bringing together the spatially and temporally distant case studies from the Pacific and northern England can, I suggest, lead to some different directions in interpreting petroglyphs. The Pohnpaid site, in the first instance, appears to fit well with an understanding of petroglyphs located in a landscape dominated by visual associations, sitting as it does above and with a clear view of the valley bottom settlement areas. But this vista is not one of intervisibility, because at the human scale the dense agroforest restricts all but the briefest of glances of the outcrop from below. This is, and probably always has been, in Gell's terms a soundscape that restricts human visual acumen to the most intimate and local world. The wider world involves a sound system in which the soundmarks are either the known places in the landscape where stone regularly beats against stone—whether in the production of *sakau* or in the creation of petroglyphs—or the mobile utterances of people as they create an ephemeral soundscape as they pass from place to place. It is in the process of engagement with place that the rock-art was created, and I suggest that it is the process of engagement, involving socially meaningful sound production, that requires some attention here, at least as much as the artistic end product. In the neighboring islands of Chuuk Lagoon, I have previously suggested that the hilltop enclosures ought not to be interpreted in terms of simple functionalist notions of defense, but as places where the elements of the air (rain and wind) are free to arrive from the horizon, unsullied by the enclosing forest below the peaks (Rainbird 1996). Taking this farther, these hilltops may have provided havens above the day-to-day soundscape, serving as places where the unusual phenomenon of distant views created a new, different, and possibly heightened sense of being. These soundscapes are different, but mundane places; in the Pohnpei and Chuuk examples it is an expansive visual landscape that is different and strange. Perhaps this was one reason for choosing the Pohnpaid outcrop as a place for inscription—a clearing that has become a special place, where silence may activate and accentuate other senses.

Where the Ilkley Moor top engravings were located out of visual range of the nearest valley bottoms, at the Badger Stone or Haystack Rock, for example, the boundaries were easily transcended by sound. Indeed, in a changeable climate, where distant views of valley bottoms could easily be concealed by mist or rain (or nightfall in most phases of the moon), the ability of sound to overcome such elements, or even be enhanced by appropriate prevailing winds, allows the local soundscape to be maintained when landscape would be lost.

Such concerns also enable us to refocus our attention on landscapes as constructed in the process of social participation. We are used to treating the evidence of past human behavior as a long-lasting archaeological record, and in this capacity we often bypass real-life experience and its temporal dimensions. In focusing on soundscapes we are reminded that landscapes are lived in. In the process of everyday participation, each of the senses is called upon to bear witness to landscapes that are as much a matter of people-people relations as they are of people-land relations. Although in long-term time scales, such as archaeologists often concentrate upon, sounds may appear to resonate and disappear, here I have suggested otherwise: as socially entangled products, sounds linger in the way that they guide human understanding of the moment, in the process serving to reproduce social relations and knowledge of the world through time. It is not just abstract space that is "marked" by sound, but *places* as locations rich in human action and meaning.

CONCLUSION

I am not proposing here to replace a universal vision-centric interpretation of petroglyphs in contextualized archaeological studies of rock-art with universal aural-centric understandings. By focusing on the aural I wish to emphasize the potential multisensual roles of such material culture and place marking in any understanding of human existence. In doing so I have neglected the other senses and any reader who has been involved in the recording of petroglyphs cannot help but be familiar with the role touch may have played in understanding the meaning of such motifs in the past.

My experience in Pohnpaid has allowed me to explore a different approach in an attempt to get closer to understanding the role of the carvings on Ilkley Moor. It has opened up potentials previously, as far as I am aware, unexplored in relation to this particular group. If sound was a dominant factor of petroglyph production in these places, then the emphasis on the motif needs to be reconsidered or at least recontextualized. The motif is less important if the land was not being "signed," and this may explain the repetitive (and abstract) form taken by motifs of the Atlantic tradition in northern Britain and the dominant types at Pohnpaid. We must thus make sense of rock-art by exploring the multiplicity of the human senses.

NOTE

I thank Meredith Wilson and Bruno David for commenting on the chapter and inviting me to contribute to this volume. Thanks also to Vince Devine of the West Yorkshire Sites and Monuments Record for providing invaluable information. Comments from Andrew Fleming, Mark Pluciennik, Yannis Hamilakis, and seminar participants at the University of Wales, Lampeter, were gratefully received. Members of the Pohnpei Historic Preservation Office and the FSM Office of Archives and Historic Preservation and Andler Anton, the landowner of Pohnpaid, made the fieldwork on Pohnpei possible. Finally, I thank Kate Howell for her much-appreciated encouragement, enthusiasm, and priceless discussions of this topic in the field and elsewhere. I am solely responsible for any inaccuracies, misrepresentations, or overinterpretation.

REFERENCES CITED

Athens, J. S., J. V Ward, and G. M. Murakami. 1996. Development of an Agroforest on a Micronesian High Island: Prehistoric Kosraean Agriculture. *Antiquity* 70:834–846.

Bannister, J. 1985. *The Vegetational and Archaeological History of Rombalds Moor, West Yorkshire*. Ph.D. diss., University of Leeds, Leeds.

Beckensall, S. 1999. *British Prehistoric Rock Art*. Stroud: Tempus.

Bintliff, J. 1988. Site Patterning: Separating Environmental, Cultural and Preservation Factors. In *Conceptual Issues in Environmental Archaeology*, edited by J. Bintliff, D. Davidson, and E. Grant, 129–144. Edinburgh: Edinburgh University Press.

Bradley, R. 1997. *Rock Art and the Prehistory of Atlantic Europe: Signing the Land*. London: Routledge.

Charatan, K. 1998. La Pileta; a Lithophone in Its Upper Palaeolithic Context. Bachelor's thesis, University of Wales, Lampeter.

Christian, F. W. 1899. *The Caroline Islands: Travel in the Sea of the Little Islands*. London: Methuen.

Classen, C., D. Howes, and A. Synott. 1994. *Aroma: The Cultural History of Smell*. London: Routledge.

Dams, L. 1984. Palaeolithic Lithophones: Descriptions and Comparisons. *Oxford Journal of Archaeology* 4:31–46.

Dayton, L. 1992. Rock Art Evokes Beastly Echoes of the Past. *New Scientist*, 28 November, p. 14.

Devereux, P., and R. G. Jahn. 1996. Preliminary Investigations and Cognitive Considerations of the Acoustical Resonances of Selected Archaeological Sites. *Antiquity* 70:665–666.

Edmonds, M. 1999. *Ancestral Geographies of the Neolithic*. London: Routledge.

Finney, B. 1995. A Role for Magnetoperception in Human Navigation? *Current Anthropology* 36:500–506.

Gell, A. 1995. The Language of the Forest: Landscape and Phonological Iconism in Umeda. In *The Anthropology of Landscape: Perspectives on Place and Space*, edited by E. Hirsh and M. O'Hanlon, 232–254. Oxford: Oxford University Press.

Hamilakis, Y. 1998. Thinking through the Consuming Body. Paper presented at the Thinking through the Body Conference, University of Wales, Lampeter.

Ilkley Archaeology Group. 1986. *The Carved Rocks on Rombalds Moor*. Wakefield: West Yorkshire Municipal County Council.

Ingham, J., M. Purvis, and D. B. Clarke. 1999. Hearing Places, Making Spaces: Sonorous Geographies, Ephemeral Rhythms, and the Blackburn Warehouse Parties. *Society and Space (Environment and Planning D)* 17:283–305.

Keighley, J. J. 1981. The Bronze Age. In *West Yorkshire: An Archaeological Survey to A.D. 1500*, edited by M. L. Faull and S. A. Moorhouse, 93–114. Wakefield: West Yorkshire Metropolitan County Council.

Lawson, G., C. Scarre, I. Cross, and C. Hills. 1998. Mounds, Megaliths, Music and Mind: Some Thoughts on the Acoustical Properties and Purposes of Archaeological Spaces. *Archaeological Review from Cambridge* 15 (1): 111–134.

Lebot, V., M. Merlin, and L. Lindstrom. 1992. *Kava: The Pacific Drug*. New Haven: Yale University Press.

Lynch, F. 1973. The Use of the Passage in Certain Passage Graves as a Means of Communication Rather Than Access. In *Megalithic Graves and Ritual*, edited by G. Daniel and P. Kjaerum, 147–161. Copenhagen: Jutland Archaeological Society.

———. 1998. Colour in Prehistoric Architecture. In *Prehistoric Ritual and Religion*, edited by A. Gibson and D. Simpson, 62–67. Stroud: Sutton.

MacGregor, G. 1999. Making Sense of the Past in the Present: A Sensory Analysis of Carved Stone Balls. *World Archaeology* 31:258–271.

O'Connell, J. F. 1972. *A Residence of Eleven Years in New*

Holland and the Caroline Islands. Honolulu: University of Hawai'i Press. Original publication, 1836.

Petersen, G. 1995. The Complexity of Power, the Subtlety of *Kava*. *Canberra Anthropology* 18:34–60.

Rainbird, P. 1994. Prehistory in the Northwest Tropical Pacific: The Caroline, Mariana, and Marshall Islands. *Journal of World Prehistory* 8:293–349.

———. 1995. Kosrae's Place in Pacific Prehistory. *Archaeology in Oceania* 30:139–145.

———. 1996. A Place to Look Up to: A Review of Chuukese Hilltop Enclosures. *Journal of the Polynesian Society* 105:461–478.

———. 1998. Marking the Body, Marking the Land— Body as History, Land as History: Tattooing and Engraving in Oceania. Paper presented at the Thinking through the Body Conference, University of Wales, Lampeter.

———. in press. Pohnpei Petroglyphs, Communication and Miscommunication. *Bulletin of the Indo-Pacific Prehistory Association*.

Rainbird, P., and M. Wilson. 1999. Pohnpaid Petroglyphs, Pohnpei. Report prepared for the Federated States of Micronesia Office of Archives and Historic Preservation, and the Pohnpei State Historic Preservation Office, Palikir and Kolonia.

Richards, C. 1993. Monumental Choreography: Architecture and Spatial Representation in Late Neolithic Orkney. In *Interpretative Archaeology*, edited by C. Tilley, 143–178. Oxford: Berg.

Riesenberg, S. 1968. The Native Polity of Ponape. *Smithsonian Contributions to Anthropology* 10.

Scarre, C. 1989. Painting by Resonance. *Nature* 338:382.

Schafer, R. M. 1976. *Creative Music Education—A Handbook for the Modern Music Teacher*. New York: Schirmer.

———. 1977. *The Tuning of the World*. New York: Knopf.

Sherratt, A. 1991. Sacred and Profane Substances: The Ritual Use of Narcotics in Later Neolithic Europe. In *Sacred and Profane: Proceedings of a Conference on Archaeology, Ritual and Religion*, edited by P. Garwood, D. Jennings, R. Skeates, and J. Toms, 50–64. Oxford University Committee for Archaeology Monographs 32. Oxford.

Smith, S. J. 1997. Beyond Geography's Visible Worlds: A Cultural Politics of Music. *Progress in Human Geography* 21:502–529.

Steager, P. W. 1979. Where Does Art Begin on Puluwat? In *Exploring the Visual Art of Oceania: Australia, Melanesia, Micronesia, and Polynesia*, edited by S. Mead, 342–353. Honolulu: University of Hawai'i Press.

Thomas, J. 1993. The Hermeneutics of Megalithic Space. In *Interpretative Archaeology*, edited by C. Tilley, 73–97. Oxford: Berg.

Tilley, C. 1999. *Metaphor and Material Culture*. London: Routledge.

Waterman, E. 2000. Sound Escape: Sonic Geography Remembered and Imagined. *Ecumene* 7:112–115.

Watson, A., and D. Keating. 1999. Architecture and Sound: An Acoustic Analysis of Megalithic Monuments in Prehistoric Britain. *Antiquity* 73:325–336.

Westerkamp, H. 1994. World Forum for Acoustic Ecology. *Soundscape Newsletter* 7:3–5.

EIGHT

The Narrow Doors of the Desert

Ancient Egyptian Roads in the Theban Western Desert

JOHN COLEMAN DARNELL

ncient itineraries in the Eastern Desert of
Egypt have received much deserved attention,[1] but most of those in the Western
Desert remain obscure (see Leclant 1950 and Vercoutter 1970 for exceptions). The differences between the Eastern and Western Deserts explain this
incomplete image of ancient activity: the Eastern
Desert is colorful, reasonably well watered, and
teeming with life (e.g., Roquet 1985), but the Western Desert is a stark, dry, and inhospitable realm of
rocky plateaus and chains of dunes.

Though often considered the best road through
Egypt (Casson 1974), and the only connection
between central Africa and the Mediterranean world
(Bagnall 1993; Goedicke 1981), the Nile may not
always have been the ideal artery of travel. During
times of inundation the Nile seemed an extension of
the sea (see Bonneau 1964:94–96), with the channel
of the river obscured, a fact that may have discour-
aged some river traffic (e.g., Thompson 1983:
73–74). During the low Nile sandbanks were prevalent (Sethe 1933), stopping all but the smallest vessels (Bonneau 1964:96–101, 418–419; Darnell
1992:70–71). Some stretches of the river were diffi-

cult to navigate; one treacherous area was the northern part of the Qena Bend (Degas 1994). In Nubia
the cataracts were obstacles to riverine travel (Vandersleyen 1971; for reference to an ancient slipway at
Mirgissa, avoiding the rapids of the Second Cataract,
see Vercoutter 1970:13–15, 173–180, 204–214).

In fact a network of overland caravan routes criss-
crosses Egypt's Western Desert.[2] By the time of the
Old Kingdom, the ancient Egyptians were making use
of many routes to traverse the desert regions border-
ing their Nile Valley home, as is evidenced by the substantial Old Kingdom material at Dakhla Oasis (see
Churcher and Mills 1999) and the accounts of expedition leaders such as Harkhuf (Helck 1977;
Obsomer 1995; O'Connor 1986; Smith and Giddy
1985; Spalinger 1979; Vercoutter 1982). Archaeological finds in more remote areas suggest a far-reaching
command of the Western Desert in the Old Kingdom
(Banks 1980:313–314; Kuper 1995; Vercoutter
1988:16; Wendorf et al. 1976:106; Wendorf et al.
1977:217). Later references to the administration of
the oases, and remains in the oases themselves, prove
that contact continued (Giddy 1987; Valloggia 1981).
The degree to which the ancient Egyptians controlled

the Western Desert has never been fully explored (Valloggia 1989a), nor do we understand fully the impact of the Saharan peoples on Egypt, especially during its formative period (el-Yahky 1985).

THE CARAVAN TRACKS

The examination of pharaonic desert activity considered in this chapter will concentrate on two major pharaonic tracks leading west out of the Thebaïd. The southern route, the Farshût Road, leads from Western Thebes toward Hou in the northwest. The northern route—the Alamat Tal Road, named for a toponym on Schweinfurth's 1909 map of Western Thebes—leads from several kilometers north of Qurna, joining the Farshût Road at Gebel Qarn el-Gir, two-thirds of the way across the Qena Bend (Figure 8.1).

The tracks of these routes appear as grooves worn into the limestone surface. On the low desert they

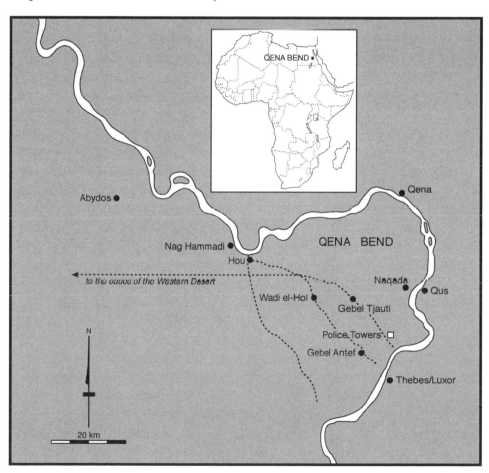

FIGURE 8.1. The Qena Bend of the Nile, showing the major pharaonic tracks of the Thebaïd, the Alamat Tal Road (northern) and the Farshût Road (southern), meeting at the Gebel Qarn el-Gir caravansary (after Davies and Friedman 1998:115).

fan out in a swath several meters wide; where they ascend the gebel (escarpment) the tracks converge, often into one narrow ribbon. The tracks disappear where they cross wadi beds (e.g., Gardiner's [1946: pl. 6, 51–52] "storm-washed roads"), and the ascents on either sides of such wadis are marked by small cairns. Even where the actual ruts have long since been eroded away, masses of pottery remain. The Egyptians recognized the often astonishingly thick pottery carpets of the roads as a type of marking of the roads. A late magical text contains a prayer that the lions of the desert and the crocodiles of the water and snakes in their holes be driven away and made like "gravel" of the desert and "broken pots" in the road (Sander-Hansen 1956:52, nos. 117–119).

Low walls of stones cleared from the tracks border the routes at several points on the various ascents, apparently an attempt to indicate the best path at the points where this might easily be washed out.[3] Similar low walls cross the tracks of the Farshût Road a quarter of the distance up the ascent out of the Thebaïd. These minor hindrances to traffic find parallels in walls that crossed the ancient roads of the Second Cataract region, controlling traffic and delimiting restricted areas (Borchardt 1923:24; Forbes 1964:61). Most of the pharaonic traffic through the Western Desert entering the Theban region was channeled into the two major roads, in contrast with the proliferation of routes during the Roman Period.

The pharaonic tracks often are steep and winding as they reach the top of the plateau; they appear to prefer the most direct route between two points. Because the travelers on the pharaonic tracks were people and donkeys, steep ascents presented no problem.[4] Postpharaonic routes prefer gentle ascents, due to the growing prominence of the camel as a beast of burden[5] (Klunzinger 1878:224–225).

Both the Farshût Road and the Alamat Tal Road, upon entering the low desert on their way to the northwest, head toward the Gebel Qarn el-Gir caravan stop (see J. C. Darnell and D. Darnell 1994:45, 1996:40–41). There tracks from Hou, Abydos, and Kharga Oasis converge with the major Farshût and Alamat Tal Roads. The presence of these roads cutting off the bend of the Nile demonstrates that the ancient Egyptians understood the geography of the area; indeed they referred to the Qena Bend as "the riverbend of the Two Lands," in Greco-Roman texts from Dendera (Meeks 1978:386, no. 78.4242).

The shortest route from the Nile to the oases of the Western Desert leaves the Nile Valley at Girga (Brugsch 1878:4–10, pl. 1; Moritz 1900:430; Paoletti 1900:476–478), and the shortest route from the Thebaïd leads north via the Farshût Road connecting to the Girga Road (Edmonstone 1822:142–144; Legrain 1897:211; Wilkinson 1835:362; Winlock 1940:160 n. 92). Ceramic and textual evidence show that the tracks leading from Thebes toward the regions of Hou and Abydos also lead ultimately to the oases of the Western Desert (D. Darnell and J. C. Darnell 1994:48–49; J. C. Darnell and D. Darnell 1996:37–38, 41; Gardiner 1933:24), and through Kharga Oasis gave access to the Darb el-Arbaîn, Darfûr, and subsaharan Africa. The high-walled Khor Battaghah/Wadi Abu Madawi, beginning behind Rizeiqat and ending behind Farshût, almost separates the gebel filling the Qena Bend from the rest of the Western Desert plateau (Schweinfurth 1901:3–4). A man going to Kharga proper, or on his way to Dakhla Oasis,[6] would be well advised to travel by the Girga Road. A trip from Luxor to Kharga is shorter than a trip from Rizeiqat/Armant to Baris, remains near the Nile as it crosses the Qena Bend, and has a much shorter portion of its length atop the exposed desert between the Nile Valley and Kharga.

Although suggested by some indistinct maps of the Thebaïd (Aufrère et al. 1994:40; Kitchen 1977:219; Lyons 1894), no track can head due west from Thebes proper for more than a short distance because of geomorphology of the desert filling the Qena Bend. The wadi systems cutting across the gebel filling the Qena Bend are oriented from northwest to southeast, and desert tracks heading west or northwest must take these into consideration.

Thebes is well placed to control access to Nubia from the north (Posener 1952), and the physical makeup of the Qena Bend gebel makes Thebes the ideal southern end of routes across the desert filling that bend. A track from Thebes also gives access to Laqeita (Cora 1891: facing p. 538), allowing control over Eastern Desert routes (see also Floyer 1891:637–638). Gebels Qarn el-Gir and Sinn el-Gir—two prongs of the escarpment extending northward in the middle of the Qena Bend—ensure that the only viable shortcuts must pass between them and originate in the Theban area. The majority of the ancient routes across the Qena Bend originate between Rizeiqat/Armant in the south and Naqada in the north, with the most heavily used post–Old Kingdom pharaonic tracks between the area of Malqata in the south and the north part of Thebes approaching Qamûla.

Midway between the Gebel Qarn el-Gir caravansary and the northeast wells of Kharga Oasis is an ancient provisioning post, in heavy use from the Middle Kingdom through the early New Kingdom (see Beadnell [1909:29–31, 39]. My excavations at this site will be published shortly). Mud seals surviving in one of the structures show that some of the provisions maintained a Theban military outpost during the Seventeenth Dynasty.

At several points the roads pass concentrations of dry stone huts, windbreaks, and tent bases;[7] most of these are associated with a standard pottery "kit" and may have been temporary bivouacs for perambulating desert patrols (see also Chartier-Raymond et al. 1994; Dunham 1967:141–142). Only a few structures appear large enough to be temporary depots for goods in transit across the road (see Kurth and Rössler-Köhler 1987:85–86). The concentrations of shelters are scattered, apparently at random, along the Alamat Tal Road. Many are too close together to suggest any stages of a journey, and many of these are probably the camps of perambulating desert patrols (Edel 1962:101), who may not have been able to keep to a strict camping schedule, resulting in more closely spaced camping sites. Most of the huts and tenting areas on the roads originated during the Middle Kingdom, as the associated ceramic remains make clear.

Some concentrations of pottery appear to be the remains of water dumps, and these appear on all of the pharaonic roads of the Theban Western Desert (Gasse 1994:174). Most of these dumps are located in fairly level areas, with the most significant concentrations at or atop the high plateau. Mountains of ceramic remains, with clear stratigraphy, bound together with a considerable amount of organic material (predominately animal dung and food remains) occur at Gebel Qarn el-Gir and over the Wadi el-Hôl. These debris mounds are peculiar to the Farshût Road. Stratigraphy reveals that the debris was periodically covered by a floor of crushed and pounded pottery, rarely by a gypsum floor.[8]

In the Wadi el-Hôl a number of Middle Kingdom inscriptions refer to runners and royal messengers using the Farshût Road. Also in the Wadi el-Hôl is the depiction of a horse and rider and nearby the Ramesside signature of a chief of the stable called "Its Fetchings are Frequent." Two stelae of the

Twenty-First Dynasty high priest king Menkhep-erre, set up at either end of the high plateau on the Farshût Road, refer to that route as the "Road of Horses" (see Caminos 1963:32, 36). Diodorus Siculus, Book I, chapter 45.7, recorded that there were once one hundred horse relay stations between Memphis and the Libyan mountains of Western Thebes. Together these bits of information support the conclusion that the main Farshût Road was, in antiquity, a major postal "pony express" route. Investigations of the debris mounds in the Wadi el-Hôl and at Gebel Qarn el-Gir reveal that these mounds began to grow dramatically during the Seventeenth Dynasty. The organic debris and the pottery are all cemented together in a matrix of animal dung. Only the Farshût Road shows evidence of having been used by horses; only the Farshût Road preserves enormous organic debris mounds with a prime dung component, and those enormous mounds begin to grow significantly at the time of the introduction of horsemanship into Egypt. The hypothesis that the debris mounds represent the sweepings from the areas of stables for relay horses is almost inevitable.

THE ROCK INSCRIPTIONS OF THE NARROW DOORS

At various points along their routes, most often near the ascent and descent of the plateau, the roads pass areas of limestone with vertically fractured surfaces. At these areas, when they directly adjoin the routes, the Egyptians were wont to carve depictions and inscriptions (e.g., Figures 8.2 and 8.3). Although the scenes and inscriptions on these routes range in date from pre-Historic drawings of animals to the inscriptions of Coptic visitors from the Coptite nome, two periods, the late Sixth Dynasty through the Eleventh Dynasty, and the late Twelfth through early Eighteenth Dynasties, are particularly well represented. Where the main track of the Alamat Tal Road ascends to the top of the high desert, it crosses a natural shelf in the mountain, backed by a multi-faceted stratum of smooth limestone well suited to inscriptions, protected by a slight overhang of stone above. Below this shelf is a large deposit of pottery, filling and flowing down two runnels in the lower slope (compare the similar Gebel Agg at Toshka East North, in Simpson 1963:36–44).

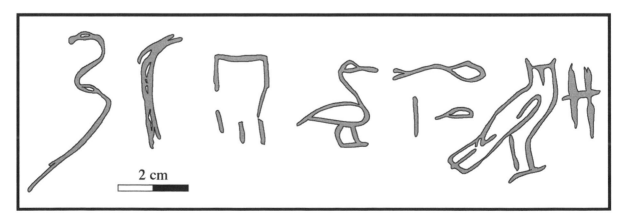

2 cm

FIGURE 8.2. The inscription of the Thirteenth Dynasty (late Middle Kingdom, ca. 1750 B.C.E.) police official Aam, from Gebel Tjauti on the Alamat Tal Road.

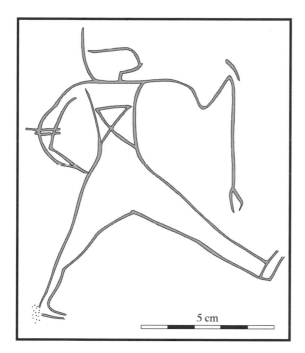

5 cm

FIGURE 8.3. Image of a desert ranger of the Middle Kingdom? (ca. 2000–1800 B.C.E.) from Gebel Tjauti on the Alamat Tal Road.

In several areas the number of inscriptions cut one over another is bewildering. At the time when a fresh inscription was cut, the whiteness of the freshly scratched limestone caused that scene or inscription to stand out from the palimpsest background. As the carved lines developed a patina, the latest text joined the jumbled mass of tangled lines over which it had been carved.

The majority of the hieratic and hieroglyphic inscriptions date to the late Middle Kingdom, a result of increased literacy at that time ensuing from growth of the Egyptian bureaucracy and administrative reorganizations of Amenemhat I (Žaba 1974:261). Many of the hieratic inscriptions, particularly those of the Middle Kingdom, show the development of a particular lapidary form of the hieratic script (for charts of lapidary hieratic signs,

see Smith 1972; Žaba 1974) and the common appearance of hybrid inscriptions employing hieroglyphic and hieratic signs.[9] Some who designated themselves as scribes may only have been semiliterate (Janssen 1992:91). The depictions and inscriptions are concerned with many things, but one may class the majority in a few major categories.

Extension of the Pharaonic Realm

Already during the Protodynastic Period, a number of the sites, prominently Gebel Tjauti, show numerous depictions of Horus falcons, serekhs, and tableaux of the Jubilee cycle, images of royal power, apparently branding the desert routes as extensions of the pharaonic realm (see Huyge 1984:5–9; for the Jubilee cycle, see Williams and Logan 1987:245–285).

In addition to the use of inscription sites as areas for promulgating unifying imagery, actual military forces marched along these routes to project physical power. At Gebel Tjauti is a large tableau dated to the reign of a Horus Scorpion (II), a ruler at the beginning of Dynasty 0. Scorpion's inscription includes a number of images with protohieroglyphic annotations and depicts an Egyptian carrying a spear in one hand and leading a bound prisoner by a rope in his other hand. The tableau appears to record a victory of an expedition from Abydos over forces in the southeastern portion of the Qena Bend.

Another of the inscriptions at Gebel Tjauti is a formal, sunk relief inscription of the Coptite nomarch Tjauti (Darnell and Darnell 1997). This inscription shows how the desert roads of the Thebaïd made Thebes so politically important during the First Intermediate Period and is an excellent example of the use of inscriptions to claim territory, and the road itself as a conduit for the expression of military authority. Tjauti's monument is a unique road construction text of the pharaonic period, and the nomarch claimed: "(I) [have] made this for crossing this mountain, which the ruler of another nome had closed. I fought with [his] nome. I flew (?) [. . .]."

The Coptite nomarch Tjauti was the last Heracleopolitan ruler of the nome north of Thebes before the Thebans took Coptos at the beginning of the final phase of the wars of reunification at the end of the First Intermediate Period. At that time, Thebes appears to have controlled all of the country to the south and was at least covertly inimical to the northern, Heracleopolitan rulers. Tjauti's predecessor User claimed the control of the Eastern and Western Deserts, but Tjauti claimed only the control of a desert pass, a "(narrow) door of the desert." Tjauti's Theban rival on his southern border, Antef, also claimed the control of a "narrow door of the desert." Apparently User controlled a plurality of routes,[10] whereas Antef and Tjauti were each concerned with one. Apparently Antef siezed the southern route west, the Farshût Road, leaving Tjauti to improve the northern route, the Alamat Tal Road.

This had important implications for Theban military conduct and strategy. By controlling the desert routes heading northwest out of Thebes, a Theban army could bypass the fifth, sixth, and seventh nomes of Upper Egypt and attack the eighth nome directly. As a result of one decisive battle, Thebes could gain control of the eight southernmost nomes of Upper Egypt. When Tjauti says the Thebans had sealed off the gebel, we should understand that they were preparing to attack the eighth nome. Tjauti, desperately trying to maintain a lifeline to the Heracleopolitan realm, improved a preexisting route.[11] This bold action of Tjauti may have set in motion the final events that led to the creation of the Middle Kingdom. The Thebans could not allow Tjauti

and the Heracleopolitans to control a route north of their tracks, a road on which an enemy army could operate on interior lines. We are fortunate to know what happened, because onto the limestone near the stela of Tjauti are boldly scratched the words "the assault troops of the Son of Re Antef" (Figure 8.4). These were apparently the Theban troops who captured the last Heracleopolitan road in Upper Egypt, perhaps on their way to the conquest of the holy city of Abydos. By early in the reign of Antef II the northern border of the Thebaïd lay between Abydos and Thinis, so apparently Antef I did indeed turn the flanks of the nomes around the Qena Bend. The first move of the Thebans as they began their northward expansion was the capture of the routes across the Qena Bend.

FIGURE 8.4. The inscription of the strike force of the son of Re Antef (ca. 2000 B.C.E.) from Gebel Tjauti on the Alamat Tal Road.

The importance of the Wadi el-Hôl during the Second Intermediate Period shows that the Thebans never forgot the lessons they learned when they fought the Coptite nomarch Tjauti for control of the roads across the Qena Bend. Wadi el-Hôl inscriptions reveal a considerable Theban presence there during the late Middle Kingdom (e.g., Figure 8.5). A late Middle Kingdom literary graffito in the Wadi el-Hôl describes the martial joys of an embattled Theban ruler and is a further strong indication that the Thebans were well aware of the importance of the roads into the Western Desert when they were again at war with the north (Darnell 1997a).

Many inscriptions belong to policemen and sol-

diers. At several sites groupings of the names of apparently unrelated Middle Kingdom men attest to the vigilance of desert patrolmen on sentry duty (Hellström et al. 1970:234–235; Obsomer 1995:284–286; Smith 1969, 1972). Numerous inscriptions of policemen and the martial nature of other inscriptions at desert passes indicate a recognition of the importance of holding the most difficult portion of a mountain ascent. An armed presence would be important at such a location, to protect a group during the vulnerable times of ascending and descending the plateau (Callwell 1990; Dennis 1985:238–239; Fischer-Elfert 1986:201–207).

Inundation Images

Many of the representations at the rock inscription and petroglyph sites depict Nilotic creatures, predominately fish, crocodiles, and hippopotamuses. The fish are often tilapia, well attested as a symbol of rebirth in ancient Egypt, particularly associated with the goddess Hathor, appropriate to desert sites (Brewer and Friedman 1989:15–19; Dambach and Wallert 1966:273–294; Gamer-Wallert 1970:109–113; Valloggia 1989b:138). Fish are also common as representations of the inundation waters of the Nile (Bonneau 1964:294–297; Edel 1976:35–43; Gamer-Wallert 1970:101–103, 111), to which the crocodiles (cf. Bonneau 1964:299–303; Gamer-Wallert 1970:104–105) and hippopotamuses also allude.

The roads reveal a remarkable number of representations of standing hippopotamus goddesses, most of late Middle Kingdom date (see Hornung and Staehelin 1976:129). As a manifestation of the eye of the sun, the hippopotamus goddess can, like Sekhmet, have militaristic associations (Bourriau 1988:163; Davies 1987:34, pl. 7). She also lights the desert path for

5 cm

FIGURE 8.5. Depiction of a royal statue with associated hieratic annotation, late Middle Kingdom (ca. 1800 B.C.E.), from the Wadi el-Hôl on the Farshût Road.

Osiris and is appropriate to these tracks, connecting with Abydos. The hippopotamus goddess, who has astronomical associations (see Verner 1969), also represents the wandering goddess of the eye of the sun returning to Egypt, again appropriate to a desert road (see also Darnell 1995, 1997a; George 1977; Nagy 1992). Hippopotamus goddesses abound on the Nag el-Birka track and on the Alamat Tal Road, essentially forming a great, magical shield protecting the northern and western boundaries of Thebes.

Religious Nature of Sites

Several sites exhibit clear religious significance. Central to worship at these sites were Osiris, deities of the desert and foreign lands (e.g., Seth, Resheph), and the goddess Hathor. The worship of Hathor predominates at these sites, and her cult may in fact explain much that we find in the protodynastic and pharaonic rock-art and inscriptions. Most of these sites are rock shelters at or near areas where desert roads ascend and descend the escarpment. Atop the plateau the sites consist of freestanding monuments, ranging from actual temples to drystone shrines, votive cairns, and small objects.

Cairns

Votive cairns occur in great abundance near the edges of the plateau, and a forest of them lies behind the shrine area of Gebel Antef.[12] Some may have been made by travelers arriving at the spot and catching their first site of the Nile or a particular temple (see also Forbes 1921:268, 289; Ingraham et al. 1981:69; Murray 1935:194–195). Demotic prayers for divine assistance from the Theban terminus of the Farshût Road show that the termini of desert roads are appropriate places for invoking divine assistance (Jasnow 1984).

Shrines

At the Theban terminus of the Farshût Road are the remains of various shrines and votive monuments. The most formal of these was a small sandstone temple dedicated to Abydene Osiris and constructed by a King Antef of the Seventeenth Dynasty. This Second Intermediate Period temple was a more formal version of the shrine at Gebel Tingar (Jaritz 1981; see also the shrine at Timna [Rothenberg 1988]), at the Aswan terminus of the Nubian High Road, and a much smaller version of the complex at Serabit el-Khadim in Sinai.

In the Wadi el-Hôl the inscription of a priest Dedusobek records his journey from Abydos to celebrate religious rituals at the temple of Monthuhotep at Deir el-Bahari. Osiris is associated with the festivals of Hathor, particularly during the Valley Festival at Thebes centered at Deir el-Bahari, sacred to Hathor and site of the nocturnal vigil for Osiris (Gutbub 1961:46). Gebel Antef was thus an appropriate location for a temple of Abydene Osiris, located on a road leading to Abydos, overlooking a site sacred to Hathor. The cult of Osiris at Abydos enjoyed a potentially chaotic popularity during the Thirteenth Dynasty (Leahy 1989:59–60), and an extension of the worship of Abydene Osiris to the Theban terminus of the Farshût Road during the following Second Intermediate Period is reasonable.

The shrine at Gebel Tingar consisted of a drystone enclosure built against a large, natural rock atop the plateau; apparently a small stone *naos* (shrine) once stood within the enclosure. This religious center itself appears to be somewhat of a combination of the formal structure of the Gebel Antef shrine and the drystone cairns with arms serving as shrines at Gebel Antef and the Chephren diorite quarries (Engelbach 1933:65–74, 1938b:369–390, particularly pl. 54; bibliography in Simpson 1963:53 n. 17).

Crescent-shaped drystone structures and cairns with radiating arms at Gebel Antef date to the time of the construction of the small temple atop Gebel Antef and appear to be lesser votive structures.[13]

Farther back along the Farshût Road is a group of cist shrines with side walls and roofs of large, flat slabs of limestone. These shrines resemble those above the workmen's village of Deir el-Medina (see a recent photograph in Bongioanni and Tosi 1991:46), in some of which were small stelae. At Semna in Nubia are tall, drystone cairns, of Middle Kingdom date, with cyst "windows" facing south, built within the upper portion of the cairns, combining the attributes of the Gebel Antef cyst and cairn shrines (Mills 1967–1968:206, pl. 39a). Similar cairns with recesses occur on the road linking the Chephren diorite quarries with the Nile (see Engelbach 1938a:525), near the quarries in the Wadi el-Hudi (Fakhry 1952: pl. 4), and atop the hill in which Seti I constructed his Wadi Mia temple, on a road to the gold mines of the Wadi Barramiya.

Statuary

There are fragments of statuary from Gebel Antef, and the base of a large Osiride statue from the vicinity of the Wadi el-Hôl. A healing statue of Ramesses III found near the Rôd en-Nahadein and the Darb el-Tuwara, east of Gebel Ahmar, once was located on a desert road, where the Nile was just visible to a traveler (Drioton 1939:86). The prophylactic nature of the statue of Ramesses III was the role filled by other royal statues on desert routes.

In the Wadi el-Hôl one late Middle Kingdom depiction shows a royal statue on a sledge (compare De Morgan et al. 1894:31), accompanied by a text promising a safe journey to those who see it. This depiction and actual remains of statuary well illustrate the statement on the late Middle Kingdom

stela of Ibia from Abydos, wherein the stela owner said he is one: "who followed the monuments of the sovereign into remote desert lands . . ." (Lange and Schäfer 1902:101–103; Lichtheim 1988:127–128). This could refer to the export of images as a demonstration of royal power (Quack 1992:41 [E 67: "send your statues into the far desert/foreign land"]) or to the dispatching of apotropaic images into foreign lands (Morschauser 1988:204).

Worship of Hathor

A number of inscriptions and finds illustrate the veneration of the goddess Hathor. Hathor, who as the red light before sunrise is the maternal womb of the sun of day, also represents the sun disk as the eye of the supreme solar deity, and as such is the daughter of the solar deity. As the sun sinks into the southern sky in winter, so the solar eye goddess left Egypt in anger, to wander the deserts and savannas of the far south as the bloodthirsty lioness Sakhmet. Deities such as Thoth and Onuris lure her back to Egypt and her father each year, where she must be placated by drinking and dancing until she becomes the benevolent Hathor, the languorous and beneficial cat Bastet (Darnell 1995, 1997b).

In the Wadi el-Hôl several inscriptions refer to "spending the day beneath this gebel on holiday." The vocabulary suggests the worship of the goddess Hathor.[14] At that site are also numerous mentions of Hathor and depictions of elaborately dressed revelers. A Ptolemaic inscription from Hou, at the northwestern end of the road, refers to a desert procession in the area (Collombert 1995:63–70). Together with references from other texts, this suggests religious revelry in the desert, veneration of the goddess Hathor at the remote desert site. The Wadi el-Hôl was probably a goal of the rite of "going out upon the desert" to welcome back the returning goddess of the eye of the sun,[15] greeting her on one of the roads along which she and her entourage return to Egypt.

At Gebel Tjauti, beneath Hathoric depictions, are the remains of a vast quantity of ceramics, including vessels with particular cultic significance for the worship of Hathor. At Gebel Antef also, below the Seventeenth Dynasty temple, are masses of pottery, many of them beer and wine jars. These areas are probably the designated "drinking places" (Franke 1994:155, 166) for the celebration of the drunken revelry in honor of Hathor.

At these desert sites, foreigners might join the Egyptians in worship of the goddess of the eye of the sun. There is considerable ceramic evidence for the presence of Libo-Nubian groups on a number of the desert roads. A site at Hierakonpolis (HK64, apparently a lookout post on the Darb Betan, running parallel to the Nile), was a place of interaction between Egyptians and people of a Libo-Nubian culture (who left deposits of ostrich feathers, offerings to the wandering goddess of the sun, more specifically in her form of Hathor) (Darnell 1999).

CONCLUSION

When we think of ancient Egyptian place markings we tend to conjure images of pyramids, temples, hieroglyphs, and vast cemeteries. Roads are rarely considered; but it is these that physically and communicatively link places along a continuous spine of human landscape. Roads represent more than pathways *between* places; they are more than routes that link towns or states. They are, to use Paul Carter's (this volume) eloquent imagery, furrows in the earth that mark an experience of space. Roads in the Egyptian Western Desert transformed the land into a landscape of human experiences. They represent paths of political control, of social rhythms, military tactics, religious observances, and economic endeavors. Inscribed with iconographic marks and at times writing, Western Desert roads were doubly built in political process, stamped with the hegemonic symbols that testified and reaffirmed existing political and religious power relations, relations of control over people, resources, and place.

There were also other ways in which processes of place making were effected. One of these was the naming of places (see also Umberger, this volume). We know very few of the ancient toponyms for sites along the desert roads through the Western Desert. Behind Thebes, on a track connecting the Farshût and Alamat Tal Roads, was a military outpost named in two inscriptions at that site "Dominion Behind Thebes." At Semna a rock at which travelers appear to have taken shelter was called "Satisfaction."[16] Clearly, place making in ancient Egypt, as elsewhere, was not a monolithic process. It involved a physical marking in the control of places—through such things as roads and rock-art—and the naming of places, all of which need be considered via the sociopolitical processes of the day. In this sense at least, rather than being an outpost of Egyptian political affairs, the Western Desert can more appropriately be treated as an organic limb of the Egyptian political, military, social, and economic machinery, without which Egypt's cities could not have existed as centers of power and international dominance.

NOTES

I thank Deborah Darnell for her assistance.

1. See, for example, Clédat 1923, 1924; Couyat 1910; Floyer 1893; Reddé and Golvin 1987; Schleiden 1858.

2. Maps in Vercoutter (1988:11, 13) show suggested early tracks, but omit the ancient routes crossing the Qena Bend.

3. Textually attested in Jasnow 1992:47, 51; figs. 4, 5. See also Fischer-Elfert 1986:197–198; Forbes 1964: 59–61; Hester et al. 1970; Petrie 1888:35, 1889: pl. 16, fig. 1).

4. On the rarity of the camel during the pharaonic period, see Midant-Reynes and Braunstein-Silvestre (1978: cols. 304–305) and Rowley-Conwy (1988). For a pharaonic representation of a dromedary, see Pusch (1996). The camel never replaced equids in antiquity—see Engels (1978:14–15), Seligman (1934:67–78), and Wainwright (1935).

5. For donkeys instead of camels on steep paths in Israel, see Dorsey (1991:13–15).

6. For routes between the Nile and Kharga, and the Darb el-Ghubari between Kharga and Dakhla, see Beadnell (1909:25–44), Giddy (1987:6–11), Maury (1979: 365–375) and Winlock (1936:7–15). Two apparently Middle Kingdom graffiti (Osing 1986:81–82; Winkler 1938:12, pl. 8, 1) suggest a route through northern Kharga, passing Gebel Teir, and continuing along the Darb el-Ghubari to Dakhla.

7. See Bienkowski and Chlebik 1991:159, figs. 16–18; Krzyzaniak 1987: 185, 190; McDonald 1991: 43, 47. Compare with Richmond 1962:146.

8. To hold down windblown waste; for such considerations compare the decree of Thutmosis III (Vernus 1979).

9. Hieratic forms in graffiti evidence training in using the pen on papyrus; hieroglyphic forms indicate a higher level of education—for scribes able to read and write hieratic, but confused by monumental signs, see De Garis Davies and Gardiner 1920:8, 27–28; Smith 1972:51; Winlock 1941:146.

10. Coptite nomarchs possibly controlled all desert routes of southern Upper Egypt (Helck 1939:23–24).

11. Tjauti probably improved a washed-out area near his inscription. The Luxor-Farshût Road has stairs cut into the rock in similar areas at Gebel Antef and the Wadi el-Hôl, and stairways are known from elsewhere—see Carter 1917:108, pl. 19 (no. 4 from p. 113 and no. 107 from p. 113); Cerny et al. 1969–1970: pl. 65b; Cerny et al. 1971: pl. 157.

12. Compare with similar cairns associated with the Gebel Tingar sanctuary (Weigall 1923:226, 233). Such cairns also occur in the Wadi Mia at the Seti I temple (Weigall 1909:163–164) and at the Hathor shrine at Serabit el-Khadim (Petrie 1906:63–65, figs. 75–76).

13. P. Szépművészeti Museum Budapest 51.1960, col. B, l. 9 may refer to a drystone shrine as an *ih3y*, "camp" (Kákosy 1990:144–145, 151, pl. 6). The discussion of terms by Schulman (1988:114–115) is oversimplified.

14. For the Hathoric overtones of "holiday," see Husson (1977:222) and Kessler (1988).

15. For going "upon the gebel with her majesty to Thebes," see Stricker (1953:19 ll. 5–6).

16. Semna graffito no. 524, in Hintze and Reineke (1989:157–158, pl. 219, ll. 16–17).

REFERENCES CITED

Aufrère, S., J.-C. Golvin, and J.-C. Goyon. 1994. *L'Égypte Restituée: Sites et Temples des Déserts*. Paris: Éditions Errance.

Bagnall, R. S. 1993. *Egypt in Late Antiquity*. Princeton: Princeton Univesity Press.

Banks, K. M. 1980. Ceramics of the Western Desert. In *Prehistory of the Eastern Sahara*, edited by F. Wendorf and R. Schild, 299–315. New York: Academic Press.

Beadnell, H. J. L. 1909. *An Egyptian Oasis*. London: John Murray.

Bienkowski, P., and B. Chlebik. 1991. Changing Places: Architecture and Spatial Organization of the Bedul in Petra. *Levant* 23:147–180.

Bongioanni, A., and M. Tosi. 1991. *Uomini e Dei nell'Antico Egitto*. Parma: Casa Editrice Maccari.

Bonneau, D. 1964. *La Crue du Nil: Divinité Égyptienne à Travers mille ans d'histoire (332 av.–641 ap. J.-C.)*.

Études et Commentaires 52. Paris: Librairie C. Kliencksieck.

Borchardt, L. 1923. *Altägyptische Festungen an der Zweiten Nilschwelle*. Veröffentlichungen der Ernst von Sieglin-Expedition in Ägypten 3. Leipzig: Otto Harrassowitz.

Bourriau, J. 1988. *Pharaohs and Mortals: Egyptian Art in the Middle Kingdom*. Cambridge: Cambridge University Press.

Brewer, D., and R. Friedman. 1989. Fish and Fishing in Ancient Egypt. Warminster: Aris and Phillips.

Brugsch, H. 1878. *Reise Nach der Grossen Oase El Khargeh in der Libyschen Wüste*. Leipzig: J. C. Hinrichs'sche Buchhandlung.

Callwell, C. E. 1990. *Small Wars, a Tactical Textbook for Imperial Soldiers*. London and Novato: Greenhill and Presidio Press.

Caminos, R. A. 1963. Papyrus Berlin 10463. *Journal of Egyptian Archaeology* 49:29–37.

Carter, H. 1917. A Tomb Prepared for Queen Hatshepsuit and Other Recent Discoveries at Thebes. *Journal of Egyptian Archaeology* 4:107–118.

Casson, L. 1974. *Travel in the Ancient World*. London: George Allen and Unwin.

Cerny, J., C. Desroches Noblecourt, and M. Kurz, with M. Dewachter and M. Nelson. 1969–1970. *Graffiti de la Montagne Thébaine I, 1: Cartographie et Étude Topographique Illustrée*. Cairo: Centre de Documentation et d'Études sur l'Ancienne Égypte.

Cerny, J., R. Coque, F. Debono, C. Desroches Noblecourt, and M. Kurz, with M. Dewachter and M. Nelson. 1971. *Graffiti de la Montagne Thébaine I, 2: La Vallée de l'Ouest*. Cairo: Centre de Documentation et d'Études sur l'Ancienne Égypte.

Chartier-Raymond, M., B. Gratien, C. Traunecker, and J. M. Vinçon. 1994. Les Sites Miniers Pharaoniques du Sud-Sinaï: Quelques Notes et Observations de Terrain. *Cahier de Recherches de l'Institut de Papyrologie et d'Égyptologie de Lille* 16:31–77.

Churcher, C. S., and A. J. Mills (eds.). 1999. *Reports from the Survey of the Dakhleh Oasis Western Desert of Egypt 1977–1987*. Oxford: Oxbow Books.

Clédat, J. 1923. Notes sur l'Isthme de Suez (suite). *Bulletin de l'Institut Français d'Archéologie Orientale* 22:135–189.

———. 1924. Notes sur l'Isthme de Suez (suite). *Bulletin de l'Institut Français d'Archéologie Orientale* 23:27–84.

Collombert, P. 1995. Hout-Sekhem et le Septieme Nome de Haute-Égypte I: La Divine Oudjarenes. *Revue de l'Égyptologie* 46:63–70.

Cora, G. 1891. La Route de Kéneh à Bérénice levée en 1873 par le Colonel R.E. Colston. *Bulletin de Société Khédiviale de Géographie*, 3rd ser., no. 7:533–538.

Couyat, J. 1910. Ports Gréco-Romains de la Mer Rouge et Grandes Routes du Désert Arabique. In *Comptes Rendus des Séances de l'Academie des Inscriptions et Belles-lettres Pendant l'Année 1910*, 525–539. Paris: Alphonse Picard et Fils, Éditeurs.

Dambach, M., and I. Wallert. 1966. Das Tilapia-motiv in der Altägyptischen Kunst. *Chronique d'Égypte* 41:273–294.

Darnell, D., and J. C. Darnell. 1994. The Luxor-Farshût Desert Road Survey. *Bulletin de Liaison du Groupe International d'Étude de la Céramique Égyptienne* 18:48–49.

Darnell, J. C. 1992. The *Kbn.wt* Vessels of the Late Period. In *Life in a Multi-cultural Society: Egypt from Cambyses to Constantine and Beyond*, edited by J. Johnson, 67–89. Studies in Ancient Oriental Civilizations 51. Chicago: The Oriental Institute, The University of Chicago.

———. 1995. Hathor Returns to Medamud. *Studien zur Altägyptischen Kultur* 22:47–94.

———. 1997a. The Apotropaic Goddess in the Eye. *Studien zur Altägyptischen Kultur* 24:35–48.

———. 1997b. A New Middle Egyptian Literary Text from the Wadi el-Hôl. *Journal of the American Research Center in Egypt* 34:85–100.

————. 1999. Pharaonic Rock Inscriptions from HK64. In Preliminary Report on Field Work at Hierakonpolis: 1996–1998, edited by R. Friedman, A. Maish, A. G. Fahmy, J. C. Darnell, and E. D. Johnson. *Journal of the American Research Center in Egypt* 36:24–29.

Darnell, J. C., and D. Darnell. 1994. The Luxor-Farshût Desert Road Survey. In *The Oriental Institute 1993–1994 Annual Report*, edited by W. M. Sumner, 40–48. Chicago: The Oriental Institute, The University of Chicago.

————. 1996. The Luxor-Farshût Desert Road Survey. *BCE* 19:36–50.

————. 1997. New Inscriptions of the Late First Intermediate Period from the Theban Western Desert, and the Beginnings of the Northern Expansion of the Eleventh Dynasty. *Journal of Near Eastern Studies* 56:241–258.

Davies, W. V. 1987. *Catalogue of Egyptian Antiquities in the British Museum, VII Tools and Weapons I: Axes.* London: British Museum Press.

Davies, V., and R. Friedman. 1998. *Egypt.* London: British Museum Press.

De Garis Davies, N., and A. H. Gardiner. 1920. *The Tomb of Antefoker, Vizier of Sesostris I, and of his Wife, Senet (No. 60).* Theban Tomb Series 2. London: George Allen and Unwin.

Degas, J. 1994. Navigation sur le Nil au Nouvel Empire. In *Les Problèmes Institutionnels de l'Eau en Égypte Ancienne et dans l'Antiquité Méditerranéenne*, edited by B. Menu, 141–152. Bibliotheque d'Étude 110. Cairo: L'Institut Français d'Archéologie Orientale.

De Morgan, J., U. Bouriant, G. Legrain, G. Jéquier, and A. Barsanti. 1894. Catalogue des Monuments et Inscriptions de l'Égypte Antique 1: Haute Égypte 1 de la Frontière de Nubie à Kom Ombos. Vienna: Adolphe Holzhausen.

Dennis, G. T. (ed.). 1985. *Three Byzantine Military Treatises, Dumbarton Oaks Texts 9.* Washington: Dumbarton Oaks.

Dorsey, D. A. 1991. *The Roads and Highways of Ancient Israel.* Baltimore: The Johns Hopkins University Press.

Drioton, É. 1939. Une Statue Prophylactique de Ramses III. *Annales du Service des Antiquités de l'Égypte* 39:58–89.

Dunham, D. (ed.). 1967. *Second Cataract Forts II: Uronarti, Shalfak, Mirgissa.* Cambridge: Museum of Fine Arts Boston.

Edel, E. 1962. Zur Lesung und Bedeutung einiger Stellen in der Biographischen Inschrift S3rnpwt's I. *Zeitschrift für Ägyptiche Aprache und Altertumskunde* 87:96–107.

————. 1976. Der Tetrodon Fahaka als Bringer der Überschwemmung und Sein Kult im Elefantengau. *Mitteilungen des deutschen Archäologischen Instituts Kairo* 32:35–43.

Edmonstone, Sir A. 1822. A Journey to Two of the Oases of Upper Egypt. London: John Murray.

el-Yahky, F. 1985. The Sahara and Predynastic Egypt: An Overview. *Journal of the Society for the Study of Egyptian Antiquities* 15:81–85.

Engelbach, R. 1933. The Quarries of the Western Desert: A Preliminary Report. *Annales du Service des Antiquités de l'Égypte* 33:65–74.

————. 1938a. The Riddle of Chephren's Diorite Quarries Answered. *Illustrated London News*, 26 March 1938, p. 525.

————. 1938b. The Quarries of the Western Nubian Desert and the Ancient Road to Tuska (Survey Expedition; February 1930, under the Direction of Mr. G. W. Murray, Director Topographical Survey *Annales du Service des Antiquités de l'Égypte* 38:369–390.

Engels, D. 1978. *Alexander the Great and the Logistics of the Macedonian Army.* Berkeley: University of California Press.

Fakhry, A. 1952. The Inscriptions of the Amethyst Quarries at Wadi el Hudi. Cairo: Government Press.

Fischer-Elfert, H.-W. 1986. *Die Satirische Streitschrift des*

Papyrus Anastasi I. Äg. Ab. 44. Wiesbaden: Otto Harrassowitz.

Floyer, E. A. 1891. Note sur les Sidoniens et les Erembes d'Homère. *Bulletin de la Société Khédiviale de Géographie,* 3rd ser., no. 7:629–643.

———. 1893. *Étude sur le Nord-Etbai, Entre le Nil et la Mer Rouge.* Cairo: Imprimerie Nationale.

Forbes, R. 1921. *The Secret of the Sahara: Kufara.* New York: George H. Doran Co.

Forbes, R. J. 1964. *Notes on the History of Ancient Roads and Their Construction.* Amsterdam: A. M. Hakkert.

Franke, D. 1994. *Das Heiligtum des Heqaib auf Elephantine.* Studien zur Archäologie und Geschichte Altägyptens 9. Heidelberg: Heidelberger Orientverlag.

Gamer-Wallert, I. 1970. *Fische und Fischkulte im Alten Ägypten. Äg. Ab.* 21. Wiesbaden: Otto Harrassowitz.

Gardiner, A. H. 1933. The Dakhleh Stela. *Journal of Egyptian Archaeology* 19:19–30.

———. 1946. Davies's Copy of the Great Speos Artemidos Inscription. *Journal of Egyptian Archaeology* 32:43–56.

Gasse, A. 1994. L'Approvisionnement en Eau dans les Mines et Carrières (Aspects Techniques et Institutionnels). In *Les Problèmes Institutionnels de l'Eau en Égypte Ancienne et dans l'Antiquité Méditerranéenne,* edited by B. Menu, 169–176. Bibliotheque d'Étude 110. Cairo: L'Institut Français d'Archéologie Orientale.

George, B. 1977. Eine löwenköpfige Nilpferdgöttin in Stockholm. *Medelhavsmuseet Bulletin* 12:38–44.

Giddy, L. 1987. *Egyptian Oases.* Warminster: Aris and Phillips.

Goedicke, H. 1981. Harkhuf's Travels. *Journal of Near Eastern Studies* 40: 1–20.

Gutbub, A. 1961. Un Emprunt aux Textes des Pyramides dans l'Hymne a Hathor, Dame de l'Ivresse. In *Mélanges Maspero I: Orient Ancien.* Mémoires de l'Institute Français d'Archéologie Orientale 66. Cairo.

Helck, H.-W. 1939. *Der Einfluss der Militärführer in der 18. Ägyptischen Dynastie. Untersuchungen zur Geschichte und Altertumskunde Ägyptens* 14. Leipzig: J. C. Hinrichs.

Helck, W. 1977. Herchuf. In edited by W. Helck and W. Westendorf, *Lexikon der Ägyptologie* 2, col. 1129. Wiesbaden: Harrassowitz.

Hellström, P., H. Langballe, and O. Myers. 1970. *The Rock Drawings 1: The Scandinavian Joint Expedition to Sudanese Nubia 1/2.* Copenhagen: Scandinavian Joint Expedition to Sudanese Nubia.

Hester, J., P. Hobler, and J. Russell. 1970. New Evidence of Early Roads in Nubia. *American Journal of Archaeology* 74:385–389.

Hintze, F., and W. F. Reineke. 1989. *Felsinschriften aus dem Sudanesischen Nubien 1.* Berlin: Akademie Verlag.

Hornung, E., and E. Staehelin. 1976. *Skarabäen und andere Siegelamulette aus Basler Sammlungen, Ägyptische Denkmäler in der Schweiz 1.* Mainz: Philipp von Zabern.

Husson, C. 1977. *L'Offrande du Miroir dans les Temples Égyptiens de l'Époque Gréco-Romaine.* Lyon: Université de Lyon.

Huyge, D. 1984. Horus Qa-a in the Elkab Area, Upper Egypt. *Orientalia Lovaniensia Periodica* 15:5–9.

Ingraham, M. L., Th. Johnson, B. Rihani, and I. Shatla. 1981. Saudi Arabian Comprehensive Survey Program: C. Preliminary Report on a Reconnaissance Survey of the Northwestern Province (with a Note on a Brief Survey of the Northern Province). *Atlal: The Journal of Saudi Arabian Archaeology* 5:59–84.

Janssen, J. J. 1992. Literacy and Letters at Deir El-Medina. In *Village Voices,* edited by R. J. Demarée and A. Egberts, 81–94. Leiden: Centre of Non-Western Studies, Leiden University.

Jaritz, H. 1981. Zum Heilgtum am Gebel Tingar. *Mitteilungen des Deutschen Archäologischen Instituts Kairo* 37:241–246.

Jasnow, R. 1984. Demotic Graffiti from Western Thebes. In *Grammata Demotika,* edited by H. J. Thissen and K.-Th. Zauzich, 87–105. Würzburg: Gisela Zauzich Verlag.

————. 1992. *A Late Period Hieratic Wisdom Text (P. Brooklyn 47.218.135).* Studies in Ancient Oriental Civilizations 52. Chicago: The Oriental Institute, The University of Chicago.

Kákosy, L. 1990. Fragmente eines Unpublizierten Magischen Textes in Budapest. *Zeitschrift für Ägyptiche Aprache und Altertumskunde* 117:140–157.

Kessler, D. 1988. Der Satirisch-erotische Papyrus Turin 55001 und das "Verbringcn dcs schönen Tages." *Studien zur Altägyptischen Kultur* 15:171–196.

Kitchen, K. A. 1977. Historical Observations on Ramesside Nubia. In *Ägypten und Kusch*, edited by E. Endesfelder, K. H. Priese, W.-F. Reineke, and S. Wenig, 213–225. Berlin: Akademie Verlag.

Klunzinger, C. B. 1878. Upper Egypt: Its People and Its Products. New York: Scribner, Armstrong and Co.

Krzyzaniak, L. 1987. Dakhleh Oasis Project, Interim Report on the First Season of the Recording of Petroglyphs, January/February 1988. *Journal of the Society for the Study of Egyptian Antiquities* 17:182–191.

Kuper, R. 1995. Prehistoric Research in the Southern Libyan Desert: A Brief Account and Some Conclusions of the B.O.S. Project. *Cahier de Recherches de l'Institute de Papyrologie et d'Égyptologie de Lille* 17:123–140.

Kurth, D., and U. Rössler-Köhler (eds.). 1987. *Zur Archäologie des 12. Oberägyptischen Gaues. Göttinger Orientforschungen* 4, vol. 6. Wiesbaden: Otto Harrassowitz.

Lange, H. O., and H. Schäfer. 1902. *Grab- und Denksteine des Mittleren Reichs im Museum von Kairo 1*. Berlin: Reichsdrückerei.

Leahy, A. 1989. A Protective Measure at Abydos in the Thirteenth Dynasty. *Journal of Egyptian Archaeology* 75:41–60.

Leclant, J. 1950. "Per Africae Sitientia," Témoignages des Sources Classiques sur les Pistes Menant à l'Oasis d'Ammon. *Bulletin de l'Institut Français d'Archéologie Orientale* 49:193–253.

Legrain, G. 1897. Étude sur les Aqabahs. *Bulletin de l'Institut d'Égypte*, 3rd ser., no. 8:203–216.

Lichtheim, M. 1988. Ancient Egyptian Autobiographies Chiefly of the Middle Kingdom, Orbis Biblicus et Orientalis 84. Freiburg: Universitätsverlag; Göttingen: Vandenhoeck and Ruprecht.

Lyons, H. G. 1894. Notes sur la Géographie Physique des Oasis Khargueh et de Dakhel. *Bulletin de la Société Khédiviale de Géographie*, 4th ser., no. 4:240–265.

Maury, B. 1979. Toponymie Traditionnelle de l'Ancienne Piste Joignant Kharga à Dakhla. In *Hommages à Serge Sauneron II: Égypte Post-pharaonique*, edited by J. Vercoutter, 365–375. Bibliotheque d'Étude 82/2. Cairo: Institut Français d'Archéologie Orientale.

McDonald, M. 1991. Origins of the Neolithic in the Nile Valley as Seen from Dakhleh Oasis in the Egyptian Western Desert. *Sahara* 4:41–52.

Meeks, D. 1978. Année Lexicographique. Égypte Ancienne 2. Paris: Imprimerie la Margeride.

Midant-Reynes, B., and F. Braunstein-Silvestre. 1978. Kamel. In *Lexikon der Ägyptologie* 3, edited by W. Helck and W. Westendorf, cols. 304–305. Wiesbaden: Otto Harrassowitz.

Mills, A. J. 1967–1968. The Archaeological Survey from Gemai to Dal—Report on the 1965–1966 Season. *Kush* 15:200–210.

Moritz, B. 1900. Excursion aux oasis du Désert Libyque. *Bulletin de la Société Khédiviale de Géographie*, 5th ser., no. 8:429–475.

Morschauser, S. 1988. Using History: Reflections on the Bentresh Stela. *Studien zur Altägyptischen Kultur* 15:203–223.

Murray, G. W. 1935. *Sons of Ishmael: A Study of the Egyptian Bedouin*. London: George Routledge and Sons.

Nagy, I. 1992. La Statue de Thouéris au Caire (CG 39145) et la Légende de la Déesse Lointaine. In *The Intellectual Heritage of Egypt*, edited by U. Luft, 449–456. Studia Aegyptiaca 14. Budapest: Innova Press.

Obsomer, C. 1995. *Sésostris Ier: Étude Chronologique et Historique du Règne*. Brussels: Connaissance de l'Égypte Ancienne.

O'Connor, D. 1986. The Locations of Yam and Kush and Their Historical Implications. *Journal of the American Research Center in Egypt* 23:27–50.

Osing, J. 1986. Notizen zu den Oasen Charga und Dachla. *Göttinger Miszellen* 92:79–85.

Paoletti, H. 1900. Route de Ghirgheh à Khargheh. *Bulletin de la Société Khédiviale de Géographie*, 5th ser., no. 8:476–478.

Petrie, W. M. F. 1888. *A Season in Egypt—1887*. London: Field and Tuer, The Leadenhall Press.

———. 1889. *Tanis Part I, 1883–4*. London: Trübner and Co.

———. 1906. *Researches in Sinai*. London: John Murray.

Posener, G. 1952. À Propos des Graffiti d'Abisko. *Archiv Orientáln* 20:163–166.

Pusch, E. B. 1996. Ein Dromedar aus der Ramses-stadt. *Ägypten und Levante* 6:107–118.

Quack, J. F. 1992. *Studien zur Lehre für Merikare. Göttinger Orientforschungen* 4, vol. 23. Wiesbaden: Otto Harrassowitz.

Reddé, M., and J.-C. Golvin. 1987. Du Nil à la Mer Rouge: Documents et Nouveaux sur les Routes du Désert Oriental d'Égypte. *Karthago* 21:5–64.

Richmond, I. A. 1962. The Roman Siege Siege-works of Masada, Israel. *Journal of Roman Studies* 52:142–155.

Roquet, G. 1985. Avant le Désert, Savanes, Vineries et Caravanes. Réflexions sur une Inscription d'Ancien Empire. In *Mélanges Offerts à Jean Vercoutter*, edited by F. Geus and F. Thill, 291–311. Paris: Éditions Recherche sur les Civilisations.

Rothenberg, B. 1988. *The Egyptian Mining Temple at Timna*. London: Institute for Archaeo-Metallurgical Studies, Institute for Archaeology, University College.

Rowley-Conwy, P. 1988. The Camel in the Nile Valley: New Radiocarbon Accelerator (AMS) Dates from Qasr Ibrim. *Journal of Egyptian Archaeology* 74:245–248.

Sander-Hansen, C. E. 1956. *Die Texte der Metternichstele, Analecta Aegyptica* 7. Copenhagen: Ejnarm Munksgaard.

Schleiden, M. J. 1858. *Die Landenge von Suês, zur Beurtheilung des Canalprojects und des Auszugs der Israeliten aus Aegypten*. Leipzig: Verlag von Wilhelm Engelmann.

Schulman, A. 1988. Catalogue of the Egyptian finds. In B. Rothenberg, *The Egyptian Mining Temple at Timna*, 114–147. London: Institute for Archaeo-Metallurgical Studies, Institute for Archaeology, University College.

Schweinfurth, G. 1901. Am Westlichen Rande des Nilthals Zwischen Farschût und Kom Ombo. In Dr. A. Petermanns Mitteilungen aus Justus Perthes' geographischer Anstalt 47:1–10.

Seligman, C. G. 1934. *Egypt and Negro Africa: A Study in Divine Kingship*. London: George Routledge and Sons.

Sethe, K. 1933. *Urkunden des Alten Reiches*. 2nd ed. Leipzig: Urkunden des Aegyptischen Altertums 1.

Simpson, W. K. 1963. *Heka-Nefer, and the Dynastic Material from Toshka and Arminna*. Publications of the Pennsylvania-Yale Expedition to Egypt 1. New Haven: Peabody Museum of Natural History.

Smith, H. S. 1969. Preliminary Report on the Rock Inscriptions in the Egypt Exploration Society's Concession at Buhen. *Kush* 14:330–334.

———. 1972. The Rock Inscriptions of Buhen. *Journal of Egyptian Archaeology* 58:43–82.

Smith, H. S., and L. Giddy. 1985. Nubia and Dakhla Oasis in the Late Third Millennium B.C.: The Present Balance of Textual and Archaeological Evidence. In *Mélanges Offerts à Jean Vercoutter*, edited by F. Geus and F. Thill, 317–330. Paris: Éditions Recherche sur les Civilisations.

Spalinger, A. J. 1979. Some Notes on the Libyans of the Old Kingdom and Later Historical Reflexes. *Journal of the Society for the Study of Egyptian Antiquities* 9:144–157.

Stricker, B. H. 1953. De Egyptische mysteri'n. Pap. Leiden T 32. *Oudheidkundige Mededeelingen uit's Rijksmuseum van Oudheden te Leiden* 34:13–31.

Thompson (Crawford), D. J. 1983. Nile Grain Transport under the Ptolemies. In *Trade in the Ancient Economy*, edited by P. Garnsey, K. Hopkins, and C. R. Whittaker, 64–75. Berkeley: University of California Press.

Valloggia, M. 1981. This sur la Route des Oasis. *Bulletin de l'Institut Français d'Archéologie Orientale* 81 Supplément: 185–190.

———. 1989a. Les Routes du Désert dans l'Égypte Ancienne. In *Le Désert: Image et Réalité*, edited by Y. Christie, M. Sartre, B. Urio, and I. Urio, 165–171. Leuven: Actes du Colloque de Cantigny 1983.

———. 1989b. Le Papyrus Bodmer 107 ou les Reflets Tardifs d'une Conception de l'Éternité. *Revue de l'Égyptologie* 40:131–144.

Vandersleyen, C. 1971. Des Obstacles que Constituent les Cataracts du Nil. *Bulletin de l'Institut Français d'Archéologie Orientale* 69:253–266.

Vercoutter, J. 1970. *Mirgissa I: Mission Archéologique Française au Soudan sous la Direction de Jean Vercoutter 1*. Paris: Librairie Orientalist Paul Geuthner S.A.

———. 1982. Balat et la route de l'Oasis. In *L'Égyptologie en 1979: Axes Prioritaires de Recherches 1*, 283–288. Paris: Éditions du Centre National de la Recherche Scientifique.

———. 1988. Le Sahara de l'Égypte Pharaonique. *Sahara* 1:9–19.

Verner, M. 1969. Statue of Twēret (Cairo Museum no. 39145) Dedicated by Pabēsi and Several Remarks on the Role of the Hippopotamus Goddess. *Zeitschrift für Äegyptiche Aprache und Altertumskunde* 96:52–59.

Vernus, P. 1979. Un décret de Thoutmosis III Relatif à la Santé Publique. P. Berlin 3049, vol. 18–19, Or. 48:176–184.

Wainwright, G. A. 1935. Review of *Egypt and Negro Africa: A Study in Divine Kingship*, by C. G. Seligman. *Journal of Egyptian Archaeology* 21:260–261.

Weigall, A. 1909. *Travels in the Upper Egyptian Deserts*. Edinburgh: W. Blackwood and Sons.

———. 1923. *The Glory of the Pharaohs*. New York: G. P. Putnam's Sons.

Wendorf, F., R. Schild, R. Said, C. Vance Haynes, A. Gautier, and M. Kobusiewicz. 1976. The Prehistory of the Egyptian Sahara. *Science* 193:103–114.

Wendorf, F., and the Members of the Combined Prehistoric Expedition. 1977. Late Pleistocene and Recent Climatic Changes in the Egyptian Sahara. *The Geographical Journal* 143:211–234.

Wilkinson, J. G. 1835. Topography of Thebes, and General View of Egypt. London: John Murray.

Williams, B., and T. Logan. 1987. The Metropolitan Museum Knife Handle and Aspects of Pharaonic Imagery before Narmer. *Journal of Near Eastern Studies* 46:245–285.

Winkler, H. A. 1938. *Rock Drawings of Southern Upper Egypt 2*. Archaeological Survey of Egypt 26. London: Egypt Exploration Society.

Winlock, H. E. 1936. *Ed Dākhleh Oasis: Journal of a Camel Trip Made in 1908*. Publication 5. New York: Metropolitan Museum of Art, Department of Egyptian Art.

———. 1940. The Court of King Neb-Hepet-Rē Mentu-Hotpe at the Shatt Er Rigāl. *American Journal of Semitic Languages* 57:137–161.

———. 1941. Graffiti of the Priesthood of the Eleventh Dynasty Temples at Thebes. *American Journal of Semitic Languages* 58:146–168.

Žaba, Z. 1974. The Rock Inscriptions of Lower Nubia (Czechoslovak Concession). Prague: Universita Karlova.

NINE

Rock-Art and Landscapes

PAUL S. C. TAÇON

It is not just artists or geographers that define, describe, and depict tracts of land—all of us create landscapes. Indeed, landscapes are more a function of the human mind than we realize, with each of us reacting to particular places or sets of places in ways defined by our individual and cultural experiences. In one sense, there is no such thing as a landscape but rather jumbles of components ordered and bounded through human thought, choice, and experience. The choice of which elements, places, and spaces are included in particular landscapes is, in turn, determined by our perceptions and conceptions. In other words, choices are affected by how we think. For many groups of people, landscapes are not constructed solely on the basis of what is seen; instead, they use a combination of visual cues mixed with sound, smell, temperature, emotional reactions, and other features (Ouzman 1998b). Thus, there can be an infinite number of landscapes, reflecting variation in human relationships to place.

Landscapes are also difficult to define in a strict scientific sense. For some people, landscapes consist of natural features only—the topography of an area of land. For others, landscapes are cultural creations or are defined as a mix of natural and cultural elements. Landscapes are political; they are contested, defended and celebrated (e.g., Ashmore and Knapp 1999; Bender 1993). They can be places called "home," exotic locations, or barren wastelands that should be avoided. To be known they must be experienced, but they can never be fully described. This is because not only are they perceived differently by each observer, but also because they constantly and continually change. The passing of seasons, weathering, human intervention, and catastrophic forces of nature combine to transform each and every landscape on an ongoing basis. Thus, for many of us, landscapes exist only as ideals held in the mind—pictures composed of key reference points woven or mapped together through experience (see Ouzman 1998a, b).

Essentially, landscapes have to do with mapping and constructing models of reality. Today, it is valid to say that there are no truly "natural" landscapes. For hundreds of thousands of years, humans have explored, charted, categorized, settled, harvested, named, and defined every corner, nook, and cranny of the globe. The process began with the emergence of *Homo erectus* about a million years ago. *Homo erectus* crafted stone tools, made ornaments from pierced ostrich shell (e.g., Bednarik 1997), engraved bone with crude designs (Marshack 1972), and sailed the first watercraft to islands such as Flores, in present-day Indonesia (Morwood et al. 1997). And *Homo erectus* may have had other human abilities, such as some rudimentary form of language (Taylor 1997:6)—perhaps first naming some of the world's landscapes. *Homo erectus* was also the first great primate explorer, with a wanderlust that took the species far out of Africa, across Europe and Asia, to islands on Australia's doorstep. Indeed, *Homo erectus* was the first human ancestor to begin the process of registering and experiencing the world's great range of natural landscapes.

There is much debate as to whether *Homo erectus* developed into *Homo sapiens sapiens* in different parts of the world simultaneously—that is, whether *Homo erectus* really was very different from ourselves—or whether fully modern humans emerged in Africa a few hundred thousand years ago (e.g., see various papers in Mellars and Stringer 1989). For those who believe in the latter, *Homo sapiens* left Africa about a hundred thousand years ago in a second great wave of migration and exploration. They colonized the *Homo erectus* lands, eventually not only making them their own, but also inheriting the Earth. Whatever the case, it appears that landscapes were first marked in a widespread symbolic way between 40,000 and 50,000 years ago, with rock paintings and engravings being among some of the more long-lasting evidence (Bar-Yosef 1998; Chase and Dibble 1987; Davidson and Noble 1989; Knight et al. 1995; Lindly and Clark 1990; Mellars 1989, 1991; Pfeiffer 1982; Taçon 1994, 2000). This occurred not only in European landscapes (see Clottes 1998), but also in those of Asia (Bednarik 1994), Africa (Wendt 1974, 1976), and Australia (e.g., O'Connor 1995). People mapped, marked, and presumably mythologized every landscape they encountered. Eventually, this behavior spread to the Americas, so that today we find the globe covered

with rich and culturally meaningful landscapes. These locations are, of course, usually populated with humans, plants, and animals, but they are often also inhabited with spirits or fantastic creatures—the elves and trolls of Ireland, the fairies at the bottom of English gardens, the Yeti "snowpeople" of the Himalayas and parts of China, the Loch Ness monster, the Mimi spirits of Arnhem Land, or the races of giants in North America, Africa, and Europe (see Taçon and Chippindale 2001 for a review).

Landscapes now have lengthy histories associated with them, with rock paintings, oral histories, topographic maps, books, movies, and computer programs commemorating some of the more significant events that took place. Some landscapes have become sacred for particular peoples or for humanity as a whole. These are often natural places, such as spectacular mountains, waterfalls, or places where incredible change is emphasized or experienced—the boundary zones between forms of vegetation, rock, water, and sky (see Taçon 1999b). Others may be cultural places of profound human experience, such as the battlefields of past wars, graveyards, or even entire villages that capture a sacred moment of the past.

As can be seen, we all have different relationships to particular places. Some of us may have a scientific, clinical, descriptive relationship; others will have one that is more creative, one that taps into the raw energy of the landscape. Relationships may be deeply personal, spiritual, historic, nostalgic, or aesthetic. The color of landscapes is important; often they are described in colorful terms (Taçon 1999a). Indigenous people may have a relationship that connects them directly not only to the land, or a particular place within it, but also to Ancestral Beings of the creative era of the "Dreamtime," to plants, to animals, to other people, and to the past. It is this totality that creates the landscape. All of these may be illustrated with rock-art (e.g., Rosenfeld 1997).

Landscape can thus be considered a key concept for defining humanity, even though language, tool use, and art traditionally have been used to define what makes us human. For it is landscape that integrates all other markers. Of course, the oldest surviving landscapes with evidence of symbolic cultural activity are usually those with rock-art, painted or engraved images made for a variety of purposes, using a range of techniques. Commonly, very special natural locations were chosen to be embellished with culturally meaningful and distinctive imagery (Taçon 1999b).

Since late in the nineteenth century, rock-art in various parts of the world has been studied in terms of its larger setting, but it has really only been in the past decade that rock-art has been studied in comprehensive landscape-focused ways. This is something Morwood (1992:65) predicted would be particularly fruitful:

> In the majority of cases, the archaeological investigation of art has, and will continue to be, based on the recognition of structural patterning, or "selectivity," in the art and its interpretation in terms of social or territorial organisation, ideology, demography, economy, and so on. The functional interdependence between art and other cultural components, so evident in ethnographic case studies, suggests that art, and changes in art (both spatial and chronological), can tell much about the complexity of prehistoric cultural systems. This same functional interdependence indicates that archaeological studies of art need to be undertaken in the light of all available evidence for systemic context, one basic component of which is resource use. I conclude that a primary focus of future research on prehistoric art should be its role in an overall pattern of land-use, and the implications of changes in art for changes in the use of natural and cultural landscapes.

Bradley (1997:213) took this further, emphasizing the uniqueness of rock-art in terms of how it can relate to or express symbolic aspects of landscape: "It is because rock art is such an obvious way of assigning special significance to a place that it is best studied as part of landscape archaeology." Special significance thus may be a key to understanding rock-art in relation to landscape in a generic sense, but there are many rock-arts, diverse meanings, and numerous different rock-art functions, as many recent case studies have shown (e.g., those in this volume; see also Chippindale and Nash in press; Chippindale and Taçon 1998). Furthermore, as Bradley (1997:213) noted for carvings, but is also true of rock paintings: "There is no reason to suppose that the importance of a particular rock was *created* by the addition of carvings; just as likely, these emphasised the meanings of somewhere that was already significant. . . ." In terms of sacred sites, the first question to consider is whether rock-art was used to mark such places or whether the approaches to such locations were marked instead? The implications for understanding landscape are very significant.

The landscapes in which rock-art can be found are naturally restricted by the nature of a region's geology; something obvious but often forgotten. Furthermore, rock-art deteriorates over time as a consequence of weathering, plants, animals, and human activity. At many sites "marks attract marks" so that superimpositioning obscures older rock-art and rock-art landscapes. Essentially, in each rock-art region two competing forces have been at work over time: *accumulation* and *deterioration*. The rock-art landscapes we study today are the result of an accumulation of marks on or in surfaces as well as a deterioration of both marks and surfaces over time. In some cases, older rock-art may not preserve well. In others, more recent marks vanish quickly because of a change to a more fragile technique, media, or method of application. The challenge is to take all of this into account when we attempt to interpret a given form, "style," or period of rock-art. It is especially important to consider these factors when examining rock-art from a landscape perspective.

RELATING TO LANDSCAPES

If we were to make a short list of the ways in which humans, both at the individual and community levels, express their relationships to places, landscapes, and geography we could start with the following:

1. unadorned portable objects
2. temporary/transient imagery (e.g., body paintings, ground drawings)
3. portable objects with imagery
4. rock-art (see definition later in this section)
5. architecture
6. monolithic sculpture
7. burials
8. settlements
9. names/labels
10. songs, stories, "mythologies," oral histories
11. performance/ritual/ceremony
12. written histories
13. fences/boundary markers/signposts
14. maps
15. multimedia

We could then cite many examples for each of the fifteen categories listed here, some exclusive, some overlapping. But to produce something a bit more

meaningful, it would be useful to further sort both the list and specific examples according to differing sorts of criteria. Thirteen ways of doing this are as follows, the first six of which are most pertinent to rock-art studies:

1. early versus recent
2. simple versus complex
3. figurative versus nonfigurative
4. marking versus mapping
5. economic versus symbolic
6. secular versus sacred
7. psychological versus physical
8. organic versus inorganic
9. conceptual versus perceptual
10. rough versus refined
11. individual versus group; community versus nation
12. oral versus written
13. visual versus performance

A particular way of expressing a relationship to landscape may fit into several categories at the same time, and more categories may need to be devised. In many cases, there will be a sliding scale between the oppositions listed here, so that examples are neither one nor the other, instead lying somewhere in between. But this is a good starting point because it covers and emphasizes a significant component of the diverse ways in which people think about and express ideas associated with landscape. However, in this chapter the focus is on rock-art: paintings, engravings, stencils, and other purposely made marks, such as abraded grooves and cupules, arranged in or on natural rock in seminatural landscape settings. The intention is to examine rock-art and landscape as a function of the first six categories just listed to explore difference and similarity in terms of how particular rock-arts have been used to highlight or express certain aspects of human relationships to place (see also Taçon and Chippindale 1998 for discussion of appropriate methods for rock-art interpretation).

1. Early Versus Recent

A crude form of rock-art classification in terms of landscape was employed when I first began to study rock-art in northern Australia (Taçon 1987, 1989b). Sites were divided into three broad locational categories, each with from two to four subcategories:

General Location:
    Plateau, plain, and interface
    Gorge

Specific Location:
    Outlier, residual or boulder(s) on plain
    Top of scree slope/bottom of escarpment
    Boulder(s) on scree slope
    Outlier, residual or boulder(s) on plateau

Type of Site and Placement of Art:
    Shelter walls and/or ceilings
    Small panel or single painting
    Vertical rock wall/face with overhang
    Cave

Significant differences were found between the locations of different manners of depiction and the ways in which particular locations were marked at different periods of time: "In general, most x-ray sites are at the base of the escarpment or below and a few are situated on the plateau or in the gorges that dissect it. The general orientation is consequently *plain* rather than *plateau*. Sites with earlier forms of painting also occur on the edge of the plain but they are just as frequent on the plateau, as has been noted by Brandl (1973), Chaloupka (1984a, b) and Lewis (1988). In general there is a different distribution pattern between sites with x-ray paintings and those with earlier forms and styles" (Taçon 1989b:112).

In other regions exposed rock platforms that incorporate engravings could be added to the list. The important point is that each region we study needs to be defined near the beginning of the project according to its geology and rock-art range so that the art may be recorded with landscape patterning in mind. For a more recent example of this see David et al. (1999:20), where a close association between "motif forms and the area and nature of rock surfaces" was found in the Wardaman region of the Northern Territory's "Top End."

Another rock-art change in landscape location over time that has been underinvestigated is related to contact with Europeans over the past five hundred years. This is something pertinent to the most recent rock-art of Australia, North America, and southern Africa, in particular. Frederick's (1999) research in central Australia is particularly revealing. She focused on the nature and patterning of contact rock-art in Watarrka National Park. Besides providing better definitions for "contact art" and describing the nature of the central Australian material, Frederick's (1999:140–41) conclusions are pertinent cross-culturally. In terms of landscape, there are three that are particularly important:

- Contact rock-art varies dramatically from region to region, and the intricacies of its production will be predicated upon the local conditions of cross-cultural exchange.
- Contact rock-art is produced both at and away from geographical points of cultural contact. This follows from the understanding that the

influences, impressions, and conditions of contact experience(s) extend beyond any spatiotemporally isolated context within which an interaction was situated. It cannot be assumed that contact art will occur only in the specific geographical location where these negotiations are actually played out.

- Changes in the use of landscape for the production of rock-art will follow long-term cross-cultural contact, particularly where colonial forces impinge on access to important resources.

Recent research in the Keep River region of northern Australia is uncovering similar sorts of changes in terms of where in the landscape people painted before and after contact (Mulvaney 1996; Taçon 1999c). In some cases, new areas were occupied for the first time. In others, certain places with lengthy histories of occupation took on new importance, with a burst of rock-art activity and new stories incorporating contact experience. It is important to note that there are many contact period designs similar to precontact motifs, as well as those that show introduced subject matter, just as Frederick found at Watarrka. Defining and interpreting similar trends in southern Africa (e.g., Smith 1995, 1997:28) and North America (e.g., Klassen 1998; Molyneaux 1989) has recently seen serious study.

2. Simple Versus Complex

One of the best recent examples of this sort of analysis is Bradley's (1997) ingenious study uniting pre-Historic art and the investigation of pre-Historic landscape, with a focus on the engraved rock-art of Atlantic Europe. Bradley's results highlight differences between the use of simple versus complex imagery in landscapes thought to be related but

spread across a vast region. One result is a remarkable difference between rock-art patterning in landscapes at opposite ends of the region: in northern Britain the more complex rock carvings are situated toward higher ground and the simplest of all, such as cup-marked stones, were associated with areas of settlement; in Galicia the opposite is true, with complex motifs close to settled areas and simple marks along the higher ground! Perhaps this is one of the ways people distinguished themselves from their neighbors, but there were likely other factors at work as well. For instance, Bradley also found both more localized regionalism and evidence that ancient paths and travel routes were marked in specific ways. Bradley's research not only increases our awareness of the symbolic properties of ancient landscapes and the ways in which simple and complex images can be differentially used, but also he shows us that previous studies, centered on territoriality and food supply, are remarkably deficient.

3. Figurative Versus Nonfigurative

A question not asked often enough is whether figurative images are distributed in landscapes differently than nonfigurative images, whether made by the same group of people or under the same contexts or not. For instance, in southern Africa it has been noted that nonfigurative engraved imagery is generally found in very different locations than are naturalistic depictions of animals, humans, and so forth. Figurative motifs are commonly found engraved in boulders that litter low hills, but geometric designs are more often found carved into rock platforms, although there is some overlap. Recent research suggested that they likely were made by two different groups of people, who used landscapes in very different ways. The figurative traditions are more closely linked to San bushfolk and similar rock paintings, sometimes with an emphasis on connecting to inner landscapes, deep inside rock (Taçon and Ouzman in press). The nonfigurative art has recently been shown to have been produced by herding peoples who entered bushfolk territories about 2,000 years ago (Smith and Ouzman in press).

Rosenfeld (1992) and Flood (1997, 1999) each remarked on the different nature, distribution, and meaning of marks such as stencils, cupules, and abraded grooves compared with figurative motifs. Forge (1991) also noted the particular significance of stencils. Although these are for the most part nonfigurative, they are arranged at sites and within larger landscapes in ways that are different from figurative rock-art and nonfigurative geometric motifs. This recently became evident in the Keep River region when a study of cupules was undertaken (Taçon et al. 1997), but more recent fieldwork has revealed that abraded grooves and stencils are also distributed in landscapes in very different ways than figurative paintings and engravings (Taçon 1999c). Like cupules, they often cluster near natural holes or tunnels through the rock (Taçon et al. 1997:957); figurative paintings and engravings are found in different sorts of locations, such as across shelter walls and ceilings. At one site a unique arrangement of cupules, abraded grooves, and stencils was found marking the approaches to a tunnel; there was no figurative art. At another, hundreds of grooves and stencils are arranged on one side of a tunnel connecting two large bowl-shaped shelters; most of the figurative art is on the other side (Taçon 1999c). Thus, two very different sorts of rock-art landscaping patterning have emerged in the same region at the same time.

Another example of dual systems operating congruently can be found across the greater Sydney region of New South Wales, Australia. Instead of contemporaneous figurative and nonfigurative traditions, McDonald (1991, 1994, 1998) found both painting and engraving traditions, at first thought to be chronologically separate, to overlap significantly in both time and space. As McDonald (1998:323) concluded: "Synchronic analyses of the two extensive regional art bodies have shown that they do represent different manifestations of the same art tradition—while demonstrating inherently distinctive stylistic traits because of their techniques. As well as striking similarities in the motif preferences, similar stylistic clines and boundaries are demonstrated by both art bodies, and there is considerable congruence in their locations."

To the north, in Arnhem Land, contemporaneous painted art traditions have been observed (e.g., see Chippindale and Taçon 1998:107; Taçon 1989b), possibly the result of different motivations, meaning, and significance. Examples of dual art systems or large traditions incorporating a range of techniques or styles can be found elsewhere, but it has been only recently that efforts have been made to tease this out of archaeological records. The lesson is to not assume a linear progression of art development in any region; the picture is usually much more complex.

4. Marking Versus Mapping

It is one thing to mark the landscape; it is quite another to map it. But mapping and marking are related pursuits and rock-art has often been considered a form of mapping (e.g., see Lewis 1998; Maggs 1998; Sutton 1998 for North America, Africa, and Australia, respectively). But first of all, it is important to understand that mapping is not something unique to particular peoples or that it is simply an aspect of Cartesian cartography: "The measure of mapping is not restricted to the mathematical; it may equally be spiritual, political or moral. By the same token, the mapping's record is not confined to the archival; it includes the remembered, the imagined, the contemplated. The world figured through mapping may thus be material or immaterial, actual or desired, whole or part, in various ways experienced, remembered or projected. . . . Acts of mapping are creative, sometimes anxious, moments in coming to knowledge of the world, and the map is both the spatial embodiment of knowledge and a stimulus to further cognitive engagements" (Cosgrove 1999:2).

Howard Morphy (1999:103) further warned that although many Aboriginal paintings may be considered or are maps of land: "It is necessary, however, to define precisely what is meant by a 'map' in this context. The danger is in transferring too literally a Western concept of topographical map on to Aboriginal cultural forms and making them into something they are not. . . ."

In reference primarily to contemporary art, Morphy (1999:106) noted: "Aboriginal paintings can only be fully understood as maps once it is realized that the criterion for inclusion is not topographical but mythological and conceptual; paintings are thus representations of the totemic geography." This is a particularly salient point when it comes to interpreting Australian Aboriginal rock-art, as Rosenfeld (1997; and see later in this section) and others have emphasized: "Marks and impressions on the ground or the person all have the potential to indicate ancestral presence" (Morphy 1999:108).

In my own research, particularly striking cases have been encountered at Roma Gorge in central Australia (Taçon 1994), across western Arnhem Land (e.g., Taçon 1989a, b, 1991; Taçon et al. 1996)

and near the Mann River, central Arnhem Land (Taçon 1994). Similar examples were found in Canada (e.g., Taçon 1990, 1993) and most recently in southern Africa. An outstanding case is the Matsieng rock-art site, in southern Botswana (Molyneux 1921; Walker 1997; Wilman 1918; 1919). This "Bushfolk" rock-art site comprises 117 engravings, mostly of human and feline footprints clustered around three natural rock holes or sumps in a sandstone plate (Walker 1997). Although the site was made by others, contemporary Tswana argue that the site is their premier creation site. It was here where Matsieng, the first or archetypal Tswana, emerged from the ground into the outer world. He left his footprints and those of the animals he brought with him on the then-soft rock of the still-new world, mapping not only the landscape but also the future for Tswana people.

5. Economic Versus Symbolic

In many regions the distribution of rock-art depictions needs to be looked at from both symbolic and economic perspectives simultaneously. This is because in many societies the two are intimately related. However, landscape patterns might also emerge that reflect larger, more purely economic pursuits or processes (e.g., for Scandinavia hunter versus farmer art compare Sognnes 1995, 1998 with Walderhaug 1995, 1998). Alternatively, the marking of landscapes might have occurred at symbolic levels unrelated to food gathering, provisioning, and economics (e.g., Whitley's 1998 discussion of bighorn sheep of western North American rock-art). Although it is difficult, wherever possible these need to be teased out.

Sometimes a feedback relationship between the economic and symbolic can be discerned that explains some of the observed landscape rock marking. For instance, in western Arnhem Land, Australia, it was found that the incidence of rock painting depictions of fish not only increased over time during the past few thousand years but also across space, from south to north. Most paintings of fish, and other animals, were done after the hunt and catch rather than before. Very few were found to relate to "hunting magic." In this sense, and at their most superficial level, animal paintings represent some of the food animals most sought after and caught by the Aboriginal hunters of the region. They would be recognized as such by most members of the group, but they also could be used in a variety of ways to teach, explain, illustrate, or pass on aspects of traditional belief and practice. Indeed, ethnographic research revealed fish to be powerful symbols of life, health, and well-being, among other things (Taçon 1989a, b). But the landscape patterning of fish depictions observable today resulted from the delicate interplay of three main factors: the incidence of actual fish in the landscape and resulting role in diet; the symbolic, totemic, and ancestral fish associations held by different clan and language groups and the histories of movement of these peoples across landscapes; and the accumulation of fish images at sites over time. For instance, as more and more fish paintings were added to shelter walls and ceilings, partly as a function of frequency of fish in the environment and diet, they began to overwhelm some sites in number. When paintings began to fade they had to be renewed with polychrome, "rainbow" color, or replaced with fresh images. Fish were added more often to replace earlier motifs, but in the process they rarely completely covered the older art. On many occasions they were placed adjacent to less-fresh fish forms or overlapped only over part of them. This has resulted in an exponential increase in the frequency of fish motifs at sites over time. Furthermore, this has also contributed to a greater emphasis on fish in the art and symbol system over time, so that for contemporary Aborigines, and their recent ancestors, it was images of fish that were more often used metaphorically to explain aspects of belief to youths and the uninitiated, including interested non-Aborigines such as archaeologists and anthropologists.

6. Secular Versus Sacred

Drawing on widespread recent ethnographic research, Rosenfeld (1997) distinguished three very different contexts of production: rock-art said to be an Ancestral creation, rock-art that is a human creation about the Dreamtime past/present; and rock-art that is "a human creation about human concerns." Each of these is distributed differently within social landscapes:

> The creation or maintenance of ancestral images is restricted to individuals according to their structurally determined identities. The art created in such contexts is narrowly constrained in terms of style and motif. Subject matter and style emphasize the nature of the artist's contextualized relationship to a locale. In its reference to appropriately expressed concepts of the dreaming it expresses his/her structurally determined interests in the locale as defined via the legitimacy of the ideational system of social relations. The creation or renovation of such paintings is an act of expressing this classificatory and contextual identity, and of relationship to place via the spiritual power of the "law." This rock art therefore expresses and mediates social relations rather than explicitly territorial affiliation. It is an affirmation of *territorial affiliation via social relations* as constructed through cosmological principles.

The execution of rock markings and of nonsacred designs is generally concurrent with rights of residence that are much more inclusive. In these contexts individual presence or concern may be celebrated in art, but this art does not evoke rights of control over place nor of ritual affiliation to it. It makes reference to the artist's individual identity but it does not visually define his/her socially constructed identity. (Rosenfeld 1997:296–297)

Rosenfeld (1997:297) concluded: "To that extent rock art in its formal variation may be thought to express and determine a social landscape." However, she also noted that the complexity is far greater than simple models of "reciprocity of access to resources between members of territorial groups" would suggest. Furthermore, she added that "formalized art systems . . . operate primarily, though not exclusively, to relate socially constructed identity-place relationships" (1997:297) and she further distinguished those that operate at the more social level from those that are more personal, such as mechanically made marks or commemorative images. But it is important to note that relationships to rock-art sites and landscapes change, with resulting shifts in socially constructed identity. A fascinating example of social landscape change has recently been detected in far northern Queensland, revealed by rock-art recording, excavation, and dating of site abandonment on an Aboriginal 'Dreaming' mountain known as Ngarrabullgan (David and Wilson 1999). There, "Around 600 years ago, relations between people and place changed to the extent that sites on and around Ngarrabullgan became systematically abandoned" (1999:186). There was then a shift in the way people engaged with their world, as well as the nature of identity in terms of how it was grounded in place. This has exciting implications for reinterpreting recent or contemporary Indige-

nous perceptions of rock-art, sites, and landscapes in various parts of northern Australia and southern Africa. For instance, it could help explain shifts in importance of Bradshaw paintings (see Taçon 1998–1999 for a review), after a period of site abandonment as proposed by Walsh and Morwood (1999). It also cautions against an overreliance on contemporary Indigenous interpretation for interpreting ancient imagery, sites, and landscapes, something Davidson (1999) warned against and Taçon and Chippindale (1998) advocated with due care. We should also remember that sites and landscapes may be accessed and reused in the present in two very different contexts: "Notions of the past are not only connected to locales created in the present, but also to features of the landscape deriving from the distant past. We are thus looking at two forms of reuse of the landscape. The first comes from the repeated use and maintenance of features with known antecedents, to which the group (or parts of it) return on a regular basis to carry out activities of a prescribed type. The second aspect of reuse derives from actions at ancient features of the landscape, given new values within the contemporary setting" (Gosden and Lock 1998:4).

For historic and contemporary ethnography used in northern Australia, North America, and southern Africa to interpret rock-art in landscape contexts, there is a mix of information resulting from both processes to disentangle.

CONCLUSIONS

There are many other ways in which landscape patterns can be identified in rock-art studies. For instance, sometimes common natural features and vantage points are highlighted with rock-art, whether they are in the Americas, Asia, Africa, Europe, or Australia—in other words, the nature of the environment setting is very important to describe. History is also always an important consideration when interpreting rock-art within landscape contexts, as many of the above examples have shown. As Feinman (1999:685) noted for landscape studies more generally: "human-environment interactions are historically contingent, dynamic and accretionary, shaped by distinct cultural perceptions and past human actions."

But we should also never forget that rock-art has always played a key role in a given people's coming to terms with landscapes as well as the transformation of landscapes from what was once true wilderness into culturally meaningful places and spaces. As Dunning et al. (1999:650) remarked "How nature was rendered culturally intelligible by landscape manipulation had important consequences for whose *voices* are heard and whose claims legitimated amid struggles over the control of vital resources." Rock-art features prominently in this sense because many forms of rock-art are about control and access: to landscapes, economic resources, histories, and even levels or forms of special knowledge. When we access already decorated sites today we do so from very different perspectives and historical circumstances than those who first marked shelter walls and ceilings, as well as those who added marks later: "We arrive many millennia after the heat and urgency of daily life has cooled and cast a retrospective view over the landscape. Our dispassionate classification after the fact is a central element of the histories we create. But for the social actors of the past, the landscape was not dead and static, but provided the possibility and necessity of action, so that sites were constantly reworked" (Gosden and Lock 1998:4).

Reinvigorated old landscapes with stories and stories from pictures is what rock-art research is all about. There are many different sorts of meaning we might derive through archaeology, some of which have been alluded to above, but ultimately these meanings are constructed in the present for use in the future. The challenge for us is to access some core of ancient meaning through the application of rigorous methods (Taçon and Chippindale 1998). That this core actually is accessible is the premise we necessarily must start with. Otherwise rock-art research is reduced to degrees of mechanical recording with little to no relevant interpretation, meaning, or significance.

REFERENCES CITED

Ashmore, W., and A. B. Knapp. 1999. *Archaeologies of Landscape: Contemporary Perspectives*. Oxford: Blackmore.

Bar-Yosef, O. 1998. On the Nature of Transitions: The Middle to Upper Palaeolithic and the Neolithic Revolution. *Cambridge Archaeological Journal* 8:141–163.

Bednarik, R. G. 1994. The Pleistocene Art of Asia. *Journal of World Prehistory* 8:351–375.

———. 1997. The Role of Pleistocene Beads in Documenting Hominid Cognition. *Rock Art Research* 14 (1):27–41.

Bender, B. (ed.). 1993. *Landscape: Politics and Perspectives*. Oxford: Berg.

Bradley, R. 1997. *Rock Art and the Prehistory of Atlantic Europe: Signing the Land*. London: Routledge.

Brandl, E. 1973. *Australian Aboriginal Paintings in Western and Central Arnhem Land: Temporal Sequences and Elements of Style in Cadell River and Deaf Adder Creek Art*. Canberra: Australian Institute of Aboriginal Studies.

Chaloupka, G. 1984a. *From Palaeoart to Casual Paintings: The Chronological Sequence of Arnhem Land Plateau Rock Art.* Northern Territory Museum of Arts and Sciences Monograph Series 1. Darwin.

———. 1984b. *Rock Art of the Arnhem Land Plateau: The Paintings of the Dynamic Figure Style.* Darwin: Northern Territory Museum of Arts and Sciences.

Chase, P., and H. Dibble. 1987. Middle Paleolithic Symbolism: A Review of Current Evidence and Interpretations. *Journal of Anthropological Archaeology* 6:263–296.

Chippindale, C., and G. Nash, eds. In press. *The Landscape of Rock-Art.* Cambridge: Cambridge University Press.

Chippindale, C., and P. Taçon. 1998. The Many Ways of Dating Arnhem Land Rock-Art, North Australia. In *The Archaeology of Rock-Art*, edited by C. Chippindale and P. Taçon, 90–111. Cambridge: Cambridge University Press.

Clottes, J. 1998. The "Three Cs": Fresh Avenues towards European Palaeolithic Art. In *The Archaeology of Rock-Art*, edited by C. Chippindale and P. Taçon, 112–129. Cambridge: Cambridge University Press.

Cosgrove, D. 1999. *Mappings.* London: Reaktion Books.

David, B., and M. Wilson. 1999. Re-Reading the Landscape: Place and Identity in Northeastern Australia during the Late Holocene. *Cambridge Archaeological Journal* 9:163–188.

David, B., M. Lecole, H. Lourandos, A. J. Baglioni Jr., and J. Flood. 1999. Investigating Relationships between Motif Forms, Techniques and Rock Surfaces in North Australian Rock Art. *Australian Archaeology* 48:16–22.

Davidson, I. 1999. Symbols by Nature: Animal Frequencies in the Upper Palaeolithic of Western Europe and the Nature of Symbolic Representation. *Archaeology in Oceania* 34:121–131.

Davidson, I., and W. Noble. 1989. The Archaeology of Language Origins—A Review. *Antiquity* 65:39–48.

Dunning, N., V. Scarborough, F. Valdez Jr., S. Luzzadder-Beach, T. Beach, and J. G. Jones. 1999. Temple Mountains, Sacred Lakes, and Fertile Fields: Ancient Maya Landscapes in Northwest Belize. *Antiquity* 73:650–660.

Feinman, G. M. 1999. Defining a Contemporary Landscape Approach: Concluding Thoughts. *Antiquity* 73:684–685.

Flood, J. 1997. *Rock Art of the Dreamtime: Images of Ancient Australia.* Sydney: Angus and Robertson.

———. 1999. Copying the Dreamtime: Anthropic Marks in Early Aboriginal Australia. In *CeSMAP—News95 Proceedings*, edited by D. Seglie. Pinerolo: IFRAO (CD Rom.)

Forge, A. 1991. Handstencils: Rock Art or Not Art. In *Rock Art and Prehistory: Papers Presented to Symposium G of the AURA Congress, Darwin, 1988*, edited by P. Bahn and A. Rosenfeld, 39–44. Oxford: Oxbow Monograph 10.

Frederick, U. 1999. At the Centre of It All: Constructing Contact through the Rock Art of Watarrka National Park, Central Australia. *Archaeology in Oceania* 34:132–144.

Gosden, C., and G. Lock. 1998. Prehistoric Histories. *World Archaeology* 30:2–12.

Klassen, M. 1998. Icon and Narrative in Transition: Contact-Period Rock-Art at Writing-On-Stone, Southern Alberta, Canada. In *The Archaeology of Rock-Art*, edited by C. Chippindale and P. S. C. Taçon, 42–72. Cambridge: Cambridge University Press.

Knight, C., C. Powers, and I. Watts. 1995. The Human Symbolic Revolution: A Darwinian Account. *Cambridge Archaeological Journal* 5:75–114.

Lewis, D. 1988. *The Rock Paintings of Arnhem Land: Social, Ecological, and Material Culture Change in the Post-glacial Period.* British Archaeological Reports, International Series S415. Oxford.

Lewis, G. M. 1998. Maps, Map Making, and Map Use by Native North Americans. In *The History of Cartography.* Vol. 2, Book 3: *Cartography in the Traditional African, American, Arctic, Australian, and Pacific Societies*, edited by D. Woodward and G. M. Lewis, 51–182. Chicago: University of Chicago Press.

Lindly, J. M., and G. A. Clark. 1990. Symbolism and Modern Human Origins. *Current Anthropology* 31: 233–261.

Maggs, T. 1998. Cartographic Content of Rock Art in Southern Africa. In *The History of Cartography*. Vol. 2, Book 3: *Cartography in the Traditional African, American, Arctic, Australian, and Pacific Societies*, edited by D. Woodward and G. M. Lewis, 13–23. Chicago: University of Chicago Press.

Marshack, A. 1972. *The Roots of Civilization: The Cognitive Beginnings of Man's First Art, Symbol and Notation*. New York: McGraw-Hill Book Co.

McDonald, J. 1991. Archaeology and Art in the Sydney Region: Context and Theory in the Analysis of a Dual Medium Style. In *Rock Art and Prehistory: Papers Presented to Symposium G of the AURA Congress, Darwin, 1988*, edited by P. Bahn and A. Rosenfeld, 78–85. Oxbow Monograph 10. Oxford.

———. 1994. Dreamtime Superhighway: An Analysis of Sydney Basin Rock Art and Prehistoric Information Exchange. Ph.D. thesis, Australian National University, Canberra.

———. 1998. Shelter Rock-art in the Sydney Basin—A Space-time Continuum: Exploring Different Influences on Stylistic Change. In *The Archaeology of Rock-Art*, edited by C. Chippindale and P. Taçon, 319–335. Cambridge: Cambridge University Press.

Mellars, P. 1989. Major Issues in the Emergence of Modern Humans. *Current Anthropology* 30:349–385.

———. 1991. Cognitive Changes and the Emergence of Modern Humans. *Cambridge Archaeological Journal* 1:63–76.

Mellars, P., and C. Stringer (eds.). 1989. *The Human Revolution: Behavioural and Biological Perspectives in the Origins of Modern Humans*. Edinburgh: Edinburgh University Press.

Molyneux, A. J. C. 1921. Note on Rock Engravings at Metsang, Bechuanaland Protectorate. *South African Journal of Science* 17:206.

Molyneaux, B. 1989. Concepts of Humans and Animals in Post-contact Micmac Rock Art. In *Animals into Art*, edited by H. Morphy, 193–214. London: Unwin Hyman.

Morphy, H. 1999. *Aboriginal Art*. London: Phaidon Press.

Morwood, M. J. 1992. Changing Art in a Changing Landscape: A Case Study from the Upper Flinders Region of the North Queensland Highland. In *State of the Art: Regional Studies in Australia and Melanesia*, edited by J. McDonald and I. Haskovec, 60–70. Occasional AURA Publication No. 6. Melbourne: Archaeological Publications.

Morwood, M., F. Aziz, G. D. van der Bergh, P. Y. Sondaar, and J. De Vos. 1997. Stone Artefacts from the 1994 Excavation at Mata Menge, West Central Flores, Indonesia. *Australian Archaeology* 44:26–34.

Mulvaney, K. 1996. What to Do on a Rainy Day: Reminiscences of Mirriuwung and Gadjerong Artists. *Rock Art Research* 13 (1): 3–20.

O'Connor, S. 1995. Carpenter's Gap Rockshelter 1: 40,000 Years of Aboriginal Occupation in the Napier Ranges, Kimberley, WA. *Australian Archaeology* 40:58–59.

Ouzman, S. 1998a. Mindscape. In *Encyclopedia of Semiotics*, edited by P. Bouissac, 419–421. New York: Oxford University Press.

———. 1998b. Toward a Mindscape of Landscape: Rock-Art as Expression of World-Understanding. In *The Archaeology of Rock-Art*, edited by C. Chippindale and P. S. C. Taçon, 30–41. Cambridge: Cambridge University Press.

Pfeiffer, J. E. 1982. *The Creative Explosion: An Inquiry into the Origins of Art and Religion*. Ithaca: Cornell University Press.

Rosenfeld, A. 1992. Changing Focus of Symbolic Expression in Late Pleistocene Australia. Paper presented at the Second AURA Congress, Cairns.

———. 1997. Archaeological Signatures of the Social Context of Rock Art Production. In *Beyond Art: Pleistocene Image and Symbol*, edited by M. Conkey, O. Soffer, D. Stratmann, and N. G. Jablonski, 289–300. Memoirs of the California Academy of Sciences 23.

Smith, B. 1995. Rock Art in South Central Africa: A

Study Based on the Pictographs of Dedza District, Malawi and Kasama District, Zambia. Ph.D. thesis, University of Cambridge, Cambridge.

———. 1997. *Zambia's Ancient Rock Art: The Paintings of Kasama*. Livingston: The National Heritage Conservation Commission of Zambia.

Smith, B. W., and S. Ouzman. In press. Introducing the Khoe Herder Rock Art of Southern Africa. *Current Anthropology*.

Sognnes, K. 1995. The Social Context of Rock Art in Trondelag, Norway: Rock Art at a Frontier. In *Perceiving Rock Art: Social and Political Perspectives*, edited by K. Helskog and B. Olsen, 130–145. Oslo: Instituttet for Sammenlignende Kulturforskning.

———. 1998. Symbols in a Changing World: Rock-Art and the Transition from Hunting to Farming in Mid Norway. In *The Archaeology of Rock-Art*, edited by C. Chippindale and P. S. C. Taçon, 146–162. Cambridge: Cambridge University Press.

Sutton, P. 1998. Icons of Country: Topographic Representations in Classical Aboriginal Traditions. In *The History of Cartography*. Vol. 2, Book 3: *Cartography in the Traditional African, American, Arctic, Australian, and Pacific Societies*, edited by D. Woodward and G. M. Lewis, 353–386. Chicago: University of Chicago Press.

Taçon, P. S. C. 1987. Internal-External: A Re-evaluation of the "X-ray" Concept in Western Arnhem Land Rock Art. *Rock Art Research* 4 (1): 36–50.

———. 1989a. Art and the Essence of Being: Symbolic and Economic Aspects of Fish among the Peoples of Western Arnhem Land, Australia. In *Animals into Art*, edited by H. Morphy, 236–250. London: Unwin Hyman.

———. 1989b. From Rainbow Serpents to "X-ray" Fish: The Nature of the Recent Rock Painting Tradition of Western Arnhem Land, Australia. Ph.D. thesis, Australian National University, Canberra.

———. 1990. The Power of Place: Cross-Cultural Responses to Natural and Cultural Landscapes of Stone and Earth. In *Perspectives of Canadian Land-scape: Native Traditions*, edited by J. Vastokas, 11–43. North York: Robarts Centre for Canadian Studies/York University.

———. 1991. The Power of Stone: Symbolic Aspects of Stone Use and Tool Development in Western Arnhem Land, Australia. *Antiquity* 65:192–207.

———. 1993. Stylistic Relationships between the Wakeham Bay Petroglyphs of the Canadian Arctic and Dorset Portable Art. In *Rock Art Studies: The Post-stylistic Era or Where Do We Go from Here?*, edited by M. Lorblanchet and P. G. Bahn, 151–62. Oxbow Monograph 35. Oxford.

———. 1994. Socialising Landscapes: The Long-term Implications of Signs, Symbols and Marks on the Land. *Archaeology in Oceania* 29:117–29.

———. 1998–1999. Magical Paintings of the Kimberley. *Nature Australia* 26 (3): 40–47.

———. 1999a. All Things Bright and Beautiful: The Role and Meaning of Colour in Human Development. *Cambridge Archaeological Journal* 9:120–126.

———. 1999b. Identifying Ancient Sacred Landscapes in Australia: From Physical to Social. In *Archaeologies of Landscape: Contemporary Perspectives*, edited by W. Ashmore and A. B. Knapp, 33–57. Oxford: Blackwell Publishers.

———. 1999c. Keep River Region Archaeological and Ethnographic Fieldwork Notebook. Housed at the Australian Museum, Sydney.

———. 2000. The Dawn of Voyagers and Past Reclaimers: 21st Century Insight into the Roots of Image Making. Paper presented at PalaeoArt 2000: Taking Stock and Envisioning the Future, Society for American Archaeology Conference, 6 April 2000, Philadelphia.

Taçon, P. S. C., and C. Chippindale. 1998. An Archaeology of Rock-Art through Informed Methods and Formal Methods. In *The Archaeology of Rock-Art*, edited by C. Chippindale and P. S. C. Taçon, 1–10. Cambridge: Cambridge University Press.

———. 2001. Transformation and Depictions of the First People: Animal-Headed Beings of Arnhem

Land, N.T., Australia. In *Theoretical Perspectives in Rock Art Research*, edited by K. Helskog, 175–210. Oslo: Novus Forlag.

Taçon, P. S. C., and S. Ouzman. In press. Worlds within Stone: The Inner and Outer Rock-art Landscapes of Northern Australia and Southern Africa. In *Landscapes of Rock-Art*, edited by C. Chippindale and G. Nash. Cambridge: Cambridge University Press.

Taçon, P. S. C., M. Wilson, and C. Chippindale. 1996. Birth of the Rainbow Serpent in Arnhem Land Rock Art and Oral History. *Archaeology in Oceania* 31:103–124.

Taçon, P. S. C., R. Fullagar, S. Ouzman, and K. Mulvaney. 1997. Cupule Engravings from Jinmium-Granilpi (northern Australia) and Beyond: Exploration of a Widespread and Enigmatic Class of Rock Markings. *Antiquity* 71:942–965.

Taylor, T. 1997. *The Prehistory of Sex: Four Million Years of Human Sexual Culture*. London: Fourth Estate.

Walderhaug, E. M. 1995. Rock Art and Society in Neolithic Sogn og Fjordane. In *Perceiving Rock Art: Social and Political Perspectives*, edited by K. Helskog and B. Olsen, 169–180. Oslo: Instituttet for Sammenlignende Kulturforskning.

———. 1998. Changing Art in a Changing Society: The Hunters' Rock-art of Western Norway. In *The Archaeology of Rock-Art*, edited by C. Chippindale and P. S. C. Taçon, 285–301. Cambridge: Cambridge University Press.

Walker, N. 1997. In the Footsteps of the Ancestors: The Matsieng Creation Site in Botswana. *South African Archaeological Bulletin* 52:95–104.

Walsh, G., and M. Morwood. 1999. Spear and Spear-thrower Evolution in the Kimberley Region, N.W. Australia: Evidence from Rock Art. *Archaeology in Oceania* 34:45–58.

Wendt, W. E. 1974. Art Mobilier aus der Apollo 11 Grotte un Südwest-Afrika. *Acta Praehistorics et Archaeologica* 5:1–42.

———. 1976. "Art Mobilier" from the Apollo 11 Cave, South West Africa: Africa's Oldest Dated Works of Art. *South African Archaeological Bulletin* 31:5–11.

Whitley, D. 1998. Finding Rain in the Desert: Landscape, Gender and Far Western North American Rock-Art. In *The Archaeology of Rock-Art*, edited by C. Chippindale and P. S. C. Taçon, 11–29. Cambridge: Cambridge University Press.

Wilman, M. 1918. The Engraved Rock of Loe, Bechuanaland Protectorate. *South African Journal of Science* 15:631–633.

———. 1919. The Engraved Rock of Kopong and Loe, Bechuanaland Protectorate. *South African Journal of Science* 16:443–446.

Part II

MONUMENTS

TEN

A Sense of Time

Cultural Markers in the Mesolithic of Southern England?

MICHAEL J. ALLEN AND JULIE GARDINER

In the introductory chapters of *Altering the Earth*, Richard Bradley (1993) explored the possible links between "Neolithic" monuments, hunter-gatherers, and the natural world. He argued forcefully that the occurrence of "early Neolithic" monuments in areas already occupied by stable hunter-gatherers is no coincidence and that monument building may actually have preceded the commitment to an agricultural economy (see Allen 1997, for example). Bradley (1993:23) stated that "many monuments were constructed in places that had already acquired a special significance" and demonstrated with numerous examples the transformations that could occur at specific points in the landscape through the "changing history of cave deposits, menhirs and rock art . . . some of those places developed into monuments themselves."

In this chapter we explore this theme a little further, but take a slightly different tack. We speculate over new evidence, in the light of past assumptions, with the aim of provoking thought rather than of making any definitive statements. Evidence is coming to light that some specific locations in southern Britain were indeed identified as special places dur-ing the Mesolithic (Figure 10.1). Bradley (1993) further reminded us that hunter-gatherer communities in various parts of the world are known to have built relatively simple monuments that embellished or emphasized natural features of the landscape and were sometimes accompanied by such ephemeral acts as carving living trees or making sand paintings. Here, we suggest that it may be possible to identify special places in the archaeological record for the Mesolithic even where no "permanent" monuments were involved, the memory of which may have persisted into the Neolithic when they may have become incorporated into monumental forms. At present the evidence is slight and enigmatic, but we offer this somewhat speculative review to draw it to the attention of others.

The Mesolithic of southern Britain is characterized by distributions of flint artifacts and debitage. Some scatters have provided evidence of specific places of activity within a region; some have been intensively studied (e.g., Cranborne Chase [Barrett et al. 1991]), enabling mapping of the distributions over large areas; still others have been studied at a more detailed, local resolution (e.g., Dorset Cursus

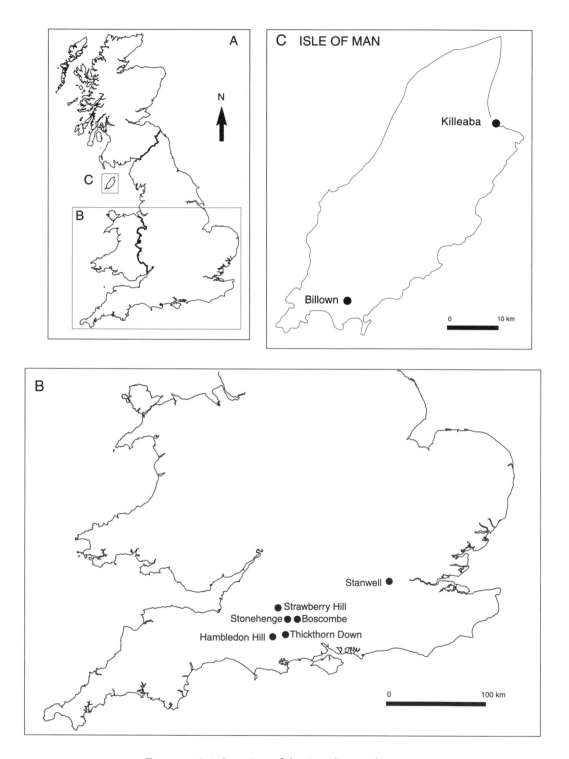

FIGURE 10.1. Location of the sites discussed in text.

[Gardiner 1985]). The archaeological record and literature assume that Mesolithic populations passed through and across the landscape in pursuit of game and plant foods, modifying the landscape only insofar as felling trees for fire or making clearings to attract and encourage game for shooting and the growth of berries, fruits, and nuts for both human and animal consumption. These populations, according to archaeological literature, seem incapable of having created any more substantial or fixed items such as fences, corrals, huts, or pits, despite their skills in knapping, woodworking, hunting, and foraging. Some suggestions of large houses in the south of England (e.g., Bowmans Farm, Hampshire [see Green 1991]) are only speculative and have now been largely questioned or discredited. There are exceptionally few convincing archaeological features of any description that can be attributed to the Mesolithic period, and none previously known to us on the chalklands of southern England.

So did these communities not even scratch the surface upon which they walked and do nothing other than walk and eat? Certainly most of the current archaeological literature suggests that they did not; further, recent constructs of social activity among Mesolithic populations have not required, nor envisaged, any permanent structures or markers in the landscape.

Yet when we look at ethnographic examples of so-called "nonsedentary" peoples, every nomadic, hunter-gathering community has, within its annual life cycle, elements of sedentism and of structures; such communities also repeatedly revisit areas or specific locations in their landscape, marking them in their minds. In many cases these markers are physical: rock-art, totem poles (American "Indians"), maypoles (English folk tradition, probably of pre-Historic origin), or natural features transformed

into sacred geographies and marking places as a structured focus of community attention. Could evidence for these markers exist in the British Mesolithic record?

THE FIRST EVIDENCE

Following an excavation in 1966, Susan Limbrey was asked to identify a fair quantity of charcoal recovered from a series of four large pits within 150–300 m of Stonehenge (Figures 10.1 and 10.2). These had been discovered during groundwork for the creation of a new visitor parking lot. Three of the four provided convincing evidence that they had held posts that had rotted in situ. They produced no artifacts and were assumed to be Late Neolithic in date (Vatcher and Vatcher 1973). Unexpectedly, the charcoal was identified as pine, a species that has not grown naturally on the chalk downlands of southern England for over 6,000 years, and certainly one that will not reach full maturity on today's thin, chalky soils (Allen 1988). Two radiocarbon dates were obtained (Table 10.1), placing the postholes firmly in an Early Mesolithic Boreal setting. A fifth pit was later revealed in 1988. It too contained evidence of the remains of a large post, and fragments of charcoal up to 60 mm in length were recovered (Figures 10.2 and 10.3).

These astonishing finds made no headlines, and it was not until we were working to produce the "definitive" excavation report for Stonehenge (Cleal et al. 1995) that the significance of these features struck home. Fortunately, though no funding had been available for analysis at the time, a column of fourteen soil samples had been taken from the 1988 pit and proved to contain not only land snails but also pollen. The charcoal fragments were again identified as pine, and the combined evidence from the

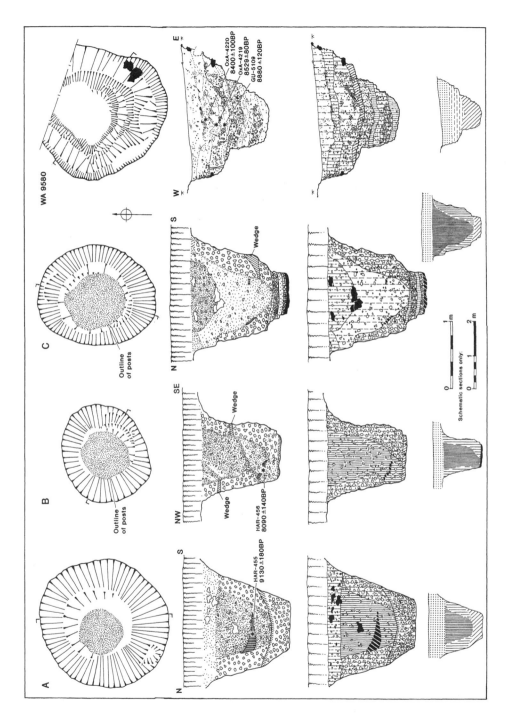

FIGURE 10.2. The post pits in the Stonehenge parking lot (from Cleal et al. 1995: fig. 25).

FIGURE 10.3. One of the Mesolithic post pits (pit 9580) in the Stonehenge parking lot (from Cleal et al. 1995: fig. 29).

molluscan and pollen analysis indicated that the post had stood in an area of open or recently cleared pine and hazel woodland, typical of the Boreal in southern England. Three more radiocarbon dates were obtained (Table 10.1) and confirmed an Early Mesolithic date for this posthole too.

What were we to make of this? No such thing had ever been reported in a Mesolithic context in Britain before, though timber posts have been noted, rarely, in Scandinavia (e.g., Skateholm, Sweden [Larsson 1989], and Vaeget Nord, Denmark [Brinch Peterson 1989]), and the fact that these extraordinary pits lay close to *the* most prestigious pre-Historic monument in the entire country, if not the whole of Europe, seemed impossibly coincidental. The date ranges show that the posts did not all stand at one time and

although the 1966 pits appear to lie in an approximate line, or on a gentle curve if the 1988 example is included (Figure 10.2), both are illusory. They are too far apart to have been joined by horizontal members, and it was calculated, from the diameters of the post pipes and surviving depths, that the posts could have stood 3 m tall. (A post pipe is the visible evidence for the actual position of the post itself in the posthole: the void left as removal or rotting of the post gets filled with soil and debris, which can be distinguished from the backfill of the larger posthole.) Our conclusions were that "the 'line' of posts may . . . represent some formal display such as a series of totem poles, or other possibly symbolic or ceremonial posts which pre-date Stonehenge by over four millennia" (Allen, in Cleal et al. 1995:56).

Table 10.1.   Radiocarbon Dates from Post Pits

Location	Material	Laboratory Reference	Radiocarbon Age (B.P.)	Calibrated Date Range (2 δ) cal B.C.E.
Stonehenge parking lot, Wiltshire				
Post pit 9580, tertiary	*Pinus* charcoal	OxA-4920	8,400 ± 100	7580–7090
Post pit 9580, secondary	*Pinus* charcoal	OxA-4919	8,520 ± 80	7700–7420
Post pit 9580, secondary	*Pinus* charcoal	GU-5109	8,880 ± 120	8090–7580
Post pit A	*Pinus* charcoal	HAR-455	9,130 ± 180	8820–7730
Postpit B	*Pinus* charcoal	HAR-456	8,090 ± 140	7480–6590
Hambledon Hill, Dorset				
Posthole F279	*Pinus sylvestris* charcoal	OxA-7845	8,400 ± 60	7580–7200
Posthole F279	*Pinus sylvestris* charcoal	OxA-7846	8,480 ± 55	7600–7380
Posthole WOWK82	*Pinus sylvestris* charcoal	OxA-7816	8,725 ± 55	8160–7590
Billown, Isle of Man				
Pit F47	Charcoal, unidentified	Beta-89312	5,650 ± 80	4710–4350
Killeaba, Isle of Man				
"Burning pit"	Oak, birch, and pine charcoal	BM-838	6,310 ± 72	5480–5070
Strawberry Hill, Wiltshire				
Ditch 15	*Pinus* charcoal	OxA-3040	9,350 ± 120	8930–8080
Ditch 15	*Cepaea* sp. land snails	OxA-3041	6,820 ± 120	5560–5140

But can we explain the coincidence? In truth, we cannot be certain, but it may be possible to throw light on one of the most vexatious questions still to be answered about Stonehenge—namely, why was it built on precisely this spot? Stonehenge lies on the top of a small, not very prominent knoll, in the middle of typical rolling chalk downland. Standing at the monument one gets a feeling of being at the center of a bowl, with Early Bronze Age monuments (mostly barrows) framing the horizon all around (see Cleal et al. 1995, chap. 3, figs. 21–23). Approach Stonehenge from almost any direction and it sits firmly and immovably on your horizon—it is a very definite focal point, but one that is far from unique on the downs. But although there is substantial evidence for Neolithic occupation and the construction of monuments in this landscape for hundreds of years before the circular ditch and bank that form the first Stonehenge were constructed, the site itself seems not to have seen any archaeologically visible Early or Middle Neolithic activity. So was the site chosen because of its views—in and out (Cleal and Gardiner forthcoming)—or was it already, somehow, special?

A clue may come from a series of animal bones placed close to the entrances on the very bottom of the encircling ditch at Stonehenge. Ox jaws, a red deer tibia, and an ox skull were radiocarbon dated and, once again, produced unexpected results. The date of the digging of the ditch can be firmly placed at between 3020 and 2910 cal B.C.E. (Allen and Bayliss 1995). The four bones, however, were very significantly older than the ditch: analysis using Baysian statistics showed that they were collected between 3900–3050 cal B.C.E. and 3020–2910 cal B.C.E. In other words, these were objects that had been curated for between 50 and 850 years, most probably for 250–350 years, before being deliberately deposited at the very bottom of a newly created monument. Where these bones were actually obtained and what they represented for the first builders of Stonehenge can only be speculated on (?skulls and hunting trophies), and that they were curated on the very spot occupied by the monument seems unlikely given the lack of other cultural evidence. We suggest that what they do show, however, is that the first builders understood the importance of ancestral belongings—that they had a keen sense of the past, a collective memory that extended over many generations.

This premonument evidence extends the sequence of activity on the exact spot of Stonehenge back over a quarter of a millennium, but leaves us a long way short of the four and a half millennia that separate the Mesolithic pits from the Neolithic monument. So is the location of Mesolithic postholes a coincidence, and, if so, is it unique? If we can demonstrate that such "coincidences" occur elsewhere, then we can explore the possibility of the remembrance of Mesolithic markers within later cultural landscapes. Now that this evidence has been discovered, shown beyond doubt, and published, we can look back at previous excavations elsewhere for undated or unrecognized features that we might, reasonably, be able to attribute to the Mesolithic. At the same time, we and other archaeologists can examine current or modern excavations in the light of this evidence. Five specific examples from recent excavations present themselves for consideration (see Figure 10.1).

At Boscombe Down, Wiltshire, on the same

chalkland and only 6 km from Stonehenge, a series of at least seven pits found in 1995 among a much larger distribution of features proved to be Late Neolithic in date. These were mostly under 1 m in diameter, were all under 0.6 m deep, and were typical of so-called "Grooved Ware" pits as seen elsewhere on the chalk of southern England, as at Fir Tree Field, and Wyke Down on Down Farm, Dorset, for example (Barrett et al. 1991; Green 1997, 2000). They variously contained placed deposits, animal bone, flints, and Grooved Ware pottery of Woodlands Style. Approximately 60 m to the south of this group was one larger, amorphous pit, ca. 1.4 m in diameter and 1.45 m deep. This did not look convincing as a natural feature, nor did it seem to be as regularly cut as the other pits (M.J.A., personal observation) though there was some suggestion of a post pipe. Despite the lack of any artifacts from this particular pit, samples for charcoal and land snails were taken for analysis. Both were highly informative. The snail assemblage contrasted with those from the Grooved Ware pits, which indicated deciduous woodland with open clearings. An impoverished, but different woodland fauna was identified, one that finds its closest parallels in assemblages from the post pits at Stonehenge. In isolation, this tentatively indicated a woodland typical of the Boreal climatic phase. The very small scraps of charcoal were difficult to identify, but produced species not present in the Grooved Ware pits: pine, birch, and willow/poplar. The analyst (Rowena Gale) stated that the species identified were typical components of Mesolithic woodland in southern Britain (Polunin and Walters 1985), suggesting, independently of the snail evidence, that these assemblages were more typical of the Boreal environment seen in the pits at Stonehenge. So here, among the least interesting and undated features, was another Mesolithic "intrusion." This site awaits full publication.

Another major center of Neolithic activity on the Wessex chalk is that at Hambledon Hill. Here an Early Neolithic causewayed enclosure complex and long barrow on the ridgelike hilltop was superseded and superimposed by an Iron Age hillfort. These overlook the surrounding low-lying clay vales. Bronze Age barrows and later Bronze Age activity are evident on the hilltop, the hill slopes, and buried under hillwash (soil moved downslope from weathering of plowed fields) and alluvium around its base. Late in the postexcavation phase *Pinus sylvestris* charcoal was identified from two isolated postholes among the myriad of pits and postholes on the hilltop. They were originally thought to be Neolithic, or at least part of the monumental complex. Neither posthole was as significant or substantial as those at Stonehenge and Boscombe but they too produced radiocarbon determinations of 8160–7590 cal B.C.E., 7600–7380 cal B.C.E., and 7580–7200 cal B.C.E.; all essentially eighth millennium B.C.E. (Table 10.1). At least one (WOWK3 F4) seems to have held a post of 0.10 m diameter, leaving a "postpipe-like concentration of charcoal" (Healy, in Mercer and Healy forthcoming). The other (HN82 F279) was less convincing and may be a natural feature (F. Healy, personal communication) or even a tree hollow.

PITS WITH ATTITUDE: SOME FURTHER EXAMPLES

Farther afield, on the gravel and brickearth of the Colne Valley, a tributary of the Thames, current excavations at Perry Oaks, Heathrow, Middlesex, have exposed a stretch (ca. 120 m) of a well-known Neolithic monument, the Stanwell Cursus. Such monuments are notoriously difficult to date (see, for instance, Barclay and Bayliss 1999; Bradley 1986). The ditches contained only a very few, nondiagnostic artifacts. Some possible Mesolithic debitage was found in this general area, but not in other parts of the excavation (Nick Plunkett personal communication). Preservation of environmental data was poor; no snails were preserved and no readily identifiable charcoal was present. Between the two ditches of the Cursus, and just to the east of it, were nine pits filled with burnt flint but, again, with very little or no charcoal. Their coincidental proximity to the Cursus suggested some association with it, and certainly some significance for this group of features was indicated. Thermoluminesence dating of burnt flint from three of the pits was arranged. These gave dates mainly in the seventh millennium B.C.E. (see Table 10.2), providing further evidence of Mesolithic activity coincidental with the siting of a later, and major, Neolithic monument.

Table 10.2. Thermoluminescence Dates from the Perry Oaks Pits in the Stanwell Cursus

QTLS Reference	Feature	Result	Range
POH21	Pit 165005	6210 ± 630 B.C.E.	6750–5490 B.C.E.
POH22	"	6750 ± 580 B.C.E.	7330–6170 B.C.E.
POH202	Pit 165009	6460 ± 700 B.C.E.	7160–5760 B.C.E.
POH151	Pit 165007	7180 ± 630 B.C.E.	7810–6550 B.C.E.

Note: If one can assume that the four dates are of flints that were heated contemporaneously, the best estimate for that event is 6670 ± 530 years B.C.E.

All of these sites reside within southern England, but our final examples are from Neolithic complexes on the Isle of Man in the Irish Sea. Recent excavations by the University of Bournemouth at Billown (Darvill 1996), in the south of the island, examined a complex Neolithic enclosure or boundary system that was accompanied by a series of vertical shafts with placed deposits at their bases; cremation deposits, including a possible cremation site; a number of large, empty jars buried upright and covered with stone slabs; and over 130 leaf arrowheads. The site was later occupied by at least one "mini-henge" with associated cremation burials. Significantly for our discussion, the site also produced an Early Mesolithic flint assemblage, a very fine later Mesolithic flint assemblage, and a pit with a clay lining and layers of charcoal interleaved with soil. Several other pits occurred close by and could be contemporaneous. A radiocarbon date of 4710–4350 cal B.C.E. (Table 10.1) was obtained. At Killeaba, ca. 25 km to the northeast of Billown, excavation of a barrow mound revealed a number of pits and cremation deposits in cists. One pit, central to the barrow mound and named the "burning pit" because it contained reddened soil and charcoal, measured 2.44 by 1.5 by 1.5 m and was assumed to relate to the Neolithic and Bronze Age burial practices (Cubbon 1978). However, it produced no cremated human bone. The burials included only charcoal of oak, but the "burning pit" contained pine, birch, and oak. It produced a date of 5480–5070 cal B.C.E. (Table 10.1). In view of the lack of any Mesolithic finds, this was dismissed by the excavator as a date from old wood. Bog oak was suggested as the culprit for the superficially erroneous date, but the nearest source is over 8 km from the site (Cubbon 1978:87). We can now identify this as another Mesolithic pit, on a site later occupied by a Neolithic ritual and funerary focus and Early Bronze Age burial ground.

With new information and interpretations at hand, archaeologists have been able to recognize Mesolithic features not previously thought to exist in the chalkland or any other British landscape. Mesolithic features, surely, have also been found in previous, published excavations, but were neither dated nor recognized for what they were. One example, again from the chalk, is of three large postholes or pits sealed beneath the Early Neolithic long barrow on Thickthorn Down, Dorset, sited at the terminal of the longest Neolithic Cursus in Britain. The excavation report described them in a rather cursory fashion, though from the plan (Drew and Piggott 1936: plan) they are the only features encircled by the ditch of the barrow. They are described as being irregular features and finally dismissed by stating that "While there was no clue as to their use or precise age, their position under the unbroken turf line indicated that they preceded the construction of the barrow by some considerable time" (Drew and Piggott 1936:81). Construction of the barrow has been radiocarbon dated to 4040–3810 cal B.C.E. (BM-2355, 5,160 + 45 years B.P.). There the story might have rested until Martin Green pointed out to us that the six fragments of charcoal from among the burnt flint in these pits had been identified and reported as mature pine, presumably Scotch pine (*Pinus silvestris* [*sic*]) by Maby (in Drew and Piggott 1936:94). Like Stonehenge, the evidence points to Boreal climatic conditions. We are currently seeking both the charcoal and any surviving soil samples from these features in the archives to verify our suspicions.

All of these sites indicate significant features of Mesolithic date, themselves anathema in the British record; there is no obvious structural or functional interpretation for any of these and all may be interpreted as marking sacred places and possibly sacred poles. All are followed, several millennia later, by Neolithic ritual or, perhaps more specifically, funerary monuments. Of course, there must always be an exception to the rule. The single exception is a dated ditch terminal sealed beneath hillwash on the scarp slope of Salisbury Plain at Strawberry Hill, Wiltshire (Allen 1992, 1994). The scarp at this point looks out over extensive views of the claylands of the Pewsey Vale. Here, in 1988, during investigations of the history of landscape development, a section was cut to expose and excavate a sequence of over 2.5 m of hillwash to study the land snail assemblages. At the base of the sequence, and cut into the chalky periglacial deposits, was a clear, shallow ditch almost 1 m wide and 0.6 m deep, terminating in a rounded end within the excavation trench. Once again the land snail assemblages produced evidence of a typical Boreal woodland (Allen 1994). Charcoal was recovered, all of which was *Pinus*, and was radiocarbon dated to 8930–8080 cal B.C.E. (Table 10.1). The combination of land snail evidence and charcoal again confirmed, with radiocarbon dates, a Mesolithic date for features cut into the chalk in an open pine woodland. At Strawberry Hill the feature does not seem to represent a pit or a post. Only 2 m of the ditch was excavated, so we have no idea how far it extended or what it described. There is no known major pre-Historic monument of any sort on or near the site, but concentrations of Mesolithic and later Neolithic flints were found on the hilltop in the shallower plowed soils. What this feature represents we cannot tell, nor is it easy to trace beneath more than 2 m of hillwash in a shallow scarp combe. It does, however, indicate the presence of other Mesolithic activity, perhaps of a more "domestic," or utilitarian nature for which we have, as yet, no other parallels in the region.

MONUMENTS AND MONUMENTS OF LANDSCAPE

Most of the sites we discuss involve the erection of isolated wooden poles or stakes. At Stonehenge, near the first three post pits, was a fourth archaeological feature (Vatcher and Vatcher 1973) that we now believe to be a tree hollow (Allen, in Cleal et al. 1995:43, figs. 24 and 27). Although it remains undated and no charcoal or other environmental or archaeological data were recovered from it, it is inviting to suggest that it may also be of Mesolithic date. Perhaps it was an important tree that was first revered and chosen as an important site before the erection of the timber artifices. At Hambledon, too, we know that one of the features may also be a tree hollow; it contained evidence not of the erection of any timber posts, but certainly of Mesolithic activity and the local burning of pine, hazel/alder, and (?)birch (Healy, in Mercer and Healy forthcoming).

A SENSE OF TIME, A SENSE OF PLACE

At Stonehenge it may seem impossible that the memory of such a place could extend over the four and a half millennia that separated the first enclosure from the pine posts of the Early Mesolithic, but, just as it was the environmental data that revealed the true date of the posts to us, so it may be the same environmental evidence that provides us with the link (see also Bradley 1991).

In a chalkland landscape covered with open pine and hazel woodlands, the floral communities of the early postglacial had still to evolve and pass through several significant climatic developments before the classic mixed deciduous woodland, so characteristic of the Early Neolithic of southern England, became established. Any interference was likely to arrest or modify this delicate process. Clearance of the woodland and the creation and maintenance of large, open glades would have provided ideal arenas for meeting and social interaction. We know that around Stonehenge the cleared area was relatively large, because it enabled the colonization and establishment of a new, different land snail fauna (Allen, in Cleal et al. 1995:55, 470–473). The establishment of the cleared area was, itself, a *biological* symbol or marker, within which more permanent artifices, such as timber posts, provided *cultural* markers. Mesolithic activity and clearance inadvertently instigated an irreversible change in the vegetation history. This change was substantial enough (both in area and biological significance) to ensure that the glade could not be immediately reassimilated within the surrounding vegetation. Vegetation composition and structure was not static, but was subject to development and flux in response to wider climatic changes. Overall there was little human disturbance, but, where it occurred on any scale, local regeneration and succession to woodland of subboreal climes may have left permanent differences in the vegetation structure of areas previously established as open, cleared land. We cannot be sure just how large an area was cleared, nor how long it remained so, but it left a permanent, or at least very long-term, visible imprint on the local vegetation pattern. Thus, once neglected, larger areas may not necessarily have become entirely revegetated or blended in with the natural foliage and may have become recognized and remembered for being "different."

Might this have been one of the attractions of the area for the siting of later monuments? Could such "different" places have an embedded "sacred" or ritual history too? Not all of the importance inherited by a locality will be embedded in its landscape history in the form of biological markers. Symbolism, among nomadic and seminomadic communities, can take many forms and be applied equally to familiar landscape features as to objects. Symbolism may persist over many generations, passed on through rituals, depiction, and oral tradition. Remembered places and sacred locations are important, and that importance becomes embedded within communities to be passed on through storytelling long after the original belief and meaning have been forgotten.

In the cases cited here, we have little idea of what the Mesolithic communities were doing and can only speculate what these pits and postholes represent. But until recently we have not even had the cause, nor evidence with which, to speculate. In southern England in the eighth and seventh millennia B.C.E., the climate was a relatively warm and dry pretemperate one (boreal, see, for example, Simmons et al. 1981), in which an open pine and hazel woodland with some birch extended over much of the land. Communities were essentially nomadic hunter-gatherers, following large "game" animals and seeking the fruits and berries of the forest when they ripened/came into season. This provided an ideal setting for the development of sophisticated, economic strategies such as those discussed by Zvelebil (1994). Societies with organized and planned food procurement strategies must also have had a level of social and economic organization not often appreciated in the published interpretations of the British Mesolithic.

In all of the examples cited, we see the excavation of pits and, in most cases, the erection of pine stakes or, at Stonehenge, large poles. Around them there is no artifactual debris, no flint artifacts or debitage that we can attribute to any visitation to the site.

Erection of these stakes and poles is a wholly new and unknown category of activity in the English Mesolithic. We assume that there was some local felling of the woodland surrounding them and, certainly at Stonehenge, there is evidence for this (Allen, in Cleal et al. 1995:41–62); but what was the activity associated with them? The sites do not seem to represent the location of utilitarian activity, such as where flint knapping or tool manufacture took place. Nor is there any evidence of butchery, bone working, nor even of fire, until the posts themselves were set alight. Though without any obvious functional role, they do represent a formal display. In recent ethnographic history hunter-gatherer societies are known to have erected posts bearing symbols that served an important ceremonial role within the complex ideology of technologically simple communities.

The features at Stonehenge have previously been likened to (but not interpreted as) totem poles (Allen, in Cleal et al. 1995:55–56, 470–477; Allen 1997). Although the term *totem pole* is strictly incorrect, it does allow us to speculate about the activity that might have taken place around the posts at Stonehenge, Boscombe, Hambledon, Thickthorn, and Stanwell. It is interesting that the totem poles of hunter-forager "Indian" communities of the northwest Pacific coast of America and Canada were usually of pine (see La Farge 1962), because these societies lived on the edge of former boreal woodlands. Their posts were embellished with heraldic signatures and iconography of peoples and history; they were erected for the ancestors—often chiefs who had passed to the other world. The locations of totem poles were sites of visitation and pilgrimage and arenas of dance, worship, belief, and symbolism. They were not a focus of settlement or mundane daily chores. The ritual activities of display and dance enhanced the significance, not of the timber uprights themselves, but of their location, ensuring that the site was a significant place in both landscape and mindscape. On leaving the site, apart from the tended and possibly painted and decorated upright timbers and the trampled and worn grass, no artifacts were left or placed—only dropped inadvertently. Another similar, simple symbolic post is the traditional English maypole. Very similar analogies can be drawn with these gaily decorated poles: set up on village greens on one day of the year for the performance of a specific ritual. This ritual no longer has any significant "meaning" to the people who dance around the pole, other than to bring them together for a communal act on an ancient festival day, the origins of which have, by and large, been forgotten. This is precisely the kind of evidence, or lack of it, that we find repeatedly at the archaeological sites reviewed here.

CONCLUSION

In summary, the following points may be made:

1. The traditional view of the Mesolithic in southern Britain does not allow for the occurrence of cut features.

2. Evidence is coming to light that such features do exist and, further, that they may have been discovered, but not recognized, during a number of excavations, both "old" and recent.

3. Where such features are identifiable, they are, with one exception to date, large pits, postholes, or even natural features, associated with indicators of Boreal woodland, which may be interpreted as marking special or symbolic places.

4. The nature of these cultural markers is not clear, but they may have been entirely organic and included decorated posts.

5. With the same exception given in no. 3, all occur on the exact spot later occupied by Neolithic monumental complexes, most of which include funerary activities.

6. The presence of cultural markers in the Mesolithic indicates the existence of belief systems involving the marking out and symbolizing of sacred geographies that probably persisted over many generations.

7. These markers may have had a significant impact on the development of natural vegetation, which served to reinforce the importance of ancestral symbolic sites even into the Neolithic, when they were absorbed by changing ideologies and transformed into a new set of monuments.

In southern England, in contrast with many of the geographical areas discussed by other contributors to this volume, we are severely hampered in our interpretation of the features we have described by the lack of physical remains other than holes in the ground, tiny shells, microscopic spores, and scraps of burnt wood. No more substantial organic remains have been found, nor any "art," nor, indeed, any direct link with the cultural groups who created them—or the monuments that succeeded them—through the survival of "primitive" Indigenous people. Yet even with our ephemeral, largely environmental evidence, we are able to argue that Mesolithic communities marked specific points in the landscape as symbolic or "special" and suggest that such localities could remain as symbolic referrents over very long time periods.

This should come as no surprise. As a number of authors note in this volume, nomadic or seminomadic communities who make regular and repeated movements through their familiar landscape mark and use points within it in specific, often highly structured, ways. In some places the knowledge, meaning, and implications of such cultural markers may persist through many generations. In others, their meanings may be lost, but the marker itself may be preserved and reused. It is not inconceivable that the endurance of special places, such as Stonehenge, over many centuries, could have been achieved through the persistence of memory rather than as a direct inheritance of cultural symbolism. Long after the reason for, and meaning of, the erection of timber posts by Mesolithic ancestors had been forgotten or transformed by changing social, economic, and ideological developments, the memory of the place in which they were erected may have persisted. Such places may only have been physically identifiable in the Neolithic by subtle (to our eyes) but significant landscape features, yet the symbolism may have remained sufficient to prompt the reestablishment of cultural/political markers though the construction of new forms of powerful monuments.

The location of these Mesolithic "monuments" in places later reemphasized by Neolithic traditions and monument building is not a coincidence (see also Bradley 1993). However, a word of caution is needed. Only on sites where later activity is easily recognized have we any real chance of finding these archaeologically more ephemeral Mesolithic features. Their true extent, however, may be much wider, as the discovery of the ditch under hillwash at Strawberry Hill indicates. For every persistent place in the landscape there may be many more that were soon forgotten and whose recovery is likely to be chance indeed.

We hope that this brief excursion shows that the hypothesis of cultural continuity between Mesolithic and Neolithic designated and marked places deserves focused research. Whether this designation is through a remembrance of things past or by successive recognition of significant features in the landscape, is not an easy question to answer. If traces of cultural markers remained visible for long periods, then perhaps the former applies; if markers disappeared, yet landscape features remained, then the latter possibility is strengthened. Either way, this seems an avenue worthy of further exploration.

NOTE

We thank Bruno and Meredith for inviting us to explore our ideas on Mesolithic features we have encountered over the past few years and Ros Cleal and Martin Green for their encouragement. We are grateful to all those archaeologists who have allowed us to refer to their unpublished data. In this respect we specifically thank Frances Healy and Roger Mercer for providing detailed information from the recent dating program from Hambledon Hill and allowing us to use those data before publication. We also thank John Lewis and Gill Andrews, Framework Archaeology, BAA and Thames Water Utilities, Ltd., for permission to use the data from the Perry Oaks excavations (Stanwell Cursus) at an early stage in the postexcavation analysis of that site; Nick Plunkett for his observations on the lithics from that site; and Andrew Fitpatrick for permission to use the information on the Boscombe pit. Richard Bradley, Nic Dolby, Frances Healy, John Lewis, Geoffrey Wainwright, and Rob Young kindly read a draft of this chapter for us. Figures 10.2 and 10.3 are reproduced by permission of Wessex Archaeology.

REFERENCES CITED

Allen, M. J. 1988. Archaeological and Environmental Aspects of Colluviation in South-East England. In *Man-Made Soils*, edited by W. Groenmann-van Waateringe and M. Robinson, 69–92. British Archaeological Reports, International Series 410. Oxford.

———. 1992. Products of Erosion and the Prehistoric Land-use of the Wessex Chalk. In *Past and Present Soil Erosion: Archaeological and Geographical Per-spectives*, edited by M. G. Bell and J. Boardman, 37–52. Oxford: Oxbow Books.

———. 1994. *The Land-use History of the Southern English Chalklands with an Evaluation of the Beaker Period Using Colluvial Data: Colluvial Deposits as Environmental and Cultural Indicators.* Ph.D. thesis, University of Southampton, Southampton.

———. 1997. Environmental and Land-Use: The Economic Development of the Communities Who Built Stonehenge (An Economy to Support the Stones). In *Science and Stonehenge*, edited by B. W. Cunliffe and A. C. Renfrew. *Proceedings of the British Academy* 92:115–144.

Allen, M. J., and A. Bayliss. 1995. Appendix 2: The Radiocarbon Dating Programme. In *Stonehenge in Its Landscape; The Twentieth Century Excavations*, R. M. J. Cleal, K. E. Walker, and R. Montague. English Heritage Archaeological Report 10:511–535.

Barclay, A., and A. Bayliss. 1999. Cursus Monuments and the Radiocarbon Problem. In *Pathways and Ceremonies: The Cursus Monuments of Britain and Ireland*, edited by A. Barclay and J. Harding, 11–29. Neolithic Studies Group Seminar Papers 4. Oxford: Oxbow Books.

Barrett, J., R. Bradley, and M. Green. 1991. *Landscape, Monuments and Society: The Prehistory of Cranborne Chase*. Cambridge: Cambridge University Press.

Bradley, R. 1986. Radiocarbon and the Cursus Problem. In *Archaeological Results from Accelerator Dating*, edited by J. A. J. Gowlett and R. E. M. Hedges, 139–141. Oxford: Oxford University Committee for Archaeology.

———. 1991. Ritual, Time and History. *World Archaeology* 23:209–219.

———. 1993. *Altering the Earth: The Origins of Monuments in Britain and Continental Europe*. Monograph Series No. 8. Edinburgh: Society of Antiquaries of Scotland.

Brinch Peterson, E. 1989. Vøget Nord: Excavation, Documentation and Interpretation of a Mesolithic Site at Vedbaek, Denmark. In *The Mesolithic of Europe:*

Papers Presented at the Third International Symposium, Edinburgh, 1985, edited by C. Bonsall, 325–330. Edinburgh: John Donald.

Cleal, R. M. J., and J. Gardiner. Forthcoming. Places and Perspectives: The View from Stonehenge. In *Ritual Landscapes: Proceedings of the 60th Anniversary Conference of the Prehistoric Society, Dublin, 1995*, edited by G. Cooney and J. Gardiner.

Cleal, R. M. J., K. E. Walker, and R. Montague. 1995. *Stonehenge in Its Landscape: The Twentieth Century Excavations.* English Heritage Archaeological Report 10.

Cubbon, A. M. 1978. Excavation at Killeaba, Ramsey, Isle of Man. *Proceedings of the Prehistoric Society* 44:69–95.

Darvill, T. 1996. Billown, Isle of Man. *Current Archaeology* 150:232–237.

Drew, C. D., and S. Piggott. 1936. The Excavation of Long Barrow 163a on Thickthorn Down, Dorset. *Proceedings of the Prehistoric Society* 2:77–96.

Gardiner, J. P. 1985. Intra-Site Patterning in the Flint Assemblage from the Dorset Cursus, 1984. *Proceedings of the Dorset Natural History and Archaeology Society* 105:87–93.

Green, F. J. 1991. Mesolithic Structures in the Test Valley: Bowmans Farm. *Past* 11:1–2.

Green, M. 1997. A Second Neolithic Henge and Neolithic Buildings Uncovered on Wyke Down, Cranborne Chase, Dorset. *Past* 27:1–3.

———. 2000. *A Landscape Revealed: 10,000 Years on a Chalkland Farm.* Stroud: Tempus.

La Farge, O. 1962. *A Pictorial History of the American Indian.* London: Spring Books.

Larsson, L. 1989. Late Mesolithic Settlement and Cemeteries at Skateholm, Southern Sweden. In *The Mesolithic of Europe: Papers Presented at the Third International Symposium, Edinburgh, 1985*, edited by C. Bonsall, 367–378. Edinburgh: John Donald.

Mercer, R., and F. Healy. Forthcoming. *Hambledon Hill, Dorset: Excavation and Survey of a Neolithic Monument Complex and Its Surrounding Landscape, 1974–86.* English Heritage Archaeological Monograph. London.

Polunin, O., and M. Walters. 1985. *A Guide to the Vegetation of Britain and Europe.* Oxford: Oxford University Press.

Simmons, I. G., G. W. Dimbleby, and C. Grigson. 1981. The Mesolithic. In *The Environment in British Prehistory*, edited by I. G. Simmons and M. Tooley, 82–124. London: Duckworth.

Vatcher, F. de M., and L. Vatcher. 1973. Excavation of Three Post-holes in Stonehenge Carpark. *Wiltshire Archaeology and Natural History Magazine* 68:57–63.

Zvelebil, M. 1994. Plant Use in the Mesolithic and Its Role in the Transition to Farming. *Proceedings of the Prehistoric Society* 60:95–134.

ELEVEN

A Place of Special Meaning

Interpreting Pre-Historic Monuments in the Landscape

CHRIS SCARRE

The earliest monuments of western Europe are characterized by their use of locally available materials such as timber, stone, and earth to create structures that by their very composition have a certain resonance with their surroundings. In some instances, there appears to have been an attempt to mimic, reference, or reproduce local landforms in the built monument (Scarre 2000; Tilley 1994, 1996). The pre-Historic communities who created these monuments did so in the context of a particular understanding of the landscape in which they lived, investing places within it with meaning, including religious or mythological significance. Conspicuous features of the land that are still visible today, such as hills, lakes, rivers, and ravines, may have been prominent in this kind of understanding, attracting mythological or sacred traditions. We may be justified in assuming that such landforms were imbued by early societies with special meaning, as is common worldwide today. In the absence of a continuous written or oral tradition or of surviving ethnographic accounts, however, it is impossible to gain direct knowledge of these early meanings (what Chippin-

dale and Taçon [1998] have called *informed* knowledge). We may, however, identify places of special significance by means of the pre-Historic monuments built on them or near them, or by associated deposits of artifacts (Chippindale and Taçon's [1998] *formal* methods).

The evidence provided by Greek and Roman writers on the nature of religious practices in northwestern Europe during the last century B.C.E. and the early centuries C.E. stresses the "natural" or nonbuilt nature of many traditional places of worship. These include, for example, sacred groves, which would be extremely difficult to identify archaeologically. The evidence of these texts must, however, be approached with caution, and one recent commentator has argued that the association of groves with Celtic religion may well be "a literary construct of the first century A.D." (Webster 1995:448). An interest in lakes and bogs, by contrast, is borne out by discoveries of precious metalwork within them and by the well-known "bog bodies," some of which at least may have been votive offerings (Glob 1969; van der Sanden 1996; but see Briggs 1995). Examples from Bolkilde Bog and Sigersdal in Denmark have been dated to the fourth millennium B.C.E. (Biennike et al. 1986), and a still older "bog body," dating to the ninth millennium B.C.E., was found at Koelbjerg on the Danish island of Fyn (van der Sanden 1996:84). Rivers, too, appear to have had a special, possibly sacred significance and were places for the deposition of polished stone axes, precious metalwork, and also of human remains, the latter going back at least as far as the second millennium B.C.E. (Bradley 1990; Bradley and Gordon 1988; Torbrügge 1971).

Whether the common names still attached to prominent hills such as the Paps (breasts) of Jura in Scotland or to stunning geological phenomena such as the Giant's Causeway in Ireland constitute evidence of a long-standing sacred or mythological significance is far from clear. The attribution of significance to such prominent features would, however, be in accordance with the behavior of people throughout the world in ethnographic contexts, as well as in Western cultures. Related to this is the question of whether pre-Historic communities may have understood certain natural features to be the work of earlier human communities; or conversely, whether they may have interpreted ruined and degraded humanly constructed monuments as natural in their origin.

Pre-Historic monuments visible in the landscape have frequently attracted popular names that interpret them as the work of giants or supernatural beings. Presumably, these names were given as a means of understanding one's surroundings, of situating it in the known world. Presumably also, these names date to a period after memory of their construction had vanished. The use of large stones, in particular, was a characteristic that generated curiosity and demanded explanation. Stonehenge was described by medieval writer Geoffrey of Monmouth as the *Chorea Gigantum* or Giants' Round (Chippindale 1994:22). Likewise, in Brittany such appella-

tions as the Roche aux Fées (the "Fairies' Stone": for the impressive dolmen angevin at Essé, among others) inscribe some of these monuments in a world of non-Christian belief and tradition (for a general survey of this nomenclature, see Reinach 1893).

Such traditional accounts, transmitted orally from generation to generation until recorded by antiquarians in the eighteenth and nineteenth centuries, are Europe's indigenous traditions. They represent the folk stories that have, in the past, explained people's experience of the world. Yet worldviews, and the stories and legends that have emerged from them, are not immutable, but have undoubtedly changed in the course of many transmissions (cf. David and Wilson [1999] with respect to Australia's Dreaming beliefs).

European folklore, as it is recorded, expresses only the latest stage in a long sequence of popular beliefs or mythologies about prominent monuments. Many of these accounts may have very shallow time depth. Whether any of them go far back into the past—let alone to pre-Historic times—must seriously be questioned. Reinach, indeed, took the view that popular names implying a funerary function for megalithic tombs postdate the first excavations at those sites (Reinach 1893:220). Cooney commented on the political motivation from early historic times that lies behind the myths associated with the Boyne Valley tombs in Ireland (Cooney 1994). The presence of Christian protagonists in a story often reveals its relatively recent formation, at least in the form we have it today. This is true, for example, of the Friar's Heel at Stonehenge (not to be confused with the Heel Stone), said to have been thrown by the Devil in a rage and to bear the impression where it struck the friar on the heel (Burl 1991). In the same category may be placed the tradition attached to the famous menhir of Saint-Samson in the Côtes-d'Armor, which holds it to be one of the three plugs that block the mouth of hell; when the Devil tried to push it away, he was prevented by the combined action of Saints Samson and Michael, who put it back in place. One feature of the Saint-Samson tradition is clearly an attempt to explain the leaning nature of the stone, which may be an ancient characteristic, but is unlikely to be original (Guénin 1936, summarized in Giot and Morzadec 1990).

The value of such folklore for an understanding of the pre-Historic monuments to which they are attached lies not in their historical accuracy but in the light they throw on the premodern or prescientific attitudes to these structures and the ways in which they attract and accrete mythologies and explanations. They underline the numinous nature of the premodern understanding of landscape features and pre-Historic monuments, suggesting that this understanding linked them with a world of beings and events both real and imaginary.

THE GRÉE DE COJOUX

Such is the general background against which we should seek to understand the significance given to particular landscape features and locales by the pre-Historic communities who inhabited them. Such an approach must rely on archaeological evidence to identify which particular areas or features may have been of special significance. Furthermore, the archaeological evidence, be it funerary, repesentational (as in the case of rock-art), or ritual deposition, must be used to guide interpretations of the nature of that significance. To illustrate this approach, we have taken the case of the Grée de Cojoux, an upland lying immediately to the west of the village of Saint-Just in the southwestern corner of the Ille-et-Vilaine *département* of Brittany (France) (Figure 11.1). The

area around Saint-Just boasts one of the largest concentrations of Neolithic monuments in inland Brittany. The aim here is to interpret those monuments in light of the topography of the Grée de Cojoux itself. What was it that led pre-Historic communities of the fifth–third millennia B.C.E. to build such a complex of monuments on this particular upland?

The principal monuments on the Grée de Cojoux are well known both from nineteenth-century accounts and from the excavations carried out by Le Roux and colleagues in 1978–1981 (Le Roux et al. 1989) and by Briard and colleagues in 1990–1992 (Briard et al. 1995). The monuments that are still visible today (others have been destroyed) include two *tertres tumulaires*, four passage graves, a lateral entry grave, four alignments, an arc of standing stones, and less-well-preserved remains of several further monuments (Figure 11.2).

In geological and topographical terms, there is nothing very remarkable about the form of the Grée de Cojoux. It is not particularly high—no higher than the other hills around it—nor (on three of its four sides) is it particularly steep-sided. Yet it is a dis-

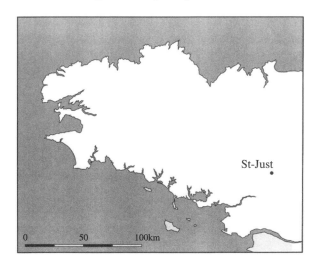

FIGURE 11.1. Location of Saint-Just within the Brittany region of northwestern France.

crete area of upland, its limits defined by topographical features and its special identity by the pre-Historic monuments that were built upon it. Monuments and topography combine to give it a special character, an elevated block of terrain set apart from the land around it (Figure 11.3).

Approaching from the east, the Grée begins as a gentle rise, flanked by steeper slopes to the north and south. On the south side the slope runs down to a narrow valley, and to the north the ground falls away to a broader plain. The surface of the upland is covered by a thin soil, with exposures of the underlying schist bedrock showing through in places. As we near the western end of the Grée, the terrain becomes steadily more accented, until at the western limit we find ourselves standing on the dramatic cliff edge overlooking the narrow, steep-sided ravine with the Etang du Val

at its base. Today this ravine is frequented by rock climbers as a recognized *site d'escalade*.

Beyond the Etang begins the Grée de Bocadève, which is effectively a continuation of the Grée de Cojoux. The two form in a sense a single elongated upland, separated only by the narrow valley now occupied by the Etang du Val. In elevation the Grée de Bocadève mirrors the Grée de Cojoux, beginning at the cliff-edged Etang du Val, rising westward to nearly 80 m, and then fading away in a gentle downward incline. If anything, the Grée de Bocadève is more impressive than the Grée de Cojoux, with steeper slopes to north and south. The southern flank of Bocadève is further emphasized by a cliff edge, notably at the southwestern corner where the outcrop known as the Rocher de Bocadève can be found. Yet apart from an east-west alignment of modest-sized standing

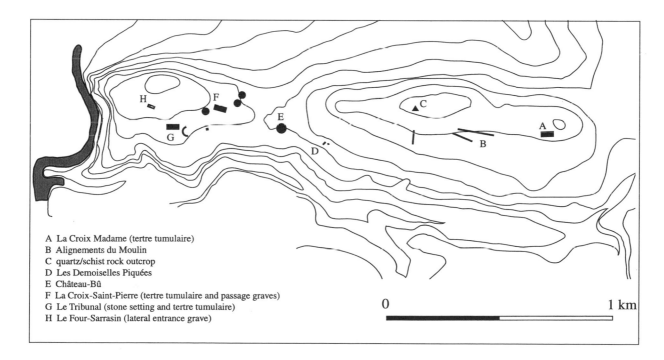

A La Croix Madame (tertre tumulaire)
B Alignements du Moulin
C quartz/schist rock outcrop
D Les Demoiselles Piquées
E Château-Bû
F La Croix-Saint-Pierre (tertre tumulaire and passage graves)
G Le Tribunal (stone setting and tertre tumulaire)
H Le Four-Sarrasin (lateral entrance grave)

0   1 km

FIGURE 11.2. Pre-Historic monuments on the Grée de Cojoux: only those currently surviving are shown.

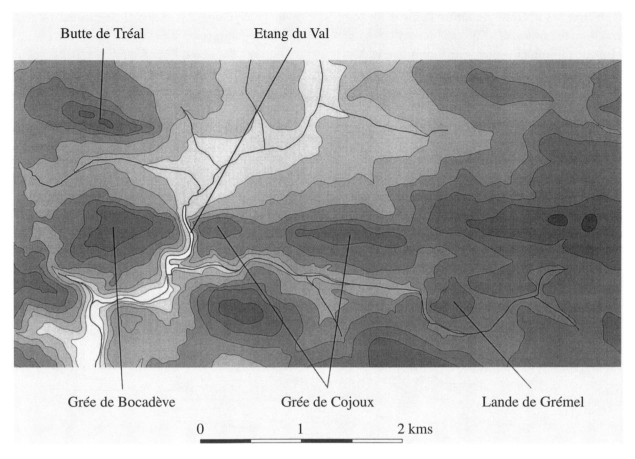

FIGURE 11.3. The Saint-Just area, showing principal landscape features: note especially the Grée de Cojoux, the Grée de Bocadève, and the intervening ravine occupied by the Etang du Val.

stones, with a second running approximately at right angles (Bézier 1883; Briard et al. 1995:151; Le Roux et al. 1989), the Grée de Bocadève has little in the way of pre-Historic monuments and certainly nothing to rival those of the Grée de Cojoux.

The greater significance of Cojoux over Bocadève, as shown by the density of pre-Historic monuments, may lie in the orientation of the hill. In Briard's view, "Il est indéniable que la Grée de Cojoux a été choisie volontairement à cause de son orientation est-ouest, idéalement placée entre le lever et le coucher du soleil. De ce fait le système des monuments de Saint-Just s'échelonne principalement d'est en ouest"[1] (Briard, in Briard et al. 1995:149). This is an interpretation to which we shall return. We may indeed go beyond Briard's observation of the east-west orientation to suggest that the crucial feature of the Grée de Cojoux is what lies at its west, toward the setting sun. It is here, at this end of Cojoux, that the ravine of the Etang du Val lies. Thus, west may have been a direction of special significance, a suggestion that may be related to the concentration of funerary monuments toward the western end of the Grée de Cojoux.

One further topographical feature should be

noted. The Grée de Cojoux has an asymmetrical profile, with the ridge that marks the crest of the upland lying toward its northern edge; thus the broader southern flank presents a gently sloping surface tilted toward the sun. This is not a characteristic unique to the Grée de Cojoux, but it may have a bearing on the deployment of monuments across its surface; the sun's movement during the course of the day perhaps played a role in the ritual practices performed there.

We may complement this account of the topographical boundedness of the Grée de Cojoux by a brief consideration of the cultural limits. Field walking by Jean-François Ducloyer has revealed a series of pre-Historic settlements around the edge of the Grée de Cojoux (Briard et al. 1995:98 ff.). These include settlement H1 at La Croix-Madame, at the east of the Grée de Cojoux, with Mesolithic and Middle Neolithic material (both Cerny and Chasséen type). The location of this settlement may mark the eastern limit of the sacred zone, though sherds and flint were discovered during excavations on the Grée de Cojoux itself, at both the Le Moulin alignments and in the body of the *tertre tumulaire* at La Croix-Saint-Pierre (Briard et al. 1995; Le Roux et al. 1989). It is significant, however, that in both cases the material (Cerny) belonged to the earliest phase of the Breton Neolithic and appeared to predate the monuments near or in which it was found. This adds a chronological dimension to the development of the Grée de Cojoux as a sacred place; a character it may have acquired during the course of the fifth millennium B.C.E.

AMBIGUITIES: THE WORK OF HUMAN HANDS?

In attempting to interpret the distribution of monuments at Saint-Just, it is important to bear in mind the degree of destruction suffered by the Grée de Cojoux

and adjacent areas in recent centuries. Already in 1864, Albert Ramé was aware of the problem: "Il est un peu tard pour tenter cette étude à Saint-Just; le nombre des pierres détruites dans ces dernières années depuis le morcellement de la lande est considérable; il surpasse, me dit-on, celui des pierres demeurées debout"[2] (Ramé 1864:82). Added to the pace of destruction is the difficulty of placing confidence in early accounts of monuments no longer extant. Twenty years after Ramé, Philippe Bézier included a description of the Saint-Just monuments in his *Inventaire des Monuments Mégalithiques du Département de l'Ille-et-Vilaine* (1883). Ramé and Bézier together provide our best evidence for the condition and appearance of these monuments in the nineteenth century, but in some cases their accounts are misleading or inaccurate, in other cases they cannot easily be reconciled, and in certain instances there are grounds for suspecting that what is being described is a natural or partly natural feature. Thus in the space between the Le Moulin alignments and the Demoiselles Piquées, both Ramé and Bézier referred to an alignment oriented east-west. Ramé described this as "un léger exhaussement du sol, ayant l'aspect d'un sillon dirigé de l'Est à l'Ouest, . . . coupé çà et là par de très-petites dalles de schiste espacées de sept à huit pas. Il semblerait indiquer une longue rangée de tombes placées à la file"[3] (Ramé 1864:90). This feature, which cannot be securely identified today, could be partly or largely natural, or an old field boundary, or a pre-Historic ceremonial structure.

In his opening description of the Grée de Cojoux, Ramé described it as "une plaine semée de plusieurs centaines de blocs, généralement en quartz blanc et luisant au soleil. Leur nombre s'augmente encore, à quelque distance, de toutes les saillies naturelles qui forment l'échine de la lande"[4] (Ramé 1864:82). This figure of a natural spine, visible in places where the bedrock protrudes on the surface, is especially appropriate for the ridge that runs along the top of the Grée, frequently exposed as a low cliff or an area of bare rock. What is most suggestive in Ramé's description, however, is the direct connection he makes between the cultural monuments and the *saillies naturelles*, the natural outcrops. It may indeed be the case that we should consider the monuments as merely additions pointing up or elaborating an existing natural "monument" or series of monuments constituted by these outcrops.

Bézier, too, had difficulty in distinguishing cultural from natural features in the Saint-Just area. This is most evident in his description of monuments situated around the periphery of the Grée de Cojoux. One and a half kilometers to the east of Saint-Just stands the cluster of hamlets of Bel-Air and Sévéroué. A number of megalithic-sized blocks

survive here, some of them perhaps abandoned from pre-Historic quarrying (Briard et al. 1995: 113; Le Roux et al. 1989). What principally drew Bézier's attention were the "dolmen" and the "roches" or "pierres" close to Le Champ-Matelin. Both are illustrated in his work (Bézier 1883: pl. XXV and XXVI: reproduced here as Figures 11.4 and 11.5). Of the dolmen, he stated "Il est incontestable que cette pierre a été placée à dessein dans la position qu'elle occupe"[5] (Bézier 1883:197). Yet modern authorities are agreed that this is a natural feature. Bézier was more cautious when it comes to the "pierres": "Ces blocs reposent sur un roc de même espèce, et l'on se demande si l'on est en présence d'un jeu de la nature ou si, jadis, ces masses ont été dressées par l'homme, ou bien si, sortant de la carrière, elles n'attendent pas là, depuis ces siècles,

FIGURE 11.4. The "dolmen" of Le Champ-Matelin, plate XXV in Bézier (1883).

FIGURE 11.5. The "roches" of Le Champ-Matelin, plate XXVI in Bézier (1883).

une destination que désormais elles ne recevront jamais"[6] (Bézier 1883:196).

More striking still than the megalithic blocks and natural outcrops around Bel-Air and Sévéroué are the features encountered at Tréal, a prominent hill a kilometer northwest of the Grée de Cojoux. This is the site of the lateral entry grave of Tréal, one of the most famous monuments of the Saint-Just complex. The monument is situated in the middle of the southern side of the hilltop, a little way from the steep southern edge. It is too far back to be visible from below, or from the Grée de Cojoux, but its position can easily be determined because of its proximity to the prominent Palette de Tréal, a conspicuous schist outcrop, heavily eroded into ridges and gullies. What Bézier drew

attention to on the Palette de Tréal is where in one place a detached slab of schist has come to rest horizontally across these ridges, forming a pseudodolmen: "dominant le ravin, la dernière tranche de roche est détachée de la masse et repose horizontalement sur la crête de plusieurs autres tranches qui lui servent de supports. Aperçue d'en bas, c'est une colossale table de dolmen que l'on croit avoir devant et à 15 mètres audessus de soi"[7] (Bézier 1883:214).

This nineteenth-century confusion between human and natural features may today be regarded as a mixture of ignorance coupled with quaint romanticism. Yet in blurring the distinction between pre-Historic monuments and natural landforms, these accounts draw attention to an ambiguity that must equally have affected pre-Historic societies. The pre-Historic communities who frequented the Saint-Just area in the Neolithic period may well have regarded prominent natural features as the specific creations of beings either human or divine, and equally may sometimes have considered the monuments built by earlier generations, in their denuded state, as part of the same category of phenomena. Furthermore, they may consciously have been mimicking in their constructions the natural outcrops or landmarks visible on the Grée de Cojoux and its surroundings. A recent study of the Kerlescan alignments near Carnac in the southern Morbihan has shown that the individual stones were raised upright near the positions where they had been lying as natural blocks (Sellier 1995). Far from being quarried elsewhere and dragged to the site, the Neolithic builders simply dug out the stones and erected them close to where they had found them, at the same time arranging them in approximately straight lines. It was as if the potential for the Kerlescan alignments was already present, only thinly concealed, in this particular locus long before the Neolithic builders began to dig out the stones and erect them. One might even suggest that the scatter of natural granite blocks was already imbued with significance, and it was this that led to their transformation into an alignment. Similarly, at the Grée de Cojoux, it could be argued that the monuments constitute simply the elaboration of an existing landform, giving emphasis to features and significances already present in the natural world.

ANCESTRAL COLORS

One prominent outcrop on the Grée de Cojoux lies upslope of the Le Moulin alignments. The alignments consist of three stone rows: two running approximately east-west and a third at right angles, taking in a north-south direction perpendicular to the slope. This north-south row, the *file ouest*, consists today of five massive quartz blocks forming a line some 25 m long. Le Roux and colleagues remarked that the direction of this alignment, if continued 100 m or so to the north (upslope), leads directly to "un saillant rocheux naturel de la ligne de crête"[8] (Le Roux et al. 1989:8). Hence the row of standing stones apears to be aligned on a natural rock formation, blending the cultural and natural in just the way we have remarked. But there is more to be said. For, approaching from the east, the outcrop appears to be of dull gray-brown schist, little different from the other outcrops at this level along the ridge; but continuing past the outcrop it is something of a surprise to find that its western face is an exposure of brilliant white quartz. The outcrop forms a kind of natural menhir or monument, combining within itself the two principal materials that are elsewhere separated in the individual standing stones of quartz or schist. This conjunction may well have betokened buried qualities of special significance hidden in the rock of the Grée de Cojoux.

The Grée de Cojoux is formed predominantly of schist, which occurs in a variety of forms. These are represented in the menhirs of Le Moulin *file sud* and in other monuments of the complex: fine-grained *schist homogène*, the coarser *schist noduleux*, and the very lumpy *schist à gros nodules*. The colors are dull reddish brown to blue gray, with brighter yellow or orange patches where erosion or the bedding of the rock has altered the surface. Textures and colors are striking; the textures in particular, though the colors are matte and muted. The possible significance of the natural shapes and textures for the pre-Historic communities must not be ignored: the flame-like profile of menhir 21 (*file sud*), for example, as opposed to the nodular menhir 3, the latter resembling a mass of fused and fossilized coral. These significances are lost to us, but that they once existed is supported by the careful alternation of nodular and fine-grained schist in the first four extant menhirs of the southern *file* at Le Moulin.

Cutting across the dull brown schist of the Grée de Cojoux are veins of brilliant white quartz. A narrow band, some 15 cm thick, runs perpendicularly across the northern *file* of the Le Moulin alignments. A more substantial seam forms part of the schist/quartz outcrop referred to earlier. Quartz seams are also exposed in the cliffs that mark the western limit of the Grée de Cojoux, above the Etang du Val. One particularly prominent vein runs vertically down the cliff face (Figure 11.6). The mixture of schist and quartz in the monuments of the Grée de Cojoux thus has resonance with the presence of both materials in the underlying rock.

The contrast in materials extends beyond color to the shapes of the stones. The schist of the Grée de Cojoux breaks up naturally to provide workable slabs. The shape of the schist menhirs is dictated by the natural cleavage of the material, giving long narrow blocks with sharp and angular profiles. The quartz and quartzite is very different in appearance, generally taking the form of squatter, more rounded blocks. Some of this was local in origin, but better-quality material was available at Plougastel, 4 km to the southwest. The large quartz uprights of Château-Bû, the central monument of the Grée, were a special case, coming from veins on the Lande de Quily, 3 km to the south, the upland on the far side of the Saint-Just valley. The largest quartz block weighed 25–30 tonnes (*file nord* menhir 2) (Le Roux et al. 1989). There is no question here of the effort involved in transporting and erecting huge monoliths on the scale of the 280-tonne Grand

FIGURE 11.6. Quartz seam in the cliffs above the Etang du Val.

Menhir Brisé in the Morbihan (Le Roux 1997). Nonetheless, the preferred use of quartz for many of the monuments on the Grée de Cojoux, involving considerable labor to bring it to the upland, implies that it held some special value or meaning. The striking appearance of the quartz blocks may have been a crucial part of that meaning.

The use of colored materials in pre-Historic monuments has recently been the subject of renewed attention (Jones and Bradley 1999; Lynch 1998). In the cairns at Balnuaran of Clava, Bradley noted the deployment of red orthostats in surfaces that face toward the setting sun, and pink or white quartz in sections facing the rising sun, the latter perhaps intentionally to reflect the light (Bradley 1998a:232; Jones and Bradley 1999). Quartz was used at the Newgrange passage grave in Ireland, perhaps to give a striking revetment to the mound, as envisaged by the excavator Michael O'Kelly and incorporated in the reconstruction (O'Kelly 1982), though other interpretations are possible (Bradley 1998b:104). Brightness, indeed, is one of the key qualities of quartz and has given it special significance in many ethnographically documented contexts. To give two examples, from Australia and western North America: Taçon remarked, "brightness and colour more generally are associated with ancestral power in northern Australia . . . and it is this power which is tapped into at sacred sites and in ceremony" (Taçon 1999:123). He also noted that quartz and quartzite have a particular association with Ancestral Beings through their brightness and iridescence. In recent times, quartzite has been considered by Aboriginal groups to be the petrified remains of the ancestors, and tools made of this material had special symbolic power (Taçon 1991). Taçon also remarked that the association with powerful Ancestral Beings extends to large, unusual outcrops of sandstone and quartzite

that dominate the landscape in western Arnhem Land (Taçon 1991:196).

Whitley and colleagues noted a systematic association between quartz and shamanism in western North America (Whitley et al. 1999:235). They noted that "quartz crystals were widely associated with, and used ritually by, shamans and sorcerers," and cited the presence of intentionally placed quartz rocks close to rock paintings and engravings in support. This association extends to the incorporation of a quartz vein in an engraved motif at Corn Springs in the California desert, and to the painting of a quartz vein at Balch Camp in the Sierra Nevada. They attributed this connection between quartz and shamanism to the physical properties of quartz rocks. The widespread belief in the American Southwest that the breaking of quartz rocks releases supernatural power may derive from the electrical qualities of quartz rocks, which can generate sparks and emit visible light when they are broken or rubbed together. This physical quality of triboluminescence "provided the natural model upon which widespread shamanistic beliefs about quartz and other crystals were based" (Whitley et al. 1999:236). They also noted the practice of wedging pieces of quartz in rock cracks at rock-art sites. The supernatural world was thought to lie within the rock, and the cracks were conceived as portals that "were believed to open up for the shaman when he entered his trance and went into the sacred realm" (Whitley et al. 1999:234). Although this ethnography relates specifically to Australia and southwestern North America, and refers mainly to small pieces of quartz, the special significance of quartz across much of the earth during recent times—including many quarters of Western society—throws light on its likely significance to early European communities as a special substance. We may in particular be led to wonder whether the quartz seams that run across the Grée de Cojoux, and especially those that are prominently visible in the sides of the ravine above the Etang du Val, were thought of as entrances into another world. The raising of quartz menhirs on the surface of the plateau may have been an attempt to harness this symbolic power.

That the schist/quartz contrast was held significant by the builders of the monuments at Saint-Just is demonstrated by systematic patterns in the use of the two materials. The quartz had the advantage of brightness, reflecting the sun's rays. We may recall here Ramé's early description of the Grée de Cojoux as "une plaine semée de plusieurs centaines de blocs, généralement en quartz blanc et luisant au soleil"[9] (Ramé 1964:82). As we have seen, most of the quartz blocks came not from the Grée itself, but from sources in the surrounding area. Its deployment in the monuments on the Grée may be an intentional reference to the quartz veins that run through the schist bedrock of this site: an emphasising of a natural (and largely hidden) feature. The locally available schist was used to form the body of the burial mounds, but both schist and quartz were employed in menhirs and alignments. In these cases the brightness and brilliance of the white quartz against the darker matte coloring of the schist slabs make a powerful contrast.

The contrast was put to good use by the builders of the Le Moulin alignments (Figure 11.7). The northern and western *files* are formed exclusively of quartz blocks of sometimes massive dimensions, but the southern *file* consists of ten menhirs of different kinds of schist (1, 2, 3, 4, 6, 12, 15, 16, 18, 21), plus three of quartz (14, 17, 19), and a series of sockets generally represented by cuttings in the bedrock with schist packing stones (*calages* 5, 7, 8, 9, 10, 11, 13, 20). That some at least of these *calages* once supported menhirs is shown by the discovery of the broken base of a schist menhir still fixed firmly in *calage* 10, and

by fragments of quartz in *calage* 20, interpreted as the remains of a menhir intentionally removed. Whether all the other holes contained upright stones is open to question. One earlier reconstruction (Le Roux 1979) envisaged the smaller holes (5, 8, 9, 11) holding timber posts rather than menhirs.

The three largest quartz menhirs (14, 16, 19) appear to be among the earliest elements of the southern *file*. Around their feet a low stone cairn was later built, extending some 50 m to the west. The schist menhirs seem in every case to postdate the cairn, because none of them descends as far as the old ground surface. This demonstrates that alongside the

FIGURE 11.7. Schist and quartz menhirs in the southern *file* of the Le Moulin alignments.

issue of the mixed media—quartz, schist, and (per-haps) timber—of which the southern *file* was formed, must also be considered the question of chronology. Thus it may be that the Le Moulin alignments originally consisted exclusively of quartz blocks, but were later elaborated by the addition of schist elements. In using these contrasting elements the builders were taking up the colors of the land, but giving greater emphasis to the brilliant white quartz.

The same contrasting use of schist and quartz is present in other monuments on the Grée de Cojoux. At La Croix-Saint-Pierre, the *tertre tumulaire* (a low, elongated mound) stands within a stone setting consisting of quartz blocks to the south and blue schist slabs to the north. In addition there is a recumbent slab of quartz at the eastern end and a 2.3-m-tall menhir at the western end. Giot and colleagues interpreted this schist/quartz opposition as a "choix à signification rituelle qui nous échappe"[10] (Giot et al., in Briard et al. 1995:39). It is mirrored by the north-south distribution of material within the mound of the *tertre tumulaire*. Small sherds of pottery were found, stratigraphically at the junction between the overlying humus and the material of the mound, and all of them to the north of the midline of the monument (Giot and L'Helgouach 1955). This pottery is now assigned to the Cerny style and hence dated to the mid-fifth millennium B.C.E. (Giot et al., in Briard et al. 1995:39). Thus the east-west axis is marked by the orientation of the mound itself, and the north-south opposition emphasized by the differential use of schist and quartz in the curb and by the varying provenance of the material scraped together to make the northern and southern halves of the mound; this must be the meaning of the way the sherds were restricted only to the northern half.

Ramé noted a similar north/south opposition of schist and quartz blocks in a structure on the northern flank of the Grée de Cojoux. This was a crescent-shaped setting of sixteen stones, opening toward the east. The eight southernmost stones were of quartz, the eight northernmost of schist (Ramé 1864:91). Ramé indicated that already in 1864 the site was "entouré de défrichements sur trois de ces côtés, est destiné à disparaître prochainement";[11] when Bézier visited it some years later only six stones survived (Bézier 1883); and neither of the more recent accounts makes any reference to it (Le Roux et al. 1989; Briard et al. 1995). It is regrettable that the *tertre tumulaire du Tribunal*, 100 m west of La Croix-Saint-Pierre, was badly damaged by the construction of a road in 1962; some of the quartz blocks that formerly edged it have been laid out in a line along its damaged northern flank. Ramé described it as surrounded by stones placed "presque contigües" (almost touching) and noted at the western end an entrance flanked by a schist slab to the north and two quartz slabs to the south (Ramé 1864:84). Here again we find the opposition of schist to north and quartz to south.

The contrasting deployment of schist and quartz in these monuments hence emphasizes the north-south distinction. At the same time, the east-west axis is taken up in the orientation of the *tertres tumulaires*, in the linear distribution of monuments across the Grée de Cojoux, and indeed in the alignment of the ridge itself. A fuller understanding of this east/west emphasis may be attained by considering the chronology and character of the individual monuments in greater detail.

TOWARD THE REALM OF THE DEAD: A SYMBOLIC CHOREOGRAPHY

Briard associated the linear, east-west arrangement of the principal monuments with an astronomical cult and with the rising and setting sun (Briard, in

Briard et al. 1995:149–151). His short discussion introduced a subject that deserves more thorough consideration.

The east-west axis of the Grée de Cojoux is not simply a chord along which the various monuments were strung. Topography strongly suggests a reading in terms of directionality, starting in the east and moving toward the west. The Grée de Cojoux is defined to north, south, and west by sharp terrain features, but on the east the approach is more gentle. This, the direction of the rising sun, also gives the easiest approach to the upland. The ascent, indeed, begins almost imperceptibly. Passing westward beyond the site of the Mesolithic/Neolithic settlement (H1), the first monuments on the upland proper are the Le Moulin alignments (Figure 11.8). These mark special directions and orientations, both in the landscape and with regard to the heavens. The *file ouest* is related to two landscape features: first, it is aligned on the schist/quartz rock outcrop to the north, already discussed; and second, it is oriented at right angles to the topography; that is, it proceeds directly downslope toward the south. It may mark a path—a physical, spiritual, or mythical route from the south leading up to this rock exposure; or alternatively a screen, because the only extant stones stand essentially across the east-west pathway along the Grée de Cojoux, marking a barrier that must be passed on the journey toward the western end of the Grée.

Proceeding in that direction, next in sequence are the stones known as Les Demoiselles Piquées; the two that are still standing are (at over 3 m) the tallest of all the Saint-Just menhirs (Figure 11.9). They are aligned obliquely to the slope in a west-south-west/east-northeast orientation. Ignoring the fallen elements nearby and taking the two upright stones alone, they form, together with the Le Moulin alignments, a kind of sundial, each successive fea-

ture marking a clockwise change in orientation: Le Moulin *file nord* at 105 °, *file sud* at 117°, *file ouest* at 195° (figures given by Le Roux et al. 1989:8), and Les Demoiselles Piquées (if we may indeed include them in this arrangement) at approximately 250°. This might suggest a solar choreography: with the *file nord* and *file sud* oriented on the morning sun in the east or southeast, the *file sud* on the southern sun shortly after midday, and Les Demoiselles Piquées on the early evening sun. It opens the possibility that these alignments are a kind of solar marker, punctuating and pacing the rhythm of actual pre-Historic ceremonies or processions proceeding east to west along the Grée de Cojoux (Figure 11.10).

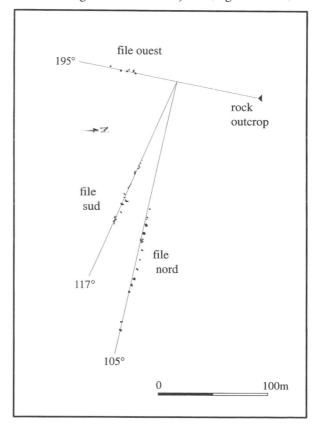

FIGURE 11.8. Plan of the Le Moulin alignments at the eastern end of the Grée de Cojoux.

FIGURE 11.9. Les Demoiselles Piquées, largest of the standing stones on the Grée de Cojoux.

For the sake of rigor, we should note the weaknesses in this argument. First, there are other blocks scattered along this hillside that may represent the remains of former alignments, now largely destroyed, that need not necessarily conform to this model. On the other hand, the pair of stones midway between Le Moulin *file ouest* and Les Demoiselles Piquées (in *parcelle* 127 [Le Roux et al. 1989: fig. 5]) seems to preserve an approximately north-south orientation, as might have been predicted. These may be the survivors of a north-south alignment of five quartz blocks referred to by Ramé in approximately this position (450 paces from Les Demoiselles Piquées [Ramé 1864:89]). Second, the Demoiselles alignment consists of only two stones, albeit massive ones, and may not give an accurate or meaningful line. It is also some distance west of the Le Moulin alignments; hence we may accept the latter with more confidence, perhaps leaving aside Les Demoiselles Piquées. As a third reservation, we must recall that the excavations at Le Moulin have shown that not all the uprights were of the same age. This may apply to other elements in these alignments, and hence the arrangement of which we see the remains

today may be representative only of a late stage in the history of the complex.

Support for the concept of an east-west progression along the Grée de Cojoux comes as we continue farther west. Beyond Les Demoiselles Piquées we leave the world of the living and enter that of the dead: the greater part of the monuments to the west of this point are funerary in nature. Indeed, the Le Moulin alignments and Les Demoiselles Piquées may mark the edges of a liminal zone between the world of the living (east of Le Moulin) and that of

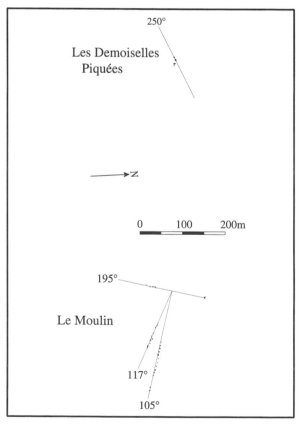

FIGURE 11.10. The Le Moulin alignments and Les Demoiselles Piquées illustrating their possible fanlike orientation.

the dead (west of Les Demoiselles). West, associated visibly every day with the decline and setting of the sun, is a natural metaphor for death and the dead.

The transition from nonfunerary to funerary functions and symbolism coincides with a break in the topography of the Grée de Cojoux. The eastern section begins with the gentle rise from La Croix-Madame to Le Moulin and ends near Les Demoiselles Piquées, where the ground falls slightly. The observer walking across the upland in this direction has the ridge that marks the crest of the Grée to the right, and to the left a view downward into the shallow valley marking the southern edge of the Grée de Cojoux. Only to the south, therefore, is there a panoramic landscape view. As the ground slopes down past Les Demoiselles Piquées, the menhirs of Château-Bû appear prominently ahead on the low rise that marks the second section of the Grée de Cojoux and on which, a little way beyond, stands the cluster of mainly funerary monuments at La Croix-Saint-Pierre.

In its Bronze Age state, Château-Bû was the largest of the mounds on the Grée de Cojoux, measuring some 25 by 35 m at the base, and surviving (before excavation) to a height of 2 m. The truly striking feature, however, was the large quartz menhirs that surmounted it and gave it an unmistakable profile. The use of these quartz menhirs—perhaps taken from an earlier monument nearby—indicates the continuing symbolism of the glistening white quartz beyond the end of the Neolithic period. It also established a link or reference to the quartz alignments of Le Moulin and Les Demoiselles Piquées. Gautier and Briard (in Briard et al. 1995:21–37) argued that the Château-Bû menhirs may have been markers for the Early Bronze Age tombs within this enlarged mound. Their excavation showed that this Bronze Age structure had been

raised over an earlier passage grave with two successive phases, the first dating to ca. 4000 B.C.E.

Château-Bû stands at the point where the northern ridge of the Grée falls away, forming a lower saddle giving distant views both to north and south. The impression as one crosses this saddle is of a more-open, less-confined world. Beyond this point the northern ridge rises once again to block the view to the right. Here, at La Croix-Saint-Pierre, are three small passage graves (northern, southern, and western [excavations described by Leroux et al., in Briard et al. 1995:49–63]); an early pit grave with stone and timber elements (Leroux et al., in Briard et al. 1995:65–71); and the two *tertres tumulaires* (of La Croix-Saint-Pierre and the Tribunal) already described (Figure 11.11). Beyond these again stands the lateral entry grave of the Four Sarrasin, the most westerly of the monuments on the Grée (Figure 11.12). All of these monuments are funerary in nature.

The ground climbs steadily here, with each monument placed higher than the last, until eventually we reach the Four Sarrasin, "posé à l'endroit où commence la pente abrupte qui descend à l'étang de Saint-Just"[12] (Ramé 1864:83), and are presented with broad views to the west across the Etang du Val. The steep cliffs along this edge of the plateau form a natural boundary; the funerary zone—the zone of the dead—ends at this ravine. Thus we began at the east where the alignments of standing stones may mark successive stages in the daily movement of the sun. We may even speculate that specific pauses or rituals were associated with the key solar moments marked out by the *files* of menhirs at Le Moulin. We end at the west at a cluster of funerary monuments and a cliff-lined ravine.

One final feature remains to be mentioned. Among the monuments at La Croix-Saint-Pierre stands the

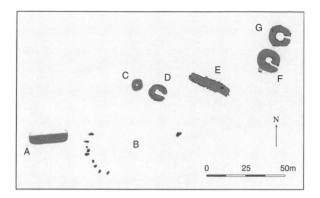

FIGURE 11.11. Complex of Neolithic monuments at La Croix-Saint-Pierre on the Grée de Cojoux: note in particular the two *tertres tumulaires* and the arc of stones of the Tribunal, with the isolated "judge" to the east. A, *tertre tumulaire du Tribunal;* B, *Tribunal;* C, pit grave with timber setting; D, western passage grave; E, *tertre tumulaire* of La Croix-Saint-Pierre; F, southern passage grave; G, northern passage grave.

FIGURE 11.12. The lateral entry grave of the Four Sarrasin on the western summit of the Grée de Cojoux.

THE WHEEL COMES FULL CIRCLE: CHANGING PRACTICES ON THE GRÉE DE COJOUX

stone setting known as the Tribunal. It consists of an arc of quartz blocks, facing toward the east. Ramé last century reported fifteen stones, but only nine survive today (Ramé 1864:85; Le Roux et al. 1989:12). A further large stone of the same material stands isolated some 50 m to the east of the arc and has popularly been identified as the "judge" facing toward his "tribunal." Briard (in Briard et al. 1995:151), pursuing his astronomical interpretation of the Saint-Just monuments, described this setting as a "hémicycle nord-sud et son gnomon oriental, organisé pour l'observation des couchers de soleil sur la ligne d'horizon ouest au délà de l'étang du Val."[13] It forms yet another element in the solar alignments of La Grée de Cojoux, a place perhaps to chart the setting of the sun across the seasons as it moved steadily north toward midsummer, or simply to observe the summer sun as it dipped toward the western horizon.

This interpretation overlooks one major dimension: it ignores the chronological succession of the Saint-Just monuments. There are in fact three separate stages in the development of these monuments, beginning in the fifth millennium B.C.E.

As noted earlier, the southern *file* of the Le Moulin alignments appears to have been built in at least two separate phases: first, the large quartz menhirs 14, 17, and 19, then the platform and the schist menhirs. None of these events is datable directly, but an indication is provided by fifth-millennium radiocarbon dates from three hearths sealed beneath the platform. The fifth-millennium dating is confirmed by finds of pottery that may relate to Cerny material farther east (Le Roux et al. 1989). The early quartz menhirs that predate the platform may also belong to this period, along with those of the *file nord*, as Le Roux and colleagues argued (Le Roux et al. 1989:27) on grounds of their morphological similarity. This gives us then a fifth-millennium complex of quartz block alignments, including elements of the southern *file* and the entirety of the northern and western *files*. The schist menhirs of the southern *file* follow later.

Contemporary with these fifth-millennium alignments are the earliest monuments at the western end of the Grée de Cojoux. The earliest directly dated monument here is the fallen menhir (now reerected) by the entrance to the northern passage grave of La Croix-Saint-Pierre. Excavation of its stone hole revealed a small hearth with charcoal and two flint flakes, and gave a ^{14}C date (on charcoal) of 6,070 ± 80 years B.P. (5270–4740 B.C.E.). This date would indeed make the menhir the earliest monument on the Grée de Cojoux. Within a few centuries followed the construction of the *tertres tumulaires*—of La Croix-Saint-Pierre and the Tribunal. The Cerny material in the earth used to create the former should itself fall in the third quarter of the fifth-millennium. The pit grave west of La Croix-Saint-Pierre, with low quartz bank and surround of timber posts, belongs in the same phase.

To these surviving *tertres tumulaires* at the western end of the Grée de Cojoux we must add the example at La Croix-Madame, at the opposite end of the upland, and the lost examples that are suggested by a reading of early accounts. Briard (1992) drew attention to one such described by Ramé, not far from Les Demoiselles Piquées (Ramé 1864:89). Both Ramé and Bézier mentioned another rectangular stone setting, perhaps the remains of a *tertre tumulaire*, lying between the Le Moulin alignments and La Croix-Madame (Bézier 1883; Ramé 1864:90). Thus around the close of the fifth millennium B.C.E. on the Grée de Cojoux there appear

to have been a series of *tertres tumulaires*, arranged east-west along the center of the upland from La Croix-Madame to La Croix-Saint-Pierre and the *tertre tumulaire du Tribunal*. If a funerary destination may correctly be ascribed to them (see, for example, Giot et al. 1998:330–336), they would represent a spread of mortuary activity that at this stage was not confined to one part of the Grée. We must furthermore note once again the evidence of Cerny sherds (fifth millennium B.C.E.) at various points along the Grée: near La Croix-Madame in the west, where they succeed or extend a pattern of Mesolithic activity (Kayser [pp. 101–103] and Ducloyer [pp. 103 ff.] in Briard et al. 1995) and may continue into the later Middle Neolithic; at the Le Moulin alignments, where one cluster of Cerny sherds lay beneath the stones of the cairn (Le Roux et al. 1989); and at La Croix-Saint-Pierre, where Cerny sherds were included in the makeup of the *tertre tumulaire* and in and among the adjacent passage graves (Leroux et al., in Briard et al. 1995). They indicate small-scale settlement, probably transient in nature and perhaps associated with ritual activity: at La Croix-Saint-Pierre, this finds direct expression in the western pit grave, which contained a pair of intact oval-mouthed vessels of Cerny or Chambon type (Leroux et al. [pp. 65–71] and Lannuzel [pp. 115–117], in Briard et al. 1995). They illustrate the mixed nature of activities across the ridge in the fifth millennium B.C.E.

It is in the subsequent phase that the western end of the Grée de Cojoux develops an exclusively funerary character. During the fourth millennium B.C.E. a series of four passage graves was built on the Grée de Cojoux. Three of these were grouped in a tight cluster adjacent at La Croix-Saint-Pierre, suggesting perhaps a continuity of funerary function with the earlier *tertres tumulaires*. The fourth passage grave stood a little way to the west, at Château-Bû. Finally, in the late fourth or early third millennium B.C.E., the lateral entry grave of the Four Sarrasin was built. It may be no coincidence that this, the latest of the monuments on the Grée de Cojoux, is also the farthest to the west; beyond the earlier works of human hands, in the western zone reserved for the dead.

As a tailpiece to this story, we may note that the west/east distinction appears to have broken down again in the Early Bronze Age, when the Le Moulin alignments became a focus for funerary activity. A small cist grave was built around the foot of menhir 5 in the *file nord*. An Early Bronze Age urn buried south of *calage* 20 in the *file sud*, and Beaker sherds and a polished stone ax from a small cist near the same stone hole are also interpreted as funerary in nature (Le Roux et al. 1989:16–17, 19). Other *tombelles* referred to by Ramé may also be Early Bronze Age cists under small mounds, now destroyed.

This chronological evidence encourages us to envisage activity on the Grée de Cojoux not as a static series of practices and attitudes, but as a dynamic pattern of change. The earliest monuments were spread along the ridge from east to west and may have associated funerary function with standing stones and adjacent transitory settlement. The next phase saw the removal of settlement from the Grée and its symbolic division into two ritual zones, the easternmost characterized by alignments and the westernmost by a series of passage graves. During the later third millennium this symbolic division was eroded, as burials were inserted at the foot of the Le Moulin alignments. Hence we return in the second millennium to where we began in the fifth, with an intermingling of funerary and nonfunerary activity across the Grée de Cojoux.

RECOVERING SIGNIFICANCE

This interpretation of the monuments on the Grée de Cojoux has attempted to draw connections between the monuments themselves and features of the natural landscape in which they stand. These natural features includes quartz seams that run across the schist upland and outcrop prominently in the cliffs that mark its western end. The special qualities of quartz, and its association in many traditional societies with shamanism and/or the ancestors, add another dimension to this observation. The intentional use made of quartz blocks—visually striking in appearance, and mostly brought to the Grée from sources beyond—in many of the monuments on this upland suggests that the pre-Historic communities were making intentional reference to the quartz seams and perhaps also indicates a symbolic recognition of the special qualities and associations of the quartz.

A key aspect of this study has been the quest to understand why the Grée de Cojoux became a focus for ritual practice and monumental elaboration during the fifth–third millennia B.C.E. The veins of quartz may be one element in that special significance, though such veins are by no means limited to the Grée but are indeed quite widely present in the Breton crystalline massif. There may ultimately be no way of decoding the precise significance of this location, which was perhaps derived from mythology and tradition as much as from any natural features of the land. Yet the east-west orientation of the Grée does seem to have been of importance, as shown by the disposition of monuments across its surface, which follows this major axis, by the alignment of individual monuments (notably the stone rows of Le Moulin and the semicircular setting of the Tribunal), and by the distinction argued earlier between a western funerary zone and the nonfunerary eastern half of the upland. An association with the daily cycle of the sun makes plausible sense of these observations, and we may envisage ceremonies involving westward progress across the Grée de Cojoux, eventually entering the zone of the dead.

Last but not least, the likely significance of the ravine now occupied by the Etang du Val at the western limit of the Grée de Cojoux must be emphasized. This cliff-lined gorge with steep sides and prominent rock outcrops is the most striking topographical feature of the Grée and may have had special meaning in the landscape understanding of the pre-Historic communities. In describing the sacred geography of the Wintu of northern California, Theodoratus and Lapena (1994:23) remarked that "Localities of unusual configuration, such as distinctive rock outcrops . . . caves, knolls, whirlpools in a river, and seepage holes, often house spirits." They noted that shamans visit such places "seeking transcendence in order to achieve another level of jurisdiction over a domain more potent and supreme in its influence than that found in the everyday world." Georgia Lee (this volume) also notes the significance of prominent landforms, in particular caves and collapsed lava tubes, in ancient Hawaiian thought. Culturally and geographically remote, these two examples need not have direct relevance to the Neolithic landscape of Saint-Just, and there is no proposal here that the widespread recent evocation of shamanism need be extended to the Grée de Cojoux. The argument is that careful consideration of the monuments and their topographic setting together can inform interpretations of their meaning, and of the ritual practices associated with them, which are persuasive, though they may never claim to be conclusive. The Saint-Just case discussed here clearly shows the construction of social and cultural identity. By marking place, people not only express their worldviews, but construct them as well.

NOTES

All translations from French are my own.

1. It is beyond question that the Grée de Cojoux was chosen intentionally because of its east-west orientation, ideally situated between the rising and setting of the sun. For this reason, the series of monuments at Saint-Just is laid out principally along an east-west axis.

2. It is a little late to attempt this study at Saint-Just; the number of stones destroyed in recent years, since the parceling up of the moor, is considerable; I am told that it exceeds that of the stones that remain standing.

3. [A] slight rise of the ground, resembling in appearance a furrow running from east to west, . . . interrupted here and there by very small schist slabs spaced seven to eight paces apart. It would seem to indicate a long row of tombs placed in a line.

4. [A] plain sown with several hundred blocks, generally in white quartz and gleaming in the sun. Their number is increased still further by all the natural outcrops close to hand that form the backbone of the moor.

5. It is beyond question that this stone has been placed intentionally in the position that it occupied.

6. These blocks rest on a rock of the same kind, and we find ourselves wondering whether we are in presence of a freak of nature or whether these masses were originally raised there by human action, or indeed whether, having left the quarry, they have not been waiting ever since, over the centuries, an employment that they will never now receive.

7. [O]verlooking the cliff, the last ridge of rock is detached from the massif and rests horizontally on the apex of several other ridges that serve to support it. Seen from below, one might believe that it is a huge capstone that is in front of one, and 15 meters above.

8. [A] natural rocky outcrop of ridge.

9. [A] plain sown with several hundred blocks, generally in white quartz and gleaming in the sun.

10. [A] choice with a ritual significance that now eludes us.

11. [S]urrounded by clearances on three sides, and destined very shortly to disappear.

12. Positioned in the spot where the steep descent toward the Saint-Just lake begins.

13. [A] north-south semicircle and its eastern gnomon, designed for the observation of sunsets on the western horizon beyond the Etang du Val.

REFERENCES CITED

Bézier, P. 1883. *Inventaire des Monuments Mégalithiques du Département d'Ille-et-Vilaine*. Rennes.

Biennike, P., K. Ebbesen, and L. B. Jørgensen. 1986. Early Neolithic Skeletons from Bolkilde Bog, Denmark. *Antiquity* 60:199–207.

Bradley, R. 1990. *The Passage of Arms: An Archaeological Analysis of Prehistoric Hoards and Votive Deposits*. Cambridge: Cambridge University Press.

———. 1998a. Architecture, Imagination and the Neolithic World. In *Creativity in Human Evolution and Prehistory*, edited by S. Mithen, 227–240. London: Routledge.

———. 1998b. *The Significance of Monuments: On the Shaping of Experience in Neolithic and Bronze Age Europe*. London: Routledge.

Bradley, R., and K. Gordon. 1988. Human Skulls from the River Thames, Their Dating and Significance. *Antiquity* 62:503–509.

Briard, J. 1992. Les Tertres Tumulaires Néolithiques de Bretagne Intérieur. In *Paysans et Bâtisseurs: Actes du 17e Colloque Interrégional sur le Néolithique, Vannes, 1990*, edited by C.-T. Le Roux, 55–62. *Revue Archéologique de l'Ouest*, Supplément 5.

Briard, J., M. Gautier, and G. Leroux. 1995. *Les Mégalithes et les Tumulus de Saint-Just, Ille-et-Vilaine*. Paris: Comité des Travaux Historiques et Scientifiques.

Briggs, C. S. 1995. Did They Fall or Were They Pushed? Some Unresolved Questions about Bog Bodies. In *Bog Bodies: New Discoveries and New Perspectives*, edited by R. C. Turner and R. G. Scaife, 168–182. London: British Museum Press.

Burl, A. 1991. The Heel Stone, Stonehenge: A Study in Misfortunes. *Wiltshire Archaeological and Natural History Magazine* 84:1–10.

Chippindale, C. 1994. *Stonehenge Complete*. London: Thames and Hudson.

Chippindale, C., and P. Taçon. 1998. *The Archaeology of Rock-Art*. Cambridge: Cambridge University Press.

Cooney, G. 1994. Sacred and Secular Neolithic Landscapes in Ireland. In *Sacred Sites, Sacred Places*, edited by D. L. Carmichael, J. Hubert, B. Reeves, and A. Schanche, 32–43. London: Routledge.

David, B., and M. Wilson. 1999. Re-Reading the Landscape: Place and Identity in Northeastern Australia during the Late Holocene. *Cambridge Archaeological Journal* 9:163–188.

Giot, P.-R., and J. L'Helgouach. 1955. Le Tertre Tumulaire de la Croix-Saint-Pierre en Saint-Just (Ille-et-Vilaine). (Fouilles de 1953–1954). *Annales de Bretagne* 62:282–292.

Giot, P.-R., and H. Morzadec. 1990. Contribution à l' Étude de l'Ère Monumentale Préhistorique: Les Lapides Stantes de Saint Samson. *Dossiers du Centre de Recherches Archéologiques d'Alet* 18:43–52.

Giot, P.-R., J. L'Helgouach, and J. L. Monnier. 1998. *Préhistoire de la Bretagne*. Rennes: Ouest-France.

Glob, P. V. 1969. *The Bog People: Iron Age Man Preserved*. London: Faber and Faber.

Guénin, G. 1936. Le Folklore Préhistorique de la Bretagne. In *Corpus du Folklore Préhistorique de France*, edited by P. Sainyves. 3:273–563.

Jones, A., and R. Bradley. 1999. The Significance of Colour in European Archaeology. *Cambridge Archaeological Journal* 9:112–117.

Le Roux, C.-T. 1979. Informations Archéologiques: Circonscription de Bretagne. *Gallia Préhistoire* 22:525–556.

———. 1997. Et Voguent les Menhirs . . .? *Bulletin d'Information de l'Association Manche-Atlantique pour la Recherche Archéologique dans les Iles* 10:5–18.

Le Roux, C.-T., Y. Lecerf, and M. Gautier. 1989. Les Mégalithes de Saint-Just (Ille-et-Vilaine) et la Fouille des Alignements du Moulin de Cojou. *Revue Archéologique de l'Ouest* 6:5–29.

Lynch, F. 1998. Colour in Prehistoric Architecture. In *Prehistoric Ritual and Religion*, edited by A. Gibson and D. Simpson, 62–67. Stroud: Sutton.

O'Kelly, M. J. 1982. *Newgrange: Archaeology, Art and Legend*. London: Thames and Hudson.

Ramé, A. 1864. Le champ funéraire de Cojou (Ille-et-Vilaine). *Revue Archéologique* 9:81–93.

Reinach, S. 1893. Les Monuments de Pierre Brute dans le Langage et les Croyances Populaires. *Revue Archéologique* 21:195–226.

Scarre, C. 2000. Forms and Landforms: The Design and Setting of Neolithic Monuments in Western France. In *Neolithic Orkney in Its European Context*, edited by A. Ritchie, 309–320. Cambridge: McDonald Institute for Archaeological Research.

Sellier, D. 1995. Eléments de Reconstitution du Paysage Prémégalithique sur le Site des Alignements de Ker-lescan (Carnac, Morbihan) à Partir de Critères Géomorphologiques. *Revue Archéologique de l'Ouest* 12:21–41.

Taçon, P. S. C. 1991. The Power of Stone: Symbolic Aspects of Stone Use and Tool Development in Western Arnhem Land, Australia. *Antiquity* 65:192–207.

———. 1999. All Things Bright and Beautiful: The Role and Meaning of Colour in Human Development. *Cambridge Archaeological Journal* 9:120–123.

Theodoratus, D. J., and F. Lapena. 1994. Wintu Sacred Geography of Northern California. In *Sacred Sites, Sacred Places*, edited by D. L. Carmichael, J. Hubert, B. Reeves, and A. Schanche, 20–31. London: Routledge.

Tilley, C. 1994. *A Phenomenology of Landscape*. Oxford: Berg.

———. 1996. The Power of Rocks: Topography and Monument Construction on Bodmin Moor. *World Archaeology* 28:161–176.

Torbrügge, W. 1971. Vor- und Frühgeschitliche Flussfunde. *Bericht der Römisch-Germanischen Kommission* 51–52:1–146.

van der Sanden, W. 1996. *Through Nature to Eternity: The Bog Bodies of Northwest Europe*. Amsterdam: Batavian Lion International.

Webster, J. 1995. Sanctuaries and Sacred Places. In *The Celtic World*, edited by M. J. Green, 445–464. London: Routledge.

Whitley, D. S., R. I. Dorn, J. M. Simon, R. Rechtman, and T. K. Whitley. 1999. Sally's Rockshelter and the Archaeology of the Vision Quest. *Cambridge Archaeological Journal* 9:221–247.

TWELVE

Monuments in the Pre-Historic Landscape of the Maltese Islands

Ritual and Domestic Transformations

SIMON STODDART

The Maltese Islands (Figure 12.1), located to the south of Sicily in the central Mediterranean, provide a fine and relatively well-preserved example of pre-Historic landscape inscription. The islands are rich in monumental architecture, including temples, megaliths, mortuary complexes, terraces, enclosures, and domestic structures. But these have not remained constant over time: major changes in monument building have taken place over the millennia, implying changes in social, political, and religious life. In this chapter I explore these architectural changes and their broader social implications.

Constructional conditions in the Maltese Islands were favorable for long-term archaeological survival: the geology of the Maltese Islands presented local communities with major stone resources for building and rebuilding. This comprised substantially two types of building material: soft Globigerina limestone suitable for architectural embellishment, and a coralline limestone suitable for more solid blocks and infill. Other, more fragile forms of constructional material, such as wood, were less readily available and consequently played a lesser role in monumental architecture.

Creative conditions were also favorable. Island conditions conspired to produce a cycle of complexity in the treatment of the built environment and a subsquent cycle of reinterpretation of that built environment. A period of agricultural colonization and consolidation (ca. 5500–4100 B.C.E.) was followed by a phase of ritualization (ca. 4100–2500 B.C.E.) and, in turn, by a radical reworking of the material remains of that ritualization (ca. 2500–800 B.C.E.) until the process was truncated by the intervention of Phoenician influence (Stoddart 1999a). The Maltese Islands thus constitute a good case study for the consideration of some current approaches to material display, inscribed in landscapes. They provide a palimpsest of inscriptions and reinscriptions where traces of the previous landscape can provide an important foundation for the new. This, in essence, is the force of inscription.

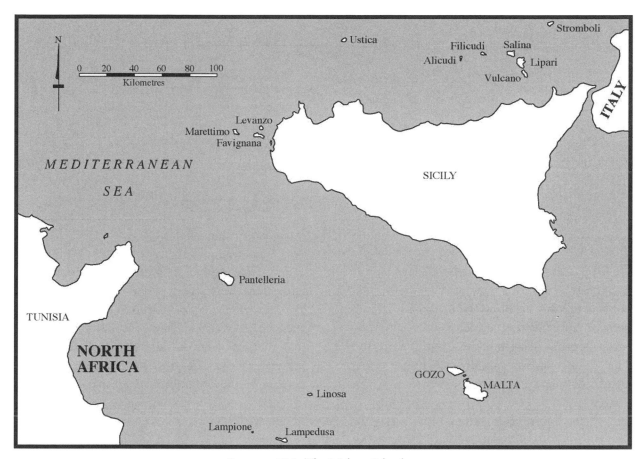

FIGURE 12.1. The Maltese Islands.

MATERIALIZATION

One recent treatment of the place of inscriptions in social landscapes has been defined as the materialization of ideology (De Marrais et al. 1996). Those authors emphasized that "ideology is materialised in the form of ceremonies, symbolic objects, monuments, and writing systems to become an effective source of power" (De Marrais et al. 1996:16). They further developed the likely presence of a series of tangible and material products in the archaeological record associated with such monuments: the presence of feasting discard and the skilled manufacture of portable and nonportable ceremonial objects. The critique that Hodder (1996) and others have used against this approach addresses many current issues in the treatment of monuments in landscapes. Hodder particularly critiqued culture-historical approaches that present culture as a series of progressive evolutionary stages (e.g., Bronze Age Denmark, Moche chiefdoms, and the Inca imperial state). He also criticized, as did Clark (1996), the lack of engagement with the real individual implicit in such an approach. This, however, is much an issue of analytical scale. A further key issue is the extent to which the ideologies within which those monuments occur are enduring. Monuments may themselves last long periods of time—indeed that is a prominent part of their definition—but not only are such monuments not static in the landscape, they are re-interpreted, even contested, by different generations.

The Maltese landscape provides a test case for the study of such issues. The peak of ritualization ca. 3600 to 2500 B.C.E. appears to be a classic example of monumental materialization (see Table 12.1 for chronology of change in the Maltese Islands). The subsequent period (ca. 2500–1500 B.C.E.) appears to have been a period of radical change in the use of the preexisting monuments where iconoclasm may have been a powerful force influencing social and political life. In this historical phase of Maltese settlement, there is clear evidence of many types of anthropogenic place markings (writing excepted). The Maltese landscape is fully pre-Historic until the eighth century B.C.E.

EUROPE IN THE FOURTH AND THIRD MILLENNIA B.C.E.

In this section I situate Malta within a broader European context, paying particular attention to chronological detail.[1] How and when did Malta first attain its lasting communal or ritual monuments? Is the ritualization of Malta a unique case, or is it part of a series of nodes of ritualization in a broader European setting? Is Maltese ritualization a case of relative isolation or a product of intense interaction? One scholar (Mezzena 1998) has suggested a pattern of widespread nodes of communication across much of western and southern Europe, coinciding with the concentration of statue menhirs and rock engravings across the region. He defined these nodes as islands and peninsulas, the mouths of major navigable rivers, and great valleys through mountain chains. On the whole this interpretation appears to simplify and collapse disparate phenom-

Table 12.1 The Chronology of Successive Landscape Types and Associated Pottery Styles in the Maltese Islands.

Landscape Type	Absolute Chronology (B.C.E.)	Pottery Style
Domestic	5500–4100	Ghar Dalam Grey Skorba Red Skorba
Bipartite	4100–3800	Zebbug
Tripartite	3800–2500	Mgarr Ggantija Saflieni Tarxien
Iconoclasm Ideological transformation	2500–1500	Tarxien Cemetery
Agriculture intensification Defensive	1500–800	Borg in Nadur Bahrija
State intervention	800	Phoenician

ena in space and time. Moreover, Malta's archaeological remains are sufficiently distinctive from those of Brittany, the south of France, the Alps, Sardinia, the Tavoliere, the Crimea, and the Caucasus to focus on their differences rather than similarities.

The small island of Malta (310 km²) was precocious in terms of the dramatic way in which a whole landscape was radically transformed. In Malta, as we shall see here, we are not dealing with statue menhirs or engravings seen all over Europe, but with incomparable, massive architectural constructions well over 6 m in height set in ritual landscapes that interconnect the rituals of the living and the dead.

A DOMESTIC LANDSCAPE
(CA. 5500–4100 B.C.E.)

The Maltese Islands were first occupied on a more or less permanent basis in the sixth millennium B.C.E. Groups from Sicily crossed the 80 km to Malta, bringing distinctive incised pottery with a strong resemblance in form and decoration to contemporary Stentinello styles in Sicily (see Table 12.1 for a list of the pottery styles of this period). These were agricultural communities; recent work has shown the improbability that an island community of ca. 310 km² could sustain a hunter-gatherer community (including the improbability of long-term maintenance of a viable population) (Malone 1999). It is unlikely that potential access to deep-sea marine resources would have compensated for the lack of terrestrial territory to support hunting and gathering activity.

Few settlements are known from this period. On Malta, occupational evidence has been preserved in caves (Ghar Dalam) or under later constructions (Skorba). On Gozo (the smaller of two main islands), survey by the Cambridge Gozo Project and by Dutch and Maltese amateurs has provided a more detailed pattern. Both mesa tops and lower areas appear to have been occupied by domestic structures. The land continued to be occupied as a domestic landscape into the subsequent period of agricultural consolidation (4500–4100 B.C.E.), with some evidence for enlarged settlements and demographic growth.

A BIPARTITE LANDSCAPE
(CA. 4100–3800 B.C.E.)

This domestic landscape was replaced by what has been termed a bipartite landscape in the subsequent period (Stoddart 1999b). Many of the later temples, including Skorba, have domestic deposits underneath them that provided points of growth for the temples (Bonanno et al. 1990). This domestic landscape of 4100 to 3800 B.C.E. ran in parallel with clusters of small, extended-family shaft burials. Typically, a central shaft was cut into the bedrock, giving access to two side chambers housing the remains of successive members of a local descent group. In two significant cases (Hal Saflieni and the Brochtorff Circle at Xaghra, Gozo), these modest family tombs gave way to dramatic mortuary complexes, as part of a completely transformed and complex landscape.

A TRIPARTITE LANDSCAPE
(CA. 3800–2500 B.C.E.)

The funerary landscape of the bipartite period was in turn replaced by a complex tripartite landscape of life rituals (in structures usually designated temples), death rituals, and domestic structures, all inscribed in stone after around 3800 B.C.E. Six new clusters of monuments appear to have been the focus of life rituals, most probably focused on a central funerary monument. The domestic structures, altogether more modest in size, have been more elusive and are still known from only three locations (Skorba on Malta, and Ghajnsielem Road and Ta-cawla on Gozo) that fail yet to form a definitive geographical pattern, although it may be significant that the only relatively recent excavation of a temple produced an early domestic structure contemporary with other temples underneath (Trump 1966).

The clusters of temples at the approximate center of hypothetical territories can be readily established. It is more difficult to be certain that each of these had an associated mortuary complex. Only one-third of the clusters have such a clear association. At the beginning of the twentieth century the Hal Saflieni underground mortuary complex was found in association with the temples of Tarxien and Kordin. More recently, the Brochtorff Circle has been found to occur in association with the temples of Ggantija and Santa Verna on the Xaghra Plateau in Gozo, strengthening considerably this pattern of landscape organization (Attard Tabone 1999; Bonanno et al. 1990; Stoddart et al. 1993).

These two clusters make an important and revealing comparison. In each case we can consider the funerary complex to form a naturally prominent monument on a physical eminence rising above the culturally prominent temples. There would have been approach routes that would almost certainly have been interconnected by processional ways, interlinking other megalithic markers in the landscape. Recent work at the Hal Saflieni complex shows the presence of a circular surface feature that contained megalithic blocks. Unfortunately, the location of this

site in the middle of an urban area has prevented a full reconstruction of the local landscape.

The Xaghra Plateau, although itself the focus of one of the more important villages in Gozo, is today less heavily occupied than other areas. It is thus possible to make a more detailed reconstruction of patterns of pre-Historic land use (Figure 12.2). This mesalike structure, in comparison with the Malta landscape, enhances the prominence of this region in ritual behavior during the tripartite period. The mesa provides a natural setting for ritual action: an approach from low ground brings the Ggantija temples into view just below the lip of the plateau on a prepared terrace. At least two significant locations link components of a ceremonial way from this temple complex to the circular mortuary structure (Brochtorff Circle) on the summit of the plateau. One is a cave (North Cave) filled with the debris of ritual largesse. The other is a megalithic structure that has some templelike affinities (Ta Ghejzu). Beyond the Brochtorff Circle is another definite temple structure (Santa Verna), which survey has shown to be at the center of a concentration of temple-period debris, suggesting a residential complex encircling the megalithic remains.

These clusters of temples have been generally explained in terms of chiefly territorial behavior (Renfrew 1973; Renfrew and Level 1979): the centralized power of chiefdoms enabled a mobilization of labor toward the construction of focal places in the landscape. However, the nature of the temple clusters on Malta and Gozo requires some modification to this explanatory model. Drawing on modern ethnographic analogy from the Maltese Islands, it seems more plausible that each community consisted of factions competing (at least locally) for the prominence of their particular interpretation of the local religion (Boissevain 1969). Put another way,

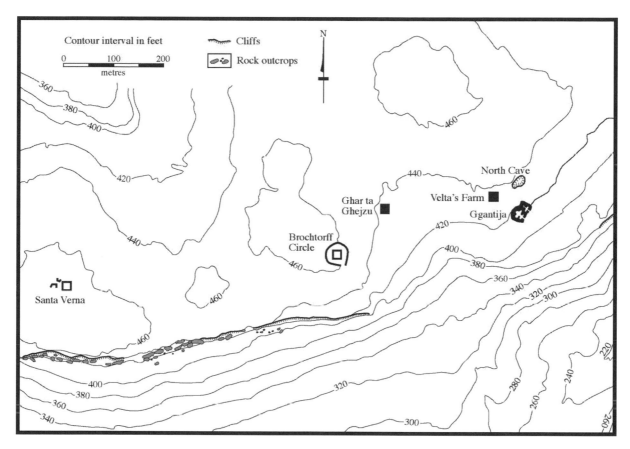

FIGURE 12.2. The Xaghra Plateau.

the intense social networks posited by Boissevain (1969) and Blanton et al. (1996) allow us to explain the presence of several contemporaneous temples of various sizes and local history across the landscape, in association with a single major funerary monument. The building statigraphy of these temples is difficult to interpret, but it appears that monuments with open access, typical of public ritual structures, were subverted by a priestly class toward the end of the Tarxien period (3000–2500 B.C.E.) while secret knowledge was increasingly preserved in the inner parts of the temple (Stoddart et al. 1993). Transformations in the way temples were fitted out enabled

parts to be selectively excluded from the eyes of the congregations outside.

Vision was a key factor in the control of knowledge both within and about the temples. The classic temples had a central line of rising sight to the main altar. Outside was generally a concave facade containing a paved or prepared area for what may be inferred to be the majority of participants. Activities could be brought in and out of sight across the main axis of vision from this external vantage point. Inside, many devices were employed to enhance the effect: screens, portholes, moving heads on static bodies, prominent areas of decoration, small objects indistinctly viewed from a distance, fire, and smoke. Many of these acted as metonyms and metaphors to give symbolic redolence to visual symbols. Certain colors of metaphorical value were most probably prominent. Red ochre was clearly favored, as indicated by temple iconography, and white and black were other colors recorded from different temple contexts.

It is natural for archaeologists to emphasize the visual as a key to the maintenance of power in the monuments of the Maltese Islands, but it is highly probable that other senses were also involved in the manipulation of secret, ritual knowledge. Sound has recently been emphasized both in the wider context of megalithic monuments and their powers of resonance (Watson and Keating 1999) and in the funerary rites of Malta (Stoddart 1999b) (see Rainbird, this volume, for further discussion of the role of sound in inscriptive behavior elsewhere). The importance of sound has long been appreciated underground at the Hal Saflieni monument, where a low-pitched voice achieves a high degree of resonance. Shells discovered in some funerary deposits at the Brochtorff Circle at Xaghra also suggest acoustic potential. However, these same principles have not yet been transferred above ground to the temples. Although the temples are remarkably well preserved, it would probably require a computer reconstruction of potential roofing to achieve models of acoustic performance (Chalmers and Stoddart 1996). However, Watson and Keating (1999) made illuminating remarks about the effects of narrow, constricted entrances on acoustic resonance (specifically, the Helmholtz resonance), a resonance that might lead to altered states of mind. They suggest the use of drums and other acoustic devices. It would thus be interesting to test the sound-transmission qualities of the large stone bowls in the tem-

ples. The reconstructed Tarxien example was potentially used as a drum. The beaded rim would have allowed a hide to be stretched across its opening, secured below the rim. Now that it appears from engineering experiments that the temples were most probably roofed, the full effect of a restricted entrance, a series of interlinked resonating chambers, and smoke-filled partial darkness would have been impressive in terms of controlling the mind and, thus restricted, specialist knowledge.

The power of taste should also not be underestimated. That taste would have played a part is clearly present in the provisions of ritual largesse. The thresholds of temples often contain hollows. Other hollows are also prominently located outside temples such as Tarxien or Tas Silg. A communal grinding stone is located inside Kordin III. All these may have supported the needs of ritual congregations in the form of ground cereal. This would have been supplemented by meat from the sacrifices of animals, most clearly demonstrated from the preserved remains in the recess of an altar in the outer temple at Tarxien. All the temples abound with offering bowls of a standard typological form that would have facilitated distribution to the majority of the population located outside. In some cases, such as the North Cave of Ggantija, disposal areas of the products of this largesse have been uncovered. Smell is more difficult to assess, but much can be imagined from the brazier platforms found within many of the temples (e.g., Ggantija).

The aboveground temples were linked to the belowground mortuary structures by some organizational principles and shared features of material culture. Both Hal Saflieni and the Brochtorff Circle at Xaghra (at least in its latest phase) appear to have had a central area for principal rituals and a range of peripheral areas for the placing of the dead. The central ritual area comprised many templelike constructional features, but not the axial emphasis of the aboveground temples. Each site had an inner, screened-off area where at least in the case of the Brochtorff Circle the symbolic artifacts of the ritual specialists were kept. The peripheral burial areas in each case consisted of a series of modular compartments with different combinations of human bones, animals bones, and figurative art. The shared features of material culture not only comprised the corpulent figurative art, but also offering bowls; stone spheres of various sizes; varied fittings such as rope holes, hollows, and portholes; and decoration in pecking and paint.

Not all of the temples followed the simple axial structure seen in some. This simple observation may help us understand the location of the third element of the tripartite landscape: the domestic. If we reject conjectures over its nineteenth-century reconstruction (Mayrhofer 1996), Hagar Qim seems to represent an atypical monument from a number of perspectives. It is accessible from five directions and has considerable internal networks of intercommunication. Most classic axial temples have one entrance and one line of internal communication. Hagar Qim also has a number of adjunct structures of nonaxial form. The whole complex may suggest an elite residential complex. Similarly, Borg, in Nadur temple, comprises a four-lobe structure, but also has many outer enclosures that do not conform to the standard type. Kordin III has a number of adjunct structures near the temple itself. Three other less-monumental structures have also been considered domestic (structures under Skorba temple and the Ghajnsielem Road and Tac Cawla structures on Gozo). Considered together with the atypical temples they compose a range of forms that show a complex domestic pattern.

A LANDSCAPE OF ICONOCLASM AND IDEOLOGICAL TRANSFORMATION (CA. 2500–1500 B.C.E.)

The monumental statements in stone before 2500 B.C.E. were abandoned in a complex ideological transformation whose explanation remains controversial. Whereas before 2500 B.C.E. the stylistic repertoire of the Maltese Islands was insular and profoundly Maltese, after 2500 B.C.E. the Maltese Islands were strongly interlinked with the rest of the Mediterranean. The traditional explanation is that the Maltese Islands became abandoned ca. 2500 B.C.E. after an ecological and demographic crisis, to be reoccupied by a fresh invading population accustomed to the martial climate of the Mediterranean of the time (Magro Conti 1999). Support for this interpretation has called upon dramatic changes evident in the material culture and the presence of a sterile silt layer between the pre-2500 B.C.E. levels of the Tarxien temple and its subsequent reuse as a burial complex (Zammit 1930).

An intriguing range of information is currently being assembled that suggests a dramatic incidence of iconoclasm before 2500 B.C.E., followed by the deliberate reuse of many of the focal monuments from the pre-2500 B.C.E. landscape. The recent excavations at the Brochtorff Circle have produced substantial evidence to suggest that features of the monument were deliberately dismantled around 2500 B.C.E. On the upper level of the site, three actions took place, which suggest an outward rejection or resistance to a previous social order as expressed through the monument area.

A small shrine, placed prominently at the entrance to the site, was badly damaged. This in itself is difficult to date because of its proximity to the surface, but appears to be just before 2500 B.C.E. rather than later activity. After 2500 B.C.E., two circular features were set into the upper deposits and filled with what appears to be domestic rubbish: broken-down mud brick, animal bones, obsidian, and loom weights. At the same time small distinctive offering vessels were placed on the lip of the mortuary cave system lying below. In the lower cave system filled with mortuary remains, there also appears to be evidence of iconoclasm immediately before 2500 B.C.E. (Malone et al. 1995:7, fig. 3) because a meter-high statue was broken up and incorporated in the pre-Historic deposit (Figure 12.3). It is also plausible that the inverted position of the twin figures on a wicker bed and damage to a large stone bowl from the same site could have been the consequence of deliberate iconoclastic action.

In light of the work at this site, evidence from other, older excavations can be reassessed. At Hagar Qim a truncated standing pair of corpulent figurines was reincorporated into the inner wall of the ritual complex. At Tarxien, the truncation of the whole monument and more particularly the very large corpulent statue at the entrance of the main temple—usually interpreted quite plausibly as the product of agricultural activity—could be a deliberate product of iconoclasm. This same site was then reused as a cremation cemetery. Both Skorba and Borg in Nadur temples were reused after 2500 B.C.E.. However, it is at Tas Silg that the most detailed reanalyses of older excavations have been undertaken. It has been suggested that a ca. 1.15-m-high statue was deliberately desecrated at what appears to be a pre-Phoenician date, most probably ca. 2500 B.C.E. (Vella 1999:234, fig. 3). Vella's twin argument of iconoclasm and deliberate reuse for ideological reasons is compelling, both in terms of the 2500 B.C.E. and the later 800 B.C.E. transitions (see later in this chapter). Both involved major political changes where the occupation of place was fundamental to establish political legitimacy (Bradley 1987; Bradley and Williams 1998).

In this same post-2500 B.C.E. era, the placing of dolmens in the landscape suggests a new experience of space. Although no clear funerary purpose has ever been established for these monuments, their smaller scale and different configuration and orientation suggest a radical reworking of the landscape compared with the pre-2500 B.C.E. arrangements.

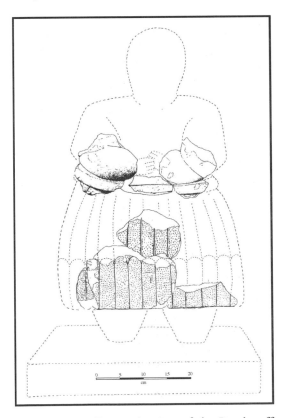

FIGURE 12.3. Reconstruction of the Brochtorff Circle at Xaghra standing figure.

AN INTENSIVELY EXPLOITED (AGRICULTURAL) AND DEFENSIVE LANDSCAPE (CA. 1500–800 B.C.E.)

Two features of the modern rural landscape demonstrate the intensive utilization of this new landscape: terraces and cart ruts. Both are probably indications of both increased intensities and modes of mitigation that most probably started in the Bronze Age, but continued over a much longer period (Grima 2000). Cart ruts (Trump 1998) are deeply engraved into many of the bare, particularly coralline, limestone surfaces of the island; they probably represent a long history of attempted repair (moving soil) and exploitation (extracting stone) of the land. The terraces, which also probably date from the same period, represent an attempt to stabilize these currently densely occupied islands. At the same time, a new domestic landscape was instituted. The naturally defended eminences of the two main islands were occupied and have continued to be occupied into modern times.

THE CONCLUSION OF STATE INTERVENTION (800 B.C.E.)

The intervention of external power in the form of the Phoenicians ca. 800 B.C.E. ended over 4,000 years of Maltese independence—Maltese political independence was not to return for nearly another 2,800 years. At this point the seascape impinged, turning a previous barrier into a bridge facilitating the islands' incorporation in broader colonial enterprises. Settlements were established in areas close to the natural ports of the Valletta and Marsaxlokk, and habitation continued on the natural eminences of Mdina and Victoria (Gozo) that had been occupied since the Bronze Age. Headlands were ritualized (or reritualized) in preference to other locations.

The multiple pre-Historic inscriptions in the Maltese landscape are remarkable in their intensity. Over a period of some 7,500 years places were inscribed and reinscribed, indicating a dynamic history of signification and use. The period of peak monumentality before 800 B.C.E. marks a time of considerable insularity and profoundly distinctive identity. Against this—at least in this reading of the landscape—there was an equally severe reaction to internal developments and to relative isolation that probably involved cases of iconoclastic force.

We will never know the full personalities of those who inscribed the Maltese landscapes. What is clear, however, is that over the thousands of years of use and reuse, the islands were inscribed with monuments of various kinds, creating foci of social activity that incorporated rituals of life, death, and links between the two.

NOTE

1. In this chapter, the complex cultural terminology of the Maltese Islands is avoided and absolute dates are employed exclusively, to allow comparison. This chronology is based largely on the radiocarbon dates calibrated by Renfrew and recently updated by AMS dates submitted by Dr. Malone for the Cambridge Gozo Project (Trump 1995–1996) and Dr. Mifsud (Bronk Ramsey et al. 1999). Table 12.1 summarizes these interrelationships.

REFERENCES CITED

Attard Tabone, J. 1999. The Gozo Stone Circle Rediscovered. In *Facets of Maltese Prehistory*, edited by A. Mifsud and C. Savona Ventura, 169–181. Mosta: Prehistoric Society of Malta.

Blanton, R., G. M. Feinman, S. A. Kowalewski, and P. N. Peregrine. 1996. A Dual Processual Theory for the Evolution of Mesoamerican Civilisation. *Current Anthropology* 37:1–14.

Boissevain, J. 1969. *Saints and Fireworks: Religion and Politics in Rural Malta*. London: Athlone Press.

Bonanno, A., T. Gouder, C. Malone, and S. Stoddart. 1990. Monuments in an Island Society: The Maltese Context. *World Archaeology* 2:190–205.

Bradley, R. 1987. Time Regained: The Creation of Continuity. *Journal of the Royal Archaeological Association* 140:1–17.

Bradley, R., and H. Williams (eds.). 1998. The Past in the Past: The Re-use of Ancient Monuments. *World Archaeology* 30.

Bronk Ramsey, C., P. B. Pettitt, R. E. M. Hedges, G. W. L. Hodgins, and D. C. Owen. 1999. Radiocarbon Dates from the Oxford AMS System. *Archaeometry Datelist* 28:422–423.

Chalmers, A., and S. Stoddart. 1996. Photorealistic Graphics for Visualising Archaeological Site Reconstructions. In *Imaging the Past: Electronic Imaging and Computer Graphics in Museums and Archaeology*, edited by A. Higgins, P. Main, and J. Lang, 85–93. London: British Museum.

Clark, J. 1996. CAA reply to De Marrais et al. 1996. *Current Anthropology* 37:51–52.

De Marrais, E., L. J. Castillo, and T. Earle. 1996. Ideology, Materialization, and Power Strategies. *Current Anthropology* 37:15–31.

Grima, R. 2000. Naxxar: An Archaeological Profile. In *Naxxar: A Village and Its People*, edited by P. Catania and L. J. Scerri, 27–64. Gutenberg Press: Hal Tarxien.

Hodder, I. 1996. CAA reply to De Marrais et al. 1996. *Current Anthropology* 37:57–59.

Magro Conti, J. 1999. Aggression and Defence in Prehistoric Malta. In *Facets of Maltese Prehistory*, edited by A. Mifsud and C. Savona Ventura, 191–205. Mosta: Prehistoric Society of Malta.

Malone, C. 1999. Processes of Colonization in the Central Mediterranean. *Accordia Research Papers* 7:37–57.

Malone, C., S. Stoddart, and A. Townsend. 1995. The Landscape of the Island Goddess? A Maltese Perspective of the Central Mediterranean. *Caeculus* 2:1–15.

Mayrhofer, K. 1996. *The Mystery of Hagar Qim*. Malta: Union Print Co.

Mezzena, F. 1998. Le Stele Antropomorfe in Europa. In *Dei di Pietra: La Grande Statuaria Antropomorfa nell'Europa del III Millennio a.C.*, edited by F. Mezzena and G. Zidda, 14–89. Milano: Skira.

Renfrew, C. 1973. *Before Civilisation*. London: Jonathan Cape.

Renfrew, A. C., and E. V. Level. 1979. Exploring Dominance: Predicting Polities from Centres. In *Transformations: Mathematical Approaches to Culture Change*, edited by A. C. Renfrew and K. C. Cooke, 145–167. New York: Academic Press.

Stoddart, S. 1999a. Long-Term Dynamics of an Island Community. Malta 5500–2000 A.D. In *Social Dynamics of the Prehistoric Central Mediterranean*, edited by R. H. Tykot, J. Morter, and J. E. Robb, 137–147. Accordia Specialist Studies on the Mediterranean. Vol. 3. London: Accordia Research Institute.

———. 1999b. Mortuary Customs in Prehistoric Malta. In *Facets of Maltese Prehistory*, edited by A. Mifsud and C. Savona Ventura, 183–190. Mosta: Prehistoric Society of Malta.

Stoddart, S., A. Bonanno, T. Gouder, C. Malone, and D. Trump. 1993. Cult in an Island Society: Prehistoric Malta in the Tarxien Period. *Cambridge Archaeological Journal* 3:3–19.

Trump, D. 1966. *Skorba*. London: Society of Antiquaries.

———. 1995–1996. Radiocarbon Dates from Malta. *Journal of the Accordia Research Institute* 5–6:173–177.

———. 1998. The Cart Ruts of Malta. *Treasures of Malta* 4 (2):33–37.

Vella, N. 1999. Trunkless Legs of Stone: Debating Ritual Continuity at Tas-Silg, Malta. In *Facets of Maltese Prehistory*, edited by A. Mifsud and C. Savona Ventura, 225–239. Mosta: Prehistoric Society of Malta.

Watson, A., and D. Keating. 1999. Architecture and Sound: An Acoustic Analysis of Megalithic Monuments in Prehistoric Britain. *Antiquity* 73:325–336.

Zammit, T. 1930. *Prehistoric Malta: The Tarxien Temples*. Oxford: Oxford University Press.

THIRTEEN

Imperial Inscriptions in the Aztec Landscape

Emily Umberger

In this chapter I explore the hegemonic nature of place marking in the Aztec state.[1] When Spaniards arrived in the Valley of Mexico in 1519, they found a highland basin occupied by about one million people (Figure 13.1). At its political and demographic center, the Mexica city of Tenochtitlan and its satellite Tlatelolco, sharing an island in the lake filling the Valley bottom, together probably had 100,000 inhabitants. Other zones of the Valley were occupied by some fifty city-states of lesser size. These city-states consisted of an urban capital, the *altepetl* (literally, water-mountain, plural *altepeme*), with one or more hereditary *tlatoque* (plural for *tlatoani*, speaker), adjacent lands, and dependent towns, villages, and hamlets. At an altitude of 2,200 m above sea level (7,200 feet), the Valley was intensively worked to support this population. Productive zones consisted of the lake itself, where products like birds, fish, and algae were gathered; the lakeshore, with its salt-collecting areas and artificial *chinampa* gardens; the rich Valley bottomlands, with corn, beans, and other crop fields, plus forests; and the terraced maguey fields on the foothills of the surrounding volcanic ranges.[2]

NATIVE LINKS BETWEEN NATURAL AND CULTURAL TERRAINS

The annual travels of the sun marked the parameters of time and space, and the gods of crops and weather, whose powers waxed and waned according to season, were the objects of human petition through contracts of reciprocity. Despite constant rituals, the rains could be unpredictable and agriculture precarious. Documented in Aztec historical sources (all dating from the early colonial period) are a number of years when too much runoff from the hills led to flooding or too little rain led to drought. The basin had no natural outlet and all waters settled in what was actually a group of five lakes in the center. One system of aqueducts brought potable water from lakeshore springs to the islands, and another system brought water to the Acolhua-Texcoco region from the piedmont of Mount Tlaloc to the east. The gods who controlled water were the rain god Tlaloc (He Who Is Made of Earth) and Chalchiuhtlicue (Jade Her Skirt), the goddess of surface water, lakes, and rivers. Other deities were concerned with weather, like Ehecatl (Wind),

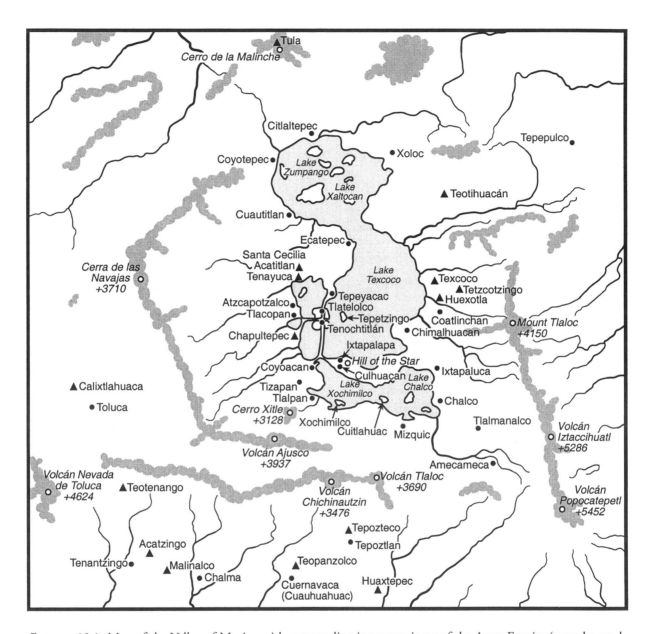

FIGURE 13.1. Map of the Valley of Mexico with surrounding inner provinces of the Aztec Empire (now the modern states of Mexico, Hidalgo, Morelos, and Puebla). Solid circles: modern settlements; open circles: important mountain peaks, most of which have pre-Hispanic remains, with height indicated in meters; solid triangles: ancient settlements (after Pasztory 1983: pl. 10; courtesy of Harry N. Abrams, New York).

who preceded the rains. These gods were petitioned at shrines on the hills and mountains dedicated to them. Hills were considered the containers of water and seeds and their caves were mythical sites of human and agricultural origins.[3] Local and imperial polities controlled the shrines themselves; concern with the solar cycle and water were very much the prerogative of the *tlatoque* of the various *altepeme*. Rulers were the negotiators between their subjects and the gods; and their continued rule depended largely on food production and associated prosperity. Thus, earth, water, and solar imagery figured large in the architecture and monuments of city centers and in the shrines and rock carvings at springs and hilltops.

Perhaps the images most expressive of the ruler's relationship to these cosmic powers are those carved in relief on a pyramid-throne found in 1926 beneath the foundations of the National Palace in Mexico City (Umberger 1984). The National Palace is on the site of the former governmental palace (*tecpan*)

of the last Mexica Aztec *hueitlatoani* (great speaker), the emperor Motecuhzoma II (ruled 1502–1520), and this throne bears his name. The throne takes the form of a pyramid, an artificial mountain, with an "earth monster" serving as the seat and a solar disk on the seat back (see miniature versions of such thrones in Figure 13.2). On the reverse side of the monument the hieroglyphic symbol of Tenochtitlan, a prickly pear cactus, names the city itself, rising from the waters of the lake. In placing himself on this throne, the ruler sat on the earth-mountain surrounded by water; he carried the emerging sun on his back. The successes of the Mexica Aztec ruler and his patron god Huitzilopochtli (Hummingbird, left) were intimately associated with the sun, as expressed in verbal metaphors comparing success to the rising sun (Sahagún 1950–1982, book 1, 2nd ed.: 83–84; Umberger 1987a:424–428). Thus, small figures of the god and the ruler flank the solar disk on the seat back.[4]

FIGURE 13.2. Clay figurines representing costumed figures (gods or rulers as gods Xipe and Ehecatl) (from Seler 1960–1961a, 3:454–455, figs. 3–5; courtesy of the Akademische Druck- und Verlagsanstalt, Graz).

This monument provides the key to the relationship of rulers to the landscape and, by extension, the cosmos. The Aztecs also marked the actual landscape in many ways and brought natural features into urban centers in the form of built structures. The pyramids and platforms represented artificial mountains and hills; basins, pools, and aqueducts represented lakes, springs, and rivers; and gardens of food plants, trees, and flowers represented fields and forests. Birds and fish abounded in these gardens and together with flowers made the gardens images of the rain god's paradise, Tlalocan,[5] placed in close proximity to the ruling family. Zoos incorporated other animals or their sculpted images (Nicholson 1955). All of the city's structures established links with different parts of the landscape, and some were probably used as altars directed at corresponding areas.[6] The centralmost of these city shrines was the main temple of Tenochtitlan, the Templo Mayor (Boone 1987; Broda 1988), standing for the origin-mountain of Coatepec (Serpent Mountain) where the tribal god Huitzilopochtli was conceived as born like the sun from the earth in the morning (Matos Moctezuma 1988). At the time of the god's "birth," Coatepec seems to have been the locus of a preexisting shrine.[7] One would suppose that this shrine was dedicated to the rain god Tlaloc and was a prototype of the Tlaloc temple next to Huitzilopochtli's on the platform of the Templo Mayor. Reinforcing the connection with the powers of sun and rain, the Templo Mayor as a whole was oriented so that the mountain dedicated to Tlaloc in the volcanic range to the east of the city was seen on the horizon behind it. The temple was oriented more precisely so that the equinox sun rising in the east appeared between its two shrines, and it faced west toward the sun's place of sinking below the earth-mountain at night (Aveni et al. 1988). On the summit of Mount Tlaloc, in turn, a temple in a walled precinct with a long passageway formed an imitation cave, an entrance to the underworld. This would have been like the passage from which the sun emerged, as well as a visual representation of one interpretation of the rain god's name, "Road under the Earth" (Sullivan 1974:213). Every year at this mountain shrine children dedicated to the rain god were sacrificed by the major *tlatoque* of the Valley of Mexico together with their traditional enemies from the neighboring Valley of Puebla during a time of forced armistice (Durán 1967, 1:81 ff.; Townsend 1991; Wicke and Horcasitas 1957). Remains of smaller shrines, some with altars and deity images in the round and some with rock-art images directed at various gods, have been found on many of the mountains surrounding the Valley (e.g., Aveni 1991; Broda 1991; Carrasco 1991; García Moll 1968; Iwaniszewski 1986; Krickeberg 1969; Lorenzo 1957; Pijo and Hernández 1972). Certainly they once existed on all such rises, and no doubt local shrines were controlled politically by the communities adjacent to them, just as the better-known imperial and "international" shrines, like the one on Mount Tlaloc, were controlled by the dominant cities. In addition, deserted, ancient sites like Teotihuacan, with their artificial pyramid-mountains, were used for ceremonies affirming inheritance by present polities of ancient cosmic responsibilities.

DYNASTIC MOUNTAIN SITES

Important natural hills in the Valley between the high mountains and the cities were the sites of the country "pleasure" palaces of the dominant polities (see Evans 2000). These palace sites, consisting of partly natural and partly built or modified forms, expressed dynastic contracts with natural forces even more clearly than the built structures in cities. The Aztec Empire of 1519 was the creation of three cities, the Triple Alliance of the powerful Tenochtitlan with the smaller cities of Texcoco and Tlacopan. Texcoco (population about 60,000) was the capital of the Acolhua area of the east Valley, and Tlacopan (population unknown) was the capital of the Tepanec area of the west Valley. Little is known of the Tlacopan area, but much was recorded about the areas dominated by Tenochtitlan and Texcoco. In both cases a small, free-standing mountain of conical shape served as the "dynastic mountain" palace site. Located at a strategic point along the aqueduct system that supplied its city, each made obvious physically the link between the *altepetl's* dynasty

and water control. Chapultepec, the mountain retreat of the Tenochtitlan rulers, was located on the west lakeshore, and the main aqueduct of Tenochtitlan originated in springs at its foot (Lombardo de Ruíz 1973:193–196). Tetzcotzingo, the mountain retreat of the Texcoco rulers, was east of their capital—midway between it and its water source, the springs at the foot of Mount Tlaloc—and the channel that supplied water to Tetzcotzingo branched off from the main channel to the city (Figure 13.3).

Both sites had palaces, gardens, waterworks, and nearby forests for hunting. These are of course the typical necessities for a luxurious country stay, but colonial documents make clear the crucial symbolic underpinnings of all of these features. The connection with water sources, in particular, was not solely a mat-

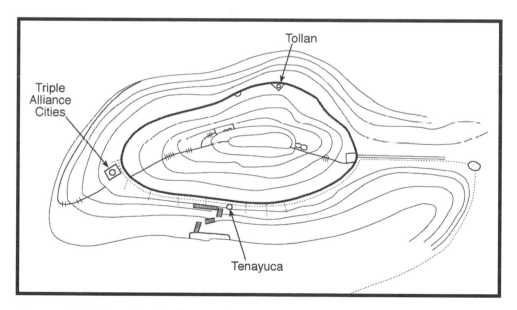

FIGURE 13.3. Plan of the Acolhua royal retreat on the mountain of Tetzcotzingo. The locations of remains are from archaeological survey; their labeling is from Alva Ixtlilxóchitl's (1975–1977) description. The dashed line indicates the canal; steps lead east to west over the top of the mountain and down the south side from the canal to the palace area (after Parsons 1971: fig. 24, modified).

ter of need. According to *The Titles of Tetzcotzingo* (McAffee and Barlow 1945–1948), the complex at Tetzcotzingo as a whole was conceived as a monumental testimony to the people of the area commemorating the ruler Nezahualcoyotl's bringing of the vital element to his domain. Remains and modifications to the hill itself reveal that, like Motecuhzoma's pyramid-throne, Tetzcotzingo represented an *imago mundi*, incorporating the world-mountain, water, and sun (Townsend 1982a, 2000; Umberger 1981:156–157, 1987b:96). A water channel still extends along the south side of the hill, halfway between the base and the summit. Parallel to this and over the summit is a path, formed partly of rock-hewn steps and marking the east-to-west passage of the sun, as if the top of the hill were the summit of the sky. The channel itself probably represented the surface of the earth, with a pool at its westernmost end being the lake around which the Triple Alliance cities were once represented by three frogs, according to an early seventeenth-century description of the place (Alva Ixtlilxóchitl 1975– 1977, 2:114–116). On the north side of the hill a temple front with another pool represented the ancient Toltec city of Tollan. A corresponding pool along the channel on the south side represented the ancient Chichimec city of Tenayucan (the Aztecs of the Valley considered themselves descendants of both Toltecs and Chichimecs). The area below the path may have been conceived as the "other world" paradise of the rain god. Within it were, reportedly, a palace and a tropical garden on the south side of the hill. Many sculptures and inscriptions documenting events in the lives of the kings of the dynasty were located all over the hill. Accounts about Tetzcotzingo describe it as a place of dynastic beginnings as well as the realization of dominion. It was the hiding place of the fugitive prince Nezahualcoyotl before he defeated his enemies and was reinstated on his hereditary throne.

The Chapultepec hill was no doubt also a site of a palace and exotic gardens, but, unfortunately, little remains of these because of the hill's propinquity to colonial and modern Mexico City, which was built on Tenochtitlan-Tlatelolco. Postconquest structures included a church and later the Castillo palace, which is still on its summit (Linné 1948:100–103). Still remaining in the bedrock of the hill, however, are the traces of the royal portraits (Figure 13.4) carved near the end of each Mexica king's reign (Nicholson 1959; Umberger 1981:147–151). Accounts about Chapultepec tell of its association also with both the beginning and end of Mexica hegemony in general, as well as myths involving water control. Chapultepec had been the locus of the humiliation of Huemac, an ancient Toltec ruler, who, upon winning a ball game against the representatives of Tlaloc, had dared to choose as his prize the symbols of fertility—jade and quetzal feathers—over the actual corn crop that sustained life. This important incident led to the fall of the Toltecs and the subsequent inheritance by the Mexica Aztecs of the responsibility to sacrifice children to the rain god (Leyenda de los Soles 1975:126–127). Later in the adventures of the Mexica tribe, Chapultepec was the place where they suffered defeat at the hands of their lakeshore enemies before swimming to the island site of their future city Tenochtitlan-Tlatelolco. Finally, it was the place where Motecuhzoma II went to hide in a cave when the fall of his empire appeared imminent (Durán 1967, 2:37 ff., 495–496).

Chapultepec then was a site rich in references to Mexica politics and the obligations underpinning that power. The first account contains a warning to kings that dominion was dependent on fertility and water, not riches. The second account, like the story of the young Nezahualcoyotl at Tetzcotzingo, illustrates how these palace sites were intimately connected with a

FIGURE 13.4. Remains of the portrait of the ruler Motecuhzoma II at Chapultepec, carved into a rock at the base of the hill in about 1519 and destroyed in the mid-eighteenth century (photograph by the author, courtesy of the Instituto Nacional de Antropología, Mexico).

tribal dynasty, as places of early humiliation later to be transformed into places commemorative of power. In Aztec thought, the mountain form itself, like the pyramid-throne described earlier, served as a visual embodiment of political success, which was comparable to the sun at the zenith. Failure was conceived as like the disappearance of the sun—its fall from the zenith. For Motecuhzoma II, the return to a cave in the dynastic mountain was a return to the underworld, an acknowledgment of the impending fall of his house. The cave was a place of endings as well as beginnings.

ROCK CARVINGS WITH POLITICAL IMAGERY

As the Aztecs moved into foreign territories outside the Valley they appropriated for their own usage the ancient deserted cities with pyramids and the sacred mountain sites that had served previously as areas of cult focus for the local inhabitants. The best-known distant urban site was Tula, called Tollan by the Aztecs. Evidences of Aztec appropriation of this place abound in written records and archaeological remains (Umberger 1987b). Best known of the foreign hill sites is Malinalco, where the Codex Aubin (1963) says the Aztecs built their own temples in the early years of the sixteenth century (Townsend 1982b), apparently over preexisting local temples (Galván Villegas 1984:167 ff.). Less well known are figurative rock reliefs on hills and mountains that give more explicit information about the relationship between sites and historical events and personages in the imperial capital of Tenochtitlan. The two described here, although outside the Valley of Mexico, were used at times of crisis in Tenochtitlan to appeal to supernatural beings dwelling in the vicinity.

The first site consists of reliefs on four adjacent rock surfaces on the hill of La Malinche (Figure 13.5) across the river from the abandoned city of Tula, believed by the Aztecs to have been ruled by Quetzalcoatl (Feathered Serpent). In Aztec sources, Quetzalcoatl provided the model for ruler comportment (Florescano 1999; López Austin 1973; Quiñones Keber 1993). Depicted on two facing surfaces on the left side are the framed date 8 Flint, referring to the year 1500 when a great flood swamped the city of Tenochtitlan, and a frontal image of Chalchiuhtlicue, the goddess held responsible for unleashing the rampaging waters of the lake. On the remaining two surfaces to the right of these are a profile image of Quetzalcoatl, posed and dressed as a penitent ruler drawing blood from his ear, and the unframed date 4 Reed next to him, referring to a day. As a deity, Quetzalcoatl is labeled by a calendric name glyph, 1 Reed (Ce Acatl, one of his names in Nahuatl, the Aztec language). From the evidence of written sources on the great flood (Durán 1967, 2: chaps. 48

and 49), the deified ruler probably stands in for the unfortunate Aztec king, Ahuitzotl (ruled Tenochtitlan 1486–1502), whose actions had led to the flood (Umberger 1981:157–164). In the previous year, 1499, Ahuitzotl had had his representatives murder the lakeshore lord of Coyoacan to use a spring in his territory to supply a new aqueduct to Tenochtitlan (apparently the aqueduct from Chapultepec was no longer sufficient). The people of the Valley in general conceived of this murder as unjustified, probably because of the strong proprietary link between a ruler and the water sources in his domain. They blamed Ahuitzotl and his aqueduct for the flooding that continued for a year and nearly overwhelmed the city.

Finally, the repentant king sent his priests on a pilgrimage to make offerings at the offended spring.

The flooding ceased, or so Durán stated. Aztec written accounts tell of other occasions when priests went to Tula to make offerings to Quetzalcoatl or to seek the advice of Huitzilopochtli's mother, who lived at a nearby hill (Durán 1967, 2:215 ff., 511). They do not mention a journey to Tula at the time of the flood, but the reliefs near the ancient city point to the possibility. The final motif on the carved rock, the date 4 Reed, the traditional day of an Aztec lord's installation, probably stands as a further sign of Ahuitzotl's contrition, when he had the son of the murdered lord put on his hereditary throne. This, in effect, was an acknowledgment of the local dynasty's rights and the illegitimacy of the Mexica ruler's aggression. That the deity image is of an ancient ruler petitioning the water goddess is not

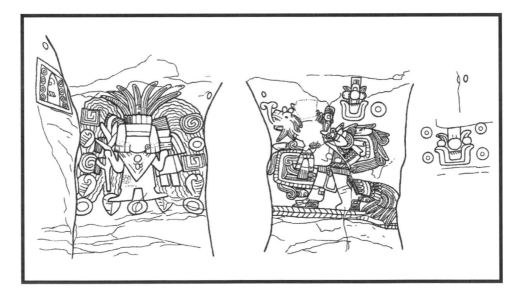

FIGURE 13.5. Low reliefs on four surfaces of rocks on the hill of La Malinche, facing ancient Tula/Tollan. Represented from left to right are the year date 8 Flint (1500); the lake water goddess Chalchiuhtlicue (the object of petition); the deified Toltec ruler Quetzalcoatl (the model for Aztec rulership) accompanied by his calendric name 1 Reed (*Ce Acatl*) and drawing blood from his ear in petition; and the date 4 Reed, the day of royal installation (drawing by the author).

accidental, given the link between rulers and water control. The reliefs' location on a hill near Tula probably has more to do with the association of the site with Quetzalcoatl than anything relating to the lake water goddess, because the hill is not known to have been dedicated to her (although a local resonance is not ruled out).

Ahuitzotl died two years later, reportedly as the result of a head injury sustained during the flood (Alva Ixtlilxóchitl 1975–77, 2:167). This was the probable reason for the reactivation by the Aztecs of another sacred site in foreign territory. The site is the temple called the Tepozteco, built on a high volcanic ridge above the modern town of Tepoztlan (Saville 1896; Seler 1960–1961b). It was the traditional seat of the powerful pulque god Tepoztecatl, who controlled the imperial province of Huaxtepec (Berdan et al. 1996:328; Seler 1960–1961b; Umberger 1981: 139–141). Ahuitzotl's nameglyph (Figure 13.6) and the year date of his death, 10 Rabbit (1502), were carved on plaques set into the base of the pyramid, a newly built or renovated structure on an old sacred site.[8] Here the choice to commemorate the emperor's death at a provincial shrine comes from the association of 8 Reed, the year date of the flood that led to his fatal injury, with the pulque god, whose ceremonial day was 8 Flint.[9] The event causing Ahuitzotl's death was seemingly connected by Aztec priest-seers to this god's domain, and his distant temple became the site of a final, penitential ceremony. Again, the use and marking of the site were specific to Tenochtitlan's internal needs, not in any way an overt proclamation of victory over the area or relating more specifically to the local territory.

The rock carvings and hill monuments discussed here are among many found in Aztec territories. Others emphasize the mythical associations of a place in Aztec thought without clear historical ref-

FIGURE 13.6. Relief carving of Ahuitzotl's name glyph, originally set into the Tepozteco. Museo Nacional de Antropología, Mexico (photograph by the author, courtesy of the MNA).

erences; or commemorate Aztec aggression; or combine imagery of mythical precedents and current Aztec hegemony. Still others may be more a matter of local than imperial marking; or consist of fragmentary, abbreviated inscriptions, unrelated to each other and pertaining to multiple uses of a site (see, for example, Marcus 1982; Umberger 1981: chap. 4). The monuments emphasized here are the ones that reveal perhaps a less obvious, underlying aspect of Aztec expansion, their concern with the powers of local cult sites and their use of these in relation to crises in the imperial capital. The examples chosen also can be linked to particular historical events, highlighting the political responsibility of a territory's lords to control the elements of nature. Most preserved mountain and rock carving sites are in the Valley and the inner empire surrounding it, but no doubt similar ideas operated in the farther distant provinces, where preservation of monuments, Aztec-period archaeology, and recordation of Aztec motivations in colonial texts are scarcer.

Although speaking of the original peopling of a territory, Alfredo López Austin's (1997:259) words about the appropriation of local hills can be applied aptly to Aztec aggressions into already inhabited areas. He said, "When a town was established, the patron gods occupied hills or changed themselves into hills. . . . Taking possession of a territory implied extending the different manifestations of divine force to it."[10] To this it must be added that the sacralization of a territory was a political act, and the people most invested in it were rulers. The act of inscribing the landscape was central to this hegemonic process.

NOTES

1. Much is owed to R. F. Townsend's work on Aztec architectural symbolism and Aztec sites at Mount Tlaloc, Tetzcotzingo, and Malinalco (see Townsend 1992, chap. 8, and other references cited). See also Carrasco 1991.

2. For overviews of the Aztec Valley of Mexico, see Gibson 1964; Lockhart 1992; and Sanders et al. 1979. For the Aztec Empire, see Berdan et al. 1996.

3. On the rain god, fertility cults, and ceremonies, and associated hills, see Aveni 1991; Broda 1982, 1987, 1991; Carrasco 1990, 1991; Heyden 1973; Krickeberg 1950; López Austin 1997; Pasztory 1988; Townsend 1982a,b, 1992.

4. More abbreviated references to the sun-on-mountain cosmogram took the form of small platforms called *momoztli*, placed like altars in market plazas and along roads (Heyden 1968; Noguera 1973; Umberger 1984; see also Cook de Leonard 1955); these were probably "seats of authority" in the places where they were located.

5. I refer to Burkhart's description of this paradise (1992); see also Lopez Austin 1997.

6. I am adopting Reinhard's (1985) approach to the relationship of altars to mountains.

7. I suggest this because the god's mother, Coatlicue, was sweeping there as an act of devotion. This would have been the sweeping of a shrine, not an unadorned mountaintop (Sahagún 1950–1982, book 3, 2nd ed.: 1–2).

8. The date of the pyramid is unknown (Michael Smith, personal communication, 1986); but the reliefs are definitely Aztec period.

9. Flint was one of four Aztec day names that were also used as year names. The associations of days and years of the same name were correlated, if possible. The connection of 8 Flint with a disastrous flood would have been added to its preexisting associations by functionaries who kept the history books.

10. This was probably the case of all Aztec towns, but ironically we have only fragments of such practices in archaeological remains on the peaks surrounding the Valley of Mexico. The most complete example of an Aztec town with hill shrines retaining some of their sculptures into modern times is the colony site of Castillo de Teayo, probably once in the Atlan Province, now the northern part of the modern state of Veracruz. When the town was studied in the early twentieth century, several hills still had pairs of fertility deity images on their summits (Seler 1960–1961c: pl. 7; Umberger 1996:171–178).

REFERENCES CITED

Alva Ixtlilxóchitl, Fernando de. 1975–1977. *Obras Históricas*, edited by E. O'Gorman. 2 vols. México: Universidad Nacional Autónoma de México.

Aveni, A. F. 1991. Mapping the Ritual Landscape: Debt Payment to Tlaloc during the Month of Atlcahualo. In *To Change Place: Aztec Ceremonial Landscapes*, edited by D. Carrasco, 58–74. Niwot: University Press of Colorado.

Aveni, A. F., E. E. Calnek, and H. Hartung. 1988. Myth,

Environment, and the Orientation of the Templo Mayor of Tenochtitlan. *American Antiquity* 53 (2): 287–309.

Berdan, F. F., R. E. Blanton, E. H. Boone, M. G. Hodge, M. E. Smith, and E. Umberger. 1996. *Aztec Imperial Strategies*. Washington: Dumbarton Oaks.

Boone, E. H. (ed.). 1987. *The Aztec Templo Mayor*. Washington: Dumbarton Oaks.

Broda, J. 1982. El Culto Mexica de los Cerros y del Agua. *Multidisciplina* 3 (7): 45–56.

———. 1987. The Provenience of the Offerings: Tribute and Cosmovision. In *The Aztec Templo Mayor*, edited by E. H. Boone, 211–256. Washington: Dumbarton Oaks.

———. 1988. Templo Mayor as Ritual Space. In J. Broda, D. Carrasco, and E. Matos Moctezuma, *The Great Temple of Tenochtitlan: Center and Periphery in the Aztec World*, 61–123. Berkeley: University of California Press.

———. 1991. The Sacred Landscape of Aztec Calendar Festivals: Myth, Nature, and Society. In *To Change Place: Aztec Ceremonial Landscapes*, edited by D. Carrasco, 74–120. Niwot: University Press of Colorado.

Burkhart, L. 1992. Flowery Heaven: The Aesthetic of Paradise in Nahuatl Devotional Literature. *Res: Anthropology and Aesthetics* 21:88–109.

Carrasco, D. 1990. *Religions of Mesoamerica*. San Francisco: Harper and Row.

———, (ed.). 1991. *To Change Place: Aztec Ceremonial Landscapes*. Niwot: University Press of Colorado.

Codex Aubin. 1963. *Historia de la Nación Mexicana: Reproducción a Todo Color del Códice de 1576 (Códice Aubin)*, edited by C. E. Dibble. Madrid: José Porrúa Turanzas.

Cook de Leonard, C. 1955. Una "Maqueta" Prehispánica. *El México Antiguo* 8:169–191.

Durán, D. 1967. *Historia de las Indias de Nueva España e Islas de la Tierra Firme*, edited by Angel María Garibay. 2 vols. México: Editorial Porrúa.

Evans, S. T. 2000. Aztec Royal Pleasure Parks: Conspicuous Consumption and Elite Status Rivalry. *Studies in the History of Gardens and Designed Landscapes* 20 (3): 206–228.

Florescano, E. 1999. *The Myth of Quetzalcoatl*. Baltimore: Johns Hopkins University Press.

Galván Villegas, L. J. 1984. *Aspectos Generales de la Arqueología de Malinalco, Estado de México*. México: Instituto Nacional de Antropología e Historia.

García Moll, R. 1968. Un Adoratorio a Tlaloc en la Cuenca de México. *Boletín del Instituto Nacional de Antropología e Historia* 34:24–27.

Gibson, C. 1964. *The Aztecs under Spanish Rule*. Stanford: Stanford University Press.

Heyden, D. 1968. Algunos Elementos de Momoztlis. *Boletín del Instituto Nacional de Antropología e Historia* 31:43–45.

———. 1973. What Is the Significance of the Mexican Pyramid? *Acts, Fortieth International Congress of Americanists* (1972) 1:109–115.

Iwaniszewski, S. 1986. La Arqueología de Alta Montaña en México y su Estado Actual. *Estudios de Cultura Náhuatl* 18:249–273.

Krickeberg, W. 1950. Bauform und Weltbild im Alten Mexico. *Mythe, Mensch und Umwelt . . .* , *Paideuma* 4:293–333.

———. 1969. *Feldsplastik und Felsbilder Altamerikas II*. Berlin: Verlag von Dietrich Reimer.

Leyenda de los Soles. 1975. In *Códice Chimalpopoca, Anales de Cuauhtitlan y Leyenda de los Soles*, translated by Primo Feliciano Velázquez, 119–128. México: Universidad Nacional Autónoma de México, Instituto de Investigaciones Históricas.

Linné, S. 1948. *El Valle y la Ciudad de México en 1550*. Stockholm: Statens Etnografiska Museum.

Lockhart, J. 1992. *The Nahuas after the Conquest: A Social and Cultural History of the Indians of Central Mexico, Sixteenth through Eighteenth Centuries*. Stanford: Stanford University Press.

Lombardo de Ruíz, S. 1973. *Desarrollo Urbano de México-Tenochtitlán según las fuentes Históricas*. México: Instituto Nacional de Antropología e Historia.

López Austin, A. 1973. *Hombre-Díos, Religión y Política*

en el Mundo Náhuatl. México: Universidad Nacional Autónoma de México.

———. 1997. *Tamoanchan, Tlalocan: Places of Mist*. Niwot: University Press of Colorado.

Lorenzo, J. L. 1957. *Las Zonas Arqueológicas del los Volcanes Ixtaccihuatl y Popocatepetl*. México: Instituto Nacional de Antropología e Historia.

Marcus, J. 1982. The Aztec Monuments of Acalpixcan. In J. R. Parsons, E. S. Brumfiel, M. H. Parsons, and D. J. Wilson, *Prehispanic Settlement Patterns in the Southern Valley of Mexico: The Chalco-Xochimilco Region*, 475–485. Memoirs of the Museum of Anthropology 14. Ann Arbor: University of Michigan.

Matos Moctezuma, E. 1988. The Templo Mayor of Tenochtitlan: History and Interpretation. In J. Broda, D. Carrasco, and E. Matos Moctezuma, *The Great Temple of Tenochtitlan: Center and Periphery in the Aztec World*, 15–60. Berkeley: University of California Press.

McAfee, B., and R. H. Barlow. 1945–1948. Titles of Tetzcotzingo. *Tlalocán* 2:100–127.

Nicholson, H. B. 1955. Montezuma's Zoo. *Pacific Discovery* 8 (4): 3–11.

———. 1959. The Chapultepec Cliff Sculpture of Motecuhzoma Xocoyotzin. *El México Antiguo* 9:379–443.

Noguera, E. 1973. Las Funciones del *Momoztli*. *Anales de Antropología* 10:111–122.

Parsons, J. R. 1971. *Prehispanic Settlement Patterns in the Texcoco Region, Mexico*. Memoirs of the Museum of Anthropology 3. Ann Arbor: University of Michigan.

Pasztory, E. 1983. *Aztec Art*. New York: Harry N. Abrams.

———. 1988. The Aztec Tlaloc: God of Antiquity. In *Smoke and Mist: Mesoamerican Studies in Memory of Thelma D. Sullivan*, edited by J. K. Josserand and K. Dakin, 290–327. Oxford: British Archaeological Reports.

Pijo, V., and C. Hernández. 1972. Pinturas Rupestres Aztecas en el Popocatepetl. In *Religión en Mesoamerica: XII Mesa Redonda de la Sociedad Mexicana de Antropología*, edited by J. L. King and N.

Castillo Tejero, 85–90. México: Sociedad Mexicana de Antropología.

Quiñones Keber, E. 1993. Quetzalcoatl as a Dynastic Patron: The "Acuecuexatl Stone" Reconsidered. In *The Symbolism in the Plastic and Pictorial Representations of Ancient Mexico*, edited by J. de Durand Forest and M. Ensinger, 149–155. Amsterdam: Estudios Americanistas de Bonn.

Reinhard, J. 1985. *The Nazca Lines: A New Perspective on Their Origin and Meaning*. Lima: Editorial Los Pinos.

Sahagún, B. de. 1950–1982. *Florentine Codex: General History of the Things of New Spain*, 12 books, translated and edited by A. J. O. Anderson and C. E. Dibble. Santa Fe: School of American Research and the University of Utah Press.

Sanders, W. T., J. R. Parsons, and R. S. Santley. 1979. *The Basin of Mexico: Ecological Processes in the Evolution of a Civilization*. New York: Academic Press.

Saville, M. H. 1896. The Temple of Tepoztlan, Mexico. *Bulletin of the American Museum of Natural History* 8:221–226.

Seler, E. 1960–1961a. *Gesammelte Abhandlungen*. 5 vols. Graz: Akademische Druck- und Verlagsanstalt.

———. 1960–1961b. Die Tempelpyramide von Tepoztlan. In *Gesammelte Abhandlungen* 2:200–214. Graz: Akademische Druck- und Verlagsanstalt.

———. 1960–1961c. Die Alterthümer von Castillo de Teayo. In *Gesammelte Abhandlungen* 3:487–513. Graz: Akademische Druck- und Verlagsanstalt.

Sullivan, T. D. 1974. Tlaloc: A New Etymological Interpretation of the God's Name and What It Reveals of His Essence and Nature. *Acts, Fortieth International Congress of Americanists* (1972) 2:213–220.

Townsend, R. F. 1982a. Pyramid and Sacred Mountain. In *Ethnoastronomy and Archaeoastronomy in the American Tropics*, edited by A. F. Avenui and G. Urton, 37–62. Annals of the New York Academy of Sciences 385. New York: New York Academy of Sciences.

———. 1982b. Malinalco and the Lords of Tenochtitlan. In *The Art and Iconography of Late Post-classic*

Central Mexico, edited by E. H. Boone, 111–140. Washington: Dumbarton Oaks.

———. 1991. The Mt. Tlaloc Project. In *To Change Place: Aztec Ceremonial Landscapes*, edited by D. Carrasco, 26–30. Niwot: University Press of Colorado.

———. 1992. *The Aztecs*. London: Thames and Hudson.

———. 2000. Pilgrimage and Renewal at the Hill of Tetzcotzingo. Paper presented at the Pre-Columbian Studies Symposium, Pilgrimage and Ritual Landscape in Pre-Columbian America, Dumbarton Oaks, Washington, D.C.

Umberger, E. 1981. *Aztec Sculptures, Hieroglyphs, and History*. Ph.D. diss., Columbia University, New York.

———. 1984. El Trono de Moctezuma. *Estudios de Cultura Náhuatl* 17:63–87.

———. 1987a. Events Commemorated by Date Plaques at the Templo Mayor: Further Thoughts on the Solar Metaphor. In *The Aztec Templo Mayor*, edited by E. H. Boone, 411–450. Washington: Dumbarton Oaks.

———. 1987b. Antiques, Revivals, and References to the Past in Aztec Art. *Res* 13:62–105.

———. 1996. Aztec Presence and Material Remains in the Outer Provinces. In *Aztec Imperial Strategies*, edited by F. F. Berdan, R. E. Blanton, E. H. Boone, M. G. Hodge, M. E. Smith, and E. Umberger, 151–180. Washington: Dumbarton Oaks.

Wicke, C., and F. Horcasitas. 1957. Archaeological Investigations on Monte Tlaloc, Mexico. *Mesoamerican Notes* 5:83–95.

FOURTEEN

Negotiating the Village

Community Landscapes in the Late Pre-Historic American Southwest

Michael Adler

The ancestral pueblo peoples, or Anasazi, of the American Southwest are noted for their exquisite masonry and adobe structures, silent edifices that were left to fall apart after their inhabitants migrated elsewhere. These early apartment complexes, built into cliff-side alcoves or commanding mesa-top locations, now provide mystery and elegy to packs of migrating tourists. Early anthropologists working among descendant populations, including the Hopi, Zuni, and other pueblo-dwelling peoples, depicted the historic Pueblos as the inheritors of a long history of peaceful, agrarian village life (Benedict 1934; Cushing 1974). Pueblo peoples have occupied the arid lands of the Southwest for centuries (Figure 14.1), over which time they have created a culturally inscribed landscape full of history, conflict, and migration. In this chapter I describe settlement and land use patterns utilized by ancestral pueblo peoples to create and reproduce social boundaries within and between largely agrarian communities between 700 and 1400 C.E. One substantial change over this time

was the nearly wholesale movement into large, aggregated village communities following centuries of relatively "rural" settlement typified by geographically widespread occupation of small, dispersed agrarian communities. Despite this change in household settlement patterns, puebloan peoples recognized and expressed their community identity and integration through the construction of monumental architectural features, including great kivas, great houses, and formalized plaza spaces. These monumental products of community effort created long-lasting symbols of group history and identity that marked, and continue to mark, the Southwestern cultural landscape. This chapter investigates these built expressions of community organization and concludes with a discussion of intracommunity organization, specifically the architectural evidence for internal segmentation and social factionalism.

My approach recognizes the important roles that the human-built environment plays in defining, constraining, and informing ongoing landscape use by human groups and individuals (Everson and

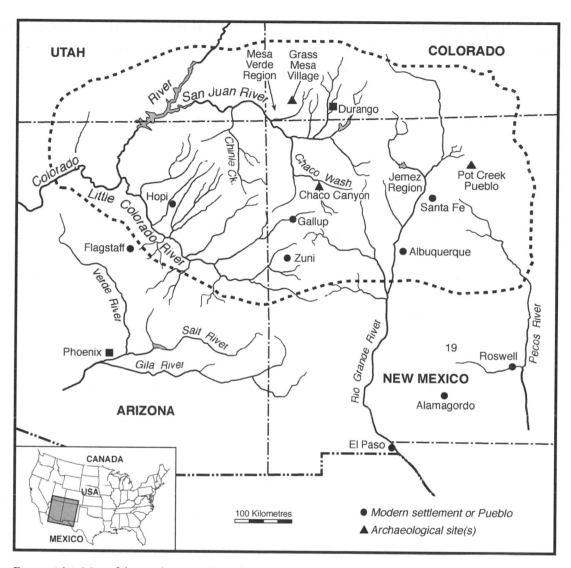

FIGURE 14.1. Map of the southwestern United States. The dashed line indicates the maximal extent of ancestral pueblo occupation at about 1050 C.E.. Sites and regions mentioned in the text are located on the map.

Williamson 1998; Topping 1997). Cross-cultural research on land use and land tenure practices indicates that general regularities exist in the relationships between subsistence practices, community organization, group size, and boundary maintenance (Adler 1996; Netting 1982; Stone 1994). Archaeology provides valuable lines of enquiry through which we can assess the applicability and explanatory strength of cross-cultural generalizations. These assessments, however, rest upon our ability to identify pre-Historic social groupings, subsistence practices, and other variable states of past human strategies.

THE ENVIRONMENTAL SETTING: HOW TO MAKE A LIVING IN THE ARID SOUTHWEST

My primary geographic focus here is the southern portion of the Colorado Plateau and the Rio Grande drainage (Figure 14.1). This region encompasses the arid canyons, mountains, and mesas of the northern Southwest, a rugged and varied terrain ranging in elevation from 5,000 to 13,000 ft (1,515–3,940 m). Yearly rainfall amounts average 8–16 inches (21–42 cm) in the altitudinal zones with sufficiently long growing periods to support corn and bean agriculture. Paleoclimatic records across this region are among the most precise in the world due to substantial amounts of dendrochronological, palynological, and paleoethnobotanical research (Dean 1988). Reconstructions of rainfall and temperature regimes indicate periods of significant drought, as well as long stretches of relatively low climatic variability and consistent levels of sufficient moisture. Averaged over the long term, paleoclimatic data show that at least one of every three years will not provide sufficient moisture to bring a crop of cultigens to maturity.

In other words, the risk of running short of cultivated foods in any given year was high, so it is no surprise that ancestral populations employed a variety of technological and social strategies to reduce the risk of food shortage. The most obvious from an archaeological standpoint was a heavy reliance on storage strategies. Developed largely in concert with an increasing reliance on cultigens after about 1000 B.C.E., food storage in the form of subterranean pits and later aboveground storage rooms ensured that more than a single year's supply of food was available. Based upon ethnographically derived estimates, agricultural peoples in the northern Southwest probably had a goal of at least a three-year supply of food.

COMMUNITY ORGANIZATION IN THE PUEBLOAN SOUTHWEST

Pre-Historic agriculturalists not only modified their built environment to offset bad crop years, they also developed social organizational strategies aimed at averting these same shortfalls. Among the most important is the social formation we call the "community," a level of social organization and identity that we take for granted in today's industrialized and economically integrated world. The community is variously defined, but its primary role is the integration of social groups above the household and kin-group level. In other words, it is a social formation comprising people related less by blood and kinship than by spatial proximity, a shared set of localized resources, a social identity, and very often by a history of sharing these same three criteria. The community is a socially inclusive grouping that serves as the basis for what we call "tribal," "middle-range," or "segmentary" social organization. It differs from the local organization of foraging peoples because it ties primary productive groups (the household) to a localized, bounded set of resources and is contingent on the exclusion of others from that same set of resources. The community is united by engaging mutually recognized inscriptions—villages, gardens, roads—creating a sense of place that guides experience and behavioral expectation. This does not mean that exclusion and protection of resources is not practiced by foraging groups or that nonfood-producing peoples lacked social identities that went beyond the local kin group, because the ethnographic record shows many exceptions to this generalization. My point is that the community is much more evident as a durable, transgenerational social grouping among food-producing peoples than among mobile foragers.

The link between community organization and the reliance on food production is grounded in an understanding of risk, and landscape inscriptions are loaded with such social understandings. Communities are not simply aggregates of people; they are also aggregates of shared risks, interdependence, and identities, particularly among food-producing peoples such as those in the ancestral and historic pueblo worlds. The Southwest is a landscape of fluctuations in precipitation, water tables, erosion, and aggradation: environmental changes that still make food production in the Southwest a risky business. For the past three millennia the dependence on cultigens and agricultural production has supplanted subsistence strategies based upon the collection of wild plants and animals. The community, as a suprahousehold integration strategy, has served to justify, reproduce, and defend the sets of social relationships that underlie individual, household, and multihousehold access to productive resources across the local landscape.

If we think of risk as the potential for failure created by the investment in one set of decisions and strategies over a different set of strategic decisions, we have to realize that the community strategy does not come cheap. The costs of being a part of a community and its social milieu are borne by the household units that, once invested in a fixed locality or region, exchange the uncertainties of making a living outside the social boundaries of a community for the risks associated with investing in the relationships, resources, and people that compose the interdependent, local community. Within any landscape, as the number of people vying for limited resources increases (with intensification an expected part of the equation), there is a competitive advantage afforded to those whose access rights are recognized and reproduced within an established community. This contrasts with mobile foraging groups reliant upon short-lived resource utilization strategies and short-term access rights. These groups achieve less of an advantage from the institutional buffer, and associated costs, that come with an investment in a geographically constrained community structure (Adler 1996).

The community, then, is a group-based risk-buffering strategy that establishes and reproduces access to resources, social identities, territorial boundaries, and interdependent relationships on a local level. The group investing in the strategy generally shares some decision making above the level of the primary economic group. From an archaeological standpoint, it is important to understand that the *social community* does not always live together as an *architecturally identifiable settlement*. It is not difficult to find food-producing communities in the greater Southwest comprising many dispersed households that recognize a common identity and share a local resource base but do not coreside in a single settlement, including the Tarahumara (Merrill 1988), Havasupai (Weber and Seaman 1985), and other groups. Fortunately for pre-Historians, ancestral pueblo peoples commonly constructed large-scale community buildings, particularly during the past millennium. These structures were domestic structures "writ large," providing evidence of how communities were organized in time and space in the Southwest.

COMMUNICATING THE COMMUNITY: MONUMENTAL ARCHITECTURE IN THE ANCESTRAL PUEBLO REALM

Communities of agricultural households created and utilized durable monuments beginning as long ago as the seventh century C.E., with the construction of large pit structures variously called "great kivas" or "oversized pit structures." Such structures not only served as meeting and ritual foci of the community, but the construction and use of the facilities also reproduced systems of local identity and social relationships between constituent groups within each community. Although not as impressive as the later, masonry-lined great kivas of Chaco Canyon (Lekson 1984), these early great kivas were commonly immense, circular structures excavated a meter or more into the ground, covered by a massive, timber-supported roof (Adler and Wilshusen 1990:138–139). An example of one such structure was excavated at Grass Mesa Village, a ninth-century C.E. settlement in southwestern Colorado (Figure 14.2). The Grass Mesa great kiva had a diameter of 22.5 m, sixteen to eighteen times larger in floor area than the contemporaneous residential pit structures at the village. Lightfoot's (1988) reconstruction of the structure estimated that the roof would have weighed a minimum of 227 metric tons and would have required 8,850 person-hours of labor to construct. Clearly these labor requirements are beyond the household level and probably involved the pooled labor and cooperation of many local household groups.

Great kivas are associated with agricultural communities, but the residential patterns within these communities span a wide range of spatial configurations. Most great kiva construction occurred between about the seventh and twelfth centuries C.E. and was associated with highly dispersed residential settlement patterns. There are some shorter-lived "experiments" with the construction and occupation of large villages in the San Juan River drainage of southern Colorado and northern New Mexico during the eighth and ninth centuries C.E., but most great kivas

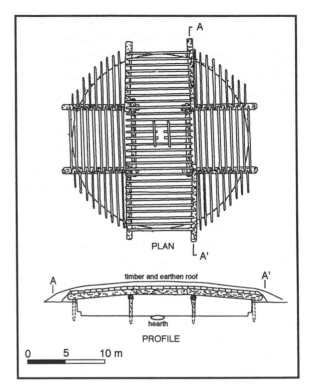

FIGURE 14.2. Reconstruction of great kiva at Grass Mesa Village, southwestern Colorado (adapted from Adler and Wilshusen 1990).

were built in localities across which are scattered many, small household-sized residential settlements. These monumental ancestral pueblo great kivas were likely utilized for community-wide activities such as rituals, dance, and other ritually integrative activities. Great kivas generally lack common domestic features, and those features present tend to be symbolic and religious, including foot drums, *sipapu* (symbolic spirit or emergence holes), and directionally oriented wall niches (Adler 1989; Adler and Wilshusen 1990; Lekson 1984).

Cross-cultural research among food-producing tribal societies illustrates that large-scale manifestations of community labor, ritual behavior, and identity often coexist with what have been called "low-level" or "generalized" ritual structures (Adler 1989). These are structures that are used for ritual activities, but not to the exclusion of day-to-day, domestic activities. In the historic pueblo world and, as detailed here, the pre-Historic pueblo realm, smaller kivas served as low-level ritual structures for factional constituencies within communities. In fact, the smaller "clan" kivas in the Hopi pueblos are just such structures, serving as meeting places and general-use structures that act to integrate smaller portions of pueblo communities.

The construction and use of high-level community integrative structures was not relegated to the subterranean great kiva. Rather, the aboveground "great house" that serves as the built icon of the Chacoan period (ca. 1000–1150 C.E.) is a touchstone that served as the architectural and ritual focus of the community (Figure 14.3). During the Chaco era, massive "great houses" were built throughout the San Juan Basin of northwestern New Mexico, southern Colorado, and western Arizona. The type sites for Chaco-era great houses include Pueblo Bonito and other structures in Chaco Canyon that were built as planned, large-scale construction events (Lekson 1984; Stein and Fowler 1996). Structurally, Chaco great houses are scaled-up renderings of the common residence of the time, the unit pueblo (see Figure 14.3). Great house design includes a number of architectural "canons" that differentiate these structures in scale, labor expenditure, and formality from the smaller residential sites that fill the surrounding landscape. Great house architecture utilizes standardized masonry styles (often called core-veneer construction), oversized rooms, multistory construction built on preplanned site layouts, enclosed plazas, formalized midden areas (some of which are sculpted to form platform-topped mounds), and lin-ear features (roads) that formalized the access routes into the structure.

Enduring debates continue to question the degree to which these community integrative edifices were utilized as domiciles (Lekson 1984; Fowler and Stein 1992; see also Doyel 1992). Similarly contentious is the argument over community and regional leadership. Some attribute the growth of the regional system of great house organization to stratified sociopolitical leadership that controlled multiple communities through economic redistribution, elite-based exchange, and coercive force (Schelberg 1992; Sebastian 1992; Wilcox 1996). Others model this regional landscape as one of autonomous, relatively egalitarian communities competing and contesting productive landscapes, with each local community marking its territory and history with monumental architectural features such as great kivas and great houses (Adler 1990; Varien 1999).

Both models of great house use recognize that these structures were the centerpieces of dispersed agrarian communities. Population estimates of these communities vary across time periods and regions, with most numbering in the hundreds of individuals. For example, full-coverage archaeological surveys of several eleventh- to twelfth-century great house communities in southwestern Colorado indicate momentary populations of between 145 and 400 people per community.

CONCENTRATING THE COMMUNITY: THE PUEBLOS COME TO BE

Communities comprising spatially dispersed households and household clusters best characterize time periods of approximately 0–700 C.E. and 1000–

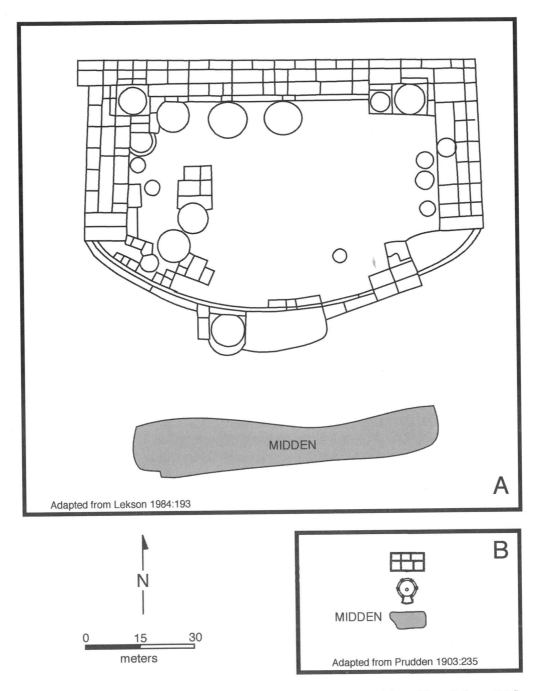

MIDDEN

A

N

0   15   30

meters

B

MIDDEN

FIGURE 14.3. *A.* Pueblo Alto great house, Chaco Canyon, New Mexico (adapted from Lekson 1984). *B.* An example of a "unit pueblo," the small residential settlement occupied throughout the northern Southwest during the time of great house construction (adapted from Prudden 1903).

1150 C.E. across the northern Southwest. The most momentous alteration in the spatial structure of ancestral puebloan settlement patterns occurred largely during and after the thirteenth century in the form of widespread population aggregation. The massive, contiguous architectural complexes that typify historic pueblo community layout became the rule rather than the exception across the Southwest about that time (Figure 14.4). The impetus for the transregional movement into aggregated villages has been attributed to warfare, labor needs, ritual belief systems, and resource competition (Adler et al. 1996). There was probably no single driving cause, because these influences are not necessarily mutually exclusive. Whatever the cause(s), community populations generally forsook their formerly dispersed residential settlement patterns and moved into large villages.

Population estimates of aggregated villages are more numerous given the spatial concentration of residential space. Population size and spatial configuration of ancestral pueblo communities exemplifies quite a range of variability across time and space. Across the northern Southwest, village populations vary between 250 and 1,400 people, with most falling below 500 people. The spatial layouts of the postthirteenth-century aggregated villages carry on some of the same architectural characteristics of the community-level great houses and great kivas of the earlier, dispersed communities. Smaller kivas continue to be constructed within and between larger blocks of surface rooms. Large, open plaza spaces are bounded by residential architecture and enclosing walls. In other words, these large village aggregates are "zoned" so that built spaces are conjoined to form open plazas, spaces that are used for public ceremony and work areas in historic pueblos.

Place marking with architectural features is not constrained to the boundaries of the residential settlements in the Southwest. In fact, there are wonderful examples of spatial clustering of community-level architecture indicating that "localities" were marked by the consistent placement and replacement of community monumental architecture. Full-coverage survey of ancestral pueblo communities in parts of southwestern Colorado shows that, for example, the aggregated Sand Canyon Pueblo community (1225–1285 C.E.) was built a kilometer from the Casa Negra Great House (1050–1200 C.E.), a massive structure that served as the community center for an earlier, dispersed agrarian community (Adler 1990). The Casa Negra Great House was, in turn, built 200 m from a great kiva dating between 930 and 1080 C.E., replacing this subterranean centerpiece of a still earlier dispersed community. These civic monuments could have been built anywhere within the Sand Canyon community locality, but like monuments elsewhere in the Neolithic world were placed and replaced to create a sense of place that transcended the lives of those individuals composing the community (Adler 1990; Varien 1999).

INSCRIBING THE PRODUCTIVE LANDSCAPE

Pueblo settlements and public architecture were not the only visible aspects of pre-Historic social landscapes. Agricultural strategies in the arid Southwest require significant investment in diversion and conservation of surface water. It is not surprising, then, that we find widespread evidence of terracing, diversion dams, some canalization and channeling of runoff water, gravel mulch gardens, field house construction, and use of reservoirs. All of these features

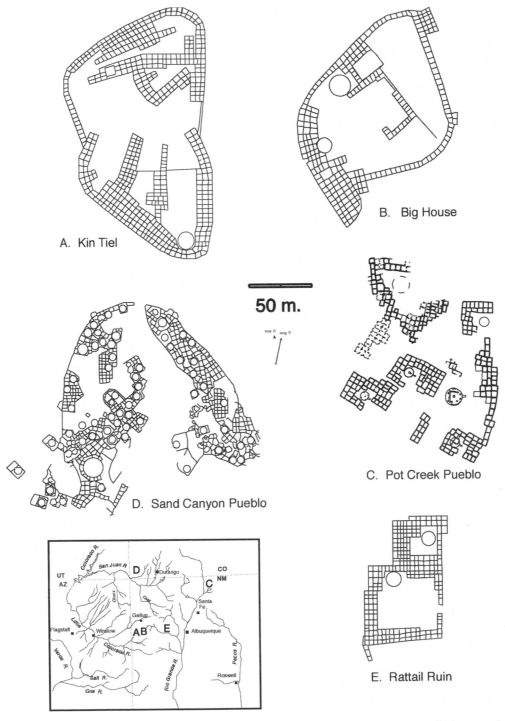

A. Kin Tiel

B. Big House

50 m.

C. Pot Creek Pueblo

D. Sand Canyon Pueblo

E. Rattail Ruin

FIGURE 14.4. Large, aggregated ancestral pueblo villages dating to the thirteenth–fourteenth centuries (adapted from Adler et al. 1996: fig. 3).

are constructed of soil and stone, providing yet one more avenue by which the ancestral pueblo peoples culturally inscribed their landscape (Figure 14.5). It is interesting that there is less evidence for significant investment in permanent agricultural technologies, including features for collecting and diverting water across fields or use of field houses, during the periods of dispersed community organization than during periods of aggregation. In contrast, concomitant with the move to aggregated village life after about 1150 C.E. is a widespread reliance on more permanent agricultural features. Rock-lined grid gardens, terraced soils, check dams for diverting and slowing water, use of gravel mulches to retain soil moisture, and other water conservation techniques are common in places surrounding the newly minted pueblo aggregates (Anscheutz 1998; Lightfoot and Eddy 1995).

FIGURE 14.5. Stone-lined agricultural terraces and gridded gardens, Locality 1, near Picuris Pueblo (from Woodbury 1999, used with permission of Clements Center for Southwest Studies, Southern Methodist University).

There is good reason for this relationship between increasing residential aggregation and an increasingly marked productive landscape. During periods of dispersed community settlement, smaller household-based settlements were located next to, or on top of, agricultural fields. Population aggregation changed this configuration, because the number of agriculturalists in each large village outstripped the availability of arable land directly associated with the village, meaning that at least a portion of the village had to travel to their now-distant fields. Agricultural strategies had to account for the fact that people often lived farther from their fields, necessitating the construction of features that would protect crops, channel and preserve the much-needed water, and retain soil moisture levels even when the fields were not actively tended.

At the same time, however, we have to question why modifications to the landscape were purposefully constructed of durable materials such as stone rather than wood or vegetal material. One answer rests with the idea of inscribing the natural landscape with evidence of human land use and ownership. Permanence of agricultural features provides lasting, visible evidence of land modification: an important hegemonic strategy within an increasingly contentious social landscape. Stone (1994) called this practice "perimetrics," where humans inscribe place with more permanent boundaries and symbols of use and control.

There is a similar trend in the increased use of more permanent field structures, usually one- to two-room facilities located on or near arable lands (Preucel 1990). For example, the upland areas of the Jemez region are dotted with an estimated 3,750 field house structures surrounding the large community aggregates, most of which were occupied after about 1300 C.E. The density of field houses in the agricultural areas between settlements reaches a density of forty-four structures per square kilometer in some parts of the region (Elliott 1989). Although all these seasonally utilized features were not in use contemporaneously, their presence on the landscape served as territorial markers and indications of past (and, perhaps, future intended) land use and territoriality.

BUILDING COMMUNITY: ARCHITECTURAL CLUES TO COMMUNITY ORGANIZATION IN THE NORTHERN RIO GRANDE REGION

To this point, ancestral pueblo communities have been treated as unified social groupings that constructed integrative facilities, shared local resources, and marked their place on the landscape through settlement and agricultural features. The community was probably the socially most inclusive group at the local level in the Anasazi region, but each community comprised many smaller groups, including households, lineages, ceremonial societies, and other social aggregates.

Though it is always risky to generalize over such a large region, there is substantial architectural evidence of multiple scales of social identity and integration that can be gleaned from these past settlements. Thus, although I think it is helpful to model the community as an important agent of regional social integration, we have to account for the "building blocks" that composed these larger social groupings. Fortunately, ancestral pueblo architectural configuration preserves patterns of settlement growth and planning, particularly when we have substantial excavated samples of built space. One such example is Pot Creek Pueblo, located near Taos, New Mexico.

Pot Creek Pueblo (LA 260) contains the architectural and artifactual remains of a large ancestral pueblo community that occupied the settlement between about 1260 and 1320 C.E. (Adler 1997; Wetherington 1968). The modern Taos and Picuris Pueblo peoples trace ancestral ties to this large architectural complex, a settlement that at its height of occupation housed between 300 and 500 or more people. Over 150 of an estimated 350 ground-floor rooms have been excavated over the past four decades (Figure 14.6), yielding an exceptionally well dated record of site growth, architectural layout, and subsequent residential abandonment. Several "levels" of social interaction and integration can be inferred from this architectural record, including household and multihousehold residential units. We can identify two major trends that mark the growth of this settlement. First is the overall trend toward decreased access to the settlement, primarily through the construction of residential architecture that limited access routes into the settlement. At the same time that the community is clearly demarcating "outside" from "inside," there is a simultaneous segmentation and separateness evident in the architectural layouts of domestic architecture at the settlement. So although we reconstruct pre-Historic communities as social entities, each community comprised a large number of smaller factions that likely competed for resources and negotiated their roles within the larger community context.

The initial stages of population aggregation at Pot Creek Pueblo took place largely between 1260 and 1290 C.E., when several separate architectural complexes were constructed. Nearly complete excavation of Roomblock 6 provides a model for architectural growth (Figure 14.7). Each roomblock comprised several contiguous rooms built in an L or C shape, surrounding a small plaza in which was

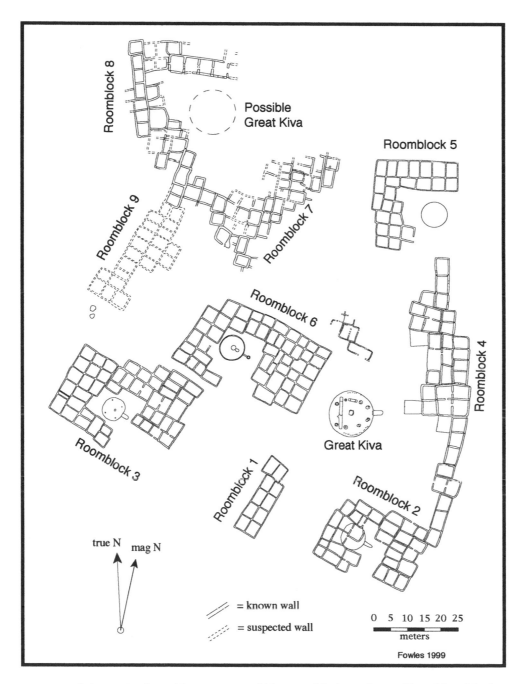

Roomblock 8

Possible
Great Kiva

Roomblock 5

Roomblock 9

Roomblock 7

Roomblock 6

Great Kiva

Roomblock 4

Roomblock 3

Roomblock 1

Roomblock 2

true N   mag N

/// = known wall

/// = suspected wall

0 5 10 15 20 25
meters

Fowles 1999

FIGURE 14.6. Pot Creek Pueblo, an ancestral Tiwa pueblo located near Taos, New Mexico.
Roomblocks 7, 8, and 9 are largely unexcavated.

built a subterranean structure (kiva). Subsequent construction later in the 1200s and early 1300s added new rooms onto the extant roomblock, building onto the back side of the existing rooms.

The dynamics of construction and reconstruction within this single roomblock are complex, but a few general patterns appear to hold. First, there are "household suites" that are identifiable as two or more rooms that were constructed simultaneously and share at least one wall segment (Crown and Kohler 1994; Wetherington 1968). Household suites were added on through the construction of multiple, ground-floor rooms, as well as the addition of second- and third-story rooms onto existing ground-floor rooms. Roomblock 6 began as a group of four to six households, growing to perhaps twelve to fifteen households by the end of the site occupation about 1320 C.E. It is important to point out that though each roomblock grew accretionally during the site occupation, each core roomblock remained spatially coherent through the retention of plaza space between each roomblock. Similarly, each set of coresiding households constructed and utilized one smaller kiva, a subterranean structure used for both ritual and domestic activities.

Population aggregation at Pot Creek Pueblo probably included both local and migrant populations (Crown and Kohler 1994). We cannot currently ascertain the relative contribution of local and nonlocal populations to the growth of the settlement; my own bias is that most of the settlement population derived from the relocation of local households. Recent research comparing the size and layout of earlier, dispersed unit pueblos with the subsequent roomblock layouts at Pot Creek supports this contention (Diemond and Fowles 2000; Fowles 2000). The founding roomblocks at Pot Creek Pueblo are nearly identical in room count, roomblock orientation, placement of kivas, and presence of internal features to those built throughout the Taos area during the twelfth and early thirteenth centuries. What makes this particularly exciting is that oral historical accounts from Taos Pueblo describe the process of aggregation at Pot Creek Pueblo (Espinosa 1936), emphasizing that the founding clans at the settlement came from differ-

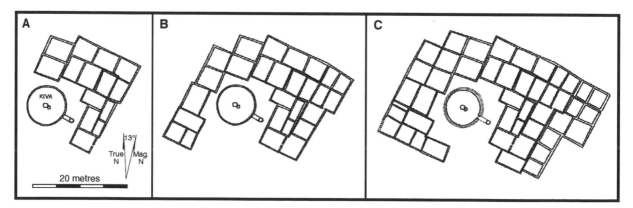

FIGURE 14.7. Pattern of Roomblock 6 architectural unit growth. *A*. Roomblock 6, 1260–1280 C.E. *B*. 1280–1300 C.E. *C*. 1300–1320 C.E. Roomblock 6 grew by accretion of additional households surrounding a small plaza and subterranean kiva.

ent directions and, we would assume, different localities within and outside the Taos region.

The architectural layout of the entire settlement preserves and reproduces the social segments that came together during the thirteenth century to form this large settlement. It is important to point out that as architectural accretion occurred at the site, new structures were added on to existing, separate roomblocks. Open areas between roomblocks were left open, presumably because of their use as public plaza areas utilized for communal activities including ceremony and shared work projects. Also significant are the two major plaza spaces left open on the southern and northern margins of the site. Excavations in the southern large plaza uncovered a great kiva, a massive subterranean structure 16 m in diameter that yielded tree-ring dates that are among the latest on the site (1319 C.E.). The northern portion of the site, which remains largely unexcavated, has a similarly large plaza space, and limited test excavations indicate the likely presence of a second, large subterranean structure (Fowles 2000).

A second great kiva at the site would not be unusual, because both Taos and Picuris Pueblos exhibit dual social organizational groupings. For example, the entire population of Picuris is divided into two units: a Northside moiety and a Southside moiety (Brown 1999). Both men and women belong to these units, with the women retaining their original membership even after marriage. There appears to be a patrilineal basis for these units, and it is possible for a man to change his group affiliation if he wants to do so. Affiliation in either of these groups in no way determines possible marriage choices. One can marry either within or outside of one's own group. Two kivas are associated with the dual organization groups. Sky kiva, located in front of the roundhouse north of the pre-

sent village is the Southside kiva. Cloud kiva, located in the upper plaza area, is the Northside kiva. Each dual organization group is led by a headman, usually referred to as the cacique. These headmen are responsible for the performance of various activities within their respective moieties.

Focusing back on Pot Creek Pueblo, it is clear that architectural change at the site also was organized over time to decrease access to the interior of the settlement. Through the architectural conjoining of formerly separate roomblocks, access routes into the site on the eastern and western sides were closed or significantly restricted. Expansion of room blocks on the northern and southern margins of the site significantly altered access from those directions.

CONCLUSIONS

The ancestors of the modern Pueblo peoples engraved a complex history of settlement, land use, abandonment, and migration across the American Southwest. Like their Neolithic counterparts in the Old World, the ancestral pueblo agrarian communities erected both residential and ceremonial structures that served to reinforce local group identity, honor their own ancestors, and claim important local resources through overt monumentality. Many of their ancient monuments to community residence and integration now provide the focus of national parks and other modern monuments to the American past.

My main points in this chapter point to the fact that community organization, manifested archaeologically as dispersed and aggregated settlement configurations, changed in the American Southwest between the seventh and fifteenth centuries C.E. What is at stake is not just the materially marked landscape, but the experience and sociality of place. In common with agrarian households throughout the world, each local community comprised several levels of potentially competing and cooperating social groupings. Fortunately we have preserved at sites such as Pot Creek Pueblo a detailed record of household and multihousehold architectural growth, change, and, finally, abandonment.

The community landscape in the pre-Historic Southwest was not simply relegated to monumental architecture and residential settlements. The interstices between these constructed focal points were filled with additional evidence of human activity, subsistence strategies, and potential future uses. More permanent agricultural features became the rule, rather than the exception, as puebloan peoples moved their residences off the landscape into large aggregated villages during the thirteenth century C.E. This system of village aggregation and extensive landscape use remained the primary strategy for puebloan occupation through the period of European contact and still provides the means for community survival in the Native American Southwest to this day.

REFERENCES CITED

Adler, M. A. 1989. Ritual Facilities and Social Integration in Non-rank Societies: A Cross-cultural Perspective. In *The Architecture of Social Integration in Prehistoric Pueblos*, edited by W. D. Lipe and M. Hegmon, 35–52. Occasional Papers of the Crow Canyon Archaeological Center 1. Cortez: Crow Canyon Archaeological Center.

———. 1990. Communities of Soil and Stone: An Archaeological Investigation of Population Aggregation among the Mesa Verde Anasazi, A.D. 900–1300. Ph.D. diss., University of Michigan, Ann Arbor.

———. 1996. Land Tenure, Archaeology, and the Ancestral Pueblo Social Landscape. *Journal of Anthropological Archaeology* 15:337–371.

———. 1997. Report of Excavations at Pot Creek Pueblo (LA 260) by the SMU Archaeology Field School. Manuscript on file, Fort Burgwin Research Center, Taos.

Adler, M. A., and R. H. Wilshusen. 1990. Large-Scale Integrative Facilities in Tribal Societies: Cross-Cultural and Southwestern US Examples. *World Archaeology* 22:133–146.

Adler, M. A., T. Van Pool, and B. Leonard. 1996. Ancestral Pueblo Population Aggregation and Abandonment in the North American Southwest. *Journal of World Prehistory* 10:375–438.

Anscheutz, K. F. 1998. Not Waiting for the Rain: Integrated Systems of Water Management by Pre-Columbian Pueblo Farmers in North-central New Mexico. Ph.D. diss., University of Michigan, Ann Arbor.

Benedict, R. 1934. *Patterns of Culture*. Boston: Houghton Mifflin.

Brown, D. 1999. Picuris Pueblo in 1890: A Reconstruction of Picuris Social Structure and Subsistence Activities. In *Picuris Pueblo through Time: Eight Centuries of Change at a Northern Rio Grande Pueblo*, edited by M. A. Adler and H. W. Dick, 19–37. Dallas: Clements Center for Southwest Studies, Southern Methodist University.

Crown, P., and T. Kohler. 1994. Community Dynamics, Site Structure, and Aggregation in the Northern Rio Grande. In *The Ancient Southwestern Community: Models and Methods for the Study of Prehistoric Social Organization*, edited by W. H. Wills and R. D. Leonard, 103–118. Albuquerque: University of New Mexico Press.

Cushing, F. 1974. *Zuni Breadstuff*. New York: Museum of the American Indian, Heye Foundation.

Dean, J. 1988. Dendrochronology and Paleoenvironmental Reconstruction on the Colorado Plateaus.

In *The Anasazi in a Changing Environment*, edited by G. J. Gumerman, 119–167. Cambridge: Cambridge University Press.

Diemond, R., and S. Fowles. 2000. Dispersed Settlements of the Taos District: Results of Recent Research. Paper presented at the 65th Annual Meetings of the Society for American Archaeology, Philadelphia.

Doyel, D. (ed.). 1992. *Anasazi Regional Organization and the Chaco System*. Anthropological Papers 5. Albuquerque: Maxwell Museum of Anthropology, University of New Mexico.

Elliott, M. L. 1989. Guadalupe Prescribed Burn Cultural Resource Inventory, Jemez Ranger District, Santa Fe National Forest. Manuscript submitted by Jemez Mountains Research Center (Report 88–11), Albuquerque, to the Santa Fe National Forest (1989-10-019), Santa Fe, New Mexico.

Espinosa, M. 1936. Pueblo Indian Folk Tales. *Journal of American Folklore* 49:69–133.

Everson, P., and T. Williamson. 1998. *The Archaeology of Landscape: Studies Presented to Christopher Taylor*. New York: Manchester University Press.

Fowler, A., and J. Stein. 1992. Anasazi Ritual Landscapes. In *Anasazi Regional Organization and the Chaco System*, edited by David Doyel, 87–100. Anthropological Papers no. 5. Albuquerque: Maxwell Museum of Anthropology.

Fowles, S. 2000. Archaeological Research into Migration and Settlement, Taos Area, New Mexico. Paper presented at the 65th Annual Meetings of the Society for American Archaeology, Philadelphia.

Lekson, S. 1984. *Great Pueblo Architecture of Chaco Canyon, New Mexico*. Publications in Archaeology 18B, Chaco Canyon Studies. Albuquerque: National Park Service.

Lightfoot, D., and F. Eddy. 1995. The Construction and Configuration of Anasazi Pebble-mulch Gardens in the Northern Rio Grande. *Geoarchaeology* 8:349–370.

Lightfoot, R. R. 1988. Roofing an Anasazi Great Kiva: Analysis of an Architectural Model. *The Kiva* 53 (3): 253–272.

Merrill, W. A. 1988. *Rarámuri Souls: Knowledge and Social Process in Northern Mexico*. Washington: Smithsonian Institution Press.

Netting, R. McC. 1982. Territory, Property, and Tenure. In *Behavioral and Social Science Research: A National Resource*, edited by N. J. Smelser, D. J. Tremain, and R. McC. Adams, 446–502. Washington: National Academy Press.

Preucel, R. 1990. *Seasonal Circulation and Dual Residences in the Pueblo Southwest: A Prehistoric Example from the Pajarito Plateau, New Mexico*. New York: Garland Publishing.

Prudden, T. M. 1903. The Prehistoric Ruins of the San Juan Watershed in Utah, Arizona, Colorado, and New Mexico. *American Anthropologist*, n.s., 5 (1): 224–288.

Schelberg, J. 1992. Hierarchical Organization as a Short-term Buffering Strategy in Chaco Canyon. In *Anasazi Regional Organization and the Chaco System*, edited by D. Doyel, 59–74. Anthropological Papers 5. Albuquerque: Maxwell Museum of Anthropology, University of New Mexico.

Sebastian, L. 1992. Chaco Canyon and the Anasazi Southwest: Changing Views of Sociopolitical Organization. In *Anasazi Regional Organization and the Chaco System*, edited by D. Doyel, 23–34. Anthropological Papers 5. Albuquerque: Maxwell Museum of Anthropology, University of New Mexico.

Stein, J. R., and A. Fowler. 1996. Looking Beyond Chaco in the San Juan Basin and Its Peripheries. In *The Prehistoric Pueblo World*, A.D. 1150–1350, edited by M. A. Adler, 114–131. Tucson: University of Arizona Press.

Stone, G. 1994. Agricultural Intensification and Perimetrics: Ethnoarchaeological Evidence from Nigeria. *Current Anthropology* 35:317–324.

Topping, P. (ed.). 1997. *Neolithic Landscapes*. Oxford: Oxbow Books.

Varien, M. 1999. *Sedentism and Mobility in a Social Landscape.* Tucson: University of Arizona Press.

Weber, S. A., and P. D. Seaman (eds.). 1985. *Havasupai Habitat: A. F. Whiting's Ethnography of a Traditional Indian Culture.* Tucson: University of Arizona Press.

Wetherington, R. 1968. *Excavations at Pot Creek Pueblo.* Fort Burgwin Research Center Report 6. Dallas: Southern Methodist University.

Wilcox, D. 1996. Pueblo III People and Polity in Relational Context. In *The Prehistoric Pueblo World, A.D. 1150–1350,* edited by M. Adler, 241–254. Tucson: University of Arizona Press.

Woodbury, R. 1999. Evidence of Prehistoric Farming in the Vicinity of Picuris Pueblo. In *Picuris Pueblo through Time: Eight Centuries of Change at a Northern Rio Grande Pueblo,* edited by M. Adler and H. Dick, 141–148. Dallas: Clements Center for Southwest Studies, Southern Methodist University.

PART III

BEYOND THE MARK

FIFTEEN

Anchoring Mobile Subjectivities

Home, Identity, and Belonging among Italian Australian Migrants

Mariastella Pulvirenti

The possession of a house is for many the final and most lasting signifier
of rootedness and is the exemplification of a fixity–the end of a long
metamorphosis from impermanence
M. Thomas, *Discord Dwellings: Australian Houses
and the Vietnamese Diaspora*

Immigrants are defined by their mobility. They are always and forever distinguishable from those born in the host country. On a day-to-day basis they negotiate ways around experiences and memories of homeland and experiences and realities in the host country. Making a home, establishing a sense of belonging for themselves and their families while retaining heartfelt attachment to the place of birth is challenging. In this chapter I argue that home ownership is crucial to meeting this challenge, not because the edifice itself can be read as an inscription on the host landscape, but because of the meaning attributed to ownership and its consequences.

As only one of many migrant groups, there is no doubt that the high levels of Italian Australian home ownership (Kee 1992) have left an indelible mark on Australia's and, significantly for this chapter,

Melbourne's urban landscape.[1] In the period after World War II and then in the 1970s (Burnely 1976), Italian migrants entered and moved within the housing market through a trajectory that left distinct patterns in inner suburban areas like Carlton and outer/middle suburban areas like Doncaster. These patterns, which may be read as inscriptions, imply a patterned association with place. But it is home *ownership*, I argue, that confers a sense of anchorage. Through ownership the house is transformed into home, becoming more than a mark in place. Such a process is mediated by gendered parent-child relationships and driven by the achievement of *sistemazione* (settling down). The house becomes a site where personal roots, ambitions, and attachments are laid, where pasts can be rested and futures unfolded.

PLACE MAKING AMONG ITALIAN AUSTRALIAN MIGRANTS

In "Place and Community: The Construction of an Italo-Australian Space," Pascoe (1992) charted the contribution of Italian immigrants to Australian culture through processes that simultaneously created a sense of community and place for the immigrants.

He argued that the "markers" of community were "a popular language, shared public ceremonies, and a recognised territory" (Pascoe 1992:86). The latter he defined as "an inviolable sense of Italian 'space' in the midst of an Australian city" (ibid.). For Pascoe, place making is a "quality" of the immigration process and an "outward expression" of immigrant identity (ibid., 94). This expression is made evident through naming, rituals, and institutions that mark neighborhoods like Carlton in Melbourne as "ethnic," as "Little Italy" (see also Marcia Langton, this volume).

Mapping place making as the creation of a "Little Italy," as Pascoe did, shows the nature of attachment to the host country, but can deny continued attachment to homeland. Such an account of attachment to the host country suggests a bounded territory of belonging. However, place is a process, not necessarily contained by boundaries that define it, but also defined by what is outside and beyond (Massey 1994). Places "can be imagined as articulated moments in networks of social relations and understandings, but where a large proportion of those relations, experiences and understandings are constructed on a far larger scale than what we happen to define for that moment as the place itself" (Massey 1994:154). This conceptualization of place as a process can inform an understanding of immigrant identities as continually in a process of "migration," linked simultaneously to "host" and "origin."

In an example of such an approach, Baldassar (1997:71) demonstrated how "return visits inform what it means to be Italian in Australia." Migrants, she argued, "develop identities in response to both their home and host societies" (ibid.). This is explained through the notion of *campanilismo*, the "attachment to, and identification with, place," a "loyalty to birthplace" (ibid., 74, 77). Baldassar (1997) argued that *campanilismo*, strengthened by return visits, consolidated migrants' Italian identities or a sense of their own Italian-ness in Australia. Those who returned infrequently, or not at all, she argued, "began to adapt to their host country," in part because they "felt they had a superior *sistemazione* [feeling of being settled down] in Australia" (ibid., 81).

This *sistemazione* is primarily evident in the children of migrants or, more important, in their children's Australian-ness. Baldassar (ibid., 82) thus noted, "Emigrants would take their families back to visit their grandparents and show off their Australian-born Italian children as proof that they had achieved a successful sistemazione." In addition, children's *sistemazione* binds Italian migrants to Australia because "Children may leave their parents but parents cannot leave their children" (ibid., 84). The home and house are fundamental to this complex process of creating attachment to the host country. Not only is home ownership important to the achievement of *sistemazione* (Baldassar 1997, Pulvirenti 2000), but the home is the locus of the relationship between parent and child, where creating a sense of belonging to the new place and nostalgic attachments to the country of origin can be negotiated and even reconciled. "[F]or those dislocated from a homeland, the house is often the concrete manifestation of the more abstract notion of 'home.' . . . The house is . . . a fundamental conceptual and tangible cultural nucleus and the conjunction between the global and the local. The home is able to signify both connectedness to the land of a new country and affinities with other times and places. For this reason the home is strategically chosen as the idiom through which many deal with the loss of both their homeland and the physical and emotional worlds which that land encompassed" (Thomas 1997:96–97).

My intention in this paper is to demonstrate how the home, experienced as home ownership, anchors Italian Australians to Australia.

ANCHORING

The title of this paper borrows Ferguson's (1993: 158) concept of mobile subjectivities: "I have chosen the term *mobile* rather than *multiple* to avoid the implication of movement from one to another stable resting place," thus problematizing "the contours of the resting one does." Quite apart from the metaphoric appeal of mobility, this concept allows a venturing into the complex linkages and movements that constitute subjectivities built on nostalgic and actual circular journeys between homeland and host-land. Yet this type of theorizing has raised a concern with deterritorialization. Mobile subjectivities can appear to be perilously and forever afloat, apparently untouched by the local. Such a danger is remedied with "careful attention" to the way "identities are territorialised" (Pratt 1998:27). The way "place and social processes are complexly intertwined" (Jacobs and Fincher 1998:20) must be understood.

Although the task at hand addresses such a project, I am interested in using this discussion about subjectivity as a metaphor for the way migrants cre-

ate a sense of belonging. Put simply, I am interested in how migrants are "grounded." Here I follow a rich history of research on immigration and place, including those mentioned earlier (Silvey and Lawson 1998). In recent years studies (like Baldassar's) have resisted thinking about the migration process as movement from "one to another stable resting place" (Ferguson 1993:158) (see, for example, Pulvirenti 1997). The migration process is not sealed off by acts of departure and arrival. The "resting" must be made. Here I find Pratt's (1998:27) summation that "subjectivities do get anchored" instructive. The notion of anchorage encapsulates how the resting is made. This is an active process of anchoring to that which resists mobility. A mooring is enacted to experience a stability from which flows the right to be in the host country. Through such a process, identities are continually negotiated. Specifically, the Australian "side" of the first generation (immigrant) Italian Australian identity is constructed through an anchoring to the Australian-ness of the second generation (their children), a process that manages simultaneously to construct the Italian "side" of the second-generation Italian Australian identity.

Ultimately my concern is how first-generation migrants develop a territorialized sense of belonging, a sense of being in place, in the host nation, while negotiating nostalgic attachments to their country of origin. More specifically, I am interested in how this making of place, marking of place, is negotiated within the first- and second-generation relationship through home ownership.

Anchoring: The First Generation

To first-generation Italian Australian migrants, belonging in a place, in a nation, is achieved primarily through birth.[2] They see their own and their children's belonging as different. They do not share the same history with, and therefore attachment to, Australia. They did not turn their backs on Italy through the act of immigration. Their hearts and their identities were still in Italy. Many had lost faith in Italy; they were angered, even disgusted at the corruption they had witnessed; in later years many even regretted not benefiting from the growth in postwar reconstruction that they might have enjoyed had they stayed. However, they did not migrate to find a place to replace Italy. The migration was an escape, pursuing the possibility of prosperity. Most achieved this through what they called "sacrifices."

For the first generation, what engenders a connection to a country is being born there or having immediate family there. Belonging is, in this sense, established by birth. There is virtually no connection to Australia because they had left their family behind. This is particularly the case for women who migrated with their husbands, often reluctantly, leaving their own families, arriving in Australia knowing, as Bianca (2:13)[3] explained, "I don't have any family here at all." Her sense of isolation was intense: "I left all my people," "all the bonds that I have are over there, in my land." This is powerful imagery, a complete sense of belonging in and to Italy.

The connection to Italy is spoken about in terms of belonging, to "my land," "my people." The disconnection with Australia is spoken of in similar ways: "this is their land" (Bianca 2:13). This country is seen as belonging to "Australians": those who were already here when they arrived. The sense of belonging, or not, was understood in terms of the metaphor of the "master of the house" and his guests: "they think this land is theirs . . . they make themselves master of it" (Caterina 4:20). This is an articulation of *campanilismo* as explained by Baldassar (1997). One always belongs and is loyal to the place of birth.

There are two other factors that Baldassar (1997) did not note that strengthen the loyalty of *campanilismo* for Italian Australians: the experience of racism in Australia and the perceived illusiveness of an Australian identity in all its diversity. In a joint interview, Gianna and Miranda (7:17) explained the "intolerance" they experienced as migrants in Australia. Looking back, Miranda said, "they couldn't really stand us much . . . slowly they got used to it and they tolerate us . . . now they treat us differently." Gianna concurred, "now they are kinder to us." They saw themselves as, at best, tolerated. This is not an articulation of belonging, an articulation of "my place." They saw themselves as always the unwelcomed guests in the master's house.

The feeling that they do not belong is further complicated by the cultural diversity in Australia. To what exactly are they belonging? Lisa was born in Italy but migrated at age eight in 1956. She lived most of her life in Australia. After marrying, her husband's occupation took them to live in Paris for two years and then on a separate occasion to Italy for five years. Then they returned to Australia. Because she "fitted in well" when she was living in Italy, she felt able to state: "I identify myself as an Italian," "I *say* I am Italian. I feel Italian. . . . I am an Australian citizen, but I am really Italian." She described herself as a stranger in Australia: " . . . sometimes, here I feel like a stranger . . . you look at all the people going past and you see so many nationalities and you often say 'well, what am I? What is this?' you know? . . . Sometimes I feel like a stranger . . . there's no cohesive, um, community" (12:43). Of course this also brings into question the value of a so-called Italian community, but the focus for Lisa is still the lack of cultural continuity in the Australian community. These respondents do not feel they belong in Australia.

It is their children, however, who connect them to Australia. It is appropriate to think of this connection as anchorage. For some Italian Australians, this anchorage is not necessarily a positive force and feels like entrapment or "exile" (Baldassar 1997). Diana (5:20), for example, explained: " . . . you have a family, and then you start making your house, and then how can you leave? That's it. When you close yourself into this land you are never able to leave. Even until today, I feel homesick for Italy."

The nature of the anchoring and its occurrence or operation can be witnessed in the following examples, both referring to parental roles. The parenting of children directly assisted Italian Australians in establishing anchorage by extending social networks (for example, through baptism of children). Bianca did not have any friends, knew no one, when she came to Australia. Her friends became kin when they accepted the invitation to become godparents to each other's children. This is the role of *commare* for a woman and *compare* for a man: " . . . with friendships there's always someone you feel closer to, that you have something in common with and so that friendship grows. And then often those friendships become *commare* when the children are born and baptized" (Bianca 2:9). This was a common experience. It was not just a matter of making friends, but of making family, for the *commare/compare* relationship brought people closer together through a shared sense of care for the children. This was especially the case because the godparent is seen to be the spiritual, and therefore moral, guide for the children. Such a relationship is extremely important, especially for women who are completely isolated from their families, because

they, more than anyone else, need to re-create the kind of close relationships they describe as having only with family. In particular, this is the case because the request to be a godparent is expected to be reciprocated; asking a friend to take on this role means you too will be asked to take this role on: "through work we met, and then . . . once you know one another you ask each other 'Be godmother for a son, I will be godmother to your son.' And then you see, you become even closer" (Diana 5:25).

Primarily, though, the anchorage is more about the relationship between parent and child and especially the fact that the parents *belong* with the children. Thus the anchorage is not simply about having to stay in Australia, but simultaneously (as Baldassar's earlier quotation elucidates) about not being able to leave. For Diana it was an impossible anxiety: "I just didn't want to stay here. Now I have children, what can I do? I have a married son, two grandchildren . . . my twenty-one-year-old daughter is engaged. I have a thirty-year-old son who isn't married. How can I return to Italy?" (5:20). Staying is not enforced by her children's dependence on her (they are not young and fragile), but the staying is enforced by her understanding of her role as a mother: "I always feel homesick thinking 'Must I die in this land? Must I die in this land? I want to go.' . . . My husband would say, 'If you feel this way we'll go and we will never come back.' But I have my children here now, so how can I? He says 'You left your mother, didn't you?' (nodding) [yes], but I cannot leave my children" (Diana 5:21).

This responsibility and thus the anchorage is exacerbated with age. It is significant that first-generation respondents were senior citizens. The anchorage had been strengthened in later life. The loss of relatives in Italy left them unhinged. As Bianca explained, "after my mother's death, I convinced myself to stay here.

It was as if I had already lost a tie, as if the thread with my land had broken" (2:14). This is particularly the case for women who had to leave their families behind. This was not the case for men who often followed or were followed by other members of their families. Such anchorage is further gendered because it is distinctly about mothers *mothering* correctly. A parenting relationship led by hegemonic power relations and guided by the principle that a parent cannot leave his/her child is much more about a mother not leaving her child than a father. His primary role as provider may be fulfilled, within those relations, even if he leaves the child, a condition permitted in many circumstances, not the least of which is immigration.

However, there is a similar principle regarding attachment to family that impacts on men as brothers and sons. The men I interviewed were not as forthcoming about these issues, and I felt less comfortable pursuing them too; however, both Nicola and Franco gave insight into how anchoring through their family role worked for them. Nicola explained that his mother had talked (or more accurately, prayed) him into emigrating: "my mother wanted me to come to Australia to keep my sister company . . . she would say 'My poor daughter has no one. You are single and could keep her company' . . . and I said, 'I don't want to go there. I am working here. I am comfortable' . . . eventually one day I resolved to emigrate, but with an ache in my heart" (Nicola 14:2). Nicola's sister had not emigrated alone; she was living with her husband in Australia, but his mother believed that "having her own blood nearby is more of a consolation" (Nicola 14:3). Later his sister repatriated, and he explained her decision through the fact that she did not have children. His children and wife kept him here, but she had no children, so she returned to Italy. For Nicola it was a logical decision.

This anchorage marks place, their place, through home ownership. Home ownership facilitated parents staying with their children and symbolizes family unity and stability. Home ownership means security. Put simply, home ownership symbolizes first-generation Italian Australians' anchorage to Australia as home. Home ownership symbolizes the Australian part of the Italian Australian identity. Nowhere is this better demonstrated than, as Baldassar has suggested, in explanations of the connection between *sistemazione*, home ownership, and migration. Elsewhere (Pulvirenti 2000) I detailed how *sistemazione* impacted on the achievement of home ownership by the way it drove a moral imperative to work and achieve. The family was at the heart of this drive: "sistemazione is important in life, whether in the sense of having a family, or in the sense of knowing how to manage responsibility for your children . . . gathering together your children and knowing how to raise them and to be able to give them a future" (Diana 5:33). The sense of anchorage achieved in the parent-child relationship is strengthened by home ownership because it symbolizes *sistemazione* and therefore belonging and home. It is only through the experiences of the second generation that this becomes clear.

The Second Generation

The role home ownership plays in belonging, place, and home for first-generation Italian Australians is articulated in second-generation experiences of home ownership expectations put upon them. Among the second generation that I interviewed, it was clear that there was a learned understanding of a specifically Italian Australian attitude to home ownership. This was not an Italian attitude, because those who had been to Italy or met Italian relatives here on visits knew that their ideas were quite different. It was also an attitude distinctly different from those who were called or thought of as "Australians": "I think Italian Australians, being first-generation Australians, believe that renting is a waste of money. I think that they see it as an Anglo-Saxon thing. I think they see it as a derogatory thing. I think they see it as showing a lack of planning, [a lack of] sense [and] all the rest of it" (Nadia 34:31). Christine explained the distinction between Italians and Italian Australians: "I see people in Italy. I don't think it's the same thing . . . my relatives rent over there but as soon as they come to Australia they seem to want to come to Australia to better themselves, and . . . [that] means owning a house . . . and I think that's why they come here. . . . I think most Italians are interested in buying rather than renting" (Christine 25:9). Overall, the attitude as they understand it is that Italians expect to own when they are in Australia—indeed that some undertook the move abroad to secure home ownership.

This attitude is not just about first-generation ownership, but also about second-generation ownership. There are basically two principles to this attitude. The first is "buy as soon as you can" (Fede 28:3). The second principle is staying in the parental home until marriage or for some, after marriage, until their own home is available. Nadia explained: "Most of them would expect their kids to stay at home until they marry and most of the kids, from what I can tell, do" (Nadia 34:30). The second principle was especially a concern articulated by those second-generation women and men who did not want to marry or who wanted to live in their own rented homes before marriage (Pulvirenti 1996).

Both male and female children felt the pressure to abide by both principles, but female respondents expressed more intense pressure over the second principle, and male respondents expressed more intense pressure over the first. The pressure applied

from this attitude overall is a means of anchoring the children to the family, strengthening the anchor that constitutes the first-generation sense of place. This is more than just an instance of the "apron string" phenomenon expressed and experienced by many Australians. Without the children, the first generation has no place or belonging in Australia.

The magnitude of the anchoring or, at least, its magnitude as interpreted by the second generation may be understood through a consideration of the means by which this attitude is "learned." Home ownership was not simply an expectation. Granted, for some, the parents' attitude was "going to rub off onto their kids" (Adrian 20:6); it was something they had "been brought up to believe" they would do (Bruno 23:6), simply received "from our parents" (Fede 28:3). For others the information was transmitted more forcefully. Both Peter, who was single, living with his parents and putting travel at the top of his list of priorities, and Leonora, who had bought a house and was living with her mother after marriage to afford renovations, spoke of being "brainwashed." "I think within the, um, Italian community, um, they sort of brainwash their kids from when they're like two foot high [laughing]. You know, 'You've got to buy a house one day and you've got to settle down and you've got to do this' " (Leonora 30:9). Peter thought this brainwashing was so coercive that it extended beyond the family home to "Anglo-Saxon Australian" friends who own: "They've sort of probably been brainwashed by a few of us 'cause we've sort of come from a mixed environment" (Peter 35:8). For Alex the brainwashing was a longer-term process of conditioning, similar to Rosemary's description of parents "constantly drumming this idea into your head" (Rosemary 37:23). Others described the expectation of ownership as inevitable. Claudio described it as "that little mold that they'd set up for me," "my planned destiny by my family" (Claudio 26:12). It had been "a part of growing up; you know that that's what you're going to be doing or what you're expected to be doing" (Claudio 26:15).

Home ownership is taught as the moral thing to do. Typically it is reported as what the "good Italian girl" or "good Italian boy" should do. Respondents speak of this process of ownership as "the right thing to do." Alex, who moved out of his parents' home to rent, told of an Italian Australian friend who asked him: "Why don't you just live at home and do the right thing?" Alex put this questioning down to: "the way they've been brought up; you see, you do the right thing. You don't knock the system around, you know, you don't shock, you don't do anything you're not supposed to do. You just do what you're supposed to do, which is probably the biggest sort of thing that the Italian community tend to use" (Alex 21:10).

Nothing symbolized a refusal to do the right thing more than moving out of the parental home. This was especially the case if moving into rental accommodation and for women moving into either rental or even their own purchased homes. Given what parents had invested in their children, it is not surprising that the second generation described their parents as taking it personally. For example, Anna's mother took her and her siblings' move out of the house personally, exclaiming: "Why do you want to go away from me?" (Anna 22:18). The first time Rosemary moved out of her parents' home they didn't speak to her for six months; "it was a big thing" (Rosemary 37:8). It was not her intention to "sever those contacts. They're actually very important to me and important to my life and to my culture and so I would've liked to keep that intact" (Rosemary 37:9). Even though they resumed communication, Rosemary explained that her parents "never visited me, ever" (Rosemary 37:9).

For the first generation to continue to feel anchored, the second generation has to be seen as part of the family and not just Australian but *Italian* Australian. Otherwise the first generation loses their own Australian-ness, which is the rationale for staying in Australia and is as close to belonging as they get. This anchorage is clearly played out around, and indeed facilitated by, home ownership. The ideals that keep the first generation anchored to the second (that is, staying with your children) are understood to be Italian ideals. Because staying at home is thought of as the moral Italian Australian way, moving out is thought of as non-Italian (Australian) behavior. Thus second-generation women and men who do move out lose a degree of their Italian-ness. In part this is because it is understood by friends and family to be something that makes them "less" Italian. Anna, for example, described an "Italian" friend's response to her renting: "she's an Italian who lives at home, and I think that she finds the whole setup a bit weird and thinks that, you know, perhaps if I lived at home, then my financial situation would be much better and blah, blah, blah. And, perhaps in some ways, she sees that action as Anglo-cizing me, in some ways; you know, like it makes her read me as a bit more Anglo than if I lived at home" (Anna 22:11). Nadia even explained her own and her brother's choice of rental as a result of the influence of the "Anglo" suburb they were raised in: "I think what has possibly affected us is the fact that we've been brought up in the eastern suburbs in an Anglo environment" (Nadia 34:29).

In part the move is taken personally because it is considered an embarrassment, scandalous, a disgrace. This is because home ownership so thoroughly symbolizes monogamous heterosexuality, and renting liberal sexuality, particularly for women. Anna, like Rosemary, spoke of her mother's reaction to the first move as *una disgrazia*, a falling into disgrace

(Anna 22:12). Even Leonora, who had bought when she married, explained: "Basically I think the Italian parents are more, you know, it's a disgrace if you don't own your house, you know, your own home when you're like thirty something. You know, it's like 'What did you do with all your money all these years?'" (Leonora 30:9). This is not just a sexual morality, but also one based on a specific work ethic. Gina was single when she moved into her own home. She had stayed in her parents' home for several years while renting her home to tenants. She described her move as "traumatic" for her parents: "My mother would talk of, you know, going and living on an island . . . where no one would be able to talk badly about her daughter. . . . They had genuine concerns for me, as well as feeling that it really wasn't going to be good for my reputation to be living here on my own" (Gina 29:13). Sara had also moved into her own flat as a single woman. Her parents thought of it as "scandalous" (Sara 38:21). More important, this scandal would have reflected directly onto her mother, who believed she herself would have been judged as "a 'bad' mother" (Sara 38:21). Indeed the embarrassment was often coped with by hiding the move from family and friends: "mum never admitted to the *paesani*, you know, that I had moved out. If they came to visit it was 'Oh, you know, Sara's, um, yeah, she's gone to a meeting,' or 'She won't be home 'til late'" (Sara 38:9). Lidia's family, on the other hand, could not hide her move because she had bought the house next door. So they told relatives that her father had bought her the house. In this way it did not reflect on her reputation as immoral or as wanting to separate from the family.

For many second-generation women and men, the path laid out by the Italian Australian home ownership attitude is not only helpful but also moral. Put simply, some second-generation women

and men hold the first generation to a moral code of helping them to achieve their own *sistemazione*, again symbolized in home ownership. Vicki and Leonora were in similar situations, staying on after marrying. Both were grateful for the financial and emotional support they received. For them it was a means of being closer to the family, particularly for Leonora, whose mother had been recently widowed. Despite the fact that Gina's move was not condoned, she too was grateful to have stayed in her parents' house for as long as she did, explaining that she would not even have been able to afford buying her own house without it.

It is in the process of leaving or staying in the parental home that second-generation women and men resist or accept the anchorage of the first generation. In so doing, because that anchorage is acted out over Italian Australian ideas about home ownership, they are also effectively negotiating their identity as Italian Australians. The second generation comes to feel "placed" in relation to the immediate family. And yet simultaneously they also negotiate their own sense of place anchored not only around the parental house, but beyond to the wider community and the role of Italian ways of operating in settings abroad. Because the second generation may feel negative about staying in the parental home and resist that process, the anchorage that the first generation has is not stable. On the one hand, Alex, Nadia, and Rosemary spoke of living at home (in short, acting out the anchorage) as a negative experience. Primarily they described it as a disempowering experience through either what they experienced or what they saw their friends experiencing. Rosemary explained how she had nothing to do at home because her parents did it all: "they wanted to do everything for me and I wasn't actually quite used to that. But not *do* everything just to be nice and nurturing, but to actually take all your responsibilities away somehow. It does that, and it's very disempowering and you don't actually have control of anything in the house" (Rosemary 37:9). Alex believed this served to "starve you of your independence as an individual," that it was "not *psychologically* good for you" (Alex 21:10).

Abiding by the moral induces idleness. Speaking of friends who live with parents, Rosemary exclaimed: "they don't do anything!" (Rosemary 37:18). Alex described a friend in a similar situation who has "never been anywhere, done anything" (Alex 21:1); described as unmotivated, "they just sort of sit at home 'cause it's easy, you know, it's easy 'cause you've got that security that you don't have to worry about screwing up" (Alex 21:3). For Alex, staying at home is allowing yourself to be manipulated: "I think that the biggest frustration that a lot of people have is the way their parents try to manipulate. You know, it's the hardest thing they find about getting away from the house. It's this idea of, you know, 'Oh, we brought you up, we looked after you, we did all these things for you.' But there's also this expectation that you return something, you know, even if it's just your presence" (Alex 21:3). That presence effects first-generation anchorage.

CONCLUSION

It is not surprising that home ownership symbolizes and means security to first-generation Italian Australians. To first-generation Italian Australian women and men, home ownership symbolizes the Australian part of their Italian Australian identity. This is because home ownership unifies the family, literally uniting them under the one roof. It symbolizes the achievement of *sistemazione*, which represents belonging as being "*a posto*" (in place) and therefore as being "home." In so doing, home ownership confers a sense of anchorage to Australia, a right to be in the land that is not inherently theirs.

This anchorage is experienced differently by women and men, whose roles in families differ dramatically. Women have much more invested in the anchorage children provide, not just because many left their families in Italy to migrate with husbands, but also because it connotes "correct" and "moral" mothering. Their children's birthright, transferred in a "united" family to the parents, provides moorage. Home ownership facilitates the unity and symbolizes the right to belong. Although the second generation expects or is challenged by their role as anchors, the pressure put upon them to own symbolizes an "Italian" part of their identity to negotiate their way around. By transforming the house into home, mobile subjectivities become anchored in place.

NOTES

I extend my deepest gratitude to the women and men interviewed for this research. I am also grateful to Ruth Fincher for assistance with the original research, Kay Anderson for comments on an early draft of this chapter, and Bruno David for editorial support.

1. See, for example, Anderson (1993) on the making of Chinatown in Melbourne.

2. The material presented in this and subsequent sections is based on research carried out in Melbourne, Victoria (Australia), in 1992–1994. In-depth interviews sought to explain the meaning of home ownership to first- and second-generation Italian Australians. Forty interviews were carried out overall. Four first-generation men and sixteen first-generation women were interviewed. These were men and women who had migrated from Italy to Australia in the postwar period. This group of twenty included only two couples; the rest were not related, nor did they share households. The gender ratio was due to three factors: the concentration of women involved in social clubs through which interviewees were

sought, the demographic makeup of that cohort, and the reluctance of men to be involved in the research (Pulvirenti 1996).

The second-generation interviews were of women and men born to parents who had migrated from Italy to Australia in the postwar period. In both sets of interviews, a snowball technique was used to identify respondents. Eight were males whose ages ranged from twenty-three to thirty-five years, and twelve were females ranging from seventeen to forty-two years of age. None of the second-generation interviewees were children of first-generation interviewees. Fourteen were single, two of whom self-identified as lesbian. Six were married or in long-term de facto relationships, two of whom self-identified as gay. Six of the interviewees lived with their parents; another two lived with their parents while owning a house they did not live in. Three were renting in shared households, and two were house-sitting—one on a long-term basis, the other temporarily. Five owned their residences outright and two were purchasing them. The interviewees included three sets of siblings. First-generation respondents were sought from inner-city areas, but the search for second-generation respondents was not bounded geographically. This improved the chances of participation in the research by recognizing research showing that second-generation men and women moved beyond the inner-city areas where parents lived (Burnely 1976).

3. The individuals whose voices are cited are based on the interviews I undertook (see note 2). The reference stipulates transcript number followed by page number. The names of the individuals have been changed to ensure anonymity.

REFERENCES CITED

Anderson, K. 1993. Otherness, Culture and Capital: "Chinatown's" Transformation under Australian Multiculturalism. In *Multiculturalism, Difference and Postmodernism*, edited by G. L. Clark, D. Forbes, and R. Francis, 68–89. Melbourne: Longman Cheshire.

Baldassar, L. 1997. Home and Away: Migration, the Return Visit and Transnational Identity. *Communal/Plural* 5:69–94.

Burnely, I. 1976. Southern European Populations in the Residential Structure of Melbourne 1947–1971. *Australian Geographical Studies* 14:116–132.

Ferguson, K. 1993. *The Man Question: Visions of Subjectivity in Feminist Theory*. Berkeley: University of California Press.

Jacobs, J. M., and R. Fincher. 1998. Introduction. In *Cities of Difference*, edited by R. Fincher and J. M. Jacobs, 1–25. New York: Guilford Press.

Kee, P. 1992. *Home Ownership and Housing Conditions of Immigrants and Australian-Born*. Canberra: Australian Government Publishing Service.

Massey, D. 1994. *Space, Place and Gender*. Cambridge: Polity Press.

Pascoe, R. 1992. Place and Community: The Construction of an Italo-Australian Space. In *Australian's Italians: Culture and Community in a Changing Society*, edited by S. Castles, C. Alcorso, G. Rando, and E. Vasta, 85–97. Sydney: Allen and Unwin.

Pratt, G. 1998. Grids of Difference: Place and Identity Formation. In *Cities of Difference*, edited by R. Fincher and J. M. Jacobs, 26–48. New York: Guilford Press.

Pulvirenti, M. 1996. Home Ownership, Identity and Social Polarization. In *Restructuring Difference: Social Polarization and the City*, edited by K. Gibson, M. Huxley, J. Cameron, R. Fincher, J. Jacobs, N. Jamieson, L. Johnson, and M. Pulvirenti, 59–66. Melbourne: Australian Housing and Urban Research Institute.

———. 1997. Unwrapping the Parcel: An Examination of Culture through Italian Australian Home Ownership. *Australian Geographical Studies* 35:32–39.

———. 2000. The Morality of Immigrant Home Ownership: Gender, Work and Italian-Australian *Sistemazione*. *Australian Geographer* 31 (2): 237–249.

Silvey, R., and V. Lawson. 1998. Placing the Immigrant. *Annals of the Association of American Geographers* 89 (1): 121–132.

Thomas, M. 1997. Discordant Dwellings: Australian Houses and the Vietnamese Diaspora. *Communal/Plural* 5:95–113.

SIXTEEN

Inscriptions as Initial Conditions

Federation Square (Melbourne, Australia) and the Silencing of the Mark

Paul Carter

> Bun-jil had . . . an instrument named Ber-rang, with which he could open any place or any thing, and in such a way as to make it impossible for any one to know how or whether or not it had been opened. No one could see the opening he made.
> R. B. Smyth, *The Aborigines of Victoria*

On 1 January 1901 the Australian colonies federated and a new nation was born. In 1997, in the lead-up to celebrating the centenary of this event, the conservative Liberal-National coalition government of Victoria awarded a London-based architectural firm, Lab, the commission to design and build Federation Square, a new civic complex located at the hub of the state's capital, Melbourne, adjoining the central business district, the major railway station, and overlooking the Yarra River. The final design, released in June 1997, illustrated a geometrically intriguing ensemble of spaces and buildings, accommodating the new headquarters of the Special Broadcasting Service, a Cinemedia Center, and a new Museum of Australian Art, as well as the usual mix of restaurants and shops. A particular feature of the design was a number of "shardlike structures," some embedded in the buildings, others freestanding. Two of the shards, at the northwest of the site, were designed to frame a new view of the cathedral facade to the north from the Civic Plaza. At the heart of the complex, and stretching irregular fingers into the interstices of the surrounding buildings, a Civic Plaza was to be created, unusual both for its irregular outline and its hill-and-dale topography. In addition, I was commissioned to design an artwork that would be incorporated into many of these architectural features (Figure 16.1). The artwork's aim was to mark the site as a focus of historical, social, and political negotiation. In this chapter I explore the implications of this marking process.

Under the coalition the project proceeded more or less smoothly, but not without its conservative critics, until, in November 2000, rather to the surprise of the pundits, the Liberal government was thrown

FIGURE 16.1. Federation Square, Melbourne, civic complex during construction, 5 March 2001.

out of office, and the Labor party came to power. Labor, opposed on principle to most if not all of the previous administration's activities, promised to review all large public works infrastructure projects, including Federation Square. Shortly after, with perhaps indecent haste, it ordered the removal of the so-called West Shard, one of the two freestanding structures diagonally opposite the cathedral. This is not the place to examine the political motive behind the government's determination to remove the so-called West Shard, nor is it the occasion to pull aside the thin heritage veil behind which it concealed its desire to settle a score with the previous government responsible for commissioning the Square.[1] In the context of my own involvement in the Square's conception, devising and designing a place marking artwork (named *Nearamnew*) for the Square, it is the language invoked to defend the incoming government's intervention that is of immediate interest. Heritage groups urged the replacement of the West Shard with a foun-

tain or "foundational statue" commemorating Federation, a proposal supported by the new planning minister, who complained that there was "nothing in the design to commemorate Melbourne's part in Federation" (*Herald Sun*, 13 February 2000, and *The Age*, 15 February 2000). It was reliably reported that ministers were saying that the government had from the time of its election been determined "to leave its mark" on Federation Square (Peter Davidson, principal of Lab, personal communication). Accordingly, Federation Square has become not just a place where history—Australian Federation—is memorialized, but a contested site of contemporary politics, its construction symbolizing and affirming the power and stance of opposing political parties in decision making. Federation Square, as a contemporary inscription of space, is a confronted and (re)negotiated political territory. It is the underlying language and logic of this territorial engineering that is the theme of this chapter.

PLACE MAKING
AT FEDERATION SQUARE

Two ideas of place and place making were invoked at Federation Square. The monumentalist lobby, represented by heritage groups and a disaffected minister, understood the site as an empty page for writing and as a ready-made medium of communication. This attitude is perhaps best captured by the Pan-Slavist poet Velimir Khlebnikov, who explained that monuments "serve to provide a dialogue between the government and the people . . . they are storehouses of sense, just like elements of written language and hieroglyphics" (Khlebnikov 1987, 1:237).

Despite being a medium of communication, monuments can also conceal messages. Certain connotations of the monument merge into ideas associated with the mark: Vico derived the Latin word for a city, *urbs,* from the curvature of the plowshare (Vico 1977:98). In classical times the boundaries of a new settlement were usually marked by plowing a furrow (Edlund-Berry 1994:18). Later, when Australia's first Governor Phillip ordered a furrow to be drawn in the ground at Sydney Cove, he created a new class of functionary, the gatekeeper, dedicated to controlling transgressions. The landmarks favored by surveyors and hikers are perhaps essentially cuts; they find their analogue in the Aboriginal initiatory practice of cicatrizing the skin. Here a division, valley, or cut is made to puff up, elevate, or render prominent the zones on either side of the declivity. A true mark signifies a desire of access and is an intimation of territory (see also David and Wilson, this volume); it creates a stepping-off point; it suggests imminent change, even erasure. In this regard it can be used to *unfound* places. The Labor government, symbolically invading a territory they associated with the predecessors, "cursed and doomed" it.

The terms *mark* and *monument* refer to the beginnings and endings of historical events,[2] but they frequently merge into each other, reflecting certain paradoxes inherent in the ideology of place making to which they belong. In its Western conception ground marking involves an act of destruction: to cultivate the land (to plow it) is to clear away obstacles to progress. Even more radically, the mark that makes a place appear may make its mark by growing invisible. Here, critically, the Western architect departs from the indigenous cicatrizer, *as she/he also flattens the ridges that spread either side of her/his incision.* Monuments divert attention from the founding violence that made the space for them. Their piety is amnesiac. "Monuments," as Khlebnikov (1987, 1:237) wrote, "convey to the people that life is an end in itself." In that sense, monuments are inherently hegemonic.

The culturally schizoid behavior that flattens a space, only to resurrect it as a monumental place, in this way engineering a double forgetfulness, belongs to the tradition of "violent" thinking that Italian philosopher Gianni Vattimo (1993:5) identified as our legacy from the Greeks. Evidently, in the heritage rhetoric directed toward the Federation Square design, this tradition was alive and well. But counter intuitions about the site were also active. Although the project had its origins in a typically violent conception of place making, in which the engineering instinct would be fully licensed to transform part of Melbourne's historic heart in the name of heritage (this was the political appeal of undertaking the development in the name of *federation,* as if by going forward we merely went back), features of the selected design suggested that, against the original rhetoric of foundations, account might be taken of the experience of beginnings usually repressed in place making.

Nearamnew represents a nexus between the federal system of government and the design principles informing Lab's approach to the spatial organization of Federation Square. Lab's projects, "designed not as freestanding buildings but as interconnected assemblages of associated programmatic entities" (Hays et al. 1996:113), suggest the kind of interorganizational networking characteristic of federal systems of government (Figures 16.2, 16.3, and 16.4). If we substitute "buildings" for "actors" (in this context signifying executive and legislative "subsystem 'wholes' " within the federal system), then political scientist Ralph Chapman's (1993:71) comment that "The actors are continuously involved in mutual transfers creating thereby an additional set of structures and processes, extra-constitutional and, in many cases, extra-parliamentary" applies with uncanny accuracy to Lab's own project.

Here was a comprehensive analogy that lent a

FIGURE 16.2. *Nearamnew*, the plaza whorl pattern, plan view computer drawing (by permission of artist and Lab).

rhetorically imposed name a poetic resonance. *The assemblage of structures forming Federation Square were federated forms.* Simply to state this is not, though, enough. Retrospectively to attribute to Lab's design a symbolic intent would be to trap it in the discourse of commemoration, classifying it as a monument in advance. If Cartesian geometry spatializes, a postgeometrical, in practice, fractal, design (such as *Nearamnew*) retemporalizes definitions of place. It shares with federal systems a desire to create the initial conditions of heterogeneity. Excess could easily be mistaken for waste (witness the fate of the West Shard) when, in reality, it is the condition of the organizational vitality of the government over time. No complex is simply the sum of its parts. Lab's proposal to abandon an economically linear structure in favor "of textures and fields of lines produced out of redundancy, superfluity, and excess," and their advocacy of "architectural lines . . . increasingly multitudinous and excessive" (Bates and Davidson 1996:103) is a graphic analogue of the "redundancies, overlap, disproportions, inconsistent distribution of powers" that, wrote Frenkel, characterize federal systems (Frenkel 1986:141).

Here, then, the character of the artwork emerges: by creating a mythform that inscribes federal principles of organization into architectural design. Federal systems (like marks) are kinds of strange attractors. Socially, politically, and geographically, they transform the neighborhoods they infiltrate; unleashing civic potentialities, they create new spaces of local dialogue, volatile and transgressive. The significance of initial conditions, then, in comparison with the idea of origin represented by the mark and the foundation stone, is that they act on the environment as a strange attractor drawing out energies, identifying and transforming shapes, galvanizing and channeling tendencies, overturning

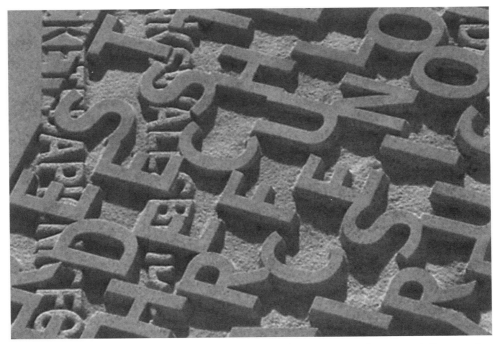

FIGURE 16.3 *Nearamnew,* ground figure no. 8, detail as it appears when carved (by permission of artist and Lab; photo by McMurtrie, Orange.).

amnesias, to produce patterns that, although unpredictable from a linearist perspective, strangely reincorporate neglected dimensions of the human and physical environment. In this sense Federation Square achieved its mythic anonymity and unique localization when these energies resident in the neighborhood were drawn into its field.

Melbourne's postfoundational history could be characterized as the consolidation of a linearist myth of progress in which the Indigenous peoples and their environment were subjected to the master-slave classification of Western science. However, evidence exists to show that in the turbulent prefoundational period of white settlement (ca. 1835–1837) quite different ideas were harbored along the Yarra River basin in the vicinity of the Federation Square site. Assistant

Aboriginal Protector William Thomas reported that "long ere the settlement was formed the spot where Melbourne now stands and the flat on which we are now camped . . . was the regular rendezvous for the tribes known as Waworangs, Boonurongs, Barrabools, Nilunguons, Gouldburns" (letter by William Thomas, 1840, cited in Presland 1985:25). At these rendezvous on the flats adjoining the Yarra River differences were settled, objects traded, and ceremonies exchanged. The neighborhood of Federation Square was ground all parties had ceded as part of a federal covenant; granting power to the decisions made there, those signatory to them guaranteed their own liberties. This also explains, in part at least, how the white settlement of Melbourne came to be located on this rendezvous ground,

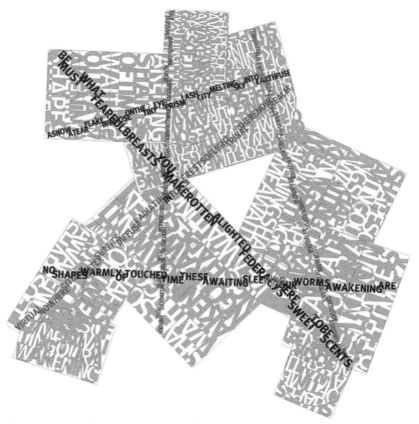

FIGURE 16.4. *Nearamnew*, ground figure no. 4, showing different layers and scales of text, plan view computer drawing (by permission of artist and Lab).

because the Aboriginal men who accompanied the first settlers overland from Geelong would undoubtedly have sought to travel extraterritorially, threading their way along tribal boundaries, directing the Europeans toward common places.

As I have documented elsewhere (Carter 1992a, b), after the arrival of the white pastoralists, a pragmatic biculturalism was essayed that contained within it the potential to create the initial conditions of a society that, instead of resembling another colonial clone, had the capacity to produce politically and socially imperceptible mergings, overlaps,

and doublings up. An example—it furnished my place marking artwork with its name—was the early history of the term *Narr-m*, defined in early word lists as the Aboriginal name for the "Place on which the city of Melbourne is built."[3] There must be considerable doubt about this: it is most unlikely that the word *Yarra*, for example, applies to Melbourne's river (now known as the Yarra River). Although this uncertainty embarrasses the makers of monuments who cannot abide regions of doubt, it is in the context of creating a mark that it comes to be understood as initial condition. In the first couple of years

of Aboriginal-European exchange, before the name
Melbourne was imposed, effectively silencing a plurality of voices, opinions, and dialogues, *Narr-m* cir-
culated as a signifier whose signified had yet to be
determined. Differently heard, pronounced, and
understood, it signified exactly because its semantic
boundaries were porous, mobile, and situational.
Among the numerous different renderings preserved in diaries and early charts, the rendering
"Nearamnew" illustrates that, in this state of non-
equilibrium, it could easily be transformed into a
utopian pidgin, evoking a new kind of neighborhood, even a novel kind of place making process (see
Carter 1992a:146; see also Billot 1985:175, where
another spelling, "Neramnew," is reported).

The sense in which I settled on the word *Nearamnew* is usefully elaborated by the ethnographer
Roy Wagner in his discussion of naming theory and
practice among the Daribi people of Papua New
Guinea. If, he wrote, "we treat names as merely
names, points of reference, then symbolism becomes
a matter of reference: a microcosm of names is coun-
terposed to a macrocosm of referents." This, inci-
dentally, describes the conventional relationship of
monuments to the places where they are located. But
if, Wagner continued, "we treat 'names' as relationships, the microcosm of names is no longer a microcosm; it becomes immersed in a microcosm of analogic construction. Not only do we have an analogy
that encompasses name and named, but the analogy
suggests, and tends to enter us into, analogic relations among macrocosmic constructs" (Wagner
1986:15–16). One result of understanding naming
as the production of relationships on the basis of
analogy is that it leads naturally to a federal organization of reality: "all people have an infinite range of
'names,' all are in some sense 'named' all things, and
all of these names and people are one" (Wagner

1986:16). Naming, in this view of things, emerges
concurrently with a widening discovery of one's surroundings. The totality of names is both the history
of the world's coming into being mythopoeically and
of one's part in this.

In this mode of place making it is the capacity of
the name to generate new names that counts: where
a sign has to be grasped in its materiality, as a performative utterance, it marks, if it marks nothing
else, the place where it was uttered. As signs, names
and monuments of this kind are always the traces of
dialogues, referring to a relationship ephemerally
placed in time and space. Unfixed, performative,
they harbor the initial conditions of a sociability
whose vitality depends on the meaning of terms not
being sharply demarcated but remaining porous,
blurred, context-permeable. Such signs are not only
verbal. They can equally be iconic. To return to my
opening remarks: landmarks are frequently selected
on the basis of their eidetic appeal. An unusually
shaped hill may not signify anything, even less commemorate an event, but its formal qualities lend it
symbolic potential. Purely by analogy it can achieve
an iconic status; and, not unnaturally, the basis of
the analogy is often the human body. Rock-art similarly features duplicated grooves, bundles of lines
and ribbons that, although they do not appear to
signify anything, clearly trace out a relationship
between the marker and the rock face.

Similarly, what unifies the artwork *Nearamnew* is
a bundle of lines signifying nothing, but, in compensation, implying a participatory ritual, whose
initial conditions it supplies. Because federal systems of political organization operate globally,
regionally, and locally, the tiers of influence overlapping to produce redundant regions of unpredictable growth, mutation, and renewal, the three
components of *Nearamnew* are organized federally.

At its broadest spatial scale, *Nearamnew* consists of nine sandstone surface figures or designs, created by configuring its nine letters in nine different ways, distributed through the plaza at Federation Square. On the federal analogy, the letters in each figure are divided into three groups of three. The largest letters are a third larger than the medium-sized letters; the medium-sized letters a third larger than the smallest. As the letters migrate from group to group through the nine figures, they create the initial conditions for new patterns to emerge. At a finer spatial scale, *Nearamnew* consists of nine federal texts carved into the sandstone: as the pages of the surface figures overlap, regions of the federal text also overlap, creating, on the analogy of redundancy in federal systems, nonlinearist zones that, although not easily legible, have a heightened haptic and eidetic appeal. At a *global* level, however, the texts and surface figures ride inside a thumbprint whorl, a meandering mythform picked out in cobbles and running throughout Federation Square's plaza.

With Vico's emphasis on invention in mind, it might seem indiscreet to ask the provenance of the mythform. But the incubator of a common place has to be more than a metaphor. Indeed, its power to act as a strange attractor depends on its not standing in for something else, not being the servant of a design. To explain that *Nearamnew*'s mythform is derived from a design grooved into the charcoal-coated inner bark of a gum tree—the whole decorated field (of which the whorl forms a small part) serving at the time of its execution as the roof of a temporary shelter—is not to suggest that ours is a copy or representation. The artist of the bark design (collected near Lake Tyrrell in northern Victoria ca. 1860) is unknown, but his brilliantly rendered juxtapositions of European and Indigenous motifs suggest that his work originated in a bicultural milieu

not unlike the one in which the word *Nearamnew* emerged.[4] There is circumstantial evidence to suggest that the artist's design may allude to the sky as well as the earth, that it not only images the whirling, infolding eddies of water in flood but the nebulous zone of the Magellanic Clouds.[5] These considerations obviously influenced the choice: but the chief appeal of the design was formal. Its duplication of lines, some merging into others, others folding under, and yet others excessively drawn out, produced a graphic form that, although suggestive of place making, rendered a process rather than an outcome. It was the integrity of the graphic trace that *Nearamnew* sought to carry over. Preserving its irregular and asymmetrical character was a way of avoiding inventions of our own or imposing upon it a symbolic rationalization.

Evoked here are the initial conditions of a different place making. The contrast I have drawn between the clearly demarcated and monumentally attired *urbs* and a ground marking that is "iconographic in a participatory, ritual, ceremonial, mythical or narrative" (Marshack 1977:316) way invites a reconsideration of the mark. It suggests the possibility of a place marking that does not have as its inevitable corollary a heritage of statues, artworks, and plaques. Bunjil, who in Kulin tradition[6] created the land around Melbourne and fashioned from clay the first man, was obviously a master of cleaving: with the *Ber-rang*, he "could open any place or any thing, and in such a way as to make it impossible for any one to know how or whether or not it had been opened. No one could see the opening he made" (see Smyth 1878, 1:423). He could make the ground open and simultaneously close it up again, in this way place making. Bunjil's place making mimicked the violence of Benjamin's (1985) destructive character, who might destroy even the signs of his destructiveness. But instead of causing the land it cut to lie flat and supine, Bunjil's instrument produced the lie of the land, a manifold of swellings, openings, gradually multiplying in the wake of his passage and spreading out in topographical eddies. In this way the entire environment was understood to participate repeatedly in the process of creation and to be its spatial narrative.

THE MARK AS BOUNDARY

Obviously, in this conception of space the mark is always in motion, establishing the initial conditions of a historical space in which it is always implicated. In his commentary on the *Parmenides*, Miller (1986) made a territorial point of direct relevance to the conception of Federation Square. In Plato's dialogue, nature, he pointed out, comes into being through a double participation, both involving the setting of boundaries: "The concrete sense of *peras* is boundary. A boundary, in turn, is the property line which first delimits—and so makes definite, determinate—an otherwise indefinite terrain" (Miller 1986:133). Parmenides also speaks of "*peras* in relation to," and, as Miller indicated, this has geopolitical implications, because "A boundary . . . defines the terrain on both sides, differentiating an area into definite regions and relating these to one another within that area as a whole. Or, considering it from the point of view of the particular regions, each is not only bounded-off, made a distinct entity for the first time; each is also set into relation, as the distinct entity it is, with the other region for the first time" (ibid., 134). If we attend to the communicative function of the boundary as the place where difference makes a difference, there emerges even in Plato's writing a distinctively *federal* conception of territory, one in which the parts simultaneously differentiate themselves into self-governing units and voluntarily participate in the one, the overarching federal covenant that preserves them in their difference.

It is an acute irony that, in ordering the removal of the West Shard, the Labor government singled out a unit of Federation Square's architectural assemblage that embodied that excess of connectivity that characterizes federal systems. In the interests of heritage or, rather, in the interest of leaving a mark, they foreclosed on participation in a widening conversation. If it is ever built, the fountain that replaces it will be a monument in advance. Its muffled voice will accurately commemorate the hush of censorship. The forces that have worked destructively to preserve a precinct of monuments picturesquely framed in nostalgia's past could have learned from Bunjil, the place maker, whose *Ber-rang* is, I speculate, in the absence of contemporary testimony to the contrary, connected with the Woiworung word *Brrering*, a name applied to the Yarra Valley and the water flowing in it, and meaning *mist*, and which in another mutation furnishes *Prahran*, the current name of a Melbourne suburb (Smyth 1878, vol. 2:188; Carter 1992a: 205 n. 7). To think of a place coming into being incrementally, its parts woven together like the hair of water, here eddying, there turbulent, now shallow now deep, and to observe the tidemarks briefly ringing the ground during its period of retreat—this is to observe the initial conditions of a process in which making and marking are contemporaneous; where, because nothing has been destroyed, nothing has to be monumentally restored.

NOTES

1. The decision attracted considerable media attention in February and March 2000; the report on which it was based can be accessed at www.shards-yes.com.

2. Etymologically *mark* has connotations of boundary and zone thus demarcated; *monument* is derived from a Latin root meaning to recall or remember.

3. "Garryowen" implied that the name would have been officially adopted except that it "was such a consonantal barbarism as could not be conveniently mouthed by Europeans" (Finn 1967:14).

4. An appreciative description of the drawing occurs in Smyth's (1878) *The Aborigines of Victoria*, vol. 1:286–287. Morieson (1996:168) speculated that the "thumbprint" represents Lake Tyrell itself, and that "The placement of the wattle and daub hut near where the creek enters the lake at the bottom of the picture is where the original Stanbridge cottage is believed to have been constructed at Lake Tyrrell." William Stanbridge, who published an article about the skylore of the Boorung, also collected the bark design and sent it to the Museum of Victoria, Melbourne, where it is now held.

5. The Boorung word *Tyrille* signified both sky and space. The idea is that the stars were observed through their reflections in the surface of the lake or, to quote a contemporary Kimberley elder, "Everything under creation is represented in the soil and in the sky" (Morieson 1996:1–2).

6. Presland (1985:25) described the four tribes of the Port Phillip Bay region as forming the "Kulin confederacy."

REFERENCES CITED

Bates, D., and P. Davidson. 1996. Textural Order: Two Recent Projects by Lab. *Assemblage* 29:103–114.

Benjamin, W. 1985. *One Way Street and Other Writings*, translated by E. Jephcott and K. Shorter. London: Verso.

Billot, C. P. 1985. *The Life and Times of John Pascoe Fawkner*. Melbourne: Hyland House.

Carter, P. 1992a. *Living in a New Country*. London: Faber and Faber.

———. 1992b. *The Sound In-Between*. Sydney: New Endeavour/University of New South Wales Press.

Chapman, R. J. K. 1993. Structure, Process and the Federal Factor: Complexity and Entanglement in Federations. In *Comparative Federalism and Federation*, edited by M. Burgess and Alain-G. Gagnon, 69–93. New York: Harvester Wheatsheaf.

Edlund-Berry, I. E. M. 1994. Ritual Destruction of Cities and Sanctuaries. In *Murlo and the Etruscans: Art and Society in Ancient Etruria*, edited by R. D. de Puma and T. P. Small, 16–28. Madison: University of Wisconsin Press.

Finn, E. [pseudonym "Garryowen"]. 1967. *The Chronicles of Early Melbourne: 1835 to 1852. Historical, Anecdotal and Personal*. 2 vols. Facsimile ed., Melbourne: Heritage Publications.

Frenkel, M. 1986. *Federal Theory*. Canberra: Australian National University Centre for Research on Federal Financial Relations.

Hays, K. M., C. Ingram, A. Kennedy, and S. Allen. 1996. Postscript. *Assemblage* 29:113.

Khlebnikov, V. 1987. Monuments. In *Collected Works*, V. Khlebnikov, translated by P. Schmidt. 2 vols. Cambridge: Harvard University Press.

Marshack, A. 1977. The Meander as a System: The Analysis and Recognition of Iconographic Units in Upper Palaeolithic Compositions. In *Form in Indigenous Art*, edited by P. Ucko, 286–317. London: Duckworth.

Miller, M. H. 1986. *Plato's Parmenides*. Princeton: Princeton University Press.

Morieson, J. 1996. *The Night Sky of the Boorung: Partial Reconstruction of a Disappeared Culture in Northwest Victoria*. Master's thesis, University of Melbourne, Melbourne.

Presland, G. 1985. *The Land of the Kulin*. Melbourne: McPhee Gribble/Penguin.

Smyth, R. B. 1878. *The Aborigines of Victoria: With Notes Relating to the Habits of the Natives of Other Parts of Australia and Tasmania*. 2 vols. Melbourne: John Ferres, Government Printer.

Vattimo, G. 1993. *The Adventure of Difference: Philosophy after Nietzsche and Heidegger*, translated by C. Blamires. London: Polity Press.

Vico, G. 1977. *La Scienza Nuova*. Milan: Rizzoli.

Wagner, R. 1986. *Symbols That Stand for Themselves*. Chicago: University of Chicago Press.

SEVENTEEN

Sarawak on Stage

The Sarawak Cultural Village and the Colonization of Cultural Space in the Making of State Identity

SALLIE YEA

Burkhart and Medlik (1981:v) defined "tourism" as "the temporary, short-term movement of people to destinations outside the places where they normally live and work and their activities during the stay at these destinations. Much of this movement is international in character and much of it is a leisure activity." In *ethnic* tourism, cultural groups other than that of the visitor's are the target of attention. Unlike *cultural* tourism, which is an overarching term that embraces all tourism activities that concern cultural matters (incorporating heritage places, ancient cities, museums, performances, and so forth), ethnic tourism is restricted to tourism in traditional places where people can (supposedly) be seen to live out their cultures.

Ethnic tourism may be understood as a means of authoring, controlling, and (re)constructing places and peoples through the disembodied gaze of the tourist. Various studies have thus appeared that explore ways in which "traditional," usually non-Western cultures are constructed in the public eye through the gaze of the tourist (Urry 1990). Many ethnic tourism experiences play upon the exotic, romantic, and "primitive" character of the host communities, firmly positioning those communities as accessible objects of the colonial imagination. In the process, tourism is often a means by which individuals and groups appropriate or colonize the cultural space of "minority" groups, constructing them as an accessible (but imaginary) Other.

Notably absent from research on ethnic tourism, however, are explorations of relationships between processes of state building, place making, and ethnic tourism. There is a need for empirically based research that attends to the ways in which states mediate and influence the presentation of ethnic tourism through multiple sites as places of political influence, including constructed cultural spaces such as the Sarawak Cultural Village (*Kampung Budaya Sarawak*) in Malaysian Borneo. Places, including sites of ethnic and cultural display, convey political messages—intended and unintended, consciously and subconsciously—that achieve their salience through people's engagements with them. To date, studies that do focus on agents of cultural construction in the tourist arena tend to target almost exclusively the formative role that tourist operators play (e.g., Adams 1984; Silver 1993), leaving the role of the state in scripting tourist sites largely unexamined.

Wood and Pichad's recent study (1997) of the dynamic interactions between tourism, ethnicity, and the state in Asia provides an important exception to this general rule. In that study, Wood (1997:5) foregrounded the significant but much neglected relationship between ethnic tourism and the state when he suggested that "the state plays a central role not only in structuring the tourist encounter but also in shaping and controlling the visible contours of ethnicity." Although Third World governments are increasingly drawn to tourism for economic benefit, there is nonetheless a significant affinity between state-building processes and ethnic tourism (see also Leong 1989, 1997; Ritcher 1989; Wood 1984). Wood (1984:365), in discussing the role of the state in marketing cultural meanings, suggested that the choice of which parts of a country's cultural heritage are to be developed for tourism constitutes a statement about national identity that is conveyed both to tourists and locals. This process of selecting particular elements of cultural heritage (and by implication of forgetting or leaving out other aspects) can be extended to ethnicity. Thus, ethnicity comes to be (re)constructed and (re)produced in the tourist arena through a kind of "sorting procedure," or filtering process that targets culturally marked places as *state* symbols of local, ethnic identity. Agencies of the state play a crucial role in this process of cultural identification and place making.

The growing importance of the relationship between the state, marked places, and ethnic tourism raises numerous questions that form the basis of this chapter. Beyond the broad desire to promote Sarawak's ethnic identities through tourism, what role does the Sarawak state play in diffusing particular concepts of, and ideas about, ethnicity and culture within the Sarawak Cultural Village (a folk village that inscribes the landscape with cultural identity)? What kinds of ethnic labels, identities, and relationships are sanctioned by the state in the context of the Village? How, in particular, does the state represent ethnic groups in the Village in ways that depart from the "reality" of ethnicity that exists outside the Village? How does the state choreograph ethnic tourism at the Sarawak Cultural Village, and how does this choreography help to construct the nation's own cultural identity?

According to Wood (1997), in Malaysia, as elsewhere in Asia, these questions have not been given much consideration to date. King (1993a:109) touched on the issue when he referred to the creation of the Ministry of Culture and Tourism, the naming of which, he suggested, is indicative of a nontourism role, or a "national purpose" behind tourist promotion efforts. Specifically, King suggested that the state's task "is to engender a local awareness of cultural matters and national identity and heritage, and to enhance national pride and commitments" (ibid.). In other words, the selection of "uncontentious" cultural elements to define Malay culture is indicative of a broader concern to be cautious in the characterization of a multiethnic society. Although King identified an important process that informs state tourist promotion efforts, the role of the state is not always confined to a passive process centering on a concern for representations that do not offend. Taking King's argument further, I suggest that the Sarawak state not only selects certain politically correct cultural elements for state-building purposes, but actively attempts to canonize a particular version of the state through carefully chosen ethnic representations inscribed in places. Let us explore such inscriptions, and in the process unfold how the state appropriates local identity in (re)defining the state's own.

CULTURAL AND FOLK VILLAGES AS POLITICAL SPACES

There is considerable scope for extending explorations of the interface between ethnic tourism, place ma(r)king, and state building, especially in an era in which state-directed tourism is becoming increasingly prominent in the Third World. This is the case in multiethnic and rapidly developing states of Southeast Asia such as Malaysia, where questions of ethnic identity and development have a considerable institutional history, and where tourism is now a booming industry. Cultural and folk villages provide excellent sites for explorations of this because they have become a central tourist attraction in much of the Asia-Pacific region, appearing in numerous countries including China, Indonesia, Thailand, South Korea, and the state of Hawai'i. These reconstructed villages are almost always conceived, funded, and operated by government tourist authorities.

Cultural theme parks or villages are deliberately framed to contain all the desired features of the ethnic and cultural makeup of the nation in one clearly bounded and demarcated place. The self-proclaimed role of the Sarawak Cultural Village, for example, is as a "microcosm" of the state's cultural and ethnic landscape. In one of the Village's promotional brochures the tourist is told that she/he can "Experience Sarawak in half a day" with a visit to the Village, much as at the Polynesian Cultural Center in Hawai'i, where "Visitors can experience the charm and beauty of seven authentically replicated South Pacific Island villages in just one day" (Polynesian Cultural Center web site). In other promotional material for the Sarawak Cultural Village the tourist is told that, if on a limited schedule, the Village offers visitors to the state the opportunity to experience Sarawak's cultural diversity without having to visit actual living Dayak villages and communities. In fact the Sarawak Cultural Village was conceived out of the state government's desire to portray "live" the state's rich cultural and ethnic diversity in one single place for the consumption of visitors and tourists. Ethnicity is thus made both compact and accessible by circumscribing place and marking it with the hallmarks of ethnic symbolism, giving the visitor the feeling that she/he can know all of Sarawak's populations through a half-day encounter with the reconstructed ethnic display in the Village. The Village becomes an appropriation by the state of particular cultural behaviors, allowing the visitor superficial entry into those cultures as a state-controlled right to cultural space. This right is expressed in the state's ability to control culturally inscribed spaces.

In these present-day cultural and folk villages several parallels with earlier imperial exhibitions, such as the World's Columbian Exposition, can be drawn in which, "Together with their artefacts, houses, and even complete villages, so-called natives or primitives were made available for visual inspection by millions of strolling and staring Western citizens" (Corbey 1995:57). Corbey could just as easily have been describing any one of the cultural or folk villages in the Asia-Pacific region, which are strikingly similar in their attempts to capture the essence of national ethnic minorities by exhibiting religious rituals and dances, clothes, household and farming implements and techniques, dwellings, and other constitutive elements of minority cultures.

China's Folk Culture Village in Shenzhen, for example, attempts to include all of China's officially recognized national minority cultures in a constructed village of ethnic exhibition (Oakes 1997). Similarly, Hawai'i's Polynesian Cultural Center houses seven Polynesian villages for the tourist gaze (Balme 1998). South Korea, although relatively homogeneous ethnically and linguistically, has also constructed a Korean Folk Village (Tangherlini 1997). However, rather than displaying the various ethnic groups of the nation, the Village represents distinctive regional cultures through typical dwellings, farming practices, and ritualistic events. In Sarawak, too, the Sarawak Cultural Village allows visitors, both Malaysian and international, a brief stereotypical glimpse of the seven major ethnic groups of the state, possible through a half-day stroll around a village of (re)constructed ethnicity. Although each of these folk villages therefore claims a certain uniqueness that derives from distinctive national and subnational cultures, ethnic groups, or regions, the reproduction of this form of ethnic display is nonetheless remarkably consistent across national boundaries and appears as yet another manifestation of the tendency toward disciplining and homogenizing space inherent within global economic relations. The Village is thus about inscribing space with symbols of the stereotypically local. But the formula is unmistakably extralocal: although purporting to represent the unique cultures of Sarawak, the conception and construction of the Sarawak Cultural Village, for example, is explicitly based on, and imitative of, Hawai'i's Polynesian Cultural Center.

Beyond tourism, these (re)constructed spaces of ethnicity have come to play a significant role in state-building processes. Cultural and folk villages can thus be at least partially located within, and understood as contributing to, statist efforts aimed at forging an imagined national community (cf. Anderson

1983) and at representing a particular version of the nation-state rich in cultural identity (cf. Wood 1984). In these villages place is inscribed with a local cultural identity in the making of a national identity, a process that extends beyond the tourist realm within which the villages are overtly framed.

The state-building agenda is an integral part of the operation of the Sarawak Cultural Village. Aside from the obvious objective of portraying Sarawak's major ethnic groups for locals and tourists alike, at a broader level of the conception and realization of the Sarawak Cultural Village there is little explicit mention of tourism. Instead, in the "vision" for the Sarawak Cultural Village it is stated that the Village is "a unique and dynamic cultural centre preserving Sarawak's rich cultural heritage and sharing a global cultural harmony towards human understanding and brotherhood" (Sarawak Cultural Village web site). In the realization of their vision, the "mission" of the Sarawak Cultural Village is given a threefold task: the dynamic enhancement of the uniqueness of Sarawak's rich multicultural heritage through its Research and Development Programme; regenerating an interest and inculcating an appreciation of Sarawakian cultures among "our" younger generation; and to present the Sarawak Cultural Village as a model village with a community living and working together. None of these three goals relates to tourism per se, but can be understood within the domestic political-developmental context of Sarawak.

A JOURNEY THROUGH THE SARAWAK CULTURAL VILLAGE

Of all of Malaysia's twelve states, Sarawak is touted by the government as the most attractive and fascinating destination for the tourist. The promotion of Sarawak in these terms is driven partly by the need to generate revenue in the state and partly by the growing popularity of Sarawak as an international tourist destination. The promotional efforts of the Sarawak Tourism Board and Ministry of Culture and Tourism have rested on a threefold characterization of Sarawak's tourist product, including Culture, Adventure, and Nature, encapsulated in the CAN acronym. The Sarawak Cultural Village and (Iban) longhouse tours constitute the two main elements of the cultural component of CAN. In both cases culture is equated with the ethnic minority, Dayak culture.

The Sarawak Cultural Village is located on a 17.5-acre site approximately 25 km from Kuching near Damai Beach and Santubong Mountain. In 1997 the Sarawak Cultural Village attracted over 60,000 visitors, of whom the vast majority (45,503 or 76%) were Malaysian (6,796 others were Asian; 1,324 were Australian or New Zealanders; 96 were African; 15 were Middle Eastern; 4,751 were European; 402 were North American; 81 were Latin American; and 1,120 Others).

Upon reaching the Village and paying the entrance fee, the visitor receives a "passport" that allows her/him "safe passage" through the village and entry into each of the seven ethnic dwellings contained therein. The passport—a central metaphor for collective territorial belonging—is also intended to situate the Sarawak Cultural Village firmly within the symbolic realm of the nation-state. The passport also provides a brief summary of the essential features of each of the seven ethnic groups housed within the village, as well as a sketch of a traditional dwelling of each community. The seven dwellings located in the Sarawak Cultural Village include an Iban longhouse, a Bidayuh longhouse, a Penan hut, an Orang Ulu longhouse, a Melanu Rumah Tinggi (Malay house), and a Chi-

nese farmhouse, all of which are "built according to authentic styles" (Sarawak Cultural Village web site). These houses are sited around an artificial lake that, according to information contained in the passport, is symbolic of Sarawak peoples' dependence on the rivers as a means of communication and livelihood.

After passing through the reception area, the visitor's passport is stamped at a "security check point," thus further contributing to the authenticity of the feeling that one is experiencing the nation. Upon clearing the checkpoint the visitor may proceed around the village along the marked path, visiting each of the seven dwellings in turn. Inside each house there are traditional artifacts, reenactments of daily practices and tasks, and members of each particular ethnic group who perform local dances and ritualistic practices. The intention of such a visual cultural display is clearly articulated in the Village web site: "The village will promote various traditional activities such as handicraft-making demonstrations by skilled craftspeople, the preparation of ethnic foods, tattooing, blowpipe making, and coconut de-husking. Traditional games such as gasing (top spinning), tibau swinging and kite flying will also be demonstrated. Full-time dancers and musicians will provide eclectic performances blending the very best elements of each ethnic group's traditional dances and music."

For each of the seven ethnic groups displayed in the Village the visitor is provided with "essential" information. For example, with regard to the Iban the visitor is told that "The Iban, once known as 'sea Dayaks,' built their longhouses to last fifteen to twenty years, or until the farm land in the surrounding area was exhausted. Then they packed up their goods and chattels and moved inland, upriver, along the coast, wherever fresh farm lands looked promising. About one-third of all Sarawakians are Iban; while some of them live in individual houses, a large number still prefer longhouses."

The paragraph that follows describes the longhouse structure and associated Iban social system. In the Sarawak Cultural Village brochure emphasis is placed squarely on the material elements of culture, including drums and gongs, *pua* weaving, and *tuak* (rice wine), and the past, as in the "hanging skulls [that] carry tales of days gone by."

Just as Iban culture and lifestyle are promoted in the Village as a "live" display, so the Penan are similarly represented. The information about the Penan provided in the Village passport describes them in the following way: "The shy nomadic people of the jungle, the Penans, live in the dense virgin jungles of the Central Borneo, among some of the state's valuable timber resources. Some are 'coming out' and learning to farm the land, others still prefer their roaming lifestyle."

The description of the Penan continues by detailing their special expertise at blowpipe production and use—an experience in which the visitor to the village may also indulge, if they are game.

In the other dwellings, selected elements of material and performed culture are also displayed for consumption by the visitor. Visiting the Orang Ulu longhouse, housing the Kayan, Kenyah, Kelabit, and other less-populous Dayak groups, the visitor can witness and experience the production of intricate beadwork, the tune of the *sape* (a stringed musical instrument), body tattooing, *parang ilang* (a fighting sword), and *kliigieng* (a burial pole). The Melanau house boosts sago processing and the *tibau* swing, used as a fertility rite during the Pesta Kaul ritual.

Once the tourist has completed the village circuit, having visited each of the dwellings and gained

a brief insight into the essential characteristics of the various ethnic groups contained therein, she/he arrives back at the reception area in time to see the Cultural Show that takes place twice daily in the Village theater (at 11:30 A.M. and 4:30 P.M.). Seated in front of a stage, the visitor views a 45-minute performance of dances from six of the seven Dayak groups represented in the Village (Chinese dances are not performed in this show). According to the information contained in the Village passport the dances are reflective of peoples whose music and dances embody a spirit of harmony and happiness: "The people of Sarawak are cheerful and friendly in their disposition. They are a very happy people and they translate a lot of their daily chores and activities into graceful and interesting dances. All their dances tell stories of happenings amongst and around them in their daily living."

Each performance group appears in turn, with the meaning of the respective dances of the groups explained for the tourist in the passport. The dances are based on themes such as the agility of a warrior or victorious battle (Iban Ngajat Lesong and Ngajat Pahlawan, respectively), celebrating or anticipating a successful harvest (Bidayuh Rajang Be'uh and Tolak Bala, respectively), a hunting trip in the jungle in which blowpipes are used (Orang Ulu Kanjet Ngeleput), and daily activities, such as processing of sago flour (Melanau Tarian Menyak).

After the individual dances of each Dayak group there is a group performance involving a de facto "state anthem" provocatively titled "Fascinating Sarawak." The anthem is sung in unison by members of each of the seven Dayak groups represented in the Village. During the performance the representatives of the Dayak groups clasp hands with each other in a physical gesture of harmony and unity, echoed by the words of the anthem:

Here we are living as one
Beneath our crescent, stripes and star
People everywhere throughout the land
Love Sarawak and together, together
Let's make our land of beauty
The best.

Come and enjoy, come let's all learn
To appreciate the richness of our cultures
To experience our friendship and our grace.

Peace and Harmony, Love and Unity
Let's share our world with one another
We are proud of this great place Sarawak.

The visitor can thus leave the Village with a sense of having both witnessed and experienced Sarawak's ethnic diversity and gained a broad understanding of the essential characteristics of the seven major ethnic groups contained therein. In addition to this sense of appreciation of the individual traits of Sarawak's ethnic groups, the visitor also leaves with a sense that in Sarawak there are well-defined, cohesive community structures among the Dayak communities, sustainable household economies, and sustainable environmental relationships. In addition, the visitor is able to form an impression of harmonious (or at least non-conflictual) relationships existing between the groups. The multiethnic harmony is particularly evident in the staged performance at the conclusion of the visitor's tour through the Village.

THE SARAWAK CULTURAL VILLAGE AND STATE-LED DEVELOPMENT

The Sarawak Cultural Village draws on indigenous ethnicity while simultaneously constructing a sense of individual ethnic markers, playing on such elements as the unique culture, dwellings, lifestyles, and practices of each Dayak group. The Sarawak Cultural Village representations of ethnicity rest on a number of reified and romanticized images that have no equivalent within the general thrust of state development policies aimed at these groups. In fact, the state's view of Dayak communities outside and inside the Village are at such variance that broader state-level Dayak development programs work to actively undermine the claim that representations of Dayak culture and lifestyle contained in the Village depict real "living" communities.

Development policies targeting Iban and Penan are cases in point. The representation of both the Iban and Penan in the Sarawak Cultural Village, in which traditional elements of material and performed culture are assigned an intrinsic value and promoted as markers of distinctive cultural identities, provides a stark contrast to the ways these groups are framed within broader state development discourses. The Sarawak state government's developmental programs aimed at these minority groups rest on the enduring premise of Dayak underdevelopment. Implicit in this view of Dayak groups as underdeveloped is the assumption that their poverty is attributable primarily to the persistence of traditional agricultural practices and attitudes toward education, land, and housing, precisely those elements of Dayakism that are promoted within the Sarawak Cultural Village. The assistant minister for tourism, speaking to a group of Iban leaders in Lubok Antu, a small trading town near Sarawak's northern border, announced recently, for example, that "The majority of rural Dayaks are still resorting to traditional farming methods like shifting cultivation to earn a living. . . . Because of these old methods of farming, the community is not able to reap greater profits which would otherwise help to raise their standard of living. *And so they remain backward*" (emphasis added) (*Sarawak Times* 1998).

In the case of the Penan, a new ten-year development program specifically targeted toward Penan development was announced in December 1998 in the eastern city of Miri. According to the then minister for industrial development, the program was formulated as part of a continuous effort to bring Penans into the mainstream of development. The minister was quoted at the time as saying, "The Penans, once nomadic and leading a subsistant lifestyle, must be motivated to recognise and exploit opportunities in a common effort to raise their standard of living" (*Borneo Post* 1998b). The program represents one strategy to develop the Penan that is part of the state-level Committee on Penan Affairs, established to promote awareness among Penan so that they "discard their nomadic and unsettled lifestyle . . . and catch-up in mainstream development" (ibid.). The Sarawak Cultural Village information on the Penan nonetheless constructs their lifestyles in terms of a *choice* between learning to lead a sedentary farming lifestyle and their traditional "roaming lifestyle."

Rural Iban communities have been characterized similarly as in need of development interventions to raise their standard of living and ensure their participation in broader state-driven development efforts. The assistant minister for Tourism, speaking in Saratok, Krian District, stated in late 1998 that "Iban people must be able to adapt themselves to new changes in order to benefit from the various development projects implemented by the government . . . [they] must cooperate with the private sector to develop NCR [Native Customary Rights] land" (*Borneo Post* 1998a). Native Customary Rights land has traditionally been the basis of shift-

ing cultivation farming practices described in the Sarawak Cultural Village passport. According to Ngidang (1997:63), "This age-old farming practice is an integral part of longhouse lifestyle, and symbolises what most people call the Dayaks' identity in Sarawak." Despite this important cultural role of Native Customary Rights land, there have been a series of state policy interventions related to the development of this land over the past thirty years that act to both compromise and reconfigure this relationship (see Ngidang 1997).

Development policies aimed at agricultural modernization and commercialization of Native Customary Rights land and associated policies aimed at the resettlement of minority ethnic communities are examples of a very different reconstitution of Sarawak's minority groups than that inscribed in the Sarawak Cultural Village's propaganda. Thus, although for example the Sarawak Cultural Village passport information hints at the changing lifestyle of the Penan as they "come out" of their traditional geographical and socioeconomic homes, the passport overlooks the uneasy tension that this process is generating between Dayak communities and the state, as well as some of the more negative impacts of this process on the communities themselves. Specifically, the Village passport fails to link the process of Penan "coming out" with the government programs of active resettlement and the associated development of Native Customary Rights land for commercial agriculture.

The same tensions that exist around agricultural development policies are also evident in the state's policies aimed at the extraction of timber resources. For both Sarawak and Kalimantan (Indonesia), timber extraction is a major revenue earner. Nonetheless, the extraction of these resources tends to conflict with traditional resource usages assigned by

Dayak communities who continue to live in these rich resource areas (recall the Sarawak Cultural Village passport's description of the Penan that locates them geographically as living "in the dense virgin jungles of the Central Borneo, among some of the state's valuable timber resources"). This conflict is embodied in the growing currency of the phrase *politik pembangunan* (timber politics) (see King 1993b). The conflicts that are part of this timber politics revolve around the uneven distribution of benefits of timber exploitation (with the timber companies, state government, concessionaries, timber contractors, and subcontractors being the major beneficiaries). Dayak land rights have also become a sensitive issue because many Dayak groups see logging activities as infringing on a number of their rights, especially the destruction of their fruit trees, farmlands, burial sites, and sometimes the actual displacement of entire communities, by logging roads and works (see Lian 1993 for an overview of Dayak marginalization through logging). For the Penan and Orang Ulu in particular, the exploitation of forest resources, much of which is still classified as Native Customary Rights land, has had dire consequences for the ability of affected communities to maintain traditional community structures and lifestyles. Yet, in the main tourist brochure for the Sarawak Cultural Village the potential visitor is told that they need look no farther than the Village to see "the real Borneo."

In sum, the most blatantly promoted aspect of Dayak culture(s) in the Sarawak Cultural Village concerns the way place is marked by cultural practices, such as shifting and swidden agricultural practices (e.g., slash and burn hill *padi* cultivation) and traditional dwellings (e.g., the Iban longhouse or Penan "hut"), as well as "traditional" elements of Dayak lifestyle (particularly the distinctiveness of the groups, their unique customs, lifestyles, and community organization). In marked contrast to this, in broader state development discourses these practices are devalued for their role in apparently retarding Dayak socioeconomic mobility. The demise of traditional agricultural practices, and housing and social arrangements, is to be actively facilitated through state-led programs aimed at resettlement of communities and commercialization, transformation, and consolidation of Native Customary Rights land. Such programs are premised on the demarcation of Dayak communities as "impoverished" and "backward." This scission between the presentation of an apparently harmonious cultural situation as inscribed by the Village and political circumstances beyond the Village is masked by a state narrative steeped in the subversion and marking of *state* space.

THE SARAWAK CULTURAL VILLAGE AND THE IMAGINED STATE IN SARAWAK

As Leong (1989) rightly pointed out, government efforts to actively construct the nation tend to be most intense and obvious in nation-states where no such preexisting, cohesive national community already exists. Thus, the nation, to borrow Benedict Anderson's (1983) phrase, must be "imagined into existence." For many multiethnic nation-states of the Asia-Pacific region, this is a formidable task precisely because the nation-state itself is often an arena (rather than arbiter) of conflict. Sarawak is an obvious case in point. State building in both Malaysia and Sarawak has, historically, been a difficult task precisely because of the ethnically and culturally based divisions that exist at both the state and national levels. The ethnic mix of Sarawak is more complex than that of Peninsula Malaysia. The state has a population of about 1.83 million and is home to twenty-four distinct ethnic minority groups. This ethnic makeup is subdivided along the following main lines: Iban, 29.5%; Chinese, 28.9%; Malays, 20.8%; Bidayuh, 8.4%; with other ethnic groups, collectively referred to as Orang Ulu making up the remainder.

In Sarawak, the specific issues that have perpetuated ethnic-based cleavages revolve largely around interrelated concerns of Dayak political participation and the position of Dayaks in national development, particularly their control over both developmental resources (such as land and timber) and processes (such as the commercialization of agriculture and development of large-scale plantations). Thus the inscription of an imagined community in Sarawak, through the guise of the model Village, is a subject that is closely intertwined with this development-ethnicity tension. The Sarawak state government has come under severe criticism over the last ten years (both by international and nongovernment organizations, and by disaffected groups within the state) for two reasons: first, ethnic minorities are seen to be excluded from, or disadvantaged in, access to developmental resources; and second, programs for state development often have severe negative repercussions for Dayak groups themselves (such as in dam building, logging, and Native Customary Rights land development).

The arena of education and employment opportunities further exemplifies Dayak marginalization in Sarawak. According to Jayam Jawan's (1998) study of available census material on occupational and educational opportunities, Dayak communities have been lagging behind in national development. Although the New Economic Policy attempts to restructure Malaysian society and economy in such a way as to eradicate ethnic identification with specific economic function, in practice this has not yet

been realized. In this environment of conflict, exclusion, and marginalization in development processes, state politics have taken on an ethnic flavor, which the Sarawak Cultural Village attempts to discount in its ethnic constructs.

Interethnic relations are thus an important subject of representation in the Village. Unity, racial/ethnic harmony, and the consensual relationship between the state and its minority Dayak groups are themes that emerge in part from the Village where ethnicity is displayed in a diverse but unified space, but mainly through the staged performances shown on the conclusion of a visit to the Village. The emphasis on national identity and multiethnic harmony aims to diffuse tensions between ethnic groups, generally by focusing on the trope of unity in diversity, in which ethnic diversity is promoted as not only desirable, but also as existing in harmony with the national (paternal, state) community.

The Sarawak Cultural Village offers the visitor a range of ways to engage in nation-building processes. The part of the visitor's experience at the Village that reinforces this nationalist theme most explicitly is the singing of the de facto state anthem at the conclusion of the visit. Interethnic harmony is unabashedly promoted to the audience through the luring "we are living as one" and "our world" and the phrases "Peace and Harmony, Love and Unity," "come let's all learn to appreciate the richness of our cultures" (Sarawak Cultural Village passport). Particularly seductive here are references to the flag, "Beneath our crescent, stripes and star," and the emotive attachment and pride Sarawakians have for their state.

CONCLUSION

In this chapter I have discussed the role of one particular kind of inscribed landscape—the ethnic tourism park—as highlighted by the Sarawak Cultural Village, in processes of state building. Two interconnected state building processes were identified as emerging from the text of the Sarawak Cultural Village. First, representations of traditional material and intangible cultural elements of Sarawak's major Dayak groups function to construct a view of Dayaks as able to maintain traditional practices and lifestyles, particularly in the face of rapid state-led development. The depiction of the integrity of Dayak culture acts to dissemble an increasingly critical view that sees the devaluing and eventual erosion of unique and distinctive Dayak culture by an aggressively developmental state. Timber politics, tensions surrounding the use of native customary land, and resettlement of communities have been focal points for these tensions in the recent past. Second, the articulation of an imagined state in the Village acts to portray an image of multiethnic harmony. Although ethnic tensions in Sarawak have never reached the same intensity as they have in Peninsula Malaysia, discrimination of Dayaks' educational and political processes is nonetheless a serious problem in the state.

These two nation-building processes at work in the Village are thus clearly at odds with what might be called the "wider reality" of ethnicity and Dayak development in Sarawak, even though promotional materials claim that the Village provides an accurate depiction of this reality. In this sense, the state-building processes at work through representations in the Village are negatively oriented toward effacing critical views of the state and its ability to deal with complex and sensitive issues relating to ethnicity by offering up alternative, idealized representations. Hence, with regard to the relationship between ethnicity and development, the development policies for Dayak groups adopted by the

Sarawak state government that view Dayak "traditionalism" as a barrier to development contrast markedly with the intrinsic valuing of their traditional culture in the Village. With regard to the forging of the imagined state, the reality of interethnic tensions and ethnic politics in Sarawak stands in marked contrast to the multiethnic harmony and unity depicted in the Village.

Studies that describe the construction and portrayal of local cultures through the tourist gaze often forget the role that the state plays in constructing such sites, even though, as I have shown in this chapter, the state plays an important role in the selection of ethnic and cultural "truths" open to the visitor. Seen in a context of state building, particularly in multiethnic, multicultural states, ethnic tourism culturally inscribes places as important arenas through which national identities, and desirable visions/versions of the nation, can be forged. Alternatively or additionally, such cultural places may also be places of resistance, a dimension I have not explored here and that warrants further discussion.

In sum, this discussion suggests that the Sarawak Cultural Village plays an important role in depicting cultural groups in a manner that is highly distorting of a reality that exists outside the Village—a reality that the state is effectively helping to create. This is despite the mission of the Village to display/contain "live" major ethnic groups in the state. The impacts that rapid (state-led) development programs are having on groups like the Penan and Iban are resulting in changing lifestyles, integration into the market economy, commodification of their resources, resettlement, waged (mostly off-farm/seasonal) employment, and so on. These multifaceted processes of minority transformation through state and national development efforts are actively excluded from the displays of reconstructed ethnicity that appear in the Sarawak Cultural Village. In short, the Sarawak Cultural Village presents a sanctioned vision/version of ethnicity in Sarawak. But questions need to be raised about tourist sites that purport to write ethnicity in the landscape, such as cultural and folk villages, as containers of national identity and places that are representative of the nation. The fact that they are promoted as windows on the nation, coupled with their increasing appeal to large numbers of tourists—both international and domestic—is alone a good enough reason to cast a more scrutinizing gaze in their direction.

NOTE

An earlier version of this chapter was presented at the Fifth Annual Southeast Asian Geography Association Conference, Singapore, 30 November to 4 December 1998.

REFERENCES CITED

Adams, K. M. 1984. Come to the Land of Tana Toraja, "Land of the Heavenly Kings": Travel Agents as the Brokers of Ethnicity. *Annals of Tourism Research* 11:469–485.

Anderson, B. 1983. *Imagined Communities*. London: Verso.

Balme, C. 1998. Staging the Pacific: Framing Authenticity in Performances for Tourists at the Polynesian Cultural Center. *Theatre Journal* 50:53–70.

Borneo Post. 1998a. Adapt to New Changes, Iban Told. 7 December.

———. 1998b. Forge Strategies to Uplift Standard of Living, Dayaks Told. 10 December.

Burkhart, A. J., and S. Medlik. 1981. *Tourism Past, Present and Future*. London: Heinemann.

Corbey, R. 1995. Ethnographic Showcases, 1870–1930. In *The Decolonization of Imagination, Culture, Knowledge and Power*, edited by J. N. Pieterse and B. Parekh, 57–80. London: Zed Books.

Jawan, J. A. 1998. *Leadership and Development: Identifying and Setting Priorities for the Iban in the 21st Century*. Puchong, Selangor: Jayum A. Jawan.

King, V. T. 1993a. Tourism and Culture in Malaysia. In *Tourism in South-East Asia*, edited by M. Hitchcock, V. King, and M. Parnell, 99–116. London: Routledge.

———. 1993b. Politik Pembangunan: The Political Economy of Rainforest Exploitation and Development in Sarawak, East Malaysia. *Global Ecology and Bioecology Letters* 3:235–244.

Leong, W.-T. 1989. Culture and the State: Manufacturing Traditions for Tourism. *Critical Studies in Mass Communications* 6:355–375.

———. 1997. Commodifying Ethnicity: State and Ethnic Tourism in Singapore. In *Tourism, Ethnicity, and the State in Asian and Pacific Societies*, edited by R. E. Wood and M. Pichad, 71–98. Honolulu: University of Hawai'i Press.

Lian, F. 1993. Blockades of Timber Roads in Sarawak: Assertion of Land Rights. In *Indigenous Land Rights in Commonwealth Countries*, edited by J. Overton, 154–162. Palmerston North: Massey University.

Ngidang, D. 1997. Native Customary Land Rights, Public Policy, Land Reform and Plantation Development in Sarawak. *Borneo Review* 8 (1): 63–80.

Oakes, T. 1997. Ethnic Tourism in Rural Guizhou: Sense of Place and the Commerce of Authenticity. In *Tourism, Ethnicity, and the State in Asian and Pacific Societies*, edited by R. E. Wood and M. Pichad, 35–70. Honolulu: University of Hawai'i Press.

Polynesian Cultural Center Web Site: http://www.polynesia.com/pcc/Info/Fact.html.

Ritcher, L. K. 1989. *The Politics of Tourism in Asia*. Honolulu: University of Hawai'i Press.

Sarawak Cultural Village Web Site: http://www/visitsarawak.com/scv/entrance.html.

Sarawak Times. 1998. New 10-yr Programme for Penans. 14 December.

Silver, I. 1993. Marketing Authenticity in Third World Countries. *Annals of Tourism Research* 20:302–318.

Tangherlini, T. 1997. Minsokchon and the Politics of Display. Paper presented at the First Conference of Korean Society and Culture, The University of Auckland, Auckland.

Urry, J. 1990. *The Tourist Gaze: Leisure and Travel in Contemporary Societies*. London: Sage.

Wood, R. E. 1984. Ethnic Tourism, the State, and Cultural Change in Southeast Asia. *Annals of Tourism Research* 11:353–374.

———. 1997. Tourism and the State: Ethnic Options and Constructions of Otherness. In *Tourism, Ethnicity, and the State in Asian and Pacific Societies*, edited by R. E. Wood and M. Pichad, 1–34. Honolulu: University of Hawai'i Press.

Wood, R. E., and M. Pichad (eds.). 1997. *Tourism, Ethnicity, and the State in Asian and Pacific Societies*. Honolulu: University of Hawai'i Press.

EIGHTEEN

The Edge of the Sacred, the Edge of Death

Sensual Inscriptions

Marcia Langton

In 1991, the traditional Aboriginal owners of the Lakefield and Cliff Island National Parks of eastern Cape York Peninsula in the state of Queensland, Australia, filed an application through the Cape York Land Council to have their Indigenous rights to the lands and waters of the national parks legally recognized under a new Queensland statute, the Aboriginal Land Act of 1991. The challenge for the Aboriginal claimants and the Cape York Land Council staff and consultants who were to represent them before the Aboriginal Land Tribunal was the question of how to prove that they had a traditional affiliation to the land claimed. Under Australian law, physical modifications to the land, such as expressed in monuments, roads, fences, and the like (referred to in legislation as "improvements"), are treated as tangible proof of relationships with the land. But what of peoples whose presence in the landscape leaves no such traces, no such marks, or where meaningful associations are not through such marks?

It was argued by the Cape York Land Council that the claimants were, according to their traditions, constituted as a group of families with particular regional language affiliations, and that all of these claimants' families, in turn, constituted a larger regional grouping deemed to have affiliations with and responsibilities for the land under claim, based on kinship, marriage, and cultural linkages. The land affiliations of these families, it was further argued, were derived from their original clan identities, some of which, such as with the Lamalama groups, had survived as critical organizational features of their society, and some of which were remembered if not by original language name, then at least in terms of their "*Story*" (Aboriginal English for "totemic" or "Dreaming") identifications. Although the Lamalama claimants were able to cite estate, site, and clan names from three or four of the original twenty languages their ancestors spoke before the impact of colonization, and the most senior of the Kuku Thaypan claimants were able to cite these classical place and group names from their language, claimants from neighboring groups, such as the "Koko Warra" people, provided English names for "totemic" affiliations, such as "Freshwater prawn." It was also argued that the members of these family groups regarded all their fellows as members of a larger group, the people affiliated, by custom and tradition, with the land under claim. Thus all related to each other by virtue of the marriage and kinship connections among their ancestors; in many cases, among their immediate forebears; and in some cases, among members of their own generational cohorts. Historical connections among members by virtue of their coresidence at various significant places and through their employment as stockmen on the pastoral leases also bound the members of this larger group together. In this chapter, I explain how the people's ancestral links with places can be read not through material inscriptions such as monuments, but through engagement and an inscription of the senses. It is this dimension of place making that I explore in this chapter with reference to the Lakefield–Cliff Island National Parks land claims of northeastern Australia.

ANCESTRAL LINKS

In the evidence elicited before the Tribunal in the land claim hearings,[1] all of the claimants were attributed with an affiliation to at least one place in the claim area, an affiliation that was said to be spiritual. Each of the claimants was a member of a family or a clan, and each of these entities traced their genealogical history from apical ancestors. The term *apical ancestor* is an anthropological one that refers to the deceased ancestral person from whom descent is traced by the members of a group, in this instance,

the family or clan that claims a traditional affiliation to part of the land within the Lakefield and Cliff Island National Parks. Deceased ancestors are conceived of as spiritual presences in particular places expressing both a resonating "spiritual" trace of the once-living persons returning to a *Story* place and as the "returning" to a place of an ancestor's spiritual force whose source is *Story*.

Story is conceived of as spiritual power that is ubiquitous in particular persons and places, and an essence that is immutable. The *Story* Beings are phenomenal, appearing as rainbows, the moon, and the like, and differentiated and speciated by their various characters, as in Emu *Story*, Snake *Story*, and so forth. The return of Spirit upon the death of a person to its *Story* place source, which remains unchanged, is the mystery that marks off death from life and yet infuses life and death with mystery. Each Aboriginal person (*Bama* in the various Aboriginal languages of the region), being descended from persons whose spirits returned to their origins in these *Story* Places, is imbued with some spiritual characteristics of the *Story* Beings and shares these characteristics with all his or her fellows who are likewise related to those *Story* Beings.

Here at the Tribunal, then, were Aboriginal people, most of whom had long been denied access to their traditional lands by the agency of a repressive government apparatus that had developed under a number of names and in different forms to administer the various Queensland Acts of Parliament that aimed to control the Aboriginal population of that state. In many cases, their parents, and even grandparents, had been denied access to what they recognized as their traditional lands. Many of them, along with their parents and/or grandparents, had been forcibly removed to far-distant places, to be administered as Wards of the State in government settlements, such as at the Yarrabah and Palm Island Aboriginal Reserves, and to serve in indentured employment on pastoral leases and farms (see Rosser 1987 for various stories of such experiences; see also Evans et al. 1975, May 1983, and Kidd 1997). The forcible removals had been carried out by police acting as Protectors under The Restriction of the Sale of Opium and Protection of Aborigines Act of 1897 and under the subsequent forms of that legislation. The result was a crippling depopulation of the region, with the remaining Aboriginal groups too small and beleaguered to continue the social life of their ancestors.

By the time of the Lakefield and Cliff Island land claim, the Aboriginal peoples who claimed traditional affiliations with, and ownership of, the land were led by a small band of Elders, each of whom was knowledgeable about the traditional affiliations of each family to estates and places in the region, their language affiliations, and the physical environments and life forms on which they had depended in their youth before their hunting and gathering lifestyle was brought to an end early in the twentieth century. These Elders worked with the anthropological consultants who carried out the fieldwork for the claim, Bruce Rigsby[2] and Diane Hafner, and with Cape York Land Council staff, including myself, to produce the necessary documentation to establish before the Tribunal that particular groups of people were affiliated by tradition to particular areas of land. What emerges from those documents and the evidence of the Aboriginal witnesses to the Tribunal is a strategy for the restitution of their lands experientially inscribed as particular traditions, traditions that have been challenged by the loss of members of the original societies and by the repression of their hunting and gathering ways of life and much of the social and ritual organiza-

tion that sustained them as societies. Such a strategy aimed to demonstrate the existence of ties to place in the absence of monuments as lasting legacies of past links. Their argument was that places are marked in the first instance not through physical inscriptions, but through kin and *Story* ties that inscribe the self in place and place in the self. That is, places are inscribed through metaphysical relationships and are experienced through relationships with the emplaced *Story* Beings who gave rise to the original clan ancestors. In this sense, both sense of place and rights to place are marked by ancestral connections passed down through Indigenous law, not simply through humanly created physical signposts. In their turn, the places of memory and experience are sensual proof of the truth of Aboriginal law. Through the authority of the Elders as keepers of law and customary land tenure, cultural memories become inscribed in the places of tradition, and such places become "site-markers of the remembering process and of identity itself" (Taylor 2000:27).

The key tradition that the Elders and their consultants relied on was that which establishes their own authority as knowledgeable Elders whose role it is to instruct and guide others in their presence in these lands. This tradition, which structures and constitutes land affiliation for the members of the claimant group, is a body of knowledge about the relationship among particular beings, human and nonhuman, and the places for which they bear particular responsibilities and in which they have particular rights. This body of knowledge is deemed to be held in trust by knowledgeable Elders and transmitted to the junior members of society as their right by birth into the group. It is through this knowledge that people write themselves on the land and the land in themselves. Such sacred readings of the landscape through the lens of highly localized bodies of social, ritual, and juridical knowledge is a "cosmic framework" for interpreting places, binding particular persons and places together in a sacred relationship and, therefore, a framework for reimplicating the returning members of the diaspora whose inchoate affiliation with the land is reactivated by the Elders.

Representations of people, spirits, and landscapes are symbols in a rich variety of rites, from the merely petitionary to the profoundly cosmological. The cultural map through which the landscape is reinscribed with the cultural memories, regulations, and logic of the Elders is marked and memorialized through social experience. The example I provide here arises from an event described by Howard Morphy (1995) that took place when he accompanied a famous Yolngu painter from Arnhem Land in northern Australia to the Snowy Mountains region in the Alps of southeastern Australia. This senior Aboriginal man had identified the place that he and Morphy were visiting as belonging to a particular moiety, although he had never been there before, and the place was over 2,000 km from his homeland. Morphy accounted for this transference of religio-geographical values from one place to another in this way, noting that, "One of the significant things about what I would term Narritjin's 'reinterpretation' of the Snowy Mountains landscape is that for him it was not a reinterpretation but a process of discovery or revelation" (Morphy 1995:185).

> I asked Narritjin how he knew it was Dhuwa moiety country since neither of us had ever been there before. Moreover, little was known of the mythology of the people who had once lived in the area, before their lives had been so rudely interrupted by European colonization in the middle of the last century. Narritjin pointed to the sharp pebbles that lay beside the stream that were Ganydjalala's stone spears, and he pointed out the trees that were similar to those in the forests through which Ganydjalala hunted, and finally he reminded me of how the lake she created was represented in paintings on the djuwany posts made for the Djungguwan ceremony by his brother Bokarra, and how its shape resembled the shape of the lake by which we were sitting (see H. Morphy 1991:121). Yes, we were in Dhuwa moiety country. (Morphy 1995:184–185)

SPIRITUAL ASSOCIATION TO PLACES AS AFFILIATION TO LAND

In the Lakefield and Cliff Island National Parks land claims a number of the Aboriginal Elders gave wide-ranging evidence before the Tribunal under questioning from anthropologists Bruce Rigsby and Peter Sutton, the expert witnesses, the representative of the Cape York Land Council, and the Tribunal chairperson, members, and the counsel assisting. The expert witnesses themselves, Bruce Rigsby, Peter Sutton, and Diane Hafner, each gave evidence as well.

Bruce Rigsby, during his evidence to the Tribunal as an expert, was cross-examined on his ideas about the nature of spiritual associations among the claimants to the Lakefield and Cliff Island National Parks. His account of the emotional content of these associations, as affective responses, raises the beginning of an answer to the question "what is the nature of the links and representations of people and the spiritual Beings which inhabited these particular landscapes, title to which was sought in the land claim, according to Aboriginal tradition?"

Rigsby, in explaining—in plain English to the Tribunal—the difficult problem of the nature of spiritual association as understood by the claimants, described his own understanding of the concept as consisting of two chief characteristics: a sense of them as numinous, supernatural beings of power, and a belief in and experience of the presence of the spirits of their ancestors in the landscape. He characterized the affect of this dimension of experience, the *emotional* state of this aspect of experience, as being not just personally experienced, but socially experienced. He inferred that emotion is primarily socially constructed and, in the instance of these events, that the *Bama* understanding of the emotion evoked by experience of the spiritual is shared by a community of people. Further, people are bound together. They are spiritually connected as a community by that emotional understanding.[3]

The question arises: are *Story* Beings one with the "Old People," the deceased ancestors who have returned to the land; what are we to make of the distinction? The answer lies in the nature of power in *Bama* cosmology as emplaced. If we examine more closely some ideas about the Old People and their mediating role between the sacred and the profane, between danger and safety, what is proper to being in a place and what is not, we observe that the power that they confront in life, and that they merge with in death, preexists as an explanation of the nature of being. Life lived in places is an encounter with mythical Beings whose creative energies imbue such places with particular characteristics, some dangerous and some protective and sustaining, depending on how one engages with them. Such engagements in other societies have been labeled as forms of geomancy, bodies of knowledge that are employed in encounters with landscapes inscribed with sacred eminences. I will revisit some of these points at various stages in this chapter.

The *Story* Beings and the Old People are numinous, supernatural beings of power. They spiritually mark the land through a belief in, and experience of, the presence of the spirits of ancestors in the landscape. The question raised, then, is, is emotion, as it is used in these circumstances regarding *Bama* "spiritual affiliations" with land, a juridical concept or a concept contingent with the juridical realm of land tenure? In the Tribunal it was thus argued that the land is inscribed by its spiritual affiliations—indeed, it is defined and identified by those affiliations. The land is always already here, sensual, and experienced in its spirituality. In this sense, spiritual affiliations inscribe the land with meaning, directing human behavior in the process; they are metaphysical inscriptions that, as Bruce Rigsby noted during the Tribunal enquiry, "connect the claimant group with the claimed land." And because they connect and structure, spiritual associations condition responses in people.

THE AUTHORITY OF THE ELDERS

Intriguing hints as to relationships among persons and the order of deference shown among persons emerged during the evidence given in the Lakefield and Cliff Island land claims, signaling the structure of Indigenous authority in this region as an intellectual problem of plain significance to the project of understanding person/place relationships. The Elders' reading of the powers of the landscape and of the powers and vulnerabilities of particular Aboriginal persons in places in the landscape became the defining framework for the landscapes they referred to, as they testified regarding the rules that they themselves observed and expected others to observe. Certain facts of *Bama* social life are plainly stated by the Elders:

- Elders intercede in the approach of persons to the *Story* places by appealing to the Old People and the *Story* Beings with ritual actions.
- Juniors must also undertake ritual actions to limit the deleterious effects of these spiritual beings or to enhance their beneficent effects.
- The ritual actions are specific and particular and efficacious. They can only be performed by people who are descended from the Old People, or in their presence and under their guidance.
- The Elders transmit knowledge about this engagement with places differentially to other members of the society.

Let me begin to illustrate this with an example.

George Musgrave was a key witness in the land claim. He is a senior Kuku Thaypan (the word "*Kuku*" means language) speaking man who is also known in his own language by the name of Alpulkal. Regarded by his people as senior not only by virtue of his advanced years but also as senior in status, he is said to be knowledgeable and authoritative about Thaypan matters, principally the territorial estate of this bloc of people and the places and forces therein. During his evidence before the Tribunal,[4] he confirmed that he is the most senior Thaypan owner of their traditional lands, "the main man," whose permission must be asked by anyone wishing to enter his country or a place in his country.[5] He explained his responsibilities as an Elder for the safe passage of visitors to his country. Bruce Rigsby asked about "fishing business," ceremonial actions that must be carried out before "going fishing," in a place-specific way. Precisely because fishing is a domain of emplaced activity, it was chosen by the Elders themselves as a way of explaining the rules of engagement between person and place in their cosmology.

Rigsby first of all acknowledged a place that is located within the jurisdiction of the witness: "this Saltwater Creek or Hann River." If he had asked of any other place, outside of George's jurisdiction, George would have answered in a different way. He would have deferred to those most senior people with a traditional affiliation to that place. He is not authorized to speak about the spiritual or ritual affairs of other countries.

Fishing is a favorite pastime among these people. It would be correct, in certain anthropological frameworks, to speak of fishing under the category of economic activity rather than pastime, but that is not the subsuming category for the speaking subjects themselves. Of course, the Elders expect us, the listeners, to understand that the result of fishing is, with luck, a very enjoyable meal, much more preferable than the common option of store-bought imported foodstuffs in tins or frozen beef, although not as desirable as dugong or turtle meat. To an extent, the activity is economic, resulting in the production of a meal that satisfies a basic need. But this activity was chosen as a hermeneutic device because of its power to explicate more difficult problems. This domain of fishing is a very useful one, as will be seen, for explaining the conceptual framework of the Elders' beliefs about relationships with land and water, and with the other beings in the land and waterscapes. Persons such as George, Sunlight, or Paddy, who were born and socialized in "the bush," perceive of several phenomena in the rules for and in the very act of fishing, to take just one example, the responsibilities of Elders for the safe passage of visitors to their country.

The primary law that Elders recite in asserting their authority over places is that of asking permission of appropriate Elders to enter their land. Sunlight Bassani, one of the Lamalama Elders, confirmed this primacy of asking permission of Elders by referring to his own understanding of his relations with George Musgrave:

DIANE HAFNER: Muka Sunlight Bassani, I want to ask you some questions about that permission business. A lot of people here have talked about how you got to ask permission to go onto country. Can you tell us something about that?

SUNLIGHT BASSANI: Yeah, yeah, that's true, you gotta go and ask somebody. Say we go up to Thaypan country that—eh, and see you gotta go and sort of talk to Old George, he's the eldest in the Thaypan country, and go and ask him if I can go to—up his country, like Morehead, or anything like that, just ask him before you go there.

MS. HAFNER: Can I ask you, Muka, you live in Coen, that's right?

SUNLIGHT BASSANI: Yes.

MS. HAFNER: If you were going to go—if you are driving through Laura where that Old man George lives on your way down to Cairns, and you felt like you want to go fishing, what would you do when you stopped there at Laura?

SUNLIGHT BASSANI: Oh well, first thing I'll ask him if I can go into his country, and ask him if I can go fishing there. He'll probably tell me, "Yeah, you can go there." That's the Aboriginals' way. And why you ask him that: just the sites you're looking at, in 'nother word his *Story*. See, he own the *Story*. If I go in there, well, might be a bit bad luck for me in the *Story*. Well he's the right man to see and he might give me idea, "When you go in there, just look after yourself. Don't do this. Don't do that. Don't—tell the kid don't making mark on the ground or throwing stick in the water, or throwing stones, or anything like that." "All right, I'll do that. All right, that's good idea." That's his way to tell us. . . .

ENVISIONING PLACE

The principal question I wish to address in this section concerns how personal and social relationships with place and places are envisaged and expressed in the Aboriginal societies of the region covered by the Lakefield and Cliff Island land claims. The goal of having their lands returned, of their relationship with their lands being acknowledged, their persistence in this endeavor, their tolerance of abuse for the sake of that goal, their suffering at their state of dispossession, all raise this question: what does place mean for these people, and why is it so important that they would, from a position of extreme powerlessness, disadvantage, and poverty, use the available legal instruments to claim their land as theirs by tradition and by right?

I want to deal with this problem in a different way from that of Bruce Rigsby at the Tribunal. I want to start not with the anthropological notions themselves, legally formalized as "spiritual association" or even the social construction of emotion as a spiritual understanding shared by a group of people, but rather with the notion of the subject in the cosmology of the *Bama* as I have come to understand it. I posit that personal identity among peoples of the region is constituted as spatialized being, and explore further the notion of being among the peoples of the Lakefield–Cliff Island region through the idea that emerges insistently from their statements, that being is constituted by being-in-a-place, that, in their world, being and place are constituted simultaneously as being-in-a-place. The spatialization I refer to concerns the phenomenological basis of local cosmologies.

It has been a truism in Australianist anthropology that for Aboriginal people the land has meaning; its mere physical forms are transformed into social and spiritual landscapes. Morphy (1991), Myers (1986), Rose (1992), Stanner (1966, 1979), and Williams (1986), among others, stand out in the Australianist literature in their efforts to explain how these transformations occur.

There have been various efforts in the discipline of anthropology in recent decades to undertake philosophical investigations of the project of thinking and writing about the perceived experiences of the "Other," peoples who are in very different societies than those from which anthropologists have traditionally come, and who do ordinary things in very different ways from "their" anthropologists. Drawing critically on the concerns that anthropologists and philosophers have had regarding the investigation of these Others, the problems investigated here are these: how do the peoples of the land claim area conceive of the world around them? How do they conceive of the things in their world? These two questions should crystallize the inappropriateness of privileging so-called anthropogenic place marks over other means of memorializing place in the construction of its significance. These two questions also automatically raise another problem to be investigated: how are the people themselves implicated in these conceptions? The question of how the human being, and other beings, are constructed as beings in a place, and how the place is constructed by the conceptions regarding their being, is treated as the relationship between embodiment and emplacement: how beings are embodied in place and emplaced in body. I will attempt to unfold this process for the region covered by the area of the Lakefield–Cliff Island land claims by identifying a series of social conventions through which relations between people and place are manifested.

The Old People as Mediators of Life and Death

In *Bama* philosophy, the person is conceived of as a spiritual being, spiritual by virtue of coming into being through sociality, that is, through others, in particular, through the Old People, or ancestors.

Further, the *Bama* conception of the spirituality of being is signified by places, not just that in being one can be perceived and remembered as living in particular places, being born in a place, dwelling in places, dying in a place, but by the (supposed) a priori significance of places, their spiritual meanings, which infuse all of these ordinary and not so ordinary, but everyday, experiences with a special sense of place. These a priori significances of places are the *Story* Beings, numinous, mysterious, powerful, and ubiquitous. This signification of being by place, and by symbols of place—songs, dances, expressions, designs—is crucially represented in the authority of Elders who mediate between the spirits of the dead and the living, protecting each from the other. The dead reside in, and are coterminous with, particular places. It is the perceived existence of the spirits of the deceased ancestors in places that enlivens these places as powerfully effective, dangerous places to be approached with the protection of the Elders leading the way with their rituals and expressed statements of familiarity and imploration to the spirits. Life and death, then, are implicated by each other.

If the dead can be spoken to, what is death? The resolution of this and other quandaries raised by *Bama* ways of being in places is to be found in precisely the way that they treat death through the notion of the Old People as spirit Beings that came from and returned to particular places and through the notion of *Story* as the numinous, and mysterious, power that enlivens both beings and places.

Story

Story Beings, that is "mythical" beings of *Story*-time, are conceived of as particular named beings, albeit spiritual, yet able to effect the physical world in perceivable ways. For example, in the case of Old Emu, George Musgrave noted that "he'll be howling and start kicking about and make that girl sick" if she fishes within a mile of a particular place where the Emu *Story* presides in the still water. Women and girls must go fishing, according to the law, a mile downstream from this place. If the rules of engagement (law) with the *Story* Beings, or with the deceased ancestors, are breached, or there is a failure to observe these rules, there are perceivable consequences, such as illness. Can a man give fish to a woman at that place? No. The rules are distinct and clear. The perceived consequences are also clear, as evidenced here in George Musgrave's answer to Michael Neal's questions.[6]

GEORGE MUSGRAVE: Because if he do that to give it his missus, 'cause—old, Old Emu, he'll be in—you know, he'll be howling and start kicking about and make that girl sick.

MICHAEL NEAL: Is that just for boy or for the men as well, if they catch it?

TOMMY GEORGE: No, just a point like what George mentioned; in the old days, it's what you've got to do. It's the Law.

MR. NEAL: Yes. Is that only if a boy catches a fish, or is it if a man catches . . .

GEORGE MUSGRAVE: That's any boy that catch fish top end here, not the girl, or even his missus. If you wanta fishing, all the girl, down the bottom end. Down here. There's water running down, they can fishing down the bottom end.

MR. NEAL: So if a boy catches a fish here, can he share it with a girl?

GEORGE MUSGRAVE: He have his separate here, all the boy and the girl have separate here.

TOMMY GEORGE: He not allowed to give his wife.

Local Aboriginal Law requires that a person approaching a *Story* Place must follow certain rules. Asking permission of the Elder is the primary rule,

and this is followed by various injunctions that are specific to each place. Just as women must not fish in certain places, so too there are rules for men of high degree. Some of these special places, *Story* Places, are associated with more onerous ritual requirements than other places. There is a "proper way to behave" in each place. In replying to Peter Sutton's question on this, George explained,

> Well, if you get—what the Aboriginal do—if you've got a *Story*, you must paint himself with mud. If you put the red mud, you're different stripe. You put white, that's the Thaypan. And you put the feather—cockatoo feather—in the head to look different. They push them away. The ones who put a white cockatoo on the head, you go straight inside—"You can come in." If you're different paint color, you might get sick—change your—change your mud, just tell them, "Pick up the mud and change him over and come in there."

These explanations presuppose an understanding of what is meant by *"Story,"* but this is not a straightforward or commonsense idea. George Musgrave assumed that his audience understood what he was referring to because he is quite sure about what he means. At this stage of the questioning by Peter Sutton, it had emerged that there are the spirits of one's own ancestors in places, and that there are special, sacred places where there is a more powerful spiritual presence that requires ritual decoration with white mud and a white cockatoo feather in one's hair, if one is of the Thaypan group. The white cockatoo feather worn in the hair by Thaypan coming to these places has the function of distinguishing the Thaypan person from other kinds of persons, persons of a "different stripe." There are peoples in Cape York who paint themselves with red mud, such as the Wik clan, *Putj*. If they were to arrive in red mud decoration, or to put it on in Thaypan country near these special, sacred places, a Thaypan person must tell them to change their mud, because they might get sick. This is in fact, even now, a very real possibility because the Laura Dance Festival is held near Thaypan country every year, and visitors from western Cape York who adorn themselves for certain rituals with red "mud" or ochre, and visitors from many other places, travel along the Development Road to the Festival location on a Trust area south of the township of Laura. If they are traveling from the north, they pass through Thaypan country. And as well, for many years, both George Musgrave and his younger brother, Tommy George, have carried out custodial duties toward the special places in the Laura region, which include famous art galleries on the rock faces of the ledges, gorges, and cliff faces of this area. Overlooking the Festival site is an art gallery on a hillside, which George Musgrave and Tommy George have protected by acting as guides to visitors and by giving advice to archaeologists, government officials and conservation experts.

"You Sing Out"

Speaking directly to an ancestor, "singing out"[7] to it, is an act of "looking after the country," according to George Musgrave in his evidence, answering Bruce Rigsby's questions. Elders, such as George Musgrave, describe themselves as obliged to "sing out" to ancestors who are the keepers of life forces—life's fecundity—not only for their own sakes when they enter a country or place, but also particularly for the sake of others with them. The task that falls to Elders in these circumstances is to protect those who are traveling with them from the dangerous spiritual forces emanating from emplaced spiritual beings.

When these Beings are addressed by George Mus-

grave, we are expected to know that George and the ancestor Being are on close speaking terms, as it were; George might say to the ancestor Being, "Look, old thing, it's just me. Alpulkal. You know me. I've got some friends with me. Don't hurt them." George must speak in his own language, the language of his ancestor, to reassure it that here is no stranger but someone who shares ancestry and language.

Deceased ancestors thus never depart from the landscape. The land is full of spiritual presences who are the ancestors of traditional owners, usually grandparents. That is, they were people known to the speaking subject in their own lifetimes, and they must be spoken to in the appropriate language. No matter how long a person has been absent from their country, their ancestors' spirits remain in the landscape and can be heard voicing their spirit presence. If one does not "sing out," there are dire consequences. Engaging with a place thus requires engaging with the spiritual presences therein. The aural sense and the power of sound, as Levinas (1989a, b) has noted elsewhere, (re)inscribes space (see also Rainbird, this volume).

Gender, Place, and Sharing Fish and Meat

Places are imbued with the gender of the Old People, the deceased ancestor's unceasing existence, as one of their essential attributes. Places are thus genderized and gender emplaced. There are places where only women may go, and places where only men may go, as the fishing *Story* already mentioned makes clear. The relationship of places to the births and the birthing rites that took place at them are remembered by reference to the trees that grow there. These are called birthing trees, and it is said that the tree holds some spiritual essence of the person born under it. There are particular *Story* places along the riverbanks, apart from these birthing places, where gender-specific observances are required.

"Giving Smell"

The sense of smell is engaged, assisted by spiritual agency, with the sacred as well. An olfactory signature bestowed by an Elder acts to displace the sacred, protecting the charge from the wrath of the *Story* Beings and the Old People. One of the ways in which guests are protected from the dangerous forces that these spiritual Beings emanate to strangers entering their places is thus through the ritual of the Elder "giving smell." This entails the action of the Elder wiping his armpits to obtain underarm odor, a unique signature scent in each person's case, and wiping the "smell" onto the head of each guest. Each guest is thus disguised with the Elder's signature scent and is thus perceived or sensed by the spiritual Being to be that Elder or very close to that Elder, so close that he or she smells of the Elder's bodily perspiration. The guest is thereby ritually enlisted as a member of the landholding group responsible for the spiritual Beings in their landscapes during the visit. It is intringuing that this guise of adopting the smell of another being is also an old hunting ruse, which all young Aboriginal people learn: when hunting, remember that your quarry will smell you on the wind, so stay downwind; once you have caught one of your quarry, rub yourself with the feathers or fur of the creature, or wear some of its skin or the like, so that you smell like that creature, to deceive its fellows and take more game.

Alkuperr

Q: When you go fishing—let us say on this Saltwater Creek or Hann River—somewhere you were talking about before . . .?

A: Yeah, yeah.

Q: . . .have you got any special rules for—like, fishing business too?

A: Yeah, yeah.

Q: What kind of thing are you talking about?

A: Well, you sing out—you have the what they callim alkuperr, perr mean—that's the poison tree, and you get that one and keep him in your mouth, and so you spit—push the *Story* away and you get the fish, and you talk your language.

Q: Is that just getting something out of the country, or are you looking after it the same time?

A: Looking after it.

George Musgrave was referring, throughout this evidence, to a *Story* Fish. After singing out, the ritual of *alkuperr* is enacted involving taking into the mouth the bark of a tree, *perr*, that is used to stun fish when thrown into a water hole, and then spitting the *perr* out into the water. This action will "push the *Story* away," as George put it. The act of spitting *perr* into the water, when enacted by a person such as George who is the coresident of the Fish Being's domain, stuns the Fish ancestor and distracts its attention from the fishing endeavor that George will undertake. By distracting the Being, its sacred hold of the fish in the water is removed for a while, and the fish can, and will, be caught, without bringing out of the water with the fish any of the essence of the *Story* Fish, a spiritual force that is dangerous and could make one sick. All the while, George must speak in his language, so that the Fish Being hears its own language and is reassured that its own people, and not strangers, are taking the fish in the water.

"Warming"

Warming is the reciprocal ritual action that is undertaken by guests when fishing in someone else's country. Albert Lakefield, a Lamalama Elder, explained that one must position one's body near a fire, "warming" the body in the smoke of the fire and, as well, "warm" the fishing line in the smoke of the fire. Every person in the visiting group must be "warmed." The significance of smoke as the "warming" agent is that it clears away any spiritually ambient presence that the person has carried from his own country or among his personal collection of things, including fishing lines.

Burning

Bruce Rigsby asked George Musgrave about his tradition of lighting fires to clear areas of land of dense undergrowth that is uncomfortable and shelters snakes, scorpions, and other dangerous creatures. Fire is used also as a hunting technique. George explained that although it is required to "clean" the land by deliberate burning, caution is needed. He explained that when people are cooking fish on a fire, and the fire is in danger of spreading out of control, ascertained by the direction and increase of smoke from the fire, the fire must be buried. Local Aboriginal people do not throw water on it, the way European campers do: "and they don't throw their water, they bury that, and talk same time." Water is ineffectual in extinguishing a fire that has burned deep into a log; the heat from wood is able to ignite again in the wind. Fire must be buried in these landscapes to be sure of extinguishing it. Moreover, George Musgrave explained, one must talk at the same time as burying it. Talking to the spirits who have enlivened the fire is a necessary adjunct to the task of burying the fire to extinguish it.

Human language has its own powers in the spiritual landscapes that Aboriginal people perceive. To talk is to assert the human presence. Similarly, burning is also an assertion of human authority, albeit one mediated by *Story* Law. Burning land requires the assistance of others, not simply to keep control of the fire, a strenuous task in itself, but also to ensure that the burning is carried out in the sacred way. "Well, if you want to burn the country like what you're saying now—well, you have to go and ask somebody else to help you along and the sacred land way."

People who know the sacred way know for instance that there are places that must not burn, that there are trees with particular types of bark that must not burn. There are two species of tree in particular that must not burn, George Musgrave explained: the Ti-tree and the Messmate. "If you don't go through the burn, and you'll have to call anybody to out the fire—and help you along to keep that place not to burn, or even tree or bark—the main thing is the bark, Ti-tree bark and Messmate, because the bark you can make out of houses, and that's the Aboriginals singing about."

The clear implication of George's last statement here, "and that's the Aboriginals singing about," is that the Old People, who once camped in these places, under the bark shelters made from Ti-tree and Messmate bark, are singing there, in those places. George explained that the Old People can be heard as one burns the country; that they are heard in certain places, and those places, in this instance, are where the Ti-tree and Messmate stands that they used for bark shelters grow. A particular respect for those places is required because of their presence. Hot fires would disturb the Old People and destroy the resources where their presences remain, and constitute a breach of sacred Law. And that is why the sacred way of burning the land is important. It is not permitted that a fire should get out of control and cause a hot burn in any of these places where the Old People's spirits remain. Only grass is burned with a hot burn.

DISCUSSION

Engagement with place in the *Bama* world is predicated on an understanding of the world as a biogeography of human and nonhuman presences, some living and mortal, and some spiritual and ever present. The deceased ancestors are distributed throughout the landscape in accordance with the "mythical" accounts of *Story* Beings and their nonhuman essences that permeate their descendants with the Emu-ness of emus, the Fish-ness of fishes, and so on. To be in one's own place is to have originated in that place and to share the essence of the creative Being existing and existent in the "everywhen" of that place (e.g., Stanner 1966). One returns to that place just as the ancestors did, rejoining this spatial, temporal, sentient force. One's self is spatialized and temporalized in this *Bama* ontology of place. One is sentient in common with that *Story* Being. Just as a person has senses by which to see, to smell, to taste, to feel warm, to hear, and a range of emotions as responses to stimulation, to which one might feel anger, fear, empathy, and so on, so too do the spiritual Beings. The Old People and the *Story* Beings have the same senses and emotions. They are sentient.

The land as places peopled by spirits is grasped through its spirituality. It is apprehended, marked, and memorialized through the senses, by seeing, feeling, smelling, and hearing. In (re)turn, the spiritual Beings imbuing these places with life potential apprehend the lives of the mortal through "senses." They "see," "hear," and "smell" the descendants of their essence; they see, hear, and smell all who enter, and they respond in a variety of ways. Only their own "stripe" can ward off the dangers of that engagement. This is the core idea in *Bama* perceptions of speciation. It begins with the human engagement with the spiritual world that brings immediately the idea of the human and nonhuman intertwined through common spiritual ancestry, sharing places by sacred design. *Bama* notions of the human then separate the human from the nonhuman in one domain only—the mundane; all these essences and potentials are preexisting in the primordial landscape behind the landscape—the sacred.

The way that *Bama* perceive landscapes is thus rather like the way that someone with a reasonable astronomical knowledge in Western culture perceives the night sky resplendent with twinkling stars. As one looks at the stars, there is the simultaneous sense of perceiving something that is present, the view itself sensed visually at that time, and of perceiving things that are past, the stars whose deaths many thousands of light years ago are perceived as the twinkling radiances in the black depths of space. And again at the same time, there is the knowledge behind these perceptions, that we can only know these things because of our understandings of time as past-present-future. The future is implicated in our understanding of the past and the present. These temporalities are inscribed in our being as fields of experience, memorialized as the landscapes we know. Experiences are sensual topographies of time and space not simply inscribed and affirmed through physically imposed anthropogenic marks, but through the marks of socio-ontological order and understanding.

The idea of the landscape populated and given shape by Old People is thus analogous to this astronomically informed perception of stars in the night sky as representations of the past, the present, and the future. The Old People are encountered in the landscape, just as stars are visually encountered in gazing at the night sky. Being astronomically informed, I know that stars are what can be seen now of some great cataclysmic event in the universe many thousands of light years ago, the light of the explosion emanating through time, and visible to my eyes in this present. What I see in the sky are ancient traces of light emanating across vast distances from giant bodies of fire. *Bama* likewise perceive the spiritual presence of Elders in the landscape as what has emanated through time since the demise of the ancestor and can now be understood, guided by the Elders, as one perceives the place in the landscape where their being is represented by the spiritual enlightenment that the invocations of the Elders quicken. Space and temporality are intertwined as contingent dimensions of life in *Bama* philosophy. *Bama* conceptions of the past and the future imply both temporality and space through the mediation of Old People, the deceased who infer connection or affiliation with, attachment to, inheritance and ownership of land. It is in this metaphysical construction that place is marked, inscribed with *Story*, given meaning, and guiding human movement in the process.

CONCLUSION

The *Bama* concept of land estate is simultaneously a social, physical, and metaphysical one. *Bama* beliefs about the nature of spiritual Beings residing in particular places articulate a core dimension of *Bama* biogeography, invoking death as a presence in places (see also Levinas 1989). Not death as abstraction, but death as the state of being of those

ancestors from whom the living trace their own being and whose constant presence must be contended with in places. Authority is emplaced by virtue of the embodied placement of the Elder in his country and the emplaced embodiment of his ancestor. All *Bama* are conceived of as descended from a being/place dialectic, and yet in the first instance, the place is enlivened not by the actual ancestors alone, whose spiritual presence can only enliven a place by virtue of the power of the *Story* and by virtue of their own nature resembling that of the *Story* because of their shared origination in a place. This ontological similarity is more than a symbol, inasmuch as a person's power is the same power whose source is the *Story*. I stated earlier that members of the families are descended from ancestors, and deceased ancestors are conceived of as spiritual presences in particular places expressing both a resonating "spiritual" trace of the once-living persons returning to a *Story* place and as the "returning" to a place of an ancestor's spiritual force whose source is *Story* (*Story* Being conceived of as spiritual power that is nevertheless never altered by its omniscience in particular persons and places). I then drew this contradiction to a temporary conclusion: the return of Spirit to its source, which remains immutable, is the mystery that marks off death from life and yet infuses life and death with mystery. This, then, is the mark of being in place.

Another conclusion can be drawn from this analysis, a conclusion in addition to that made by Rigsby concerning the socially constructed nature of emotion as a spiritual matter: people inscribe their landscapes through their power over it. Power is emplaced. The conception of power is inferred in the many ways used by the *Bama* witnesses to speak of their place in the social order and in relation to land. It is the consequences for the desecration of such places being beyond human agency, within the ambit of the personal influence of Elders mediating between the living and the dead. Power resides in places by virtue of the presence of Old People; their spiritual Being is emplaced and their power is emplaced. It is this emplaced source of power that Elders mediate.

In *Bama* cosmology, Mystery lies in the spirit of the dead, the known ancestors who gave them life and who quicken places in their estates. Mysterious death is knowable and unknowable and, therefore, amenable and not amenable to human agency. Their authority arises from this very engagement with death through their mediation of the power of the Old People in leading the living toward their own confrontation with that ultimate Mystery.

The intercession and mediation of Elders with the deceased and the *Story* Beings place death as the presence of others in being in places at the core of the construction of the subject among *Bama*. Emplacement is fundamentally a relationship to, and toward, death, and death is a source of power in place, which enlivens the subject. This mysterious contradiction is the ontological foundation of subjectivity and the subject's place in the physical world as both a cultural and natural phenomenon in the world as constructed by *Bama*. Thus, the ancestral landscape of the *Bama* is a conservative framework for ensuring the maintenance and replication of the physical world around them. The physical world is the legacy of the Elders' own descendants and is conserved by the cautious ritual actions of the Elders who protect the dead from the living and the living from the dead, both human and nonhuman. This engagement with the nonhuman world through the lens of the a priori sacred landscape peopled by *Story* Beings imbued with the essence of both human and nonhuman beings is the foundation of *Bama* bio-geography. The appropriation of the landscape by the geomantic reading of places imbued with *Story* Beings, a landscape full of danger and serendipity, inscribes the landscape with the laws of ritual engagement, with ancestors and *Story* Beings, by a hierarchy of Elders who have acquired the ritual knowledge from those ancestors, and with a system of property relations.

NOTES

I am grateful to the Elders and many *Bama* claimants, the Cape York Land Council, and to Professor Bruce Rigsby, Dr. Peter Sutton, and Dr. Diane Hafner, whose herculean efforts in pursuing this land claim and advice to me on many of the matters discussed here were invaluable to my work. I thank Dr. Ritchie Howitt for his generosity—intellectual, social, and material. He enabled me to hide away and think about these issues and deal with them in a way that would show the respect for *Bama* Elders and their cosmology beyond the usual confines of the role of a land council anthropologist. I thank also Professor Nancy M. Williams and Dr. Bruno David for their comments and advice on this chapter.

This chapter is a version of a chapter in my forthcoming Ph.D. thesis to be submitted to the Department of Human Geography, Macquarie University, Australia.

1. All evidence cited is from Aboriginal Land Tribunal (1994).

2. I refer to three anthropologists in this chapter. Dr. Peter Sutton is a senior anthropologist acting as an expert consultant to the Cape York Land Council and appearing as an expert witness. Diane Hafner at that time was a doctoral student supervised by Professor Bruce Rigsby, chair of anthropology at the University of Queensland; both also acted as expert consultants to the Cape York Land Council and appeared as expert witnesses.

3. An extract of his evidence on this point is included here:

"And certain—people that we will describe or have described as elders throughout the claim were particularly informative. . . . I think I learned a lot from them about their views of what a spiritual association are, and I've characterised them as a—as primarily being two things: a—a belief in and experience of the presence of the spirits of their ancestors in the landscape, and a belief in and experience of the presence of the beings that I characterise as numinous beings, beings, supernatural beings of power, and, yes, their presence and—and the experience of them in the landscape."

"And these numinous beings, are they sometimes presented as what we might refer to as *Story* Beings?" "Yes. . . . I'm not aware of any claimants that I would characterise as not having a spiritual association, and that reminds me that I should probably explain a little bit more . . . part of my study arose out of an interest in the affect of—affect of dimensions, the emotions that connect people with land . . . understanding of emotions are—are that they're not purely personal, inner states, that my view of emotions are that they are that, but they are not just those things that exist within an individual. They're, I suppose, what I characterise as that's—that as a subjective judgment that's understood, and the meaning of which is negotiated in a social—within the social world, that people have—there—there's two meanings to it. . . ."

"There's two meanings to the term emotion?" "The term emotion, yes. The one that an individual may hold themselves, and the one that is understood by a group of people to be held. So in talking about a spiritual association among the claimants, I would say that it is also to do with being understood by the community within which an individual lives that those people share a belief."

"You have used the word *emotion* where I have used the term *spiritual association*. Can you say why you have used the term *emotion*?" "It'd be difficult to characterise a spiritual association as merely a belief. It's a belief that conditions a response in people, which we would understand, I think, as an emotional response. It's something beyond that and—but nonetheless it—it causes some sort of response that I characterise as emotional in people. . . . a spiritual association to me is that understanding that is shared by a community of people. An association is something that is not purely held by an individual, but it's a common connection. It's a connection between people."

"You said earlier that in your research, you are interested in feelings that associate people with land, which I take it as being emotions that associate people with land, or spiritual associations between people and land. Are the associations that you are referring to associations that connect the claimant group with the claimed land—amongst other land, perhaps?" "Yes, amongst other land, yes."

4. Bruce Rigsby, in his questioning of George Musgrave before the Tribunal, spoke in the local form of Aboriginal English to defer to this senior witness, according to the etiquette that is observed among people of George's advanced years.

5. This was affirmed to Bruce Rigsby in the following way:

> BRUCE RIGSBY: Alpulkal, you main man for this Thaypan mob now?
>
> ALPULKAL: Yes.
>
> BRUCE RIGSBY: You the main man?
>
> ALPULKAL: Main man me, yeah.

6. Michael Neal is the legal counsel in the employ of the Cape York Land Council.

7. This refers to a communication with the ancestor whose creative actions brought things into existence.

REFERENCES CITED

Aboriginal Land Tribunal. 1994. *Transcript of Proceedings, AB93-001, AB-002, in the Matter of Aboriginal Land Claims to Lakefield and Cliff Islands National Parks*. Brisbane: Auscript.

Evans, R., K. Saunders, and K. Cronin (eds.). 1975. *Exclusion, Exploitation and Extermination: Race*

Relations in Colonial Queensland. Sydney: Australia and New Zealand Book Co.

Kidd, R. 1997. *The Way We Civilise: Aboriginal affairs—The Untold Story*. St. Lucia: University of Queensland Press.

Levinas, E. 1989. Time and the Other. In *The Levinas Reader*, edited by S. Hand, 37–58. Oxford: Basil Blackwell.

May, D. 1983. *From Bush to Station: Aboriginal Labour in the North Queensland Pastoral Industry, 1861–1897*. Townsville: History Department, James Cook University of North Queensland.

Morphy, H. 1991. *Ancestral Connections: Art and an Aboriginal System of Knowledge*. Chicago: University of Chicago Press.

———. 1995. Landscape and the Reproduction of the Ancestral Past. In *The Anthropology of Landscape: Perspectives on Place and Space*, edited by E. Hirsch and M. O'Hanlon, 184–209. Oxford: Clarendon Press.

Myers, F. 1986. *Pintubi Country, Pintubi Self*. Washington: Smithsonian Institution Press.

Rose, D. B. 1992. *Dingo Makes Us Human: Life and Land in an Aboriginal Australian Culture*. Cambridge: Cambridge University Press.

Rosser, B. 1987. *Dreamtime Nightmares*. Ringwood: Penguin.

Stanner, W. E. H. 1966. *On Aboriginal Religion*. Oceania Monographs 11. Sydney: University of Sydney.

———. 1979. *White Man Got No Dreaming: Essays, 1938–1973*. Canberra: Australian National University Press.

Taylor, A. 2000. "The Sun Always Shines in Perth": A Post-colonial Geography of Identity, Memory and Place. *Australian Geographical Studies* 38:27–35.

Williams, N. M. 1986. *The Yolngu and Their Land: A System of Land Tenure and the Fight for Its Recognition*. Canberra: Australian Institute of Aboriginal Studies.

NINETEEN

The Work of Inscription in Foi Poetry

James F. Weiner

Footprints I have made; they are broken
Osage Corn-Planting Song (E. LaFlesch, *The Osage Rite of Vigil*)

A volume dedicated to reading the material traces of people left on the Earth might be an odd venue in which to write about a people such as the Foi of Papua New Guinea, who possess no decorative art techniques. Virtually everything they manufacture is made of decomposable bush material that erodes and degrades once its user discards it or is no longer able to continue putting it to use. Those stone implements they did acquire and possess—ax blades, antique stones, and pottery remains that were adjuncts of various pre-Mission religious cults—were traded regularly to neighboring groups, so that unearthing such artifacts might very well have little to say about Foi practices of place making or place marking.

How then would such a people create a sense of what we might call monumentality for themselves? And in the absence (until fairly recently) of a written language, how could they maintain any sense of the tension between what is recorded and what is forgotten and newly remembered, or remembered again without realizing it?

Let us first accept that the traces of people's actions left on the earth and in the environment generally also leave traces in people's consciousness. Although there may be no elaborate permanent material scarring or inscribing the earth and its surfaces, there is a complex and well-developed tradition of imaginal marking in the form of the memorial song poetry, or *sorohabora*, that Foi women compose, and that men recompose in their own style—keeping the content and the imagery the same—to honor the memory of deceased male relatives.

The Foi today number about 6,000 and inhabit the shores of Lake Kutubu and the valley of the Mubi River southwest of Mendi and Poroma in the Southern Highlands Province. Their territory is large in relation to their small population and they subsist on a complex mix of sago processing, gardening, tree crop cultivation, gathering, fishing, and hunting. Since 1991, their spatial world has been significantly and dramatically transformed by the discovery of petroleum and gas west of Lake Kutubu, and completion of the Kutubu Access Road, which linked their hitherto isolated valley with the Highlands Highway system.

The Foi, in common with other people in different parts of the world, tend to perceive the passage of time in terms of human movement over and through terrain.[1] As people move, inhabit places, abandon them and move elsewhere, journey in search of food, and so on, they leave traces of themselves in the houses, gardens, and other intrusions in the environment. The landscape under such conditions becomes iconic of human history. Renato Rosaldo (1980:56), in his eloquent study of Ilongot head-hunting, noted that "the Ilongot sense of history [is] conceived as movement through space in which (and this is the usual analogy drawn) people walk along a trail and stop at a sequence of named resting places." Bachelard (1969:56) even coined the term *topoanalysis* for the "systematic psychological study of the sites of our intimate lives."

This notion of human movement as history becomes a dominant trope for artistic and imaginal elaboration. For people such as the Osage, the Ilongot, and the Foi, human history and intention is discursively re-created through the narration of movement between places: discourse delineates this movement and centers the core values of language around moving images.

In this chapter I examine the lyric content of Foi song poems. These sung poems are composed by Foi women while they are at work making sago, and in this form are called *obedobora*. They are always sung to the memory of deceased men; women are never the subject of these songs. Men either overhear their female relatives' songs or are taught them directly by their wives and other female relatives. The men then arrange them in their own musical convention, which involves groups of pairs of men and a different melody and tempo, and perform them publicly on ceremonial occasions. In this form they are called *sorohabora* (see Weiner 1991 for more detail on musical and poetic conventions of Foi men and women). Although women claim that they per-

formed their own ceremonial rendition of the songs, I only ever witnessed men's *sorohabora* performed on public ceremonial occasions in the 1980s.

The most salient and regular feature of Foi poetry is the way each song juxtaposes images of movement and nonmovement or posits an action or movement and the subsequent halting or cutting off of that action.[2] Here I describe and analyze these forms of imagery in Foi song poetry, those that focus on the tension between the movement that is the definitive heart of life, and the stillness that constitutes the finality of death. The core element of every Foi song poem is based on this contrast; it can be said to be as integral to Foi poetry as the "seasonal element" is to Japanese haiku (see Yasuda 1957).

Let us first look at some examples:

(Song 8):

1. *duma yefua sabe ya erege*
   mountain Yefua ridge bird cockatoo

   auwa fore ibaa'e
   wing broken is

   ibu sumane habo ya namuyu
   creek Sumane water end bird cockatoo

   vira hua uboba'a
   shot struck gone

2. *duma fai-[3] hesabo ya erege*
   mountain side following bird cockatoo

   auwa forabo'owa'ae
   wing broken

   duma ka'afa hesabo ya namuyu
   mountain edge following bird cockatoo

   vira huiba'ae
   shot killed

3. *ira farabo hau- bobo ya namuyu*
   tree farabo break off leaves bird cockatoo

auwa gefodiyo'owa'ae
wing spear pierced

ira sonane hau~ bobo ya namuyu
tree sonane break off leaves bird cockatoo

auwa fore iba'ae
wing broken is

1. The ridge of Mt. Yefua, the Sulphur-Crested
   Cockatoo

   Its wing is broken

   At Sumane Creek as it flows underground, the
   Cockatoo

   Its wing is broken

2. Following the side of the mountain, the Cockatoo
   Its wing broken

   Along the edge of the mountain's base, the
   Cockatoo
   Arrow shot and killed

3. The Cockatoo breaks off the leaves of the farabo
   tree as it flies
   Its wing broken

(Song 11):

1. *ibu barua ga iga*
   creek Barua source path

   iga ere'e
   path look!

   kumagi iga
   Kumagi path

   iga ereyiya'abe
   path do you not see?

2. *ba'a na'a ibu faya'a ga iga*
   boy your river Faya'a source path

   iga ere'e
   path look!

   ba'a na'a ibu faya'a ga iga
   boy your river Faya'a source path

iga ere'e
path look!

3. *kumagi tage iga*
   Kumagi mouth path

   iga kigiba'ae
   path bush covered

   sese faiyu wabu iga
   marsupial faiyu coming path

   iga aodiba'ae
   path tree covered

1. The path to Baruaga Creek
   Look at the path!

   The path to Kumagi Creek
   Do you not see it?

2. Boy, your path at the head of the Faya'a River
   Look at it now!

   Boy, your Faya'a River source path
   Just see what it looks like now!

3. The path leading to the mouth of the Kumagi
   Creek
   It is covered with bush

   The path along which the faiyu marsupial travels
   Has been covered over with bush

These pictures of halted or cutoff movement or
stillness are among the most evocative portrayals of
the practical effects of death for the Foi. Of the
forty-one men's ceremonial songs I transcribed in
the 1980s, twenty-five revolve thematically on this
literal contrast between a predicated movement and
its observed surcease.

In Song 8 the deceased, a member of the So'one-
dobo clan, is referred to as the Sulphur-Crested
Cockatoo, which is one of the primary totems of
that clan. The cockatoo, its wing pierced by an
arrow, drops suddenly to the ground. The meteoric

quality of the cockatoo's fall from the sky represents the suddeness and rapidity with which Yabokigi himself died, allegedly "struck" by sorcery.

In Song 11, we are given an image of a path through the forest as a conduit of human movement, an inscription of regular human activity. It is through making paths through the forest and repeatedly using them to visit places of habitual use and occupation that people establish proprietary rights over territory in Foi. Paths are named as "So-and-so's path" to indicate that these are the personalized routes through the forest that label or name a person in terms of the characteristic movements they engage in and the places they occupy. The song reminds us that nothing so starkly and sadly attests to the end of this activity and the implied death of a human being as the sight of the bush or forest reclaiming the path after its user ceases to maintain this inscriptive activity. The exhortative mood of the answering line in each verse urges the listener to consider the tragic implications of these abandoned and obliterated paths.

Now, let us examine two songs in which the valence or order of movement/stillness is reversed:

(Song 13):

1. *ba'a bamo ira huba gugu biri*
   boy this tree huba flower here

   hu-ga afu wahuge
   larvae butterfly alit

   ba'a bamo ira kabare gugu biri
   boy this tree kabare flower here

   hu-ga none wahuge
   larvae bumblebee alit

2. *ba'a na'a ira fayane gugu biri*
   boy your tree fayane flower here

   hu-ga afu wahuge
   larvae butterfly alit

ba'a na'a hefa bari gugu biri
boy your vine bari flower here

hu-ga none wahuge
larvae bumblebee alit

3. *ba'a na'a ira huba gugu biri*
   boy your tree huba flower here

   hu-ga afu wahuge
   larvae butterfly alit

   ba'a na'a ira fayare gugu biri
   boy your tree fayare flower here

   hu-ga none wahuge
   larvae bumblebee alit

4. *aidobo ba'a bereromo u'ubi*
   Aidobo boy Berero's child

   ba'a howare
   boy Howare

   momahu'u ka genemo
   Momahu'u woman Genemo

   dawa
   dawabo

5. *momahu'u kabo genemoka*
   Momahu'u girl Genemoka

   ba'a herere
   boy Herere

   aidobo berero
   Aidobo Berero

   kabe Howare
   man Howare

1. On the flowers of your huba palm
   The afu butterfly alights

   On the flowers of your kabare tree
   The none bumblebee alights

2. On the flowers of your fayane tree
   The afu butterfly alights

On the flowers of your hefa bari vine
The none bumblebee alights

3. On the flowers of your huba palm
The afu butterfly alights

On the flowers of your fayare tree
The none bumblebee alights

4. The Aidobo clan, the man Berero
His son Howare

The Momahu'u clan woman Genemo
Dawa

5. The Momahu'u clan woman Genemoka
Her son Herere

The man of the Aidobo clan, Berero
His son Howare

The butterflies referred to in this and other verses of the song are those that leave edible larvae in the trunks of fallen trees. A fallen tree is a common image of a dead man, particularly in Foi dream interpretation. The movement of the butterfly is briefly halted as it stops to lay its eggs, so that although the verse begins with a picture of the horizontal stillness of death, it yet promises regeneration from that death when the edible larvae mature and are sought after as delicacies by humans. Through the intervention of the constantly moving, flitting butterfly, the dead tree can once again become a source of edible "fruit."

In the next song, the Mubi River emerges as the most important means by which people themselves "flow":

(Song 27):

1. *ba'a na'a bare ga burayodi dibiri*
   boy your canoe prow rise from water curved

   na-o mihiba'ane we
   I to embark come!

ba'a na'a bare ga yo-dibi
boy your canoe prow dips into water

na-o moware do'ane we
I too to embark to speak come!

2. *ba'a na'a bare ga ya sabeyu arumaibi*
   boy your canoe prow bird cockatoo tongue-taken

   na-o moware do'ane we
   I too to embark to speak come!

   ba'a na'a bare ga ya sabeyu arumaibi
   boy your canoe prow bird cockatoo tongue-taken

   na-o moware do'ane we
   I too to embark to speak come!

   [verse 2 repeated two more times]

3. *ba'a na'a ibu faya'a wagibu*
   boy your river Faya'a mouth

   ibudawabo
   ibudawabo

   yiya amena ibu hesa wagibu
   we men creek Hesa mouth

   dawabo
   dawabo

4. *yiya amena i-bariabe sabe u'ubi*
   we men I-bariabe Ridge children

   dawabo
   dawabo

   yiya amena kana deregebo
   we men stone cliff face

   dawabo
   dawabo

1. Boy, the curved prow of your canoe lifts gently
      from the water
   Come fetch me too

The bow of your canoe dips gracefully back into the
water
Oh come and let me embark too!

2. Boy, your cockatoo-tongued canoe prow
Come and get me, I say!

   Boy, your canoe prow as beautiful as the cockatoo's
   tongue
   I too want to get in your canoe

2. Boy, your cockatoo-tongued canoe prow
Come and get me, I say!

   Boy, your canoe prow as beautiful as the cockatoo's
   tongue
   I too want to get in your canoe

2. Boy, your cockatoo-tongued canoe prow
Come and get me, I say!

   Boy, your canoe prow as graceful as the cockatoo's
   tongue
   I too want to get in your canoe

3. Boy, your Faya'a Creek flowing into the Mubi
Ibu Dawabo

   We are the men of the mouth of Hesa Creek
   Dawabo

4. We are the children of I-bariabe Hill
Dawabo

   We are the men of the stone-lined mountain
   Dawabo

The gentle up and down movement of a canoe as
it moves through water is evoked in this song. The
tapered bow of the canoe suggests to the singer the
curved tongue of the cockatoo. Journeying by water
is an image of the life course itself for the Foi: in this
song, the deceased man is traveling in his beautiful
canoe alone, and the singer implores him to let her
come with him.

The centrality of movement as the initial predi-
cate of a song poem explains why flowing water is

commonly invoked: thirteen of the forty-one *sorohabora* I transcribed make use of that specific
imagery. Let us look at a fragment from the following song:

(Song 7):

1. *ba'a na'a ibu barua ga habo duma*
   boy your creek Barua source flow into mountain

   aodoba'aye
   let bush covered

   ba'a na'a ao iburo'o
   boy your bush creek

   kigiba'aye
   let strong bush

1. Boy, your Baruaga Creek flowing into the mountain
The bush has covered it over

   Boy, your tiny creek
   The forest has claimed it back

In this heavily karstified limestone country,
underground creeks are common; indeed, the Mubi
River itself flows underground at the northwestern
end of Hegeso territory and the Foi call the cave
from which it emerges the "source of the Mubi." But
often enough, these tiny creeks become so covered
over with horizontally growing shrubs and over-
hanging growth that one only hears their bubbling
noise without seeing them. It is only through people's efforts that such small creeks stay uncovered
and swift flowing.

In the following song, it is the sound of rushing
water that constitutes what Hugh Kenner (1951:
62) called the peripeteia, the "moving image":

(Song 26):

2. *ibu dufu hua yibumena*
   creek dam planted sleep-man

uaha yiboba'ae
go-live sleeps

ibu dufu hua yibumena
creek dam planted sleep-man

uaha yiboba'ae
go-live sleeps

3. *ibu dimani hua yibumena*
water rushing strikes sleep-man

uaha yiboba'ae
go-live sleeps

ibu a~gu hua yibumena
water swiftly strikes sleep-man

bereboba'ae
is lost

4. *ibu hu~a yibumena*
water mother sleep-man

uaha yiboba'ae
go-live sleeps

ibu ka'asubagedia yibumena
water crashing sleep-man

bereboba'ae
is lost

5. *ibu hemomo'o hubagia yibumena*
water flotsam remove sleep-man

uaha yiboba'ae
go-live sleeps

ibu a~gu hu~a yibumena
water swiftly mother sleep-man

bereboba'ae
is lost

2. Near the fish dam where you habitually slept
There you have gone to rest

Near the fish dam where you were wont to stay
There you have gone to sleep the night

3. He who sleeps near the rushing water
There he silently sleeps

Near the rushing hissing water
Only the river's sound we hear

4. The man who sleeps near the sibilant water
He has gone to rest there

The soft crash of rushing water
But he is lost

5. He who removed the flotsam as he paddled
He has gone there to sleep

Near the splashing rushing water
He is lost

This song makes use of the homophony between the Foi words "*hua*," which means "struck" (from the verb *hu-*, to strike, kill, hit); "planted" (from the same verb, *mohu-*); and "*hu(~)a*" (mother), which tends to have a slightly more nasalized /u/. Crashing, rushing water strikes the stones in creek and river beds. Also, men must "plant" the stakes with which they construct fish dams across the mouths of small creeks. Finally, large bodies of water, like the Mubi, Baru, Yo'oro Rivers, and Lake Kutubu, are called "*ibu hu~a*, (the mother of waters), as in any particularly large specimen of any category (hence a *hu~a*: "mother of houses" [i.e., the longhouse]).

Hemomo'o is detritus and flotsam that bunches up and clots as it flows downstream. It also means "froth, scum," etc. The verb *hubagia-* (from *bagia-*, "to divide into parts" [see later in this section]) means two things: (1), to push aside logs and flotsam as one paddles a canoe; (2), to spread fish poison in dammed water. This fine verse thus compresses the image of spreading fish poison in still water with that of the man threading a canoe through debris-laden water.

Notice in Song 26 that the composer used different words to describe the moving water:[4] *ibu dimani, ibu a-gu, ibu hu-a, ibu ka'asubagedia, ibu hemomo'o hubagia*. Like the Eskimo and their snow vocabulary, the Foi seem to make fine distinctions between varieties of flowing water. *Dimani* apparently comes from the word *dima*, another name for women's sago song, and hence *ibu dimani* could be both "water singing like a woman's sago melody" and "water next to which women sing." *A-gu* may come from the verb "*a-godi-*," (to fill up with fish, of a trap), and refers to the action of moving water pulling fish into weirs and humanly made dams.

Some other examples are as follows:

(Song 2):

1. *ibu irama yibi wabo'ore*
   water stick carrying sleep if-gone

   ibu ka'ayamikiribi wabo'ore
   river waves caused by moving canoe come

1. The man who sleeps near the fast flowing river
   (lit. "water that carries twigs along")
   The waves caused by a canoe in motion

(Song 20):

1. *ibu hekoro yibumena*
   river bank sleep-man

   ibu hekoro bagia yibumena
   river bank debris island sleep-man

1. The man who sleeps by the bank of the river
   Twigs and branches clot in the flowing river

Bagia- means "to divide into parts" and is another one of the ubiquitous "cutting" and "dividing" words of the Foi vocabulary. Anything that is caused to branch or fan out into several strands is described

by this verb: the branching roots of a tree are called *bagi'u*. In this case, a clot of debris in the middle of a river causes the water to divide into two or more separate streams.

3. *ibu hefofore hua yibumena*
   river bank strikes sleep-man

3. The man who sleeps by the crumbling bank of
   the rushing water

Hefofore occurs in connection with "*fufu*" words, which convey a sense of held movement suddenly released in a rising, flying way. *Hefofore*, from the verb meaning "to break into small pieces," refers to the action of a rushing river crumbling its banks into pieces and carrying them away.

This use of the many synonyms for moving water more than anything else attests to the role of what Lévi-Strauss (1966) called detotalization in the poetic and discursive creation of an icon of motion. In this case, not only is a picture of moving water ostensively invoked, but the serial listing of different varieties of rushing, hissing, crashing water itself causes the verse to flow in the same way. In the next section I examine in more detail the thoroughgoing use of detotalization in the constitution of the moving image in Foi poetry.

THE POETRY OF DETOTALIZATION

Let us return momentarily to Song 11 and look at a common theme of Foi song poetry:

1. The path to Baruaga Creek
   .   .   .   .

   The path to Kumagi Creek
   .   .   .   .

2. Boy, your path at the head of the Faya'a River

· · · · · · · · · · · · · · ·

   Boy, your Faya'a River source land

· · · · · · · · · · · ·

3. The path leading to the mouth of the Kumagi
   Creek

· · · · · · · · · · · · · · · ·

   The path along which the faiyu marsupial travels

· · · · · · · · · · · · · · · · ·

Like Ilongot narratives, the Foi song unfolds a sequence of places; its impact is ostensively spatial, and, as Schieffelin (1976:184) noted for the very similar Kaluli songs, "it is possible with any song to construct a map of the region concerned, including hills, streams, gardens, sago stands, and other resources, and . . . trace a history of the area."

The sequence of places, of course, also constitutes a temporal sequence—as the singer moves from place to place in the song, he/she iconically images the movement of the deceased between those places during his/her lifetime. And as I mentioned earlier, such chaining of place names in song discursively recreates a person's life in spatial and temporal terms and preserves the sense of life's encompassing flow.

The following song is one of the few that focuses on Mubi River garden and sago areas in memorializing the life of Kabosa of the Orodobo clan:

(Song 40):

1. *ba'a na'a yebibu ibu*
   boy your Yebibu creek

   aginoba'aye
   let another steal it

   ba'a na'a yefua duma
   boy your Yefua mountain

   aodoba'aye
   let bush cover it

2. *ba'a na'a yebibu ibu*
   boy your Yebibu creek

   aginoba'aye
   let another steal it

   ba'a na'a yefua duma
   boy your Yefua mountain

   aodoba'aye
   let bush cover it

3. *na'a hu~amo ibu sumaniyu*
   your mother's creek Sumaniyu

   ibu aginoboba'ae
   creek stolen eaten

   ba'a bamo yahadenabo
   boy that Yahadenabo

   ibu aodoba'aye
   water let bush cover it

4. *ba'a na'a ibu agegenebo*
   boy your creek Agegenebo

   ibu aodoba'aye
   creek let bush cover it

   ba'a na'a yebibu ibu
   boy your Yebibu creek

   ira waba'aye
   tree let come

5. *ba'a na'a sonobo duma*
   boy your Sonobo mountain

   aodoboba'ae
   bush covered

1. Boy, your Yebibu Creek
   Let another man eat it

   Boy, your Yefua Ridge
   Let the bush cover it over

2. Boy, your Yebibu Creek
    Let another man eat it

    Boy, your Yefua Ridge
    Let the bush cover it over

3. Your Sumaniyu Creek
    This creek, let another man steal it

    This boy's Yahadenabo Creek
    Let the bush cover it over

4. Boy, your Agegenebo Creek
    Let the forest reclaim it

    Boy, your Yebibu Creek
    Let the trees cover it up

5. Boy, your Sonobo Ridge
    Let the bush cover it

    Boy, your Yefua Ridge
    Tree covered

The -*ba'aye* ending is an exhortative ending indicating "to let someone do x." "Let another man claim your territory," the composer exhorts, and there is the underlying note of contempt for those of the deceased's kinsmen who would so immediately and unfeelingly appropriate a dead man's property. It is true that the forest itself obliterates the traces of people's productive lives, but people grimly know that it is the dead person's kinsmen who far more efficiently and quickly avail themselves of the dead man's land and resources.

This serial listing of place names is only one instance of the pervasive use of detotalization as a poetic device, and Lévi-Strauss himself was aware of how easily detotalization could embody a temporal, as well as a spatial and categorical speciation, when he chose the example of the Osage Bear and Beaver chant (Lévi-Strauss 1966). In that song, the bear enumerates the signs of age visible on his body: " . . . my toes that are folded together . . . the wrinkles of my ankles . . . the muscles of my thigh, loosened with age . . . the muscles of my abdomen, loosened with age . . . my ribs that lie in ridges along my side . . ." (LaFlesch 1917–1918:160–161), and so forth. And with each refrain, the bear sings that of these signs of old age, "[W]hen the little ones make of me their bodies, they shall be free from all causes of death, as they travel the path of life" (ibid.).

The last example of this temporal moving image I consider here concerns the invocation of seasonal contrasts, as the next section details.

THE MOVING HUNTER

Traditionally, the Foi alternated between their garden sites near the Mubi River, where they located their longhouse villages, and Ayamo, the hunting area to the north, where they made no gardens and established no permanent residence. To simplify, the relatively drier months between October and April were dedicated to village life, gardening, and ceremonial, and the rainier months of May through September were the time people dispersed to the bush to hunt, fish, and gather (see Weiner 1988).

The place names of Ayamo are disproportionately featured in Foi song poetry: men are memorialized or idealized by reference to their hunting activities more commonly than in relation to their "dry season" gardening activities. Seventeen of the forty-one men's *sorohabora* I transcribed explicitly focus upon place names, and of these seventeen, nine mention place names at Ayamo, three mention places only near the Mubi, two mention both, one describes hunting territories that are not at Ayamo, and two songs make use of landscape images without specifying their location.

Why are Ayamo place names, then, the more

common theme of memorial song poetry? Ayamo is, of course, the venue for men's hunting and foraging activities, and such activities are precisely the exemplary activity of men. It is hunting, not gardening, that creates the most compelling image of male virility and aggressive vitality. And because hunting requires a constant movement over the land—whether it is the regular checking of widely spaced traps or the actual stalking of animals with dog and ax—no other activity is so starkly opposed to the stillness of death. The following song makes use of this contrast:

(Song 5):

1. *se' duma yibu kunuga*
   marsupial mountain sleep cave

   sebe'o'oyo'o
   do not search

   sese baro yibu kunuga
   marsupial baro sleep cave

   sia o'oyo'o
   search do not go

2. *sigina daba yibu kunuga*
   cassowary large sleep cave

   uaha yiboba'ae
   go-live sleeps

   sese budu yibu kunuga
   marsupial black sleep cave

   bereboba'ae
   is lost

3. *ya dabura hu–a yibu kunuga*
   bird red mother sleep cave

   sia ubihamone
   search do not keep going

   ya gibi hu–a kunuga
   bird bush owl mother cave

   sia o'oyo'o
   search do not go

4. *kuiyare yibu kunuga*
   python sleep cave

   sia o'oyo'o
   search do not go

   tuba budu yibu kunuga
   tree kangaroo black sleep cave

   sebe'o'oyo'o
   do not search

1. The duma marsupial that sleeps in the limestone
      caves
   Do not search for it

   The baro marsupial that sleeps in the caves
   Do not attempt to seek it

2. The large cassowary that sleeps in the caves of stone
   He has gone away

   The black marsupial of the stone caves
   He too is lost

3. The bush fowl mother who sleeps in the cave
   Do not go looking for her

   The red bush fowl mother who sleeps in the cave
   Do not seek her

4. The python who sleeps in the stone cave
   Do not go looking for it

   The black tree kangaroo who sleeps in the cave
   Do not try and find it

There is an ambiguity in this song—it is actually Mare, the deceased, who is spoken of as different game animals, which can no longer be found: they no longer sleep in their accustomed shelters. At the same time it is as if the deceased himself is being commanded not to find game animals.

Men's hunting is inextricably associated with the

time of year in which, in its ideal form, it is associated—the wet months of the "*kagi hu-a hase*," (the mother of rain time). Thus, when Foi sing about the creeks, caves, and mountains of Ayamo, they invoke the drizzly, cool primary forests of winter. The following song may be taken as a homage to the tree kangaroo:

(Song 4):

1. *kagi au-wa hubiwe'iya'are* [5]
   rain softly falling-come

   ba'a na'a igebe
   boy you is it?

   kunu kunuga hubiwe'iya'are
   palm wood floor rattling-come

   ba'a na'a igebe
   boy you is it?

2. *kana togebiwe'iya'are*
   stone overturn-come

   ba'a na'a iyo'oge
   boy you is

   ira waru sina irari hubiwe'iya'are
   tree waru shoots dew brushing-come

   ba'a na'a iyo'oge
   boy you is

3. *kunuga hubiwei'iya'are*
   floor striking-come

   ba'a na'a iyo'oge
   boy you is

   ira bai- sina irari hubiwe'iya'are
   tree bai- saplings dew brushing-come

   ba'a na'a iyo'oge
   boy you is

4. *oro sina ineri hubiwe'iya'are*
   bamboo shoots dew brushing-come

   ba'a na'a iyo'oge
   boy you is

   ira bai- sina ireri hubiwe'iya'are
   tree bai- saplings dew brushing-come

   ba'a na'a iyo'oge
   boy you is

5. *duma haro sese sone*
   mountain climbing marsupial Sone

   dawabo
   dawabo

   duma hau sese sawa
   mountain side marsupial Sawa

   ibudawabo
   ibudawabo

6. *duma oro sese sawa*
   mountain top marsupial Sawa

   dawabo
   dawabo

   duma fai sese sone
   mountain side marsupial Sone

   dawabo
   dawabo

1. The sound of rain falling softly while someone approaches
   Boy, is that you?

   A sound like palm wood floor beams rattling as someone comes
   Boy, could that be you?

2. You overturn the stones as you approach
   Boy, is that you?

   Your legs are wet like dew on the waru tree saplings
   Boy, could that be you?

3. The sound of rattling as someone approaches
   Boy, is that you?

Your legs are as wet as the bai- saplings covered
   with dew
Boy, could that be you?

4. You brush the dew off the bamboo shoots as you
    come
    Boy, is that you?

    You are wet from the dew of the bai- tree saplings
    Boy, could that be you?

5. Along the hillside, the tree kangaroo named Sone
    walks
    Dawabo

    Along the side of the mountain, the tree kangaroo
    named Sawa wanders
    Ibu Dawabo

6. At the crest of the mountain, Sawa wanders
    Dawabo

    Along the mountain sides, Sone travels
    Dawabo

The patter of rain, the tinkle of water on rocks, the rattling of the palm wood slats of a house floor as people walk—these are the soggy, fluid, moving, liquid sounds of the rainy season at Ayamo. And every tiny patter makes people imagine the silent padding of the marsupials as they roam through the bush seeking fruit by night, evading hunters by day in their treetops. And of course, Ayamo itself is the "high" place, the place of mountainsides and peaks. Its name literally translates as "sky + possessive"— "the sky's realm," one might say.

CONCLUSION

We can say that "inscription" is a fundamental aspect of the human "*existentielle*," a term that broadly connotes the manner in which human action leaves traces of all kinds on and in the material world. Writing, carving, and incising are the deliberate uses of inscriptive techniques, but what the Foi give voice to in their songs is something more general—the unintentional manner in which all human action "writes" itself upon its surroundings. In the process, the Foi landscape is confirmed as at once known and experienced, marked not only through physical alteration, but also in memorialization through poeticization.

The Foi make this unintentional action visible by singing it through their memorial poetry. The residual effect of this memorialization is the image of the human life course as a series of paths and a series of sites on which individuals marked their selves in various ways, mainly through productive activity of various sorts. This also serves as general aesthetic of movement and stoppage, as some of the song poems I examined here indicate.

Although the landscape and territory of the Foi are personalized in this way, this process results in no permanent marking or memorialization of the environment. Life for the Foi is such that its material traces erode, fade away, and become invisible after the individual ceases such trace-making activity. The memory of these life lines through the forest can only be made "permanent" through the repetitive singing of the memorial poetic songs that revivify in peoples' memories the visual, tactile, and aural image of these movements.

However, the reality is that these memories too are not permanent. All of the song poems I heard in my time with the Foi were sung about men who had been known in the memory of then-living members of the community. The implication is that gradually, over time, the songs of any particular man will cease to be performed. The memories of these men's historic life movements too will fade away, and the paths of association in people's embodied memory will too become invisible. Foi collective memory thus mirrors the erasive effects of the environment, an environment within which the Foi must establish historicity without the benefit of more permanent forms of memoriation, such as are found in Vanuatu for example, in the Malakulan or Massim stones (see Layard 1942; Young 1983). Ultimately, this has profound implications for the nature of sociality, a point that should be compared with the other forms of place marking, as modes of memorialization, discussed in this volume.

NOTES

1. As Gaston Bachelard once remarked, "At times we think we know ourselves in time, when all we know is a sequence of fixations in the spaces of the being's stability. . . . In its countless alveoli, space contains compressed time" (1969:8).

2. Witherspoon (1977: chap. 2) reported that the processes of motion and stoppage are central to the Navajo cosmos. He cited the following passage of Hoijer (1964:146): " . . . in three broad speech patterns, illustrated by the conjugation of active verbs, the reporting of actions and events, and the framing of substantive concepts, Navajo emphasizes movement and specifies the nature, direction, and status of such movement in considerable detail. Even the neuter category is relatable to the dominant conception of a universe in motion: for, just as someone is reported to have described architecture as frozen music, so the Navajo define position as a resultant of the withdrawal of motion."

3. The tilde (~) indicates nasalization of the preceding vowel.

4. The invocation of different qualities of flowing water was also a poetic device employed by the Wind River Shoshone in their shamanic Ghost Dance songs (Shimkin 1964:349).

5. *Hubiwe'iya'are*: The ending *-iya'are* is a nominalized form of the *-iyo'o* ending that indicates knowledge gained

of a past action from present, sensible evidence. The ending *-iyo'oge* can be translated as "was that you? (based on the evidence I see myself as I walk through the bush)."

REFERENCES CITED

Bachelard, G. 1969. *The Poetics of Space.* Boston: Beacon Press.

Hoijer, H. 1964. Cultural Implications of Some Navajo Linguistic Categories. In *Language in Culture and Society*, edited by D. Hymes, 143–153. New York: Harper and Row.

Kenner, H. 1951. *The Poetry of Ezra Pound.* London: Faber and Faber.

LaFlesch, E. 1917–1918. The Osage Rite of Vigil. In *Thirty-ninth Annual Report of the Bureau of American Ethnology*, 31–630.

Layard, J. 1942. *Stone Men of Malakuka: The Small Island of Vao.* London: Chattus and Windus.

Lévi-Strauss, C. 1966. *The Savage Mind.* Chicago: University of Chicago Press.

Rosaldo, R. 1980. *Ilongot Headhunting, 1883–1974: A Study in Society and History.* Palo Alto: Stanford University Press.

Schieffelin, E. 1976. *The Sorrow of the Lonely and the Burning of the Dancers.* New York: St. Martin's Press.

Shimkin, D. 1964. On Wind River Shoshone Literary Forms: An Introduction. In *Language in Culture and Society*, edited by D. Hymes, 344–355. New York: Harper and Row.

Weiner, J. 1988. *The Heart of the Pearl Shell.* Berkeley: University of California Press.

———. 1991. *The Empty Place.* Bloomington: Indiana University Press.

Witherspoon, G. 1977. *Language and Art in the Navajo Universe.* Ann Arbor: University of Michigan Press.

Yasuda, K. 1957. *The Japanese Haiku.* Rutland: Charles E. Tuttle Co.

Young, M. 1983. *Magicians of Manumanua: Living Myth on Kalauna.* Berkeley: University of California Press.

CONTRIBUTORS

Dr. Michael Adler is associate professor of anthropology at Southern Methodist University, Dallas, Texas. His long-term research focuses on village formation and landscape use in the American Southwest, and he has undertaken fieldwork in southwestern Colorado and New Mexico. He specializes in the archaeology of ancestral pueblo peoples, or Anasazi, of the American Southwest and has published a variety of works on the topic, including *The Prehistoric Pueblo World*, A.D. *1150–1350* (University of Arizona Press, 1996). His interests also include the role of ritual and sacred places in human societies, particularly with respect to the use of ancestral sacred sites by Indigenous peoples.

Dr. Michael J. Allen is environmental manager for Wessex Archaeology, Salisbury, England, specializing in the analysis and interpretation of subfossil land snail assemblages, soils, and sediments. His research focuses on the archaeology of landscape formation and human interaction, especially in the chalklands of southern England. Among his many publications are landscape reconstructions and syntheses in *Stonehenge in Its Landscape* (English Heritage, 1995), *The Dorchester Landscape* (Wessex Archaeology, 1997), and *Langstone Harbour* (Council for British Archaeology, 2000).

Dr. Chris Ballard is a fellow in the interdisciplinary project on Resource Management in Asia-Pacific at the Australian National University's Research School of Pacific and Asian Studies. He has conducted long-term research as an archaeologist, historian, and anthropologist in Papua New Guinea and the Indonesian province of West Papua/Irian Jaya. He is editor of *Mining and Mineral Resource Policy in Asia-Pacific* (1995); *The Ok Tedi Settlement* (1997); *Fluid Ontologies* (1998); *Historical Perspectives on West New Guinea* (1999); *Myth and History in the New Guinea Highlands* (1999); *Agricultural Intensification in New Guinea* (2001); and *Race for the Snow* (2001).

Professor Paul Carter is an artist and writer. His latest book, *True Clairvoyance: Art, Migration, Place* is scheduled for 2001 publication. Recent artworks include *Relay* (Olympic Coordination Authority, Fig Grove, Homebush Bay, 2000) and *Nearamnew* (Federation Square, Melbourne, 2001). Among his many books are *The Road to Botany Bay* (Faber and Faber, 1987) and *The Lie of the Land* (Faber and Faber, 1996). His current book in progress is *Repressed Spaces: The Poetics of Agoraphobia*. He is professorial research fellow at The Australian Centre, The University of Melbourne.

Dr. John Coleman Darnell is assistant professor of Egyptology at Yale University. He has worked for the Demotic Dictionary Project of the Oriental Institute, University of Chicago, and was epigrapher and senior epigrapher for the Epigraphic Survey of that institute for ten years, based in Luxor, Egypt. He has been

Egyptologist and director of the Theban Desert Road and Yale Toshka Desert Surveys. His specialties include Egyptian religion, ancient Egyptian cryptography, lapidary hieratic, and ancient Egyptian political and military history. His publications include *The Theban Desert Road Survey*, *The Rock Inscriptions of the Wadi el Hôl*, and *The Enigmatic Netherworld Books of the Solar-Osirian Unity*.

Dr. Bruno David is Logan Fellow at Monash University. His major research interests include an archaeology of ontology and of the Dreaming, and the archaeology and ethnography of rock-art and social landscapes. He has undertaken archaeological and ethnographic research in Australia, Vanuatu, and the United States. He is author of *Landscapes, Rock-art and the Dreaming* (Continuum, 2002) and co-editor of *Bridging Wallace's Line* (Catena Verlag, 2002).

Dr. Julie Gardiner is an archaeologist and editor of the *Proceedings of the Prehistoric Society*. Her research interests include the study of Mesolithic-Neolithic landscapes of southern England, with an emphasis on lithic assemblages. Her major projects and publications include contributions to *Landscape, Monuments and Society: The Prehistory of Cranborne Chase* (Cambridge University Press, 1991) and *Stonehenge in Its Landscape* (English Heritage, 1995). She is currently reports manager for Wessex Archaeology, Salisbury, England.

Professor Marcia Langton is chair of Australian Indigenous Studies at The University of Melbourne. Her research focuses on Native title, land rights, and resource rights in Aboriginal Australia. She is a specialist in Aboriginal land tenure and resource issues, and has published on customary law. She is author of *Burning Questions* (Centre for Indigenous Natural

and Cultural Resource Management, 1998) and *Well, I Heard It on the Radio and I Saw It on the Television* (Australian Film Commission, 1993) and co-editor of *Aborigines, Land and Land Rights* (Australian Institute of Aboriginal Studies, 1983). She was awarded a Medal of Australia in 1993 for services to anthropology and advocacy of Aboriginal rights.

Dr. Georgia Lee received a master's degree from the University of California, Santa Barbara, and a Ph.D. in archaeology from the University of California at Los Angeles. She has worked on the archaeology of rock-art of Easter Island, Hawai'i, and in several areas of California. One of her particular interests is conservation and preservation of archaeological sites. Lee is active in the Easter Island Foundation and is a research associate at the Santa Barbara Museum of Natural History. She is the editor of *Rapa Nui Journal* and the author of nine books.

Dr. Ian J. McNiven is lecturer in archaeology at The University of Melbourne. He has published widely on Australian archaeology in the areas of coastal settlement, stone artifact technology, rock-art, and cultural heritage management. He is co-editor of *Constructions of Colonialism* (Leicester University Press, 1998) and *Australian Coastal Archaeology* (Australian National University Press, 1999). His current research focus is Torres Strait, where he is investigating the development of exchange and alliance systems before and after European contact.

Dr. Mariastella Pulvirenti is a lecturer in the School of Geography and Environmental Science at Monash University in Melbourne, Australia. She teaches cultural geography and qualitative research methods. Her research focuses on immigration and housing and multiculturalism in local government.

Dr. Paul Rainbird teaches archaeology at University of Wales, Lampeter. His research interests include the archaeology and anthropology of island societies, the archaeology of colonial encounters in Australia and the Pacific, and the political use of the past in contemporary society. He has undertaken fieldwork in Micronesia, Australia, England, Scotland, and France and published in numerous books and journals, including *Archaeology in Oceania*, *Journal of World Prehistory*, *Journal of Mediterranean Archaeology*, *Journal of the Polynesian Society*, and *World Archaeology*. He is currently working on a book, *The Archaeology of Micronesia*, for Cambridge University Press.

Andrée Rosenfeld obtained a bachelor of science in physics before graduating in archaeology at the Institute of Archaeology, London. Working in the British Museum and then at the Australian National University, her interests have focused on palaeolithic art and Aboriginal pre-history, rock-art, and its conservation. Her books include *Palaeolithic Cave Art* (with Peter Ucko) (Weidenfeld and Nicholson, 1967), which has been translated into seven languages, and *Rock Art Conservation in Australia* (Australian Heritage Commission, 1985).

Dr. Lynette Russell trained as an archaeologist before shifting her research interests to history and the social construction of archaeological knowledge. She is Director of the Centre for Australian Indigenous Studies at Monash University, where she is researching the colonial history of Australian archaeology. She is the author of *Savage Imaginings* (Arcadia, 2001) and *A Little Bird Told Me* (Allen and Unwin, 2002), editor of *Colonial Frontiers* (Manchester University Press, 2001), and co-editor of *Constructions of Colonialism* (Leicester University Press, 1998).

Dr. Chris Scarre is a specialist in the pre-History of western Europe, with a particular interest in the archaeology of the Atlantic facade—Iberia, France, Britain, and Ireland. His recent publications have considered the meanings pre-historic societies may have attached to natural landscape features in Brittany and the manner in which those meanings were given material expression through the construction of burial mounds or settings of standing stones. He is currently deputy director of the McDonald Institute for Archaeological Research and editor of the *Cambridge Archaeological Journal*. His recent books include *Exploring Prehistoric Europe* (Oxford University Press, 1998), *Ancient Civilizations* (with Brian Fagan) (Longman, 1997), and the co-edited (with Colin Renfrew) *Cognition and Material Culture: The Archaeology of Symbolic Storage* (Cambridge University Press, 1998).

Dr. Simon Stoddart has studied in Cambridge, Michigan, and Rome; taught in York, Bristol, and Cambridge; and undertaken fieldwork in the Casentino (Tuscany), Gubbio (Umbria), Nepi (Lazio), Malta, and Troina (Sicily). His research has specialized in linking fieldwork to the study of complex landscapes, as represented in many of his publications, including *Etruscan Italy* (with Nigel Spivey) (Batsford, 1990), *Territory, Time and State* (with Caroline Malone) (1994), and his edited *Landscapes from Antiquity* (Antiquity Publications, 2000).

Dr. Paul S. C. Taçon is head of the Australian Museum's People and Place Research Centre and principal research scientist in anthropology. He has conducted archaeological and ethnographic fieldwork in Australia, Canada, southern Africa, and the United States. He is co-editor of *The Archaeology of Rock-Art* (Cambridge University Press, 1998) and has published over eighty scientific papers on rock-art, social identity, landscape archaeology, and contemporary Indigenous issues.

Dr. Emily Umberger is associate professor at Arizona State University, where she teaches Pre-Columbian, Colonial, Spanish, and general non-Western art history. Her research focuses on Aztec stone monuments and hieroglyphic inscriptions, the calendar, politics, and notions of history, but her interests also extend to colonial Mexico and Golden Age Spain, and she has written on seventeenth-century Spanish and Mexican paintings. She is one of six authors of the book *Aztec Imperial Strategies* (Dumbarton Oaks, 1996).

Dr. James F. Weiner is a visiting fellow in the Department of Anthropology, Research School of Pacific and Asian Studies, Australian National University. He has conducted fieldwork among the Foi of Papua New Guinea since 1979 and among Aboriginal communities of central and southeastern Queensland since 1998. He is the co-editor, with Alan Rumsey, of *Emplaced Myth: Space, Narrative and Knowledge in Aboriginal Australia and Papua New Guinea* (University of Hawai'i Press, 2001). His latest book, *Tree Leaf Talk: A Heideggerian Anthropology*, will appear in 2001 by Berg Press.

Meredith Wilson is currently completing her Ph.D. in the Department of Archaeology and Natural History, Australian National University, Canberra. Her main research interest is the archaeology of rock-art, with particular reference to Vanuatu and the broader Pacific region. She has published in academic books and journals, including the *Cambridge Archaeological Journal*, *Oceania*, *Rock Art Research*, *Conservation and Management of Archaeological Sites*, *Archaeology in Oceania*, and *Asian Perspectives*.

Dr. Sallie Yea is lecturer in international development at Royal Melbourne Institute of Technology University. Much of her research focuses on the political and cultural construction of places and groups. She has recently published papers on the representation of dissident regions in South Korea, the political inscription of a cemetery in South Korea, and the representation of mail-order brides through cybertexts.

INDEX

Aam, 108

abandonment, 131, 183, 210, 212, 213, 214, 233, 271, 273

Aboriginal people: *Aboriginal Land Act* 1991, 253; Aboriginal Land Tribunal, 253, 254, 255, 256, 257, 258, 259, 267, 268; ancestors, 3, 58, 62, 77, 123, 130, 164, 253, 254, 255, 257, 260, 261, 262, 263, 265, 266, 267, 268; and anthropologists, 32, 254, 255, 256, 258–259, 260, 267; and burning, 56, 264; clans, 3, 36, 49, 130, 253, 254, 255, 261; "clever-men," 30; country, 54, 57, 62, 66, 70, 71, 73, 74, 75, 253, 256, 257, 258–259, 260–265, 266, 268; dispossession, 34, 36, 54–57, 259; and the Dreaming, 3, 7, 36, 47–49, 52–54, 57, 58, 62, 70–73, 75, 77, 123, 130, 131, 155, 253–254, 255, 258, 259, 261, 262, 263, 264, 265, 266, 267, 268; elders, 3, 49, 53–54, 56, 255–267, 268; estates, 36, 47–48, 49, 53–54, 57, 66–67, 253, 255, 258, 263, 266, 267, 268; and European law, 55, 57, 253, 255; and fear, 56–57, 259; forcible removals of, 29, 254, 255; "giving smell," 263; and government reserves, 29, 254–255; "increase" ceremonies, 30; Indigenous law, 7, 58, 72, 130, 253–267; land, 3, 7, 32, 34, 35, 36, 37, 46–48, 53–58, 62, 235, 253–267, 268; land rights, 253–267, 268; language, 46, 47, 130, 235, 253, 255, 258, 262, 263, 264, 268; massacres of, 7, 30, 34, 54–57; "medicine men," 33, 261; Native Police, 34, 56; and night sky, 3, 265–266; Protectors, 234, 255; relations with Europeans, 7, 28–32, 33, 34, 45, 47, 49, 54–57, 234–236, 253; resistance, 7, 27–29, 45, 54–58; responses to invasion, 7, 27–32, 35, 37, 45, 49, 54, 55–57, 58, 61; *The Restriction of the Sale of Opium and Protection of Aborigines Act* 1897, 255; sacred places, 7, 65, 66, 76, 261–262, 267; "singing out," 262, 263; social organization, 47, 57; social turmoil, 7, 54–57; spirit Beings, 7, 52–54, 62, 164, 254, 255, 256–257, 259, 260, 261, 262, 263, 265, 266, 267, 268; and stars, 3, 265–266; Tasmanians, 27; *terra nullius*, 55; and time, 265–266; and tourism, 66, 72; and Wards of the State, 254; "warming," 263. *See also specific groups*; Dreaming, the; Dreaming places; territoriality

abstraction, 49, 91, 266

Abydene Osiris, 112. *See also* Osiris

Abydos, 106, 109, 110, 112, 113

access, 21, 22, 31, 54, 56, 58, 63, 65, 66, 67, 76, 106, 127, 131, 132, 181, 183, 203, 205, 210, 213, 232, 240, 242, 249, 254, 257, 258–259, 260, 261, 262, 263

accommodation, as a frontier response, 27–28

acculturation, 32, 37, 226

Aceh, 15, 25

Acolhua, 187, 191

acoustic ecology, 94, 95

Acts of Parliament. *See specific Acts*; Aboriginal people

administration, 104, 109, 231, 254

aesthetics, 2, 88, 94, 123, 282

Africa, 28, 104, 106, 123, 126, 127, 128, 129, 131, 132. *See also specific places*

Agegenebo Creek, 278–279

agency, 4, 14, 17, 23, 27, 29, 33, 210, 241, 254, 263, 264, 267

agriculture, 98, 99, 129, 139, 176, 179, 184, 187, 189, 202, 203, 204, 207, 209–210, 245, 246, 247, 248, 249, 270

Ahuitzotl, 194, 195

Aidobo clan, 273–274

Akimuga, 15, 16

Alamat Tal Road, 105–108, 109, 110, 112, 114

alder, 148

Alice Springs, 63, 67

Alkupal. *See* Musgrave, G.

alliances, 61

Alps, 179

altars, 181, 182, 190, 196

altered states of consciousness, 182

Alyawara, 71

Amenemhat I, 109

American Southwest, 5, 164, 200–214

Amungme, 15–24, 25

'Anaeho'omalu, 90–91

Anasazi, 200, 210

ancestors, 2, 3, 18, 47, 58, 62, 91, 94, 95, 96, 123, 130, 145, 150, 151,

Production Notes for David and Wilson/INSCRIBED LANDSCAPES

Cover and interior design, and composition by Bookcomp, Inc.
Text in Adobe Garamond and display type in Goudy Old Style.

Printing and binding by The Maple-Vail Book Manufacturing Group.

Printed on 60 lb. Text White Opaque.